"Seasoned travel writer David Leffman has guided us through the Middle Kingdom for decades, and in Mesny he has found his spiritual ancestor. Written with great care and attention to detail, *The Mercenary Mandarin* documents the life and exploits of one of the great overlooked adventurers of colonial-era China. A tale of war and discovery set in one of China's most tumultuous periods, it is a valuable contribution to any traveler's bookshelf."

— Derek Sandhaus, editor of *Decadence Mandchoue;*
author of *Tales of Old Peking*

THE MERCENARY MANDARIN

HOW A BRITISH ADVENTURER BECAME A GENERAL IN QING-DYNASTY CHINA

David Leffman

BLACKSMITH BOOKS

The Mercenary Mandarin
ISBN 978-988-13765-4-1

Published by Blacksmith Books
Unit 26, 19/F, Block B, Wah Lok Industrial Centre,
37-41 Shan Mei Street, Fo Tan, Hong Kong
Tel: (+852) 2877 7899
www.blacksmithbooks.com

Edited by Samuel Rossiter

For hundreds of photographs, research notes and extracts from
early versions of the book, check out "The Mercenary Mandarin"
on Facebook or visit *www.davidleffman.com*.

CONTENTS

I have often been told that rolling stones gather no moss, but I have a weakness for travelling, having contracted the habit when I was only nine years old.

— William Mesny, 1883

ACKNOWLEDGEMENTS

First thanks are due to Narrell for her unwavering support, both at home and on many long trips around China's backblocks; and to Peter and Shelagh Hardie, who have encouraged my interest in China, art and history since 1980.

Insurgency and Social Disorder in Guizhou by Robert D. Jenks introduced me to Mesny and the Miao war. Jim Thompson, a descendant of Mesny's sister, set up a website on Mesny (www.mesny.org) and generously provided scans of *Tungking* and the *Miscellany* on disc, without which I could never have begun to research his life.

Professor Gary Tiedemann and the late Keith Stevens shared hospitality and decades of hard-won research; in particular, Stevens' 1992 biography of Mesny became the framework for my original timeline, while Professor Tiedemann alerted me to Mesny's uncredited articles in the *North China Herald*, encouraging me to search elsewhere for more. Tony Hadland gave feedback via his blog (hadland.wordpress.com) about his great grand-uncle, Captain William Gill; and Joyce Hill, another descendant of Mesny's sister, supplied family reminiscences and photographs.

My research was greatly helped by staff at the British Library, the National Archives at Kew, the Royal Geographical Society, the School of Oriental and African Studies Library (University of London), the Central Library and Public Records Office in Hong Kong, Macau's Leal Senado Library and the Shanghai Municipal Archives.

I'd especially like to thank Anna Baghiani, Karen Biddlecombe and Gareth Syvret of Société Jersiaise; Martin Barrow at Matheson & Co. and John Wells at Cambridge University Library; Lorna Cahill at Kew

Gardens and Jonathan Gregson and Jacek Wajer at the Natural History Museum, London; Carol Westaway of the Royal Horticultural Society's Lindley Library; David of www.gwulo.com; Emily Walhout of Harvard University's Houghton Library; and Professor Rudolf Wagner, Ruth Wilcock and Hope Justman.

In Guizhou, Li Maoqing cheerfully interpreted from Hmong, guided me around Qiandongnan and chased down history and folklore about the Miao war. At Zhaitou village, Granny Ve Me Ou sang about the death of Guan Baoniu while Mr Wan Guoshen recited an oral history of the Dingpatang campaign and pointed out the battlefield. The Zhou family at Jiuzhou confirmed Mesny's account of the town's destruction by the Sichuan Army and retold the tale of Guo Moruo's grandfather. Villagers at Shidong located sites connected with Su Yuanchun, a cook at the canteen beside Mesny's bridge at Chong'an offered personal insights into the campaign, while Mr Wu Guomin, a farmer at Huangpiao, gave the Miao version of the Hunan Army's defeat. Two girls at Weng'an shared a late cab ride to Niuchang along the worst main road in all China and tracked down the site of the Sichuan Army camp; villagers at Bandeng fed me sour hotpot, escorted me around Zhang Xiumei's grave and set me off down the old track down the mountain towards Shidong; Mister Wu at Jiuzhou gave directions to the flagstoned post road to Weng'an; and Mr Tian Xinlong of Jiaba Niuchang village filled in details of the Jiaba campaign and told me where to find remains of the Miao stockade.

Along the way Simon Lewis, Derek Sandhaus and Paul Tomic handed out sound advice and solid backup, Wendy Van Duivenvoorde translated from Dutch and CK Lau translated from Chinese, Google Maps sometimes got things brilliantly right, and in 2012 the National Library of China published a facsimile of the complete four-volume *Miscellany*, some 107 years after Mesny brought out the final issue. My gratitude to Daniel Kadar for further translations and reading the manuscript through, Philip Kenny for hospitality, Chris Carroll and Mike Broom for their support, James Lucas for website design and Pete Spurrier for agreeing to publish the book.

Finally, thanks to the many, many people in China – foreign expats, guesthouse owners, teachers, policemen, bus and taxi drivers, students, shop staff, martial artists, villagers, passers-by and chefs – who have fed me, ferried me around, chatted to me, taught me, hit me, plied me with *baijiu* and otherwise helped out over the last thirty years.

David Leffman

Chinese characters and names

There's no alphabet in Chinese: Chinese characters embody meanings, not sounds or spellings. The idea is similar to numerals in the West, where the symbol "8" means the same thing in Britain, France or Iceland regardless of local pronunciation. This way, people from different parts of China – a country with many regional dialects and languages – can at least communicate with each other in writing.

However, without an alphabet there is no "correct" way of transliterating the sounds of Chinese characters. Various systems have been used over the years, so that the Taiping leader's name – written 洪秀全 in Chinese – appears in different English-language accounts as Hong Xiuquan, Hung-sui-tshuen, Hung sew tseuen and Hung Hsiu-ch'üan.

Some Chinese place names have also changed since Mesny's day. In Sichuan, Tachienlu has become Kangding and Paoning is now called Langzhong; Guangzhou, the capital of Guangdong province, was known to the colonial British as Canton; the island village of Hwai Yuen Hsien in Guangxi province has been renamed Danzhou, and so on. Working out which settlement Mesny was talking about often involved seeking local knowledge of the old names and hours spent picking over contemporary maps.

To minimise confusion I've used modern place names and the current standard system, *pinyin*, for transliterating Chinese. The main exceptions are where original sources are quoted and where historic or local names are still in use, such as "Hong Kong" (derived from the Cantonese pronunciation *heung gong*, instead of the *pinyin* spelling, "Xiang Gang"). This should make it easier to follow Mesny's journeys on a modern map, but these are not necessarily the spellings or place names used in the *Miscellany* or other original sources.

Brief biographies of the major players in Mesny's story can be found on pages 358-365.

FOREWORD

I'm not sure *exactly* when I first heard about the Miao Rebellion. I do know that I was very, very drunk.

It was springtime in southwestern China's Guizhou province and the Sisters' Meal festival was in full swing. Thousands of Miao girls had descended from outlying villages on the small country town of Taijiang, dressed in jackets that they'd spent years embroidering in beautiful, nit-picking detail for this very event. Defying the historic Chinese norm of arranged marriages, the girls were hunting for husbands, and everything was display and competition. Proud mothers made sure that their daughters looked their best, fixing complex hairdos in place with fluorescent pink combs or, more traditionally, long silver hairpins shaped like writing brushes. Groups danced in concentric circles in the town square, the men playing long gourd pipes and banging drums, the girls jingling as they stamped to the beat underneath huge assemblages of silver necklaces and headpieces. They sang flirty, dirty songs to one another in a strange falsetto. There were buffalo fights between bulls in the surrounding paddy fields, drawing a mostly male crowd, dragon-boat races on the river for the young men to show off their strength and lantern fights at night along the main street, where village teams attempted to torch their opponents' giant paper dragons with hand-held fireworks. Much collateral damage was inflicted on the crush of spectators.

Away from the noise and crowds, suitors tried to find a private moment to present their favourite girl with a packet of sticky rice wrapped in a lotus leaf. If she fancied the man, it would be returned with a pair of chopsticks inside; if she didn't, there would be only one chopstick or

– insultingly – a pickled chilli. Either way, sweet rice wine would be needed to celebrate or drown sorrows, and it was being consumed in vast quantities. Miao are hospitable people and outsiders at the event were dragged cheerfully into the chaos; before even entering the town I'd been stopped by a roadblock of women in festival dress and handed a buffalo horn full of wine. Knowing that if I touched the goblet I'd have to drain it, I put my hands behind my back and waited for a mouthful to be poured in. But buffalo horns are not designed for Westerners; my big nose bumped into the edge and my shirt got a soaking. "Make him do it again!" cheered a young policeman, eager to capture the moment on film. Several attempts later the policeman had his photos and I was let through into Taijiang, fuzzy-eyed and reeking of spirits. The party lasted three days.

At some point in the proceedings, somebody must have mentioned the rebellion. I had no memory of the event but later on found it written down in my notebook: "Zhang Xiumei, statue, Miao war". Details resurfaced slowly from the murk. Zhang had led the Miao in an uprising against the Chinese government during the mid-nineteenth century. He had been captured at Xianglu Shan, "Incense-burner Mountain", and beheaded. Locals still climbed the hill each year in his honour and now there was talk of erecting a statue to him at Taijiang, his hometown. I also dimly recalled being harangued with inebriated insistence about how three million people had been killed in the war. *Three million?* Even today, there are only nine million Miao in all of China. At the time, three million might have been half the total population of Guizhou province, an unimaginable slaughter. So why hadn't I heard about it before?

Guizhou made a big impression on me, not least because in over ten years of regular visits to China, the Sisters' Meal was the first time I had ever had out-and-out, unadulterated fun. And if continually returning to a country that I didn't enjoy much sounds perverse, ask anyone from that time what they thought of China and you'd find that it wasn't a matter of like or dislike. The word everybody used was "interesting", usually prefaced by "very" or even "incredibly". On my first visit in 1985, China was just opening up, having been closed to independent travel for over thirty years, and both foreigners and Chinese were rediscovering each other through a fog of mutual ignorance and confusion. Information about anywhere other than major historic sites was most likely gleaned from pre-war literature, now hopelessly outdated. Right through the 1990s Westerners were still barred from parts of the interior whose military value – or embarrassingly impoverished living conditions – made them sensitive, but these bans were slowly lifting. If you were lucky or determined enough (patient negotiators could sometimes charm travel permits for closed areas from local authorities), it was possible to become the first foreigner in decades to be allowed into a region. The boundaries to exploration hadn't yet been set. For somebody who was hooked on the whole thrill of travel for its own sake, "enjoyable" wasn't the point.

China was, however, very hard work. My first trip was crushingly unromantic. I spoke no Chinese; few people spoke English. The cities were grey, depressing, outrageously polluted and gritted with coal dust; the food was terrible; the hotels were miserably cold, disturbingly mildewed and determined not to accept foreign guests. Mao Zedong had been dead barely nine years and his doctrine that Westerners were intrinsically evil still held sway, so hotel staff wanted nothing to do with us. Every single night involved hours of arguing with receptionists before they would reluctantly admit that yes, this was a hotel, and beds were available. Out on the streets the general public were often far too interested, congregating around you in mildly aggressive, jostling crowds whose members jabbed fingers and pulled at your clothes as they discussed your more bizarre features at point-blank range. My hairy arms seemed to be a particular wonder. Toilets were a nightmare; men would wander in, gape at the sight of a foreigner squatting over the porcelain (there were never any doors on the stalls), then rush off to get their friends so that all could laugh and point at your anatomy. I used to hide behind newspapers.

Then there were train journeys. Three-hour struggles for tickets were the norm, fighting the whole time to hold your place in the scrum of a queue. Sometimes police would be employed to keep order, which they did by lashing out with steel whips at everybody within reach. If you made it to the window, requests for tickets – to anywhere, on any date, at any time, in any class – would be routinely rejected by surly, hostile staff whose rudeness had to be experienced to be believed. As state employees their jobs and wages were secure however little work they did, so customers were seen as unwelcome irritations to days otherwise spent pleasantly chatting and drinking tea with their friends. Thanks to them, *meiyou* – "don't have" – was the first Chinese word many foreigners learned. I soon gave up even trying to buy seats this way and resorted to the black-market touts who flocked like vultures outside train stations, gladly accepting their fifty percent mark-up and hoping that the tickets they sold me weren't fake. The trains themselves were so overcrowded that there were often platform riots – smashed windows, punch-ups, blood – in the rush to get aboard the "hard seat" compartments, where you were lucky if there was even standing room. Privacy was an impossible luxury: from dawn to dusk people would turn up to gape and practice their English, rummage through your bags, and demand your attention. China is as large as Europe or the US and with trains of the time topping barely 60km per hour, journeys often took days.

The other major headache involved Foreign Exchange Certificates, or FEC. China naturally had a single currency, the yuan, but this was issued in two types of banknotes. Renminbi – literally, "Peoples' Money" – was for the general population, while foreigners were issued with FEC notes. Renminbi and FEC had the same face values and were theoretically interchangeable, but as imported luxuries such as washing machines and televisions could only be paid for in FEC, there was a huge underground demand for them. Naturally, people hoarded FEC, refusing to accept payment in anything else but fobbing you off with Renminbi notes in change. You ended up with huge wads of cash that was almost impossible to spend.

Of course there were highlights too. My first sight of the Terracotta Army outside of Xi'an, the eerie ranks of life-sized, grey-brown figures emerging from the clay as if they'd been real people fossilized by some ancient disaster. The Great Wall on a clear Spring day, snaking to the horizon across rugged hills, where a young George Michael, taking time off from his groundbreaking gig in Beijing, paid me a huge compliment by complaining loudly to his entourage of photographers that I didn't look like a *Wham!* fan. There was also a memorable evening spent wrestling with fellow customers for a seat in the famous Quanjude Peking duck restaurant, one of the few worthwhile places to eat in the capital at the time. The management had squeezed in as many tables and chairs as possible, and the limited floor space was packed to bursting with salivating masses waiting their turn. Exposure to train travel stood me in good stead. The trick was to squeeze in behind a diner who was finishing their meal and, the moment they started getting up to leave, to push them sideways and sit down in their chair before anyone else beat you to it.

But on balance, I have never left another country with such an overwhelming sense of relief as I left China in 1985, almost running onto the plane and swearing I would never, ever, ever return. Yet like many people, I found that China had wormed its way under my skin. I'd like to say that this was because, in retrospect, I had been intrigued by glimpsing a completely alien view of the world and had begun to appreciate the depth of the country's history, culture, and art, or that I was hooked by the challenge of learning the language. To be honest, it was probably a combination of rose-coloured spectacles and simple bloody-mindedness. I returned for my honeymoon of all things, and then a few years later began making regular visits as part of my career as a travel writer. After a low point following the crushing of student protests at Tiananmen Square in 1989, living conditions in China seemed to improve with every trip. As the government released its hold on industry and employment, the economy grew competitive and staff in shops and hotels suddenly became attentive and helpful. Widespread TV ownership made Western faces a familiar sight; people were still curious, but you no longer drew oppressive crowds. Food, accommodation and transport infrastructure improved dramatically; FEC were abolished; travel restrictions began to evaporate; people became more open, confident and friendly. They even put doors on the toilet stalls. By the time the Sisters' Meal festival in 1999 came about, bloody-mindedness had paid off and I was finally having fun.

Meanwhile, the three million dead in Guizhou deserved some research and I soon discovered why the war rated barely a mention in most history books. Nineteenth-century China wasn't short of civil conflicts with astoundingly large body counts. The biggest of them all, the Taiping Rebellion, saw between twenty and forty million people killed, depending on whose estimates you believed. Then there was the Nian Uprising, the Tungan Revolt – during which China considered abandoning its entire northwestern frontier – and a Muslim uprising in Yunnan, possibly totalling another twenty million casualties. And these were just the major events. The Miao Rebellion, confined to one corner of a remote province and whose dead were mostly from ethnic minorities, was easily lost amongst this tally.

A hunt through library bookshelves turned up just one work in English about the war, *Insurgency and Social Disorder in Guizhou: The "Miao" Rebellion 1854–1873* by Robert Jenks. This painted a clear, concise picture of the causes and progress of the uprising, all gleaned from contemporary Chinese records which my limited grasp of the language prevented me from reading. And I was especially intrigued to discover that there had been a surprising first-hand witness to the war: one William Mesny, from the island of Jersey, who had spent five years in the Chinese military fighting against the Miao. Footnotes added that Mesny later rose to the rank of general and, between 1895 and 1905, published his experiences in a weekly magazine, *Mesny's Chinese Miscellany*.

At this stage the internet was relatively undeveloped – no Wikipedia, Facebook or Twitter – but even so a quick online search uncovered a whole website dedicated to Mesny, set up by a distant relative in Canada. This revealed that William had spent his entire adult life in China, arriving at Shanghai in 1860 aged eighteen and dying in the Yangzi port city of Hankou, not long after the end of the First World War. His employment as a Westerner in the Chinese forces wasn't unique in itself – Americans, Belgians, Germans and other British had served too – but few had written much about their exploits. Mesny's *Miscellany*, on the other hand, ran to an enormous four volumes and some two thousand pages. Originals were rare collectors' items but scans of the entire work were made available for free through the website. I ordered a set and sat down to read.

At first glance the *Miscellany* seemed disappointingly dull, obsessed with dissecting the precise meanings of long-redundant Chinese phrases, titles and professions, interspersed with diatribes on the importance of "progress" and urging investment in mining, railways and steamship navigation. The layout seemed bewilderingly random too, and the only section that really caught my eye was Mesny's serialisation of his exploits, entitled the "The Life and Adventures of a British Pioneer in China". Mesny had arrived in the country to find central China occupied by the Taiping rebels, with Imperial forces only just beginning to gain the upper hand. The main trade artery, the Yangzi River, was blockaded and inland cities were desperately short of provisions; there was money to be made as a smuggler, though the chances of being captured or killed by either side was high. Mesny took the risk, narrowly avoided being murdered by government troops and ended up as a prisoner of the Taipings. He survived, joined the customs service, grew bored, and ran off to fight the Miao in Guizhou. Accumulating military rank and decorations, he spent the following two decades roaming the country and witnessing, either directly or through their aftermaths, nearly every major rebellion in nineteenth century China. By now the conservative Qing dynasty was losing its grip on the country and progressive factions were eager to hire foreign experts who could teach them about the modern world. Several of China's most famous statesmen had employed Mesny, ignoring at their peril his visionary advice on battle tactics, the modernisation of infrastructure and foreign policy. Further larding the tale were his romances with Chinese women, which had resulted in two marriages. Finally settling down in Shanghai in the mid-1880s, his fortunes had slowly declined and he ranted bitterly against the people whom he felt were responsible. How much of all this was true was anybody's guess, but Mesny had clearly enjoyed a very full life.

These personal revelations were fascinating enough, but then so were many other things about China. And I found it hard to obsess about history, when the whole point of China in the 1990s seemed to be the pace of change. I couldn't understand Westerners who were still harping on about the misery, chaos and destruction inflicted by Chairman Mao during the 1960s when the country had clearly long since abandoned

Mao's attempts to dismember society with his Red Guards and Cultural Revolution, embracing instead the philosophy of his successor, Deng Xiaoping. "Poverty is not Socialism", Deng had declared in 1992, "To get rich is glorious". His words had sparked a free-market boom and in the rush for personal wealth China was fast forgetting the past, or at least erasing any physical evidence of it. In the frenzy to modernize and be considered an equal by the rest of the world, entire cities were being rebuilt from the ground up, inflicting far more damage to historic remains than the Cultural Revolution had ever achieved. As the country became one huge construction site, the national soundtrack was one of sledgehammers and pneumatic drills. Every year the Chinese public vote for the written character that best encapsulates current trends; my favourite for the entire period since 1985 would be 拆, *chai*, demolish. You saw the symbol painted up everywhere, often on buildings less than a decade old; citizens dreaded waking up to find it daubed on their front door by a local authority eager to clear yet more homes out the way for another monster shopping mall. All this activity kept the country employed and the economy raging, but it became the norm for so long that you wondered – would China ever be finished?

And so I carried on working as a travel writer, turning out guidebooks, articles, and a cookbook. Extended stays in China carried me right around the country, improving my knowledge of the language and all things Chinese while turning me into a generalist with many fields of interest but few in-depth skills. This wasn't necessarily a bad thing. Chinese culture is like a ball of wool with loose ends poking out all over. You get attracted to one strand and begin pulling on it, only to find it linked to another, then another, then another. Despite the ball of wool being infinitely long and tangled, you slowly gain insights into how the separate strands connect, and attain an appreciation of the whole.

During this period my mental dossier on Mesny remained open and eventually things built up to critical mass, a point where I needed to read through the *Miscellany* again. This time I felt a growing personal connection as it dawned that I had, over the intervening decade, unwittingly footstepped almost all of Mesny's journeys around China. From his descriptions I now recognised several of the villages and battle sites where he campaigned during the Miao war; I had even written about some of the very temples and guildhalls which he visited. Although widely travelled, he had – like me – spent a great deal of time in the southwestern Chinese provinces of Guizhou, Guangxi, Sichuan and Yunnan, seeing them open up to the outside world after years of isolation. I also wondered about one of the *Miscellany's* recurrent themes: that Mesny had played a pivotal role in nineteenth-century Chinese history by convincing at least one influential official to attempt Western-style modernisations on a grand scale. No other books seemed to have taken this claim seriously but, if true, Mesny surely deserved wider recognition and it was exciting to suddenly realise that I was qualified to investigate. The idea of writing a Mesny biography took shape.

Biographers are always at the mercy of their subjects. People tend to leave behind records of the most interesting parts of their lives, omitting the boring and embarrassing bits and generally presenting themselves in the way they want to be remembered. Mesny was no exception and I could see from the start that my perspective would be very limited if I relied on the *Miscellany* alone, which was opinionated and episodic and ended fourteen years before his death. By this time it was 2010 and the internet was no longer in its infancy; the trouble now was filtering the overload of information which echoed between sites. Months spent surfing through thousands of Mesny-related hits paid off, however. Online searches of archive indexes turned up the existence of unpublished manuscripts, notebooks and maps, Mesny's will, some photographs, a few letters and even one of his calling cards. The first of his two major journeys across China was made in company with the explorer William Gill, who had penned a two-volume account of their trip called *The River of Golden Sand*. In the 1880s Mesny himself had produced a book, *Tungking*, about the violent scuffle between France and China over control of northern Vietnam. Between 1870 and the mid-1880s, Mesny had also written scores of anonymous articles for contemporary English-language newspapers, whose value lay in providing honest, on-the-spot opinions of key events which he might have later revised in his favour for the *Miscellany*. There was certainly enough to be getting on with.

At this point I was brought down to earth by the discovery that other biographies of Mesny already existed. The earliest, based on an interview with his father, filled a lengthy column of *The West Briton and Cornwall Advertiser* from November 1883; it was lively reading but seemed to conflate several events. The second, a short entry in George Balleine's *Biographical Dictionary of Jersey*, was cobbled together in the 1940s from the *Miscellany* and family recollections, and suffered from being totally uncritical of either. But by far the most comprehensive was *A Jersey Adventurer in China*, a hundred-page account of Mesny's life which appeared in a 1992 journal of the Hong Kong Branch of the Royal Asiatic Society. Its author, Keith Stevens, obviously knew not only a great deal about Mesny but also about nineteenth-century China. Was another biography likely to add anything new?

On reflection, this only made it easier to choose the direction that my own take on Mesny's life should follow. I wasn't about to compete with Keith Stevens' detailed analysis of Mesny the man, in which he had unravelled the *Miscellany*'s complex, often contradictory web of autobiographical material. From it Mesny emerged as a not entirely successful chancer, spending most of his life milking a reputation for bravery and resourcefulness gained very early on in his exploits. Stevens felt that Mesny had intended the *Miscellany* – written decades after his glory days – as a platform for reviving a fading self-image, in which Mesny was never shy of touting his own position at the centre of events, his famous contacts, his specialist insider knowledge, and his many awards. While not arguing with any of these conclusions, I was more interested in the details of Mesny's adventures, capitalizing on my two definite skills: research, and a solid knowledge of travel in China. Nobody had yet pieced together the many contemporary documents relating to Mesny's life outside of the *Miscellany*, and by doing so I could retrace his journeys across the country to the borders with Central Asia, Tibet, Vietnam and Burma, searching for evidence of his presence, colouring in detail, and comparing the hardships of the road. Understanding his travels and the people he met would, of course, involve providing context by framing a solid history of nineteenth-century China, but with feet in both the Western and Chinese worlds, Mesny's life story was well-placed to provide a balanced view of the times. It seemed that I would have to knuckle under at last and study the past.

Back in the present, my career as a travel writer seemed increasingly doomed. Even as the internet blossomed, making it ever easier to chase down the details of Mesny's life, guidebook sales were withering as travellers opted instead to harvest information about their destinations for free off the web. Within weeks of deciding to write about Mesny, a book I had been about to research on Hong Kong was cancelled, leaving me with a plane ticket and six months of spare time. Hong Kong had been one of Mesny's first ports of call after reaching China in 1860, and he had spent almost a year there. I was off.

William Mesny as a third-rank military official, c. 1875.

華 英 會 通
HUA YING HUI TUNG

肝 膽 照 人

中華弟席時熙

問星都督仁兄大人政

不同羣品在虛懷

左宗棠

能將萬人無躁氣

問星尊兄都督屬

大清光緒叁拾壹年歲次乙巳

耶穌降世第一千九百零五年

Photo of the author with Complimentary Tablets
written by the late Marquis TSO TSUNG-TANG,
Viceroy of the Min-Chê Provinces and presented to
Yours truly,
W. MESNY.

THE FOURTH BOOK OF MESNY.

上 海 華 英 會 通 第 四 部

"Able to command many without impatience; Outstandingly modest in nature".

Yours very sincerely
William Gill

Left: William Gill. Above: Zhang Zhidong.

Above: Mesny's bridge at Chong'an.
Left: Li Hongzhang.

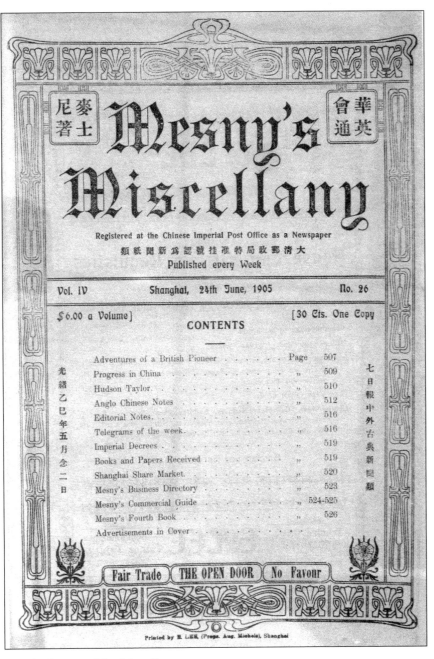

尼麥
士著

會華
通英

Mesny's Miscellany

Registered at the Chinese Imperial Post Office as a Newspaper

大清郵政局特准挂號認爲新聞紙類

Published every Week

Vol. IV   Shanghai, 24th June, 1905   No. 26

$6.00 a Volume]   [30 Cts. One Copy

CONTENTS

Fair Trade   THE OPEN DOOR   No Favour

Printed by E. LEE, (Props. Aug. Michels), Shanghai

The final issue of the Miscellany.

Above: Old flagstoned post-road, Guizhou. Below: Desert fort at Jiayuguan.

Above: Miao girls with Welcoming Wine, Guizhou.
Below: Tibetan village on the Sichuan-Yunnan border.

CHINA
PROPER.

To China

An intricate tangle of events preceded Mesny's arrival in China in 1860. The causes dated back over two centuries to the foundation of China's final imperial dynasty, the Qing, and they were all the fault of Wu Sangui.

From the outside, China appears as a unity, inhabited by generic "Chinese". Of course it is to a large extent. Over ninety percent of the population class themselves as Han Chinese, the cultural descendants of the great Han dynasty which lasted from 206 BC to AD 220. But in a country currently numbering 1.4 billion people, even the relatively small remainder make up a fair-sized population of ethnic groups. There are more than fifty of these "minorities", most of them settled around China's fringes, including Tibetans, Mongolians, Muslim Hui and Uighur, Bai, Dong, Bouyei and Miao. They haven't always peacefully coexisted with the Han: many have risen in rebellion and some have even successfully taken over China and had a go at running the country.

In 1644 it was the turn of the Manchus, who lived up near the Korean border in what is now Dongbei, northeastern China. After decades of steady expansion their troops were lapping at the Great Wall and the only thing between them and the Chinese capital, Beijing, were the armies of General Wu Sangui. Then came news that the last Ming emperor had hanged himself and that a peasant warlord, Li Zicheng, had captured Beijing and was holding Wu Sangui's father and his beautiful concubine, Chen Yuanyuan, as hostage. Wu, outraged and without a Ming ruler to defend anymore, formed an alliance with the Manchus. Their combined forces swept south through the wall, threw out Li Zicheng, and entered Beijing on 6 June 1644. It was the beginning of the Qing dynasty.

For his role in the defeat of his homeland, China's new Manchu rulers packed Wu Sangui off to help pacify the remote southwest, where he chased the last Ming princes and their dwindling band of loyal followers right into Burma. Wu became governor of "Yungui", the combined provinces of Yunnan and Guizhou, building up a private army, keeping a tight rein on disgruntled tribes and accumulating wealth and power. All went well until 1673, when Wu's Manchu overlords, having consolidated their hold on the rest of the country, became concerned over his growing regional power and recalled him for retirement. Wu decided otherwise, made a pact with the Chinese governors of Guangdong and Fujian provinces, and launched the "Revolt of the Three Feudatories". But the Manchus proved better organised – and armed with European-designed cannons – and the rebellion was systematically suppressed. Wu died in 1678 and within three years the last of his supporters had been chased west to Kunming, the Yunnanese capital, and defeated. Seen as a traitor by both the Chinese and the Manchus, there are few monuments to Wu Sangui: legend has it that his grave was obliterated and his remains dug up and scattered to the four winds.

So the Qing were a foreign dynasty and at first their rule was bitterly resented by China's Han majority, who formed secret societies dedicated to their overthrow. As a mark of their subjugation, the Chinese were forced to shave the tops of their heads and grow a long plait of hair at the back – the humiliating "pigtail". Intermarriage between Manchu and Chinese was banned. Learning from their experiences with Wu, the Manchus also forbade regional authorities from personally recruiting local militias.

On the other hand, the early Qing period was one of the most stable in Chinese history. As warfare died away, trade and agriculture flourished under a firm but open-handed administration. Three successive emperors – Kangxi, Yongzheng and Qianlong – reigned for a total of 134 years; Qianlong ran the country so sympathetically that one popular rumour refused to accept that he was of Manchu stock, inventing all sorts of ways a Chinese baby could have been smuggled into the palace and raised as emperor. But by the time Qianlong abdicated in 1796, aged 85, the peace was beginning to unravel. Prosperity had created a population boom: there were land shortages, competition for resources and unrest. Chinese began to migrate westwards into less densely settled parts of the country, coming into conflict with the minority peoples who already lived there. And then there was the growing problem of foreign trade.

Throughout its history China had swung between openness towards the outside world – when the country absorbed foreign sciences, art and culture – and similar periods of isolationism. The conservative philosophy of Confucianism, one of the three formal strands of belief in China, held contempt for all things foreign, but the Manchus, as foreigners themselves, were to some extent immune to this prejudice. In fact, European Jesuits had been living in China since the sixteenth century, and their knowledge of the sciences and practical engineering skills (including improved methods for casting cannon, which had helped to defeat Wu Sangui) were highly valued by the Manchu court. In 1747, Qianlong even commissioned Jesuit architects to build him a grand Summer Palace, which they completed in a fusion of European and Chinese styles. For their part, the Jesuits were responsible for copying detailed maps of China's interior – including places that no foreigner had ever visited – and shipping them to France during the seventeenth century.

But while the Chinese were prepared to borrow and adapt a few useful alien ideas, commercially China was a closed shop. The Portuguese, later joined by the British, Dutch and French, had established trading posts along the south China coast as early as the sixteenth century, but business was very one-sided. The Chinese were happy enough to take the Europeans' silver in exchange for tea, silk and porcelain but had no interest in purchasing foreign goods, convinced that the country already produced everything it needed. And to emphasise the fact, they held these "barbarian merchants" at arms' length, eventually confining them to the vast city of Guangzhou, located way down on the nation's distant southern fringes near the mouth of the Pearl River. Even then, trade was only conducted during certain months of the year, and the foreigners were kept inside the grounds of their waterfront "factories" (which incorporated warehouses, club facilities and accommodation), absolutely forbidden to enter within Guangzhou's city walls. Those that managed to barge in past the guarded gateways were pelted with stones and filth by angry citizens, and few saw any sights interesting enough to justify the excursion. It was also illegal – on pain of execution – for anyone to teach the foreigners Chinese, so that all business had to be conducted through intermediaries, adding to the expense.

For an up-and-coming manufacturing sea power like Great Britain, thoroughly convinced of its own superiority and keen to muscle in to such a large potential market, the situation was intolerable. In 1792, the British government sent an embassy to Beijing to negotiate for a more balanced trade agreement, but the whole idea was rebuffed by Qianlong, who was unimpressed with the mission's gifts and, in a letter to King George III, grandly ordered his British counterpart to "Tremblingly obey and show no negligence" in any future dealings with China.

Determined to open up Chinese markets anyway, Britain cast around for a more devious plan. They found it in opium, the dried sap of a particular kind of poppy which grew wild across Europe and Asia. Chinese medicine already knew about opium and used it to cure fevers, rheumatism and malaria, but from the 1700s limited quantities were also smuggled into the country as a recreational drug. The British East India Company now vastly expanded this trade, sourcing opium cheaply from their holdings in Bengal, and by 1834 (when the company lost its lucrative tea monopoly) were importing about 30,000 chests of it into China every year. The flow of silver reversed in Britain's favour and the Qing court, alarmed at this rapid draining of the Imperial treasury, made several ineffectual efforts to halt the trade. But they were undermined both by resistance from Chinese middlemen at Guangzhou, who were making a tidy profit on opium sales, and a sad ignorance of foreigners: in one attempt to force Britain to the negotiating table, the court decided to ban the export of rhubarb, which they believed that the British urgently needed to cure their chronic constipation. When this dire threat was utterly ignored, the government ordered the incorruptible official Lin Zexu down to Guangzhou to study the situation first-hand. Lin made extensive enquiries about rhubarb and foreigners in general, politely informed the court that they had been misled, and decided that rather more in the way of direct action was needed. In June 1839 he blockaded the British inside their factories, confiscated 20,283 chests of opium – weighing 1,400kg and worth around ten million silver pieces – and destroyed the lot. When the news got home, Britain declared war.

The First Opium War wasn't much of a contest. Britain had modern warships and long practice in using them, while the Chinese had no comparable vessels, firepower or organization. Having shelled cities along the China coast, the British fleet moved inland up the Bei River to threaten Beijing's port, Tianjin. In 1841 Lin Zexu was stripped of his position and banished to China's remote northwest, and the job of negotiating a peace deal with these aggressive foreigners was given to a Manchu official named Qishan. The spat had all been about the right to free trade, and Britain now demanded a suitable piece of land on which to establish a permanent base, plus financial compensation for the destroyed opium and the insult given to national pride. Qishan agreed and even before a treaty was ratified had allowed Britain to occupy Hong Kong Island, off the coast south of Guangzhou near the mouth of the Pearl River.

Qishan's actions outraged everyone. The Emperor was furious that Chinese territory had been ceded without Imperial permission and had Qishan recalled to Beijing in chains, to follow Lin Zexu into exile. The warmongering British foreign secretary, Lord Palmerston, fumed that Hong Kong was a worthless, "barren island with hardly a house upon it". Fighting resumed, but there could only be one outcome. In August 1842 the Chinese signed the Treaty of Nanking: Britain was to receive twenty-one million silver dollars in reparations, the enormous sum to be paid within three years; the cities of Guangzhou, Xiamen, Fuzhou, Ningbo and Shanghai were opened up as "treaty ports" where consulates could be established, Christian missionaries could preach, and British merchants could live and conduct business; and Hong Kong Island was to be handed over to the victors in perpetuity. Taking advantage of the situation, America and France demanded similar concessions. Despite being the cause of the war, opium wasn't mentioned and the trade continued, costing China even more silver every year than it was paying out in damages.

Being conquered again by outsiders was a humiliating blow to the Chinese, who now remembered that the Manchus were themselves foreign. The pattern throughout Chinese history is that dynasties rule through a combination of public consent and military might; some upstart is always awaiting their chance to challenge the throne and when governments become both unpopular and weak, they fall. By allowing the country to be invaded, the widespread belief was that the Qing dynasty had exhausted the "Mandate of Heaven", which is its right to rule. The court inflamed the situation by increasing taxes to raise revenue for paying off the war indemnity. Taxation created poverty; poverty led to dissent; and dissent flared into fighting. By 1855 the government had four major rebellions on its hands: the Taiping and Nian in eastern China, the Miao in Guizhou province, and Muslim groups in Yunnan.

At this point the European powers decided to squeeze China for further concessions. The problem began at Guangzhou, where British merchants had attempted to set up shop in what was now, in theory, an open treaty port. But Guangzhou's ever-assertive population had rioted, burning down the magistrate's court and driving the foreigners back to their factories outside the city walls. The situation simmered away unresolved until 1856, when the Guangzhou authorities boarded a British-registered ship, the *Arrow*, to arrest its Chinese crew for piracy. According to the Treaty of Nanking, under which foreigners and their vessels were not subject to Chinese law, they should have asked permission first. A war of words between Chinese and British officials escalated into plain war: America was drawn in by the shelling of one of their ships, the Spanish by the killing of their vice-consul, the French by the execution of a missionary in Guangxi province and the Russians because everyone else was fighting. An international force gathered and marched on Beijing, demanding that the country cede more treaty ports, more trading rights and more money. Chinese militias fought back but were eventually defeated. As foreign armies surrounded the capital, the Qing court fled northeast into their Manchurian homelands and the British High Commissioner, Lord Elgin, vindictively ordered the Jesuit-designed Summer Palace destroyed as retribution for Chinese mistreatment of prisoners of war. The palace's demolition was witnessed by Captain Charles Gordon, who was shortly to be fighting on the Imperial side against the Taiping rebels: "after pillaging it, [we] burned the whole place, destroying in a vandal-like manner most valuable property, which could not be replaced for millions… you can scarcely imagine the beauty and magnificence of the palaces we burned… it was a scene of utter destruction which passes my description". The ruins survive to this day, deliberately preserved as a showcase of barbarian aggression.

China capitulated to all of Britain's demands. On 24 October 1860, Lord Elgin and the Manchu representative, Prince Gong Yixin – looking unsurprisingly bitter and sullen in contemporary photographs – signed the Convention of Peking, ending the Second Opium War. And within weeks, an eighteen-year-old William Mesny stepped ashore in China.

Mesny was born on Jersey, one of the Channel Islands between France and England, on 9 October 1842, "when the apples are in season and cider is considered a most refreshing drink". He was the first of three children; his brother John was two years younger while his sister Mary Ann was born in 1846. The family name (also sometimes written as Mesney) was properly pronounced "may-knee", but as William's Chinese name transliterates as "*mai shi ni*", he probably pronounced the "s" in later life. The family was poor: his mother was an invalid while his father, a Methodist preacher, appeared as a "Shoemaker" on the 1851 census. Mesny always described himself as a Jerseyman, though shortly after his birth the family returned to his father's home on the smaller island of Alderney, and William grew up there.

In 1847 the British Admiralty started building a breakwater and series of forts on Alderney, and Mesny left school at the age of eight – astonishingly early for a man who was to become such a prolific writer – working first at the brickyards and then with stonecutters, carrying tools to the blacksmith to be sharpened. He picked up the basics of smithying along the way and within a few years was learning how to draw up plans, survey with a theodolite and use explosives for excavating. After the fortifications were completed and construction work dried up in 1854, Mesny helped out around the harbour until, one day, a cutter named the

Napier, bound for Cherbourg, found itself short-handed and took him on as crew. The Crimean War was then in full swing, Britain and France joining forces to fight Russian expansionism into Turkey and the Baltic, and there was a steady run of vessels taking supplies to the continent.

And so, for a wage of one pound – the foundation of his fortune, as he put it – Mesny became a sailor. He served as a cabin boy aboard the West Indiaman *Bellweather*, then spent five years in various vessels orbiting between Europe, Africa, South America and Australasia. A brief glimpse of his life at sea emerges from the pages of the Australian newspaper, the *Sydney Morning Herald*: on 4 July 1860 there was a brawl aboard the barque *Ann*, recently arrived at Sydney from London, and seaman William Mesny found himself in the Water Police court the next day for kicking his bosun, David Andrews, in the ribs, unprovoked; he was ordered to pay a fine of twenty shillings or face a week in jail. Crew lists for the *Ann* show that Mesny was one of the youngest members aboard, and his position as an ordinary seaman meant that he was still working as a general hand, without any authority. He wouldn't have had much to lose by giving up the sea.

The China that greeted Mesny a few months after this incident existed as a direct consequence of the Opium Wars. Angry and humiliated, the country was dividing into factions: revolutionaries, eager to overthrow the old order; conservatives, trying to ignore China's disintegration and attempting to hold on to power; and reformers, keen to adopt the very Western technologies which had proved so superior against their own. None of them were necessarily friendly to foreigners but it was in this unstable environment, rich with opportunity, that Mesny was to flourish. For Britain, the greatest territorial trophy of the Opium Wars had been Hong Kong. It seems appropriate that Mesny began his China career there.

In fact, that's a bit of a gloss. Mesny's first port of call after Sydney was Shanghai, where he deserted his ship in late 1860. It would be satisfying to know his reasons for quitting life as a sailor, but he wrote very little about his beginnings in China. The Shanghai area was then a battleground of marauding Taiping rebels, the Imperial forces fighting them and bands of foreign mercenaries, willing to take up arms for either cause. Lured by the chance of "not only [making] more money than by sea-faring, but also winning for themselves a name and possibly a distinguished reputation", British and American crews at Shanghai were deserting in such huge numbers that ship-owners were having trouble finding enough men to safely put back out to sea. Mesny was most likely one of the many new arrivals in town hoping to join in the fray, though – as he was to admit much later – it's possible that his plans were sidetracked by a brief addiction to opium.

Whatever the reason, Mesny resurfaced at Hong Kong in April 1861 to find that he couldn't make himself understood, despite having picked up a smattering of Chinese at Shanghai. So, despite whatever else he'd been up to, he certainly couldn't have travelled far, or he would have known that the Shanghai dialect was very local. The notion of "Chinese" as a language is as slippery as that of "Chinese" as a people, and the country is a mess of regional tongues, dialects and accents. Northerners, with their purring vernacular, are largely unintelligible to people living in the central provinces. Shanghainese is about as closely related to Cantonese, the language spoken in Hong Kong, as French is to Italian. Hong Kongers have trouble with the Cantonese dialect used one hundred kilometres away in Guangzhou. China does of course have a national language, Mandarin, which – in theory – is understood to some extent by anyone who has been to school. But even here pronunciation around the country differs by as much as spoken English varies from place to place in Britain.

Mesny's account of his ten months in Hong Kong is thin on facts but rich in Victorian melodrama. He begins the tale with two Cantonese salt merchants, named Li and Luke, who were sailing to the island from Guangzhou. They were probably smugglers. Salt was a government monopoly in nineteenth-century China, but the British at Hong Kong decided that locally harvested sea salt wouldn't be taxed and there were huge profits to be made by smuggling it to the mainland for sale. At any rate, pirates had boarded the merchants' ship and killed the crew when Mesny "turned up, gave chase, and the pirates let go their prize in order

to escape". Li and Luke gratefully took William in and arranged for him
to marry Loving Pearl, only daughter of the prosperous Huang family.
Mesny played along for a while, writing awful, slushy poems about the
girl which he later reprinted in the *Miscellany*, but eventually got cold
feet and wriggled out of the deal. Not long afterwards, Li and Luke were
arrested over a business affair that had gone awry in Guangzhou and
Mesny headed back to Shanghai to try out his luck there.

A romantic episode, but it still leaves unanswered the question of
what Mesny was doing in Hong Kong in the first place. Since the British
had taken possession nineteen years earlier, this mountainous island had
become the hub of their China trade. Though only fourteen kilometres
wide, it had a superb harbour – a broad, sheltered strait between Hong
Kong and the mainland to the north – and was well-positioned at the
mouth of the Pearl River, conveniently close to Chinese markets at the
treaty port of Guangzhou. But unlike Guangzhou, where foreigners were
still having a tough time establishing themselves, Hong Kong's main
settlement, Victoria town, was British built, British owned and British
run. Victoria was also safely isolated from the Taiping Rebellion which
was still running riot across mainland China; Shanghai itself was now
under siege, and, with Imperial armies bogged down elsewhere, it was
even possible that the city was going to fall – which as much as anything
may explain why Mesny had decided to seek his fortune in Hong Kong.

After rough, fever-ridden beginnings, by 1861 Victoria was beginning
to coalesce into a well-planned town filling the narrow band of land
between Hong Kong's north shore and the steep lower slopes of the Peak,
the island's rocky apex. Elegant stone buildings with shady colonnades and
wraparound balconies were replacing earlier ramshackle constructions;
roads were being surveyed, reservoirs dug, telegraph lines installed,
avenues of trees planted and a racetrack and botanical gardens laid out.
The resident population of some 1500 Westerners were outnumbered
a hundred to one by the Chinese, most of them Cantonese-speaking
immigrants from the southern coast, drawn by Hong Kong's burgeoning
trade opportunities; Chinese artisans and trading firms were doing brisk
business and the harbour was full of junks and European sailing ships.
Hong Kong – an approximation of the Cantonese for "Fragrant Harbour",

heung gong – is said to be named after the trade in sandalwood once conducted here, though Mesny deliberately mistranslated it as "Fragrant Streams" so that he could moan about the new town's "odiferous drains". Clearly, there were still a few sanitation issues to sort out.

Despite Victoria's commercial success, Britain soon became dissatisfied with owning such a tiny piece of Chinese territory. As the Second Opium War escalated through the 1850s, they demanded the narrow Kowloon peninsula too, lying directly north across the harbour. This was a notorious refuge for criminals, who would constantly drift south to the island and cause trouble, and the British authorities were tired of having to periodically round them up, brand them on the ear and deport them back over the harbour, to be imprisoned if they reappeared Hong Kong-side. So the Chinese government leased Kowloon to Britain in early 1860, just as the Anglo-French war fleet was looking for somewhere to reprovision itself before sailing up the coast to bombard Beijing into submission. A splendid photographic panorama taken by Felice Beato in March of that year shows Hong Kong harbour full of warships, the white tents of French and British forces encamped amongst Kowloon's vegetable plots. At the end of the war, the Convention of Peking cancelled the lease and gifted Kowloon to Britain, expanding the territory that they had forcibly taken from China.

And even this hadn't satisfied the British. In 1898, a new ninety-nine-year lease allowed them to push the Hong Kong border north again from Kowloon, by which they acquired a huge chunk of Chinese land known as the New Territories. This time the villagers fought back, but the colonial administration sent in gunboats and killed five hundred people, whose names are still posted up today in local ancestral halls. There was also resistance from a garrison outpost known to the British as Kowloon City – unflatteringly described by Mesny as a "dirty little walled town called Chinese Kowloon" – whose defiant commander insisted that the Chinese authorities be allowed to continue their jurisdiction. The British warships returned and Kowloon City fell without a fight, but general resistance to the British occupation simmered for decades. Mesny was outraged at this opposition, which he felt was being stirred up by duplicitous Chinese authorities and, in an uncharacteristically jingoistic outburst, exhorted the British government to retaliate by annexing all of southern China.

China simply outwaited the colonialists. Britain ignored Mesny's advice and left southern China alone. Hong Kong Island developed into one of the world's richest banking and business hubs, but the legal status of Kowloon City was never resolved and it became the haunt of criminals and the dispossessed, a no-go area for Hong Kong's police right up until its demolition in 1991. Today, a park occupies the site, with the original stone blocks inscribed with the characters for "Kowloon Walled Stockade" set into the south gate. The British invested so much money and infrastructure in the New Territories that they eventually became integral to the existence of Hong Kong as a whole, the source of most of its water and home to half of its population. When their ninety-nine-year lease expired in 1997, Britain had no choice but to hand the entire package back to China: the New Territories, Kowloon, Hong Kong Island, the wealth, the lot.

Mesny skips over anything as mundane as how he made a living in Hong Kong, but the China Directory residents list crisply fills in this omission with three words and an initial: "Mesney, W. turnkey, gaol". A lowly position then, which Mesny quietly edited out of his memoirs: in China, being a prison warder was considered so demeaning that even your children were barred from ever holding public office, though this particular post was a moderately well-paid one at £75 per year. His workplace was Victoria Prison, wedged uphill from the harbour between Hollywood Road and Old Bailey Street, which employed a mix of Sikh guards, European warders and Chinese office staff. In 1861 the original wooden stockade, built twenty years earlier for a fraction of the inmates that the prison now housed, was being upgraded to stone though everything remained shambolic: during Mesny's time here a new wall collapsed and, in another incident, a group of prisoners simply crawled to freedom down a drain.

Few documents relating to Victoria Prison's early days seem to have survived, the records perhaps destroyed during the Japanese occupation of Hong Kong during World War II. Another possible reason behind their disappearance involves Daniel Caldwell, Protector of Chinese during the 1850s. Caldwell seems to have protected them too well, turning a blind eye towards – or possibly even supporting – gambling, racketeering, prostitution and piracy. When one of his Chinese associates threatened to testify against him in 1860, Caldwell had him jailed on slavery charges. The affair was reported in the London *Times* and a public inquiry ordered; the Hong Kong Governor, John Bowring, was retired and replaced by reformer Hercules Robinson and Caldwell hid his tracks by destroying as many records as possible. He was eventually found guilty of consorting with pirates and dismissed from the service (though, ironically, later re-employed by the government during an anti-piracy campaign). At least, that's the story as reported in one of Hong Kong's earliest newspapers, the *Friend of China*, run by the habitually indignant William Tarrant, which detailed prison floggings, meagre rice gruel diets, abuse of inmates by the governor and poor wages paid to the warders. Tarrant had himself served time for libel and so had many axes to grind, but if this tale is true, it's hardly surprising that Mesny kept quiet about having worked for such a discredited institution.

Mesny did, in fact, make one oblique hint about his prison-warder career in the *Miscellany*. As his escapade with Li and Luke had shown, pirates were a serious menace all along the south China coast; the problem was already so acute during the early Qing dynasty that the Manchu government forcibly relocated China's entire coastal population far inland, hoping to deprive the pirates of both prey and settlements to hide out in. It didn't work. By the 1860s, Hong Kong's wealthy marine traffic had become the target of regular assaults, and contemporary newspapers were abound with tales of crews murdered and hostages taken, to be tortured and executed if ransom demands were ignored. In one famous incident, the British merchant brig *North Star* was attacked with firebombs and boarded, the captain killed and $4000 in gold stolen. By no means were all the pirates Chinese either, and Mesny – who was in town during the *North Star* incident – knew Europeans engaged in the trade, including "William Kilburn, nicknamed Fokey Bill... another was named May, *alias* Allen, and nicknamed Gentleman Jack... and also

Four-fingered Jack, because one of his thumbs were missing, having been blown off or chopped off in some fight... [There were also] Red Edwards, Kelly the Bloke and another called Kelly the Rake, all of whom I had seen personally". Fokey Bill dressed as a Chinese and was a regular patron of the notorious Taiping Shan district, the ironically-named "Peaceful Mountain" just up the road from the jail, whose gambling dens and grog-houses were the haunt of prostitutes, thieves and all manner of low-lifes. Mesny must have met these men during his stint as a warder.

There's no record of when Mesny began working at the prison – his name is missing from a staff roster compiled in July 1861 – but a letter between Hercules Robinson and the Secretary of State for the Colonies, Lord Newcastle, fixes the abrupt end to his career as late February 1862:

"My Lord, I have the honour to report that I have appointed, from 24th instant, Mathew de Chagas to be a turnkey in Victoria Gaol, in the place of William Mesney, dismissed."

Robinson never reveals why he sacked Mesney, though a large turnover in prison staff wasn't unusual; the previous year had seen a flurry of mass hirings and firings, and Mathew de Chagas himself was returning to a post he had quit eighteen months earlier. Perhaps Mesney had already planned to leave Hong Kong, as immediately after his dismissal he departed aboard the P&O steamer *Aden*, bound for Shanghai. For the first time his stated motives were clear: he hoped to join a band of foreign mercenaries who were gathering to defend Shanghai from the Taiping rebels. This must have seemed an exciting prospect after his unheroic stint at the gaol, though Mesney might have been less enthusiastic at leaving the safety of Hong Kong had he realised the role that the Taipings would play in his immediate future.

BLOCKADE RUNNING ON THE YANGZI
1862–63

The roots of the Taiping Rebellion reach back to the 1840s and the general loss of faith in the Manchu government following China's defeat in the First Opium War. Peasants in central China found themselves facing new taxes, levied to help pay off the war indemnity demanded by Britain, just as the region was brought low by drought. Left penniless and hungry, many drifted into banditry, and a succession of anti-government scuffles broke out across central China.

Amongst the disaffected was Hong Xiuquan, a failed civil service candidate and Christian convert who experienced visions in which he appeared as Christ's younger brother. Reinterpreting the bible accordingly, he converted family and friends to his version of the religion and began to preach the overthrow of the Qing dynasty. On 11 January 1851, Hong and ten thousand followers launched an armed rebellion at Jintian village in the southwestern province of Guangxi, under the banner "Taiping Tianguo", the Kingdom of Heavenly Peace. Considering the unparalleled slaughter his insurrection was to cause, Hong might have chosen a more suitable name. To emphasise their break with Manchu laws, the Taipings cut off their pigtails and stopped shaving the top of their heads, becoming known to their enemies as *chang mao zei*, the "Long-haired Traitors".

The following year Hong's army swept up into northern Guangxi, battering aside forces sent against them and swelling their ranks with fresh recruits. Crossing into Hunan province, they met their first real setback attempting to take the provincial capital, Changsha, where they were defeated by the scholar-general Zeng Guofan. Warned of the Taiping's approach, Zeng had cobbled together a rabble of local militias into what was to become the efficient Hunan Army, the first Chinese-run provincial force since Wu Sangui's time. Zeng's success against the Taipings marked the beginning of Hunan's century-long domination of Chinese politics and the military, and inspired other provincial authorities to create their own forces. Mesny himself was to later serve with the Hunan Army in Guizhou.

Chased away from Changsha, the Taipings regrouped and moved up to the Yangzi river, the huge trade and transport artery which flows eastwards right across central China, connecting the landlocked interior provinces to the sea near Shanghai. At Yueyang town they captured an enormous quantity of weapons and ships, then sailed downstream to Wuhan, capital of Hubei province. By this time the Taipings were no longer a small but feisty rural army: having looted the provincial treasury at Wuhan, they found themselves with money and upwards of half a million followers, all eager to reap the rewards of rebellion. Cruising ever-eastwards, their armada took several ports along the Yangzi's middle reaches before finally capturing the walled metropolis of Nanjing in March 1853. Nanjing became the Taiping capital and within two years the rebels had secured a power base for themselves along the lower Yangzi valley, a seven-hundred-kilometre-long stretch of the river between Wuhan and Shanghai.

It would be difficult to overstate how seriously the fall of Nanjing shocked Qing prestige: the city was not only strategically important but had deep symbolic associations too. During the fourteenth century the founder of the Ming dynasty, the former beggar-monk Hongwu, had driven the Mongol Yuan dynasty from China and then settled at Nanjing, and the city's name – meaning "Southern Capital" – stood as a direct challenge to the "Northern Capital" of Beijing. The Ming had been the country's last Han Chinese dynasty, and by making Nanjing their headquarters the Taipings declared their intent to overthrow the despised alien regime and re-establish Han supremacy, just as Hongwu had done by evicting the Mongols centuries before._

Nanjing had also been the scene of recent humiliation, where British gunboats forced the Qing government to sign the treaty that ended the first Opium War in 1842. On that occasion Nanjing's citizens had put up a stiff fight, but now the city apparently fell without a struggle: the Taipings slaughtered the entire Manchu population – men, women and children – and threw their bodies into the Yangzi. The modern scourge of opium was outlawed, along with prostitution, slavery, and the crippling practice of binding the feet of young girls, which created the tiny but grossly deformed foot considered beautiful by Chinese men. Less commendably, the Taipings, as Christians, systematically destroyed the city's temples and the four-hundred-year-old Porcelain Pagoda, a tall and elegant landmark glazed in white tiles.

At this stage, foreign powers in China adopted a "wait and see" neutrality towards the Taipings, impressed perhaps by their drive and Christian leanings but worried about the opium prohibition and preferring a weak, divided China under the Manchus to a strong, unified China under anyone else. For their part, the Qing might have found it easier to suppress the rebels if they hadn't become distracted by the Second Opium War, which was beginning to unfold. Fortunately for the beleaguered Chinese government, the Taipings were having their own internal troubles at Nanjing. In 1856 an attempted coup against Hong Xiuquan led to a purge amongst the rebel leadership, after which Hong became increasingly paranoid and left the running of his rebellion to others. With resources on both sides stretched, Taiping and Imperial forces battled inconclusively across eastern China, each struggling to gain possession of towns that they would hold for only a few months before losing again.

The stalemate continued until 1860. Early that year the Taipings launched their Eastern Campaign, first capturing Suzhou, a wealthy canal town south of the Yangzi, then attacking Shanghai. But here the rebels ran up against "Ward's Force", a well-armed band of seventy-odd freebooters, deserters and sailors led by the American mercenary Frederick Townsend Ward. Much to everyone's surprise, this ragtag militia scored a few initial successes, possibly because the rebels were under orders not to fire on foreigners, but to befriend them. Then in October the British and Manchu governments concluded the Second Opium War, freeing up China's armies to concentrate on fighting the Taipings. The foreigners now considered the valuable treaty they had just squeezed from the Qing court. How many concessions would they lose, or have to renegotiate, if the rebels won control of the country? They looked at the formerly wealthy trade along the Yangzi valley, torn apart by the conflict, and wondered how profitable their riverside treaty ports would be if the war carried on for much longer. Western missionaries, believing the Taipings' take on Christianity to be heretical, clamoured for their defeat and removal. For the first time, Britain considered taking sides.

In the Spring of 1861 – around the time Mesny left for Hong Kong – a British naval expedition cruised upstream along the Yangzi from Shanghai, installing consuls at their new treaty ports and warning the Taipings to keep away from these towns. In part the threat was effective: the Taipings dropped plans for the recapture of Wuhan and instead renewed their efforts to take Shanghai. They routed Qing forces and captured the suburbs but were again driven back by foreign militias, who were using modern artillery for the first time in China. Elsewhere, the Imperial armies began to make gains against the rebels too, systematically clearing the Taipings from satellite provinces and retaking Anqing, a key Yangzi port about halfway between Nanjing and Wuhan.

By this time Ward's Force had been virtually wiped out in a skirmish west of Shanghai. The badly-injured Ward had survived, however, and was now busy teaching modern military tactics to a Chinese brigade which became known, rather grandly, as the Ever Victorious Army. Ward was further appointed *fujiang* or colonel, the first foreigner of the times to be awarded a high Chinese military rank. His sponsor was a protégé of Zeng Guofan named Li Hongzhang, a brilliant scholar with a military bent who, in his mid-twenties, had come third in the Imperial examinations. These civil service exams, requiring years of rigorous study in the Confucian classical texts, were open to almost all Chinese, regardless of social background or wealth, and had been used to select government officials for over a thousand years. Aspiring scholars were tested at district, regional and finally Imperial level, sometimes bankrupting themselves to travel from their homes to the examination centres, where they would spend weeks walled up in solitary cells. Despite this conservative schooling Li Hongzhang had become fascinated by foreign technology, joining a growing number of similarly pragmatic military officials who had experienced first-hand the superiority of Western firepower. Li spent his life employing foreign advisors, rose to become a powerful statesman and politician, and – much later on – was to play a telling role in Mesny's career.

Away from the Yangzi battlefields, another far-reaching conflict was taking place inside the Imperial Household in Beijing. The old emperor had died and his successor, Tongzhi, was only six years old. A palace coup in November 1861 led to the regency of Prince Gong, the man who had stared angrily back at the camera whilst being forced to sign away his country's rights to Britain at the end of the Second Opium War. Prince Gong raised Tongzhi's mother, Cixi, to a position of authority as Empress Dowager, one that she used to take gradual control of the monarchy over the next fifty years. Concerned only with maintaining her own hold on power, Cixi was supported by those palace officials whose positions depended on the old ruling order and had the most to lose if it collapsed. Their stance became fiercely anti-foreign, and the political struggle between conservative and reformist factions divided the court and drew its attention inwards at a time where it should have been aggressively countering outside intervention and civil war.

But all this lay far in the future: in February 1862 Prince Gong remained in command. He had reason enough to hate foreigners and everything that they represented but decided to set aside personal feelings and support Zeng Guofan, Li Hongzhang and other reformers looking to adopt Western military methods against the Taipings. Meanwhile, the district around Shanghai was under siege, and Mesny had just returned from Hong Kong.

Britain had taken Shanghai in 1843 as one of its first batch of treaty ports, attracted by its strategic location halfway along China's eastern seaboard near the mouth of the Yangzi. A foreign quarter had sprung up alongside the original Chinese city, protected from the river by a flood-proof embankment and from the rebels by a volunteer force, some heavy-duty artillery and a rammed-earth wall. Inside these defences were warehouses, consular buildings and dirt streets that became impassably muddy during the heavy summer rain. By 1862 the city and its suburbs was bursting with refugees fleeing fighting in the surrounding countryside – half a million of them, according to one estimate – rubbing shoulders with newly-arrived Western entrepreneurs, clergy, the military and all manner of seedy adventurers.

Mesny arrived back into this melee with Major W. Brennan, a former US Cavalryman who was immediately snapped up by Ward for use in his Ever Victorious Army. For unexplained reasons, Mesny decided not to serve under Ward and instead assembled a dozen other like-minded mercenaries and a fleet of war-junks intent on liberating Ningbo, a coastal port to the northeast which had fallen to the rebels a few months earlier. Despite this, Mesny's plans fell through: crossing the ruins of the French Quarter on the evening before their departure, he was challenged by guards, answered in French, and was promptly arrested as a French army deserter. By the time he had proved otherwise, his friends had departed for Ningbo without him.

So Mesny found himself stranded at Shanghai, but with fighting raging outside the city walls it wasn't long before he found alternative employment as a blockade runner. Historically, goods had always been ferried along China's rivers in preference to using the country's appallingly-maintained network of roads, and the Yangzi – which originated on the country's distant western borders with Tibet – was the biggest of them all, widely known as *chang jiang*, the Long River. Now the foreign powers, given that their whole purpose in China was to turn a profit, saw the Yangzi as the easiest way to deliver their wares to untapped markets in the remote interior. Shanghai and the Sichuanese port of Chongqing, 1700 kilometres upstream, were the two poles of the Yangzi trade, with Wuhan, the main marketplace for central China, roughly halfway between them. Chongqing was still closed to outsiders but, despite the turmoil, river traffic between Shanghai and Wuhan was increasing and there was good money to be made for anyone willing to risk running supplies upstream through the various blockades. The work was extremely hazardous: as it was impossible to distinguish between pirates, Taipings and Imperial forces – and you were in any case likely to be robbed, sunk or murdered by any one of them – the general rule was to travel in a convoy and fire on any vessel that attempted an approach. As Mesny put it, "it was dangerous to be merciful in those days".

Ideally, you wanted to run the blockades in a foreign-registered ship. The Taipings were still unsure of the consequences of attacking Westerners, so flying the British flag might reduce the risk of being boarded, but the biggest advantage was in the matter of paying *lijin*, the hated transport taxes on goods. Chinese merchants were subject to them at all manner of toll-houses on roads and rivers, both official and unofficial; the amounts levied were unpredictable and there was the certainty of having to fork out an additional "squeeze" to greedy local authorities. In theory at least, British traders were only bound to pay *lijin* at treaty ports, where Western powers were busy helping the Chinese government establish efficient, foreign-staffed customs posts and where the tariffs were fixed. But in reality, the rules offered little protection. The British naval officer Augustus Lindley (who, along with his wife, fought for the Taiping cause and defended them passionately in his memoir *Ti-Ping Tien-Kwoh*), found firearms far more effective than the law: "Every two or three [kilometres] some wretched little bamboo hut would make its appearance round a bend of the creek, with a long pole and dirty white rag on the end, containing huge red and black characters, setting forth the official nature of the den. Then sundry opium-stuffed, villainous-looking mandarin soldiers would rush from their pipes and gambling, catch up their rusty gingalls and spears, and loudly call on my Chinese captain to "soong mow" (let go the anchor), and pay a duty, or squeeze, into their dirty hands. Upon such occasions, P— and myself would be compelled to get on deck with our fowling-pieces, and drive the harpies off, when they would sullenly retire to their opium and cards, muttering curses upon [us] and trusting for better prey next time."

Of course, there were better profits to be made by not paying any taxes at all, and Mesny knew that smuggled salt sold at Wuhan for a dozen times its purchase price further downstream. Buying salt for resale was in itself illegal (if caught, smugglers faced having their vessels confiscated and sawn in two), but given the confusion of war, there was a good chance of getting away with it. And salt was by no means the only contraband that ships carried upriver. In a slippery series of articles entitled "How I

Made My Fortune", Mesny spun an impersonal yarn about the wealth to be made from smuggling weapons, if you could sell to the right people – either Taiping or Imperial – without being double-crossed or caught. He was less coy elsewhere in the *Miscellany*, frankly admitting: "I made a few very successful speculations in the arms trade, on my own or on joint account with other like-minded people". Without a doubt, Mesny made his first big profits in China as gun-runner out of Shanghai.

Mesny's first blockade run began in March 1862, escorting a convoy of Chinese boats from Shanghai to Wuhan with a British business associate called "Captain Bob". Their ship, the *Rob Roy*, was an armed junk, a high-sided wooden Chinese vessel with a raised stern, a rectangular hand-stitched sail and a local crew. Anticipating the likely dangers ahead, the two of them invested in an ancient but powerful rifle complete with bayonet, a brace of double-barrelled pistols, a Colt revolver and a British naval cutlass; early on in the journey Mesny ran through an ostentatious weapons drill so that word would get about that they were well-armed. The thought of meeting Taipings didn't seem to worry them nearly as much as running into Imperial forces, which the *Miscellany* portrays as aggressive and bullying, and likely as not to pay off a Chinese crew to mutiny against foreign captains in order to steal their cargoes. The Taipings insultingly referred to the Chinese troops as *yao mo gui*, loosely "Imperial Devils", or, as Mesny liked to call them, "Imps".

The *Rob Roy* made it unscathed through to Zhenjiang, 250km west of Shanghai, though not without having to weather a storm and scare off a couple of pirate vessels with some target practice – incidents which terrified the crew but left Mesny and Captain Bob feeling almost heroic. The city marked the junction of the Yangzi River and the Grand Canal, one of the many oversized but functional prestige projects that Chinese rulers have indulged in over the centuries, which connects the fertile Yangzi region with China's dry northern plains. The canal's value to trade, transport and irrigation are indisputable but millions of peasants were unwillingly drafted to work in its construction, and the repressive Sui dynasty who commissioned the project lasted less than forty years.

Zhenjiang itself had fallen to the British in July 1842; the city had been thought impregnable but the Chinese had yet to grasp the superiority of foreign arms and its capture saw distraught Qing officials committing suicide *en masse*, setting fire to the Manchu quarter and slaughtering their families rather than have them fall into barbarian hands. Then the Taipings descended, and the city was again destroyed during a messy recapture by Imperial forces in 1861. Now the new British consulate had just set up shop inside a well-defended temple complex, but the inner city remained a shambles of ruins; Zhenjiang's population was starving and the surrounding war-ravaged farmland a desolate, treeless wilderness. The city later bounced back to become famous for its black vinegar and as the one-time home of the American novelist Pearl Buck, and both Mesny's brother and nephew were to spend years here working in the Imperial Maritime Customs Service – as did Charles Welsh Mason, a young Englishman whose involvement with a Chinese secret society was to have a catastrophic effect on Mesny's later career.

Back on the river, the *Rob Roy*'s next stop was Shi'er Wei, a marketplace for salt where, thanks to the rebellion, smuggling had become rampant. Much of the business was run by the "Green Gang", a fearsome cartel of former Grand Canal barge crews left unemployed after shipping grain along the waterway had been banned in case the precious cargoes fell into Taiping hands. Now the gang had turned to crime to make ends meet, and were so successful in their new career that by the 1920s they were running the Shanghai underworld. Mesny and the *Rob Roy*'s crew landed and spent everything they could afford – $20 in his case – on contraband to carry through to Wuhan. They now had to sneak past the Taiping capital, Nanjing, without getting shot up by either the menacing Imperial navy, which was beginning to mass here, or the outlying, rebel-held Mud Forts. The Taipings spotted them and seemed friendly enough, waving them over, but they decided to play safe and took advantage of a fair wind to hurry past, putting Nanjing as far behind them as possible before dark.

Crossing into Anhui province, the landscape became flat, brilliant green and very watery, with reed beds stretching in all directions; deer were grazing along the riverbank and Mesny shot a duck with his pistol. Away to the south, glowering purple storm clouds obscured Huang Shan, the Yellow Mountains – a mass of poetically worn granite summits covered in contorted pine trees. The soil here was rich and by rights Anhui should have been a major producer of crops, but it was eastern China's poorest province: the south was too mountainous, the middle too sodden and the north too dry.

At Wuhu Mesny again found ruins, starvation and friendly Taipings, all decked out in red sashes or turbans, who were openly bartering goods – most likely weapons – from the British-registered *Waterwitch*, in exchange for tea. The rebels offered Mesny silver bars on trust to buy percussion caps or gunpowder for them and called the Westerners *yang xiongdi*, "foreign brothers", in marked contrast to the derogatory *yang guizi*, "foreign devils", used by the Imperialist forces.

Upstream they heard firing and saw thousands of villagers fleeing across the Yangzi in large wooden tubs, escaping soldiers who were setting fire to their homes. Passing Tongling, they were forced to pull ashore for a government inspection and ran into serious trouble for the first time. The city was swarming with Imperial troops, and they soon had some pushy officials aboard wanting to buy arms and ammunition. The next thing they knew, a soldier was making off into a boat with Bob's pistols and Mesny realised that his dagger had been stolen. In the ensuing fracas they recovered the guns and put off into the river unharmed, if extremely angry, but the "Imps" fired arrows and rockets at the *Rob Roy* from the shore until Mesny scared them off with his rifle.

A little further on, the Zhenfeng pagoda lifted up out of the north bank, the whitewashed brick tower rising sixty metres over Anhui's capital, Anqing. Pagodas are believed to have flood-protecting properties, but just to make sure this one was also chained down by two iron anchors, their prongs were set in concrete on either side of Zhenfeng's entrance. Anqing didn't encourage a stopover, however; the city had finally fallen to Imperial forces the previous September after an appalling fourteen-month siege in which the defenders, starved beyond endurance, had resorted to cannibalism. Towards the end of the blockade the Taiping commander here, Chen Yucheng – also known as *si yan gou*, the "Four-eyed Dog", after a pair of birthmarks on his face – had been lured away on a foolhardy attempt to recapture Wuhan, which had fallen into Imperial hands. It was a bad mistake: the Taipings were chased back from Wuhan by the British and, without Chen's troops to defend it, Anqing was left open for the Qing armies to storm. The Taipings' reserve force in the city, who had been waiting for reinforcements which never arrived, almost broke through Imperial lines near the pagoda but were finally overwhelmed; tens of thousands were slaughtered and the British explorer Thomas Blakiston, on his way upstream in an unsuccessful attempt to reach Tibet and India, saw the river choked with headless corpses.

The next official customs house was at the newly-established treaty port of Jiujiang, set around two-thirds of the way to Wuhan at the borderlands of Anhui, Jiangxi and Hubei provinces. Everyone they met here was desperate to buy salt and they looked set to make a tidy profit at their journey's end. Mesny went ashore but was shocked to find this formerly wealthy city, which had once been a lively market for tea and porcelain brought up from the imperial kilns at Jingdezhen, utterly laid to waste by the rebellion: "A single dilapidated street, composed only of a few mean shops, was all that existed of this once thriving and populous city; the remainder of the vast area, comprised within walls of five or six miles in circumference, contained nothing but ruins, weeds, and kitchen gardens". Following their most recent victory, government troops had massacred the city's elderly and infirm and had taken the rest as slaves; Mesny saw a soldier leading two children through the streets on a rope, hoping to sell them. Jiujiang's tiny foreign community lived under virtual siege, forced to carry weapons for protection against the xenophobic Imperial militia now in control of the urban area. The hatred was mutual. Mesny asked the British Consular Constable how he learned to speak Chinese: "'Speak Chinese?' he said indignantly, 'I speak English to them with this Penang lawyer [cane], that's the only language the brutes can be made to understand.'"

Thoroughly dispirited, they set sail for Wuxue, a short run upstream, but this small town proved equally nightmarish. The population were gruesomely butchering packs of dogs for some festival; a "white bone" pagoda proved to be full of corpses. On the way back to the boat, hostile crowds gathered as a band of assertive prostitutes tried to drag Mesny off the street. He had to be rescued by one of his crew, who calmed the mob down and escorted Mesny safely back on board.

Later that night they ran aground in gale, but no damage was done. It had just been a bad day.

Wuhan was reached without further incident in late April 1862, after a six-week run up from Shanghai. The metropolis actually comprised of three separate, self-contained cities, facing each other at the confluence of the kilometre-wide Yangzi and smaller Han river, and the combined population – maybe two million – was matched worldwide only by that of contemporary London or Tokyo. With the war raging downstream, inland trade had focused on Wuhan and thousands of vessels clogged the Yangzi here, despite the appalling summer heat which had the city labelled – along with Nanjing and Chongqing – as one of the Yangzi's "three furnaces".

For the British, the most important of Wuhan's districts was the treaty port of Hankou, which stretched thinly along the Yangzi's north bank. An embryonic European quarter was emerging above the waterfront, though most Westerners still lived elsewhere in Chinese-style houses, raised high on piles against the inevitable summer floods. Hankou's adjacent Chinese quarter formed a tightly-packed sprawl of unremarkable white buildings perked up by a scattering of more elaborate temples and guildhalls, ornate complexes divided up into rectangular courtyards and decorated with small gardens, ponds, shrubs and oddly-shaped rocks. The city streets were shaded by overhead bamboo awnings and almost impassable with livestock, labourers, porters, hawkers, barbers, ear-cleaners, beggars and all manner of craftsmen, each of them advertising their trade with distinctive calls. Walking through this mass of humanity was so arduous that few Europeans ventured far into the city on foot, preferring instead to move around by junk, docking at private jetties.

West across the Han river from Hankou was the satellite settlement of Hanyang, later to become China's first industrial zone but for now simply a hilly outcrop scattered with temples and lookouts. South across the Yangzi was the third city, Wuchang, seat of the provincial administration.

Shacks and low houses were built right up against Wuchang's dilapidated city walls, all overlooked by the three-storied Yellow Crane Tower, a hexagonal pavilion capped in green tiles, its eaves drawn out into upcurved points hung with bells. Under repair after having been badly damaged by the Taipings (it burned down again in 1884), the tower was associated with a Taoist sage who used to drink at a nearby inn, and would bring a mural of a crane to life to entertain other customers. Eventually he flew off on his creation and the publican, doubtless wealthy enough by now, built the tower in his honour.

Despite competition from Sichuanese salt shipped down from the interior, Mesny sold his twenty dollars' worth of contraband for a tidy $260 and checked into Hankou's sole hotel, run by a Monsieur Dutronquoy, which was tucked away near the mouth of the Han. His successful escapades on the river were already the talk of Hankou's European community, and Mesny was immediately interviewed by an unnamed, but clearly British, "Tai-pan" – a foreign entrepreneur – and offered a further $120 to captain a large, newly built cargo junk carrying two hundred tons of freight down to Shanghai. Mesny named the vessel the *Hai-lung Wang*, the Sea Dragon King; the dragon is a creature of elemental power in Chinese mythology, especially associated with wind and water, and *Hai-lung Wang* is an obviously auspicious name for a ship. All the same, an antique temple to the Dragon King still stands close to the site of Dutronquoy's hotel at Hankou, and it is tempting to suggest that the vessel was christened after it.

After a cheerful farewell evening spent partying with Bob, the Taipan and friends, Mesny and the *Hai-lung Wang* cast off downriver back towards Shanghai. He had set himself up with the crew by handing out generous cash presents, and now found that one of his Chinese shipmates from the *Rob Roy* had signed up for the return voyage, unpaid, as his servant and gun-bearer. This luckless orderly was almost immediately knocked overboard by the boom but Mesny, an experienced sailor, saved him by jumping into the river with a rope and had them both back on deck before anyone else realised what was happening. Despite the night's revelries

Mesny had drunk in moderation; as the son of a devout Methodist he was generally abstemious, though admitting to an occasional wander off "the narrow path that leadeth unto salvation" by indulging in short-lived drinking and gambling binges. Without ever evangelising, the *Miscellany* often mentions Mesny's strong Christian faith and his interest in Chinese beliefs; he wrote sympathetically about Buddhism and, as required by that religion, experimented with periods of vegetarianism.

The first salvos of what was to prove a difficult journey were fired, literally, on the first day out from Hankou, when a lucky shot from a Chinese customs boat blew in the side of Mesny's cabin after the *Hai-lung Wang* failed to stop at a *lijin* duties post. There was no serious damage, and after an exchange of abuse they sailed on. At Anqing, Mesny was offered $300 – plus "tea money" for the crew – to escort a flotilla of six smaller junks safely downstream past Nanjing; he also took on board a party of three shifty, shabbily-dressed men, despite the possibility that they were pirates. Shortly afterwards the convoy was pulled up briefly by Imperialists and then fired on by Taipings, but both on both occasions the sight of Mesny, a foreigner on the deck of the *Hai-lung Wang*, was enough to get them through unharmed. At this point the mystery passengers revealed themselves to be rebels, on the run since fleeing the slaughter at Anqing the previous year. They thanked Mesny for helping them escape through the Imperialist blockade into Taiping-held territory, gave him money and red rebel sashes and made off in their own boats. The sashes came in useful soon enough, when another aggressive Taiping vessel sheered away at the sight of them trailing from the mast.

Outside Nanjing they found a shift in the balance of power. A veteran British gunboat, the *Banterer*, had moored here to keep an eye on smuggling, but at the Mud Forts – where friendly rebels had encouraged them to land on their way upstream – they now found decidedly unfriendly Imperial forces, who opened fire on the flotilla with cannons. The six junks made themselves scarce as scores of bloodthirsty "Imp" marines boarded the *Hai-lung Wang*, shooting blindly and slashing with swords and spears. There was no time to diffuse the situation and Mesny was lucky not to have been killed as he vainly fought off attempts to loot his cabin with his bare hands. After a brief scuffle he was bundled up on deck, bleeding from stab wounds, to find four of the crew had been dragged ashore as hostages; the Imperials had anyway moored the *Hai-lung Wang* mid-stream between shore batteries and gunboats, so there was no chance of escape.

The following morning Mesny went aboard the Chinese flag-ship in an attempt to negotiate, but officials pelted him with firewood and demanded an exorbitant ransom for the kidnapped crew, while a jostling crowd of angry soldiers, some of them wounded from the fight in Mesny's cabin, shouted for his immediate execution. Realising he was unlikely to escape alive, Mesny ran to the railing, jumped overboard and wrestled a nearby rowboat from its owner, dodging bullets and rockets fired by the irate Imperialists. He eventually made it back to the *Banterer* at Nanjing, which steamed down to the forts and issued the Imperialists with an ultimatum: return the kidnapped crew and release the *Hai-lung Wang* by daybreak, or be shelled. When dawn arrived without the men being handed over, the British seized a string of Imperial gunboats and the Chinese finally released their prisoners. They had all been severely beaten.

The badly battered *Hai-lung Wang*, her sails, cabins and sides shot through in scores of places, limped downstream to Zhenjiang where Mesny reported the incident to the British consul, Thomas Adkins, and rested up for a few days to allow his crew to recover; his own left arm had been seriously cut about, causing him much pain. Here, he traded tales with the skipper of another large, foreign-owned junk which had recently run into pirates further downstream but had managed to escape like the *Hai-lung Wang*, riddled with shot.

Keen to avoid more of this kind of excitement, they teamed up with a large convoy of junks for the final run down to Shanghai, where they docked in mid-June after an eventful twenty-one-day cruise from Hankou. There was plenty of news to catch up on: Ward (whom Mesny literally bumped into one night) had again got himself badly wounded on the battlefield, leading his Ever Victorious Army into harm's way; Ningbo and other key towns had been recaptured from the Taipings; while the French had lost an admiral, killed in the fighting, and had destroyed the village of Zelin in retaliation. Shanghai's arms trade was flourishing and Mesny picked up the theory of guns and gunnery from Griffith's hefty *Artillerist's Manual*, with practical instruction provided by William Nelson Lovatt, a sergeant in the British Royal Artillery. Within a few weeks, he considered himself competent in the use of naval cannon and field artillery – skills which were to prove invaluable to his later career.

Meanwhile, the *Hai-lung Wang* was repaired and the cargo, undamaged except for a few barrels of oil, unloaded and sold. Mesny was toasted by Shanghai's foreign community and his Chinese crew, who were ecstatic over the pay-out he had forced from the Imperial authorities on their behalf for damages, personal injury and everything that the soldiers had looted from the *Hai-lung Wang*. At a farewell banquet held in his honour, he spiralled off into a romantic rhapsody over a troupe of "sing-song" girls hired to entertain the company. One, named Chu Wen-ching, teased him, holding a melon seed in her teeth for him to take with his; their lips inevitably ended up glued together, Mesny swooning with joy as "invisible sparks shot forth". It had been a difficult and exciting journey from Hankou. A quick-thinking stranger announced that Mesny had somehow saved his life at the Mud Forts, and that in gratitude his mother, seeing Mesny's interest in Chu Wen-ching, would offer to buy her, adopt her as a daughter, and present her to Mesny as a wife on his return.

By the time Mesny had left Shanghai for his third cruise in July 1862, pirates were running rampant along the lower Yangzi and nobody was now foolish enough to set sail alone. As a seasoned – and lucky – runner, Mesny was much sought-after as an escort and at the mouth of the Yangzi he found over a hundred Chinese junks waiting to accompany the *Hai-lung Wang* upriver. But in fact Mesny's cabin had been robbed the night before sailing by an impoverished Englishman, who had broken into his trunk and stolen money and a revolver, and the only weapon aboard the *Hai-lung Wang* was an ancient Tower musket whose barrels had burst the first time Mesny fired it, rendering it useless. He didn't tell anyone.

Still, it turned out to be a fairly trouble-free voyage; Taiping raiders took flight at the mere sight of the *Hai-lung Wang*, winds were in their favour and the convoy made swift headway. There was a minor hitch at Zhenjiang, where the British consul, Adkins, had heard a rumour that the *Hai-lung Wang* had been captured by pirates. When Mesny presented himself to prove otherwise, Adkins bombarded him with questions: if the *Hai-lung Wang* was safe, which ship had been taken? Why was he wearing a red sash? Was his name really Mesny? Where was he from? It turned out that Mesny hadn't written home for a while and his parents back on Alderney had been harassing the British authorities for news of him. Adkins only reluctantly accepted William's assurances as to his identity.

Upstream, Shi'er Wei's salt dealers were still doing brisk trade and the crew renewed their stocks of contraband. With the situation so dangerous around Nanjing, Chinese junks were now offering $400 to be hauled up past the city under the protection of British steamers, though this time the *Hai-lung Wang* passed the Mud Forts, Wuhu and Anqing without incident. Mesny heard along the way that the Imperials were cruelly scalping any Taipings they took prisoner, forcing the "long-hairs" to conform to the Manchu dress codes. They skipped Jiujiang altogether but stopped at Wuxue to sell their salt, having been warned that the Hankou customs had begun to take a hard line with smugglers.

Hankou was reached safely in mid-August after a swift upstream run of just twenty-two days. The *Hai-lung Wang's* Tai-pan owner was pleased with profits from the ship's two voyages, but decided to put the vessel in dock for repairs, leaving Mesny temporarily unemployed. Without much difficulty he found work as a construction-site manager in Hankou's rapidly-expanding foreign concession, whose riverfront area was filling out with smart, European-style buildings. But the project was soon bogged down in complicated negotiations over land purchases; it was uncertain when work would begin, and Mesny decided to take time off to head back to Shanghai and marry Chu Wen-ching. A regular steam-boat passenger service was just starting up between the two cities, covering the distance in under a week, so he could easily return as soon as his services were required. Opening up Chinese river systems to steam navigation was to become one of Mesny's hobby-horses.

Back at Shanghai, all was not going well. Ward, never one to shirk combat, had been killed during a skirmish that September; he was later honoured with a memorial temple built in his memory. By this time his battle-hardened Ever Victorious Army had become an impressive fighting force, and the combined Imperial and European militias were finally driving the Taipings away from the city and back down the Yangzi valley towards Nanjing. Inspired by Ward's model, many Chinese generals were now actively seeking Westerners with military skills to help drill their troops in modern warfare. The Taipings were having a tougher time attracting foreign mercenaries as the Imperial forces tended to offer better pay and conditions.

More importantly, the British and French governments had finally decided to come out in support of the Imperial cause, partly because the Taiping's eventual defeat seemed inevitable, but also because the Qing government was talking about opening up all of China to Christian missionaries. The foreign powers also recognised that although the Taipings themselves were nominally Christian, many of their soldiers were in fact anti-Manchu rather than pro-Western, and might want to drive all non-Chinese out of the country if they won.

For his part, Mesny's sympathies were with the rebels. Had foreign powers not intervened, he believed that the Taipings would have defeated the Qing armies and that China would then have become a Christian country, if an unorthodox one, and open-minded to Western culture and influence. He was probably wrong but, now that British neutrality was over, the Taipings no longer had any reason to respect foreign vessels.

Mesny didn't catch the new ferry downstream. Instead, he accepted a lucrative position captaining three locally-built cargo ships down to Shanghai, where they could be sold for a decent profit. He would also be carrying a consignment of munitions for General Zuo Zongtang, then busy fighting the Taipings in coastal Zhejiang province. Zuo was another up-and-coming official, whose early failure in the civil service exams had been followed, relatively late in life, by an unexpectedly successful military career. Mesny greatly admired Zuo Zongtang and made much mileage in the *Miscellany* about this early connection with him, however tenuous it might have been. There were some concerns about the loyalties of the largely Cantonese crew, so a sizeable bond was asked of the shipping agents to ensure that the valuable cargo wouldn't "accidentally" end up in Taiping hands. Mesny's companion this time was an invalid passenger named "Portuguese Joe", who proved to be fine company, with a talent for spinning amusing yarns and being a crack shot with a pistol.

There seem to have been apprehensions about the journey even before it began in early October, just after Mesny's birthday. This was his fourth blockade run, and the number four – which in Chinese sounds similar to the word for "death" – was considered unlucky. The stretch of river between Shanghai and Zhenjiang was, as Mesny already knew, swarming with buccaneers, and friends warned him not to set off without mounting a light cannon on each ship, which would at least make any raiders think twice about attacking. For some reason Mesny ignored their advice, despite carrying only his useless musket and even after four Cantonese members of his crew asked pointedly if the vessels were armed – a likely sign that they were in league with pirates along the way.

Zhenjiang was reached without mishap, but a day upstream from there, on November 2, Mesny found his little flotilla uncomfortably isolated far out on the wide river. The crew also seemed unusually subdued, as if sensing approaching trouble. Sure enough, a heavily-armed Taiping fleet hove into view and rapidly intercepted them. Mesny tried to bluff the rebels away with his decrepit gun, but in the end had to surrender without a fight. They were all taken ashore to the tiny south-bank port of Fushan and chained up in a makeshift cell. After sword-sharpening theatrics and threats of violence designed to terrify their captives, the Taipings set Mesny's ransom at a princely $100,000, and brought him before the local commander where he refused to bow down, proclaiming pompously that "Englishmen kneel only to God". Impressed with his gall, the commander unchained Mesny and Joe and offered them dinner, at which Mesny further charmed his host by playing Chinese tunes on an accordion. The evening ended in uproar, with Mesny's captors trying to outdo each other in promising him wives and military commands.

The next morning, however, all goodwill seemed to have evaporated. First, Joe was almost cut down by a guard he had startled, then Mesny's cook was dragged in trembling, having been caught trying to escape. Some quick talking saved him from execution – though not a sound flogging – but Mesny learned that the Cantonese, whom everyone had mistrusted so much, had all been beheaded overnight (although, if they were in league with the Taipings, this could have been a lie to explain why they weren't being held prisoner too). Mesny further irked his captors by refusing to write a ransom demand, at which the commander exploded, threatening him with decapitation as well if the money wasn't paid within ten days. Then he relented, introduced Mesny to his wives and daughter, and again brought up the subject of marriage. These mood swings give the impression that the Taipings were beginning to feel that they might just have bitten off more than they could chew; they didn't want to release their foreign prisoners in case they turned out to be valuable, but were unsure of how to treat them.

The following day, Mesny, Joe and their entourage were escorted south of the Yangzi to Changshu, an elegant canal town strategically sited on a waterway between the Yangzi and the Grand Canal and within striking distance of both Suzhou and Shanghai. Changshu was ringed by an eight-metre-high stone wall running right up along the wooded slopes of Yu Shan, a ridge to the west; the defences had been built during the Ming dynasty as protection against Japanese pirates who had been sailing up the Yangzi and raiding inland. Rising over everything was Fang Ta, a tall pagoda which balanced the town's defective *feng shui*, a form of geomancy which describes the ideal arrangement between natural features and buildings. Ideally, cities should be protected from the "unlucky" north direction by high hills, with water to the south to bring along good fortune. Changshu's hills were to the west and there was a lake to the southeast, but the off-centre placement of this pagoda restored the perfect balance.

At Changshu, Mesny was handed over to General Hou Guansheng, a young Taiping commander from Guangxi known as the "Forest King". Hou's whitewashed, stone and timber mansion still stands in a narrow, mildewed back lane just southwest of Changshu's city centre.

There, Mesny was provided with a handsome suite of rooms, had his cook's injuries treated by a doctor and was generally welcomed warmly as the prospective son-in-law of a Taiping officer. The background to his capture was revealed too: the Taipings had been ordered by their leaders in Nanjing not to touch foreign vessels, fearing reprisals from modern gunboats, but a few rogue commanders – mostly urged on by Cantonese pirates – couldn't resist the temptation.

Though the marriage offer was soon withdrawn, Mesny made himself useful fixing clocks and music boxes for the ladies of Hou's household, and was taken on as an English teacher for the general's three children. He also set to work on improving his Chinese, picking up the principles of writing characters fairly quickly, though the language's tones proved difficult to master. In Mandarin, every sound is given one of four fixed tones, and altering it affects a word's entire meaning: for instance, *ma* pronounced with a high tone means "mother", while spoken with a falling-rising tone it means "horse". English uses the same tones, but for emphasising emotions – to indicate questioning, determination, patience and so on. For a native English speaker, trying to separate emotion from tone is one of the toughest aspects of learning Chinese; presumably it's made even more difficult if you're being held hostage under threat of execution. Mesny spent his spare time repairing and cleaning weapons for soldiers and various Taiping bigwigs, and after a fortnight had made himself so amenable that he was formally inducted as a *yang xiongdi*, or foreign brother, and presented with the scarlet sash and turban of the Taiping outfit.

Meanwhile, Changshu's magistrate summoned the foreigners for an interview. Mesny was ordered by Hou to feign sickness and stay behind, but Joe went along and found two more Western prisoners – presumably other captured sailors – living in the courthouse as "guests". The magistrate admitted that the British Consul in Shanghai was asking anxiously after Mesny and now wanted to send him back, worried about the consequences if he was found at Changshu. In fact, British gunboats were already on their way to shell Fushan and demand Mesny's release, but the Taipings spread a rumour, reported in China's English-language press, that he had been hacked to death and his remains fed to dogs. The

story was believed and the gunboats went home, but Hou wasn't taking
any chances: the next day Mesny, Joe and their servants found themselves
accompanying the general on a trip southeast to Suzhou.

Suzhou was a cultured city: beautiful women, whitewashed mansions
backing onto a grid of narrow canals, elegant humpbacked bridges and
exquisitely-designed gardens with poetic names such as "Blue Wave
Pavilion" and "Lion Forest". Coming ashore here in early December,
Mesny recognized two foreign arms dealers outside the gates (one,
Frank Philip de La Cour, was also from Jersey), but was prevented from
talking to them. The city had become the headquarters for the Taipings'
eastern campaigns and seat of its commander-in-chief, the "Loyal
Prince" Li Xiucheng, who had captured Suzhou from the Imperialists
two years earlier. Li had since been campaigning around Shanghai and
in Anhui, so wasn't there to meet them in person, but resident Taiping
forces turned out in Hou Guansheng's honour, lining the city walls and
cramming the canals with war craft. A succession of grizzled, battle-
scarred veterans, who had followed the rebellion since its earliest days in
Guangxi province, came to Hou's mansion to pay their respects. Mesny
was treated well, cocooned in luxurious apartments and attended by a
bevy of "bewitchingly beautiful" maids; predictably, he found his heart
melting and eyes swimming with joy in their company. Once again he
occupied his time by repairing mechanical trinkets for the women, who
he found well-bred and unusually chatty, and all with unbound feet.

After another fortnight of this comfortable but dull captivity, Joe
grew despondent and went to seed, letting his hair grow untrimmed and
becoming disagreeable; he also smoked tobacco, in defiance of a Taiping
ban on the practice. Hou Guansheng had left Suzhou to continue the war
elsewhere and Mesny never saw him again, but his younger brother – also,
confusingly, called General Hou – proved equally friendly. He quizzed
Mesny mercilessly about foreign politics and berated him for the actions
of his countrymen, saying that, as fellow Christians, the foreigners should
aid the Taipings' struggle against the Imperial forces instead of siding
with the government. Surely the British must have been beaten by the

Manchus? If not, why were they now fighting their battles for them? In retrospect, it seems likely that Mesny and Joe were being kept in Suzhou as a bargaining chip in case the Taiping cause failed, from where it would be easy to negotiate with British authorities at Shanghai about releasing them. Mesny, however, was worried that the Taipings would take him to war against British or French forces, in which case he decided to escape at the earliest opportunity. Others were more loyal to the rebel cause; the Englishman George Smith fought on the Taiping side when Suzhou fell a year later, and left behind diaries describing the siege.

As the Taipings began to lose their grip on eastern China, Hou Guansheng wrote to his younger brother with instructions to move the prisoners to his base at Baoying. Displaying a sometimes shaky notion of distance – though to be fair, he was writing decades after the event – Mesny located Baoying "not far from" Zhenjiang, though it lies over one hundred kilometres north of the Yangzi along the Grand Canal. Under normal circumstances, this would have been a pleasant enough journey through a gentle rural landscape of flat fields glowing in the sunshine, and dappled, tree-lined roads raised above the flood-levels on embankments. Here the canal was some hundred metres wide, an impressive work, plied by low-lying barges, with awnings stretched tight over their cargoes. Unfortunately, Mesny, Joe and the cook made the trip to Baoying in mid-December, a bitterly cold prospect, passing through what by now must have been familiar scenes of devastation and war. At Changzhou their vessels were fired on by Imperial forces; at Tanyang the city walls had been destroyed and human skeletons littered the landscape, remnants of a battle won years earlier by the Taipings. Approaching Baoying they were met by Hou's forces and taken to his camp, where they learned that the Imperials were expected to launch an all-out attack within the next few days. Mesny witnessed a sham battle enacted by Taiping veterans and was surprised to see that less than half were armed with modern firearms, most making do with swords, spears and tridents. These tough old soldiers, mostly from the southern provinces of Guangdong and Guangxi where the Taiping Rebellion had begun, were devout Christians after their own fashion, but locally-recruited troops weren't in the least interested in the foreign religion and followed the Taipings for their own reasons. After the performance, eight captured Imperial soldiers were beheaded.

Mesny spent two months at Baoying being entertained by military bigwigs and fowling off on his own in the desolate countryside, though it was grim work: corpses were tumbled everywhere, some torn apart by animals, others with neat pieces of flesh cut out of their arms and thighs by starving peasants. The expected assault on Baoying never eventuated, but then came news that Changshu, Mesny's first place of captivity, had been handed over to the Imperialists by the same magistrate who had interviewed Joe, and the town had become a military base for threatening Taiping-held Suzhou. Mesny was soon forbidden to leave Baoying without an escort, had his notebooks confiscated and was banned from keeping a journal. As Imperial victories began to mount, supplies of fresh food dried up and soon the Taipings were reduced to sending out scavenging parties to prise whatever they could away from the already destitute villagers. One group returned with just the skin and hooves of an old donkey, which they boiled down into jelly.

By now it mid-February 1863, Chinese New Year. Conditions inside Baoying were worsening; food was still scarce, and instead of the usual festive fare, the Taipings baked a cake made from wheat or barley flour mixed with earth, which they called *guanyin fan*, Goddess of Mercy meal. Reviewing his troops, the younger General Hou at first encouraged them by recalling the Taiping's old plan to capture Shanghai and befriend the foreigners living there, but then ended his speech by ordering everyone to prepare for a march in the opposite direction, southwest to Nanjing. It was, in fact, a retreat. Joe decided to remain behind at Baoying – once General Hou had gone, he felt sure he could slip safely away to Zhenjiang – but Mesny wanted to see a battle and was determined to accompany the army, despite the onset of a bad fever. As the troops were marching out of the city, he stole an unattended mule and followed along in the rear of the van.

The next few days were the hardest of Mesny's captivity. The Taiping soldiers travelled in an undisciplined disorder, their baggage carried by villagers who were press-ganged into service along the way; any caught attempting to escape were cut to pieces on the spot, leaving the roadside strewn with fresh corpses. Mesny's fever worsened to the point where he was barely able to hang on to his saddle or even eat a bowl of rice gruel pressed on him by his worried companions. When his faithful cook became sick too, Mesny insisted on setting him astride the mule while he stumbled along behind, hanging on to the animal's tail, and so entered under Nanjing's enormous walls on foot.

Mesny was in very bad shape, delirious and losing consciousness, and his captors – expecting him to die – bundled him into one of General Hou's mansions in Nanjing's far north. Perhaps he had caught malaria for the first time, a condition he was to suffer from intermittently throughout his life. His last memory was of a doctor feeding him an enormous, foul-tasting pill, then he woke up a week later to find himself lying on a straw mat, covered by a vermin-ridden sheepskin jacket and with his head resting on a nine-pounder cannon.

Nanjing is a huge city – the walls are thirty-six kilometres in circumference – but despite his weakened state Mesny managed to haul himself across town to view the situation from the crenellated top of the Zhonghua Men, the monumentally solid south gate. General Hou had been busy fighting outside Nanjing, re-opening supply lines and supposedly routing the enemy, though the Imperialists were still launching furious nocturnal bombardments which had left the ground at the foot of the walls littered with spent iron shot and stone cannonballs. The enemy had dug themselves in behind detached clusters of small, fortified earthworks, which they gradually moved ever-closer to the badly pockmarked city walls; the Taipings captured one or two every night but were unable to hold them for long, and these forays proved a pointless drain on men and ammunition. In fact, large areas of the city were deserted and in ruins, with most of the Taiping army tied down elsewhere along the Yangzi by the Imperials. There simply wasn't enough manpower left in Nanjing to break the Manchu siege.

By now it was some point in April 1863, five months since Mesny's capture. As before, he found himself coddled by the women of Hou's household, spending much of his time drinking tea with them, repairing their trinkets, teaching English and being quizzed about his marriage prospects. Inevitably, he fell in love again, though he finally tired of this game and even became uncharacteristically maudlin, wishing himself at home in Jersey with a British wife "whose interests and sympathies would be more akin to mine than those of any Chinese lady".

After his excursion to the south wall General Hou had forbidden Mesny to leave the house again, but his young cook – who had also shaken off his fever – was allowed a little more freedom to roam. Through him, Mesny managed to smuggle several letters out of the city and one day, unannounced, the British gunboat *Slaney* appeared mid-river outside Nanjing's north gate demanding his release. Thoroughly alarmed, the Taiping authorities refused at first to believe that Mesny was the man that the British were looking for, but a letter from the *Slaney*'s captain convinced them. Already under pressure from the Imperialist bombardments, and unwilling to risk a simultaneous shelling by a British warship, they escorted Mesny to a grand palace in the south of the city where he was finally interviewed by the "Loyal Prince" Li Xiucheng and ceremoniously handed over to the long-suffering British consul, Thomas Adkins. Despite last moment hitches – not least the problem of finding a suitable saddle so that Adkins could ride out of the city in style – Mesny soon found himself steaming down to Zhenjiang aboard the *Slaney*, utterly bewildered by his sudden freedom. Overwhelmed with nostalgic sympathy for his captors, he compared the hospitality he had received from the Taipings over the past few months to his earlier mauling at the hands of Imperialists.

Put ashore at Zhenjiang, Mesny was immediately offered three hundred dollars a month to drill Imperial troops, but felt uncomfortable putting his talents to use against his former companions. Instead, he elected to help escort a half-burned lorcha, a European-style vessel with Chinese rigging, that was being towed up to Hankou. Here, as it turned out, was another adventure: inside the lorcha's cabin he found a solitary Chinese woman, the recently widowed wife of a provincial official. She and her sister had been returning to the family home in Hunan when their boat was attacked by pirates and her sister carried off. The widow had escaped, taken passage on the lorcha and survived the fire, but her last remaining servant had abandoned her. She asked Mesny for his protection. This sort of romantic intrigue was right up William's street and, homesick longings for a British wife forgotten, he promised to chaperone her safely to Hankou.

They finally reached port in May, where Mesny found a house for his ship-wrecked charmer and spent an idyllic summer in her company, drinking rose-scented spirits, playing chess and finding that "the weather was hot, and clothing unnecessary". It turned out that she was pregnant – Mesny never says whether he or her late husband was responsible – and after giving birth she left Hankou, returning home to Hunan. With her departure, the demands of a more mundane existence descended and yet again Mesny found himself in need of employment. An enquiry cleared him of blame for the loss of the ships he had been escorting when captured by the Taipings, and at a wage of $70 a month he accepted a dull but secure post as a "tide waiter" – a junior inspector – with the largely foreign-run Imperial Maritime Customs Service. Mesny seemed ideally suited to the work: a former smuggler himself, he would have known the various ruses used to conceal contraband aboard a vessel. He had several friends already in the service and, as something of a war veteran, was well-treated by his superiors. But he felt little enthusiasm for completing the pile of paperwork that was involved in the job, and spent his spare time modifying boats and collecting firearms.

As Mesny settled down at Hankou, the Taiping Rebellion was drawing to its conclusion. Now that Ward was dead, his Ever Victorious Army had been taken over by Major Charles Gordon of the British Royal Artillery, the man who had witnessed the destruction of the Summer Palace at Beijing back in 1860. Gordon tightened up the force's discipline, established regular pay (until now, they had been mostly fighting for loot), and equipped his troops with modern uniforms, guns and artillery. Leaping into battle, he took the initiative against the Taipings by attacking Fushan and Changshu – the very places that Mesny had originally been held hostage. Indeed, Mesny believed that Gordon's choice of targets was in direct retaliation for his captivity, and that the subsequent loss of these towns to the British so unnerved the Taiping leadership that their will to fight was broken. While there might be some truth to this, it's perhaps better seen as an early example of Mesny's habit of placing himself at the centre of important events. Mesny was, in fact, approached by Gordon to join his staff as an aide-de-camp, but – still sympathetic to the Taiping cause – he declined.

Suzhou surrendered to Imperial forces in early December 1863, after Gordon engineered a general amnesty for the city. But then Li Hongzhang arrived from Shanghai and sanctioned a terrible slaughter in which perhaps thirty thousand former Taipings were butchered, leaving the city's elegant canals running red with their blood. A contemporary painting shows a victorious Li, mounted on horseback at the head of his army and wearing an Imperial yellow riding jacket; behind him Suzhou is engulfed in flames, whilst kneeling officials offer up the severed heads of the city's rebel leaders. Gordon went berserk at this breach of trust, removing the Ever Victorious Army from combat and spending a frenzied night hunting Li Hongzhang down, intending to kill him. Li escaped, however, and the Imperial court added to the insult by awarding Gordon 10,000 pieces of silver for his services, which he rejected in disgust – though he did accept back-pay owed to his men.

By the time Gordon got over his sulk and allowed his army to rejoin the fray the following February, Imperial forces were gearing up for a final assault on Nanjing. Determined that Chinese alone would be responsible for recapturing the rebel capital and ending the war, Li Hongzhang packed off the Ever Victorious Army to deal with outlying pockets of Taiping resistance along the Yangzi valley. This wasn't an easy job and Gordon himself was wounded besieging the town of Jintan; his description of the total desolation of the war-torn countryside echoes Mesny's – bleak landscapes strewn with ruins and piles of corpses, a starving population driven to cannibalism. He paints a less hostile picture of the Imperial troops, however, and noted that the Taipings were not always seen as heroes by the general population, whose lives had been utterly devastated by the conflict: "I do not exaggerate when I say that upwards of 1500 rebels were killed in their retreat from Kunshan by the villagers, who rose *en masse*".

Gordon's final campaign on Chinese soil was against Changzhou, a large and well-defended Taiping city on the Grand Canal. But the Qing forces he was relying on for support proved reluctant to launch a final assault, which would signal an end to both the campaign and their military careers. Eventually, hundreds of rebels surrendered, and on May 11 artillery breached Changzhou's walls; tens of thousands of civilians were killed before the city, like Suzhou, was set ablaze. At this point the British government rescinded an order allowing its officers to serve in the Chinese military, so Gordon stepped down and disbanded the Ever Victorious Army, making sure that his men were well-rewarded for their services – not least to stop them defecting to the Taipings.

There's a tendency (amongst British historians at least) to overplay Gordon's role in suppressing the Taipings – in truth, he appeared late in the day and it was the Chinese who had done most of the groundwork in containing the rebels along the Yangzi – but there's no doubt that his services were appreciated by the Imperial court. Li Hongzhang himself, who had managed to patch up their differences, petitioned Prince Gong to reward Gordon with the rank of Commander-in-Chief, and had him presented with a yellow riding jacket, official robes, banners and a peacock's feather, all marks of high military honour. Prince Gong even wrote a letter to Queen Victoria, asking that Gordon be further rewarded back in Britain. But Gordon, rather ungraciously, refused to be impressed, stating simply, "I do not care two-pence about these things". He did, however, pick up the sword of the Taiping "Loyal Prince" Li Xiucheng as a souvenir. This conflicted, quintessentially Victorian man of action would later die a heroically pointless death in Sudan, a fate which won him fame throughout the British Empire as "Gordon of Khartoum".

All that was left now was for Nanjing itself to fall. On 1 July 1864, Hong Xiuquan, the man who had caused the world's largest civil conflict, responsible for the deaths of at least twenty million people over the previous thirteen years, committed suicide by taking poison. Eighteen days later, the Hunan Army mined Nanjing's walls and poured into the city through the rubble; most of the population had already fled or were nearly dead from starvation, but the Imperial forces went on the rampage and "killed everyone they met, burned every house they saw, seized young women and looted valuables". Hong Xiuquan's son, Hong Tianguifu, escaped along with many of the surviving Taiping commanders, but the "Loyal Prince" Li Xiucheng was captured and executed, having written an account of his part in the rebellion, *The Autobiography of the Chung Wang*. Hong Tianguifu eluded pursuit until October, but eventually met the same fate. The last Taiping remnants were chased south into the coastal province of Fujian, where they were mopped up over the following year.

According to Chinese accounts, a brief sentence in the *Miscellany* and Lindley's *Ti-Ping Tien-Kwoh*, it seems that Hou Guansheng, the general who had protected Mesny so hospitably during his early captivity, evaded the slaughter at Nanjing, changed his name to Hou Yutian and escaped to Hong Kong. He should have been safe there, but in 1865 the British, under pressure from the authorities at Guangzhou, had him falsely convicted of piracy and extradited to the mainland for execution. He was just thirty-seven years old.

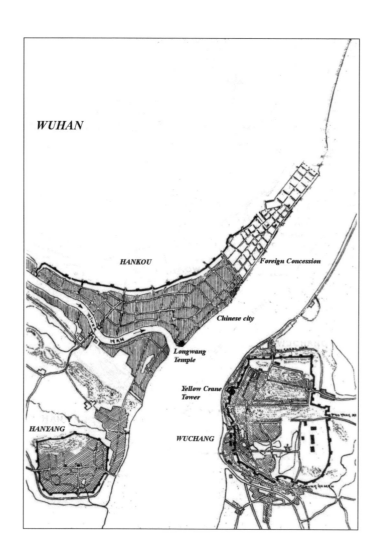

WUHAN

HANKOU

Foreign Concession

Chinese city

Longwang
Temple

Yellow Crane
Tower

HANYANG

WUCHANG

HANKOU IN THE SIXTIES
1863–68

By the time Mesny settled down at Hankou in 1863, the city had over one hundred permanent foreign residents, variously employed as consular and customs staff, merchants and missionaries. With the Taiping Rebellion drawing to a close, business was booming and the annual export trade, mostly in leaf tea, tobacco and tung oil (used for waterproofing ships' timbers) was worth over twelve million silver pieces – a turnover nearly balanced by imports of British cloth and, of course, opium. Now that the negotiations with Chinese land-owners had finally been settled, construction of the kilometre-long foreign concession was well underway above the waterfront, marked out into separate British and French districts; the Hankou Club had been founded with a library, billiard room and accommodation for its members, there was a horse market and races twice a year and soon the settlement even had a newspaper, the *Hankow Times*. Despite a new flood-proof embankment, the entire city was inundated when the Yangzi burst its banks in 1866 and Mesny, living one street back from the river behind the British Consulate, wrote laconically that he had four feet of water in his house, "so I could have a swim indoors if needing such exercise". Roofs floated like islands above the submerged concession, and Hankou's jaded foreigners spent their time organising yacht races around the flooded horse track. The river played other odd tricks too. In March 1867, a bizarre tremor along the banks knocked over a row of buildings in the Chinese city and sucked down a junk which was caught in mid-stream. The event was all so surreal and localised that Mesny, whose own house fell in on him during the quake, almost doubted the evidence of his own eyes.

Mesny's linguistic skills found him many friends amongst Hankou's Chinese, who dubbed him "Wen Kao" – an obscure nickname reflecting his "notoriety amongst the Chinese [at Hankou], if not actual fame". Even so, the city's sullen tolerance of foreigners often threatened to boil over into outright violence, and on one occasion Mesny was badly beaten and nearly drowned after getting into an argument with a boatload of soldiers during the mid-summer Dragon Boat Festival. (A friend of Mesny's, Francis Pickernell, was actually hacked to death a couple of years later during a similar incident at Zhenjiang.) In 1865, Chinese troops at Hankou mutinied over withheld pay and threatened to riot through the foreign quarter, and the following year the Nian Uprising – which, minus the religious message, had picked up from the Taipings – got within a few kilometres of the city, causing the usual influx of panicked refugees. In response to these crises the British threw a wall around their concession, ejected the Chinese and bought in howitzers to defend themselves, but one day Mesny – a member of the Hankou Volunteer Force – found that Nian sympathisers had "spiked" the cannons by hammering copper plugs into their vents. He repaired the damage and then discovered that the guns' shells had been loaded back to front and would have exploded in the muzzles had they been fired. The Nian periodically menaced the city over the next few years, but never proved a real danger to Hankou.

But if Hankou escaped unharmed, its sister city across the river, Wuchang, was not so fortunate. In December 1867, while military stores for the war were being unloaded at the dockyards, Wuchang's gunpowder magazines went up in three terrific explosions which blew roof tiles off houses two kilometres away. Mesny immediately went over to offer help and found the city's streets almost blocked with wreckage, buildings stripped by the force and the heat of the blast charred wooden frameworks, and "several deep holes in the ground, the mangled remains of human beings and cattle, and ruins far and wide in all directions". The *Hankow Times* reported that the explosion had been caused by a labourer carrying a smouldering tobacco pipe into the magazine under his jacket. Over eight hundred people were killed.

On the other side of the world, the American Civil War was creating a demand for cotton, and with prices expected to soar, Mesny left his customs job to try his luck as a cotton broker. When that scheme failed he became in quick succession a horse trader, hotelier and blacksmith, founding a small armoury which he grandly named the Hu-pei Iron and Brass Works. He and Pickernell also experimented with the relatively new art of photography (as had Pickernell's father, an engineer), and took portraits of Chinese merchants using collodion plates prepared by Mesny, who claimed to have picked up this difficult process somewhere in his travels. Money proved easy to come by, but a love of gambling and extravagance made it equally easy to spend, and Mesny accumulated no great fortune. And once again he became ensnared in marriage intrigues, as Chinese friends tried to wed him to their daughter, despite her prior engagement to a family friend. No sooner had these advances been tactfully rejected that Mesny, much to his surprise, found himself being hunted by one of the few Western women in Hankou; at the same time, he was carrying on a long-distance romance with a childhood sweetheart back home in Jersey. But, short of cash and unwilling to be tied down, in the end he declared bluntly that he "was not ready to marry either of these ladies then, and didn't".

By 1866 Mesny was back with the customs service (along with his younger brother, John, recently arrived in China) at the more senior level of Tide Surveyor. But he remained restless, aware that beyond the treaty ports China was finally opening up to adventurous travellers. Almost the entire country remained unexplored by Europeans, and you can sense Mesny's frustration as he writes about a string of early pioneers he bumped into as they passed through town: the venerable British missionary and Sinologist Alexander Wylie, on his way west to Sichuan province; Thomas Blakiston, part of an expedition that had travelled up the Yangzi from Hankou in 1861; and Thomas Thornville Cooper, who in 1868 charted a route westward towards the Burmese border that Mesny was to follow nearly a decade later. Cooper spoke no Chinese and approached Mesny to act as his interpreter, but declined his fairly reasonable terms of travelling expenses plus a share in any official honours handed out at the end of the mission. Cooper eventually set off, armed "with nothing suitable for such a journey excepting indomitable courage and athletic vigour" – enough, as it turned out, to carry him to China's borders with Tibet, beyond which war and revolution blocked his path. He later penned the exciting *Travels of a Pioneer of Commerce in Pigtails and Petticoats*; it's perhaps from this title that Mesny later took "Pioneer" as a pen-name.

The most inspiring of these early ventures into China's interior was perhaps the Lagrée mission, whose surviving members wound up at Hankou in 1868 at the end of a monumental two-year journey from Vietnam. Having struggled up the Mekong River – with a quick diversion to visit Angkor Wat in Cambodia – the expedition arrived at Jinghong, capital of the small Thai kingdom of Xishuangbanna. This region, today a mix of tropical rainforest, rubber plantations and paddy fields set firmly within Yunnan province, then constituted a vague borderland whose rulers paid tribute to both Burma and China. They had seen Europeans here thirty years before, when a Captain McLeod and six elephants had trampled through from British-held Burma; McLeod had hoped to force trade agreements on the local court, but Jinghong's rulers had sent him packing. Now Lagrée, perhaps a more tactful individual, managed to wrangle permission to leave the Mekong behind and continue overland into China.

Their first stop after Jinghong was the thoroughly Chinese town of Simao, where the expedition's ragged appearance caused embarrassment, and their lack of Chinese made it difficult to explain their presence or plan their next move. Much of Yunnan was in the grip of the Muslim Uprising and it wasn't clear which routes through the province were safe. In the end they continued northeast to Pu'er town, which they found virtually undefended and expecting an imminent assault by Muslim forces. Beyond here they eventually descended into the deep Red River valley at Yuanjiang, whose authorities welcomed them with pomp and ceremony. Constricted by a steep, straight valley, the Red River ran southeast to the sea near Hanoi in northern Vietnam, and seemed to offer a far more direct trade route into the region than the longer Mekong, with all its twists and turns. The expedition pressed on to Jianshui, where intensely curious crowds became hostile and had to be dispersed with gunfire; and finally arrived at Yunnan's capital, Kunming, just before Christmas 1867.

At Kunming the French were feted by Ma Julong, a former Muslim general who had been made the city's governor as a reward for coming over to the Chinese cause. Ma was a huge man, his body covered in honourable battle scars, who proudly paraded the modern weaponry with which he planned to besiege the rebel capital, Dali, way over in Yunnan's far west. (A few months later he'd be back in Kunming, defeated, with the Muslim armies at his heels.) French Catholic priests living at Kunming negotiated a loan to the expedition, whose funds were exhausted, and obtained permission for them to visit Dali on their way out of the province. But Lagrée had become seriously ill, leaving the charge to Dali in the hands of the expedition's capable second-in-command, Francis Garnier, a veteran of the Second Opium War. Garnier and his men made it through to Dali but were told to clear off before they had managed to enter the city itself. Lagrée succumbed to dysentery on the journey to the Yangzi, from where the remains of his mission followed the river down to Hankou.

Though Mesny failed to join any of these expeditions, there was also the possibility of adventure with the Chinese military. Despite the defeat of the Taipings, civil wars were still raging across China – the Nian Uprising in the east, the Miao Rebellion in Guizhou, the Muslim separatists in Yunnan, and the Tungan Revolt in the country's northwest – and the practice of hiring foreign military advisors was by now well-accepted. But though Ward and Gordon had won high rank and reputation for themselves in this way, serving in the military was a dubious path to career advancement in China. Common soldiers were recruited from the dregs of society and widely held to be little more than legalised bandits; even the higher ranks were popularly despised and enjoyed none of the respect given to their civil service counterparts. Even so, it was the career that Mesny decided on, and in January 1867 he was finally introduced to Zuo Zongtang, who had recently been appointed governor of Fujian province. Zuo had established China's first modern naval arsenal and shipyards at the provincial capital, Fuzhou, under the guidance of

Frenchman Prosper Giquel. (Giquel offered Mesny a post here too, but despite the good pay he decided to stay at Hankou for the time being, the first of many potentially lucrative job offers he rejected over the years.) But then, before Zuo had a chance to settle down, he was ordered off to the other end of the country to fight the rebel Tungans. Rumour had it that the Imperial court was jealous of Zuo's popularity in the south, and nervous of the firepower that the Fuzhou arsenal placed at his disposal.

Now Zuo was passing through Hankou on his way to the front, and on the lookout for fresh foreign talent. This was Mesny's first – and probably only – meeting with the man he grew to admire so much, but never managed to find employment with. Zuo was a stocky and round-faced official in his mid-fifties with sad eyes, wearing a thin goatee and a rather more abundant moustache, and Mesny found him "a pleasant old gentleman, not too proud to talk to me on terms of equality". For his part, Zuo was impressed enough to offer Mesny the entry-level post of English and French Secretary for the duration of his campaign against the Tungans. That was, of course, if Mesny was prepared to leave immediately.

This, unfortunately, was a problem. Foreigners needed permission from both the Chinese authorities and their own consulates to travel beyond the confines of the treaty ports. In practice, there was nothing to prevent you from wandering anywhere you wished, but there was always the possibility of causing trouble in unexpected ways. Not long before, a shooting party led by Hankou's French Consul had been almost lynched by angry villagers after accidentally peppering a farmer with buckshot while out hunting. The man hadn't been seriously hurt but a violent mob gathered to demand blood-money and, in a ludicrous over-reaction, French marines had stormed off into the countryside and burned down the village. Hankou's British consul, keen to avoid a repeat of this sort of incident, had also just received a letter from Mesny's parents asking to keep him out of trouble. He refused the request to follow Zuo; if Mesny wanted a permit, he would have to apply to the British Embassy in Beijing. It would take months. And almost before the consul had turned Mesny down, Zuo himself had been ordered onwards, diverted from his original mission to help suppress the Nian, whose rebellion was getting out of hand. Mesny was left behind at Hankou, fuming at this missed opportunity.

At last, in May 1868, help came from the French adventurer Jean Dupuis, a man who later, almost single-handedly, started a war between France and China over control of northern Vietnam. Nebulously described as a "merchant" in the 1867 *China Directory*, Dupuis had arrived in Hankou in 1861, just after the city had been opened up as a treaty port; he spoke fluent Chinese and, like Mesny, had tried his hand at many trades, including a little arms dealing. Plausible and sociable, he made friends with people from all walks of life, his habitual Chinese dress slightly at odds with a long, sagging moustache. Mesny had met Dupuis whilst interpreting for the *Hankow Times* over the French shooting-party fiasco, and later helped him kidnap and prosecute a duplicitous Chinese merchant who had sold Dupuis a shipment of water instead of oil.

Dupuis now introduced Mesny to a party of officers serving with the Sichuan Army. This recently-created provincial force was on its way down to pacify the Miao in Guizhou province, who had entered their fourteenth year of rebellion against the central government. Like Zuo Zongtang, the Sichuan Army was keen to hire foreign experts in modern warfare and Mesny was offered the post of military instructor; he was to proceed west up the Yangzi into Sichuan province, where he would receive further orders at the provincial capital, Chengdu. The British consul again refused Mesny permission to leave town but this time Mesny ignored him, disguised himself in local garb and snuck out of Hankou on June 18 with two "associates" (both former Taiping rebels) aboard a junk carrying weapons to the Imperial forces – and so set off for southwest China and war.

G U I - Z H O U
Zunyi
Weng'an
Jiuzhou
Zhenyuan
Zhaitou
Huangpiao
Niuchang
Chong'an
Jiaba Niuchang
Xianglu Shan
GUIYANG
Anshun
Lushan
Taijiang
Leigong Shan
Xincheng
Xingyi
Tong tse
Se-nan
Mi-tan
Che-tsien
Tong gin
Sou tchou
Nan ki
Ouei-ning
Tong-tchuen
Pogan
Tou chan
Tou-yun
SENG MIAU SE
OUEI-LING
Tong lan

THE MIAO REBELLION
1868–71

Free at last from Hankou, Mensy and his friends sailed westwards through the Yangzi's middle reaches, the river describing broad loops between perpendicular mud embankments as it crossed flat, open plains. Around eighty kilometres upstream they passed a bluff inscribed with huge red characters for "*chi bi*", the Red Cliff, site of a critical naval battle during China's turbulent Three Kingdoms period. In 208 AD the warlord Cao Cao, regent to the last Han emperor, descended from the north to take on the combined forces of his two rebel competitors: Liu Bei, ruler of Sichuan, and Sun Quan, who controlled southern China. They met here on the Yangzi, where Cao Cao, no naval tactician, chained his enormous armada together while he waited for the southern alliance to attack. But his opponents took advantage of unseasonal winds and sent a flotilla of burning hulks across the river, totally incinerating Cao Cao's fleet and, so the tale goes, permanently branding Red Cliff with the colour of the flames.

Beyond the cliffs came shallow Dongting Lake, flooding making it more of an inland sea at this time of year, the main expanse to the south clouded by the rectangular white sails of cargo junks cruising up from Hunan province. Fishing boats worked in teams on the lake, forming broad circles and then beating the surface of water with paddles as each boat sailed inwards towards the others, contracting the circle and chivvying shoals of fish into easily-netted masses at its centre. River dolphins, now extinct but then a common sight along this stretch of the

Yangzi, played around the junk's hull as Mesny passed Jinshan Island, famed for its "Silver Needle" tea, once paid in tribute to the emperor.

On the far side they re-entered the main body of the Yangzi, the river plains continuing as far as Shashi, an "abominably filthy" walled port built above the river on a stone-faced dyke. Wooden-fronted warehouses and canteens lined the waterfront, overlooking thousands of large cargo junks moored in tiers below, but it was Shashi's vicious mosquitoes that really stuck in Mesny's memory – he always suffered badly from insect bites.

Shashi was as far eastwards as Sichuanese traders would venture, held back in part by a nostalgia for their up-river homeland, but mostly because Sichuanese craft were either lightweight and elastic or heavy-hulled and sluggish – either way, built not for the lazy passage along the middle Yangzi, but for surviving the rigorous journey in and out of Sichuan through the infamous Three Gorges. This 160km-long corridor of vertical cliffs, destructive cataracts and savage shoals was where the river cut a passage through the wild mountain ranges which isolated Sichuan from eastern China; in places the current was so strong that vessels had to be laboriously hauled upstream by teams of men known as "trackers", and if the trackers slipped or their ropes broke, boats spun out of control into the rapids, often to be smashed against mid-stream boulders and sunk. As an idea of how tortuous the journey was, by 1868 it took a steamer less than ten days to cover the sixteen hundred kilometres between Shanghai and the Three Gorges, from where you needed at least another six weeks on local vessels to cover the final eight hundred kilometre stretch to Chongqing – longer, in fact, than it took to travel from Shanghai to London by sea.

Describing the tribulations of the Three Gorges became a set-piece in nineteenth-century European travel literature, though the Chinese had, naturally enough, been writing about the gorges for millennia. Back in the Tang dynasty, poets such as Li Bai were already celebrating the courage of the Yangzi boatmen, the loneliness of their wives left behind in remote villages, and the stark, terrifying scenery. But what caught the imagination of the nineteenth-century Europeans was the possibility of taming the Three Gorges by running a steamboat ferry service up through them to Chongqing. The subject had been under discussion since at least the 1850s, though the *Miscellany* sometimes reads as if Mesny, who became a passionate advocate of opening up China's interior to European markets, had not only invented the idea but championed it in the face of stiff opposition. True, plenty of European "experts" had indeed claimed that steamboats would never be able to conquer the gorges, but the only people who rejected the whole idea on principle were the Chinese themselves: the government because it had no wish to allow foreigners direct access to western Chinese markets; and the Yangzi boatmen and trackers who stood to lose their livelihoods if larger, more reliable foreign vessels replaced the 10,000 or so junks employed in ferrying goods between Sichuan and eastern China.

Transferring from the lighter craft that had ferried him up from Hankou, Mesny found himself aboard a solid Sichuanese vessel with short masts, small sails, a heavy sweep, and a front-facing rudder which projected out over the ship's bow and which was counterbalanced by a millstone – all adaptations for working through the Three Gorges' difficult conditions. The large, forty-strong crew were outwardly busy provisioning the vessel with rice and sun-dried greens, using the activity to quietly stow an illicit cargo of mercury, silk and cotton out of sight of Shashi's customs inspectors. Once everything was ready, gongs were beaten and firecrackers exploded for the noise to scare away bad luck, and a rooster was sacrificed as an offering to the protective deity Yang Tai. Departure was delayed by what turned out to be the final day of the Dragon Boat Festival, and Mesny joined Shashi's raucous riverbank crowds as they watched boat races in memory of the patriotic poet Qu Yuan, who had drowned himself in 278 BC rather than see his home state of Chu conquered by the invading armies of neighbouring Qin.

Finally they were off, passing a flood-protecting iron rhinoceros sculpture and enjoying an easy run upstream to Yichang, an insignificant, single-street town at the eastern end of the Three Gorges. In later years, Yichang became a full-blown treaty port with foreign-run customs houses and churches, but even then it never really amounted to much. The sole point of interest here was that fishermen trained otters to work for them in the same way that cormorants were used in the rest of China, the animals chasing shoals of fish into waiting nets. It was at Yichang that Mesny and his companions discovered that the Sichuanese viceroy they were supposed to have been meeting in Chengdu had died and that his replacement had decided to assemble forces for the Guizhou campaign at Chongqing, the metropolis on the far side of the gorges.

Mesny had chosen the worst possible time of the year for travelling upstream through the gorges: the Yangzi ran especially fast and swollen through the summer, fed by melting snow in Tibet and heavy rains in Sichuan. On the other hand, several dangerous shoals would be submerged, making shipwreck and stranding less likely. Even assisted by the junk's oars – and, if the wind suited, their small sail – over one hundred trackers would be needed to pull the moderately-sized vessel through some of the rapids. The men worked naked, their eerie calls ringing between the cliffs as they hauled in unison from narrow paths above the river. They were fuelled by four or five large bowls of rice at each meal, seasoned with pickles and hot chillies – a very Sichuanese relish.

Where the current was slow enough not to need the trackers' help, the junk was captained by local pilots and helmsmen, roped onto the ship in case of accidents. There were plenty of these: collisions with rocks, shoals and other vessels as they careered headlong through the rapids were simply a fact of life, everyone trusting the ships' strongly-built hulls to save them – though crews also sprinkled rice overboard at particularly bad spots as an offering to the river spirits. Everywhere Mesny saw hulks dragged up on the shingle for salvage or repair, and lifeboats were stationed at the worst rapids, painted red and hung with looped ropes for shipwrecked passengers to grab hold of. The lifeboat captains were paid a fixed fee for every corpse they recovered but only what a man could afford if he was hauled out alive, and there were rumours that some captains were none too quick in trying to do their job.

The first gorge, Xiling, was the roughest and longest, entered suddenly from the plains above Yichang between vertical, 500m-high limestone cliffs. Each part of Xiling had its own name, suggested by rock formations – Shadow-lantern gorge, Yellow-cat gorge, and Ox-liver-horse-lung gorge. There were tiny villages and patches of terraced farmland squeezed into occasional bays, with waterfalls tumbling down over the precipice from high above. During the summer the river ran all shades of reds, copper, yellows and purples, coloured by flood-borne silt.

Xin Tan, the "New Rapids" created during a landslide or earthquake during the seventeenth century, was rated one of the most dangerous shoals on the entire Yangzi; at certain times of the year there was a visible waterfall midstream where the river dropped over submerged reefs. Dragging boats up against the fierce current here was especially arduous work, the boatmen pushing the vessel around rocks with iron-shod poles while the trackers kept their ropes as tight as possible to avoid snagging them in crevices. But once through Xin Tan, there was a brief chance to rest along a suddenly calm stretch of water as they passed a small pagoda guarding the unwalled town of Badong, the poet Qu Yuan's birthplace, a visibly poor settlement sitting astride a rich seam of coal.

Then it was into the next narrow, turbulent channel at the mouth of the second set of gorges, Wu, for another forty-five kilometres of perpendicular cliffs and frantic action. With the river running fast, Mesny's junk was nearly capsized by a whirlpool, which spun them downstream and onto a beach. They laid up here for a day in the hope that the current might ease and a helpful wind pick up, but on their second attempt a tracking rope broke and they ended up stranded on rocks. During their third try, they saw another junk wrecked on a projecting shoal as it careered downstream into the rapids, the crew saving themselves as they were swept overboard by grabbing floating bales of cargo.

At the western end of the Wu Gorge they crossed the Sichuanese frontier, with still another gorge and a long stretch of river between them and their destination. The border town, Wushan, sat at the junction of the Yangzi and the little Daning river, which descends from the north past the salt-producing district of Wuxi. The Daning was another ancient trade route, one that had left the gorge wall pocked with a dotted line of post holes, marking where a now-rotted galleried plank road had once ran high above the river. Ahead were more rapids and shoals of partially submerged boulders rising up out of the swirling waters "like the teeth of a dog", forcing boats to pick their way carefully upstream along the barely navigable channels that snaked from side to side across the river.

An unexpected kink northwards brought them into the final major gorge, Qutang, just eight kilometres long but dropping sheer-sided from a backswept pinnacle and very narrow; so narrow, in fact, that submerged chains had been strung across the river here at the end of the Song dynasty to prevent the Mongol navy from invading Sichuan. The western end was known as "Wind-Bellows Gorge", where the whole turbid mass of the Yangzi tore through a tight channel barely one hundred metres wide; the immense current must have been a considerable challenge even for their hardy trackers, but Mesny's vessel passed through unscathed.

At the exit to the gorge was Baidi Cheng, where a tall black boulder, the "Goose-tail Stone", was used to gauge whether travel downstream through the Three Gorges was safe or even possible. If almost all the boulder stood clear, water levels were too low, and if nearly submerged, they were too high. Ruins on the north bank were said to be the remains of the palace where Liu Bei – the Three Kingdoms warlord who had triumphed earlier at the battle of the Red Cliffs – had died in despair at his later military failings. Sichuan had been Liu Bei's power base and, even today, the province is littered with monuments to the Three Kingdoms era.

Not far upstream was Guifu, where they pulled in for the night and found the area studded with wealthy mansions, despite being surrounded by impoverished countryside. The town had two profitable assets: brine collected from local springs, which was evaporated into rough blocks of raw brown salt and exported; and notoriously thorough customs officials, who were known to spend days picking over passing vessels for contraband. They soon detected the illicit cargo concealed by Mesny's crew at Shashi and had to be bribed. (The disgruntled captain might have drawn some consolation from the fact that a century and a half later the entire town of Guifu – buildings, salt wells and all – was permanently submerged by rising waters following the construction downstream of the monumental Three Gorges Dam above Yichang.)

With the Three Gorges behind them, the steep hills on either side of the Yangzi gradually drew back into the distance, the river calmed down and Mesny's junk sailed on past Yunyang and its Zhang Fei temple, another Three Kingdoms site built in honour of one of Liu Bei's generals. (A year later, the solidly-built temple washed away during a colossal flood and had to be rebuilt at the cost of 10,000 silver pieces.) The next town they pulled in at, Wanzhou, was the first sizeable, densely settled place they had encountered since leaving Shashi. Hemmed in by hills on a bend in the river, Wanzhou was humid, thick with mosquitoes and half-flooded – the surrounding fields coloured by opium poppies in defiance of an Imperial edict against growing the crop. Here Mesny and his associates learned that the "Herd of Swine" rapids upstream was too rough to attempt in a boat, so they decided to travel overland to Chongqing, a nine-day journey which saw them portered in sedan chairs along dangerously narrow mountain tracks.

Chongqing emerged as a hilly, cramped, ungainly city of 300,000 people which entirely filled a comma-shaped peninsula at the junction of the Yangzi and Jialing rivers. It formed a nexus between eastern and western China, where the river road from Shanghai converged with overland trade routes from distant Tibet and Burma, and was a clearing house for every imaginable type of goods; its annual exports were valued at over a million British pounds, providing nearly four percent of China's total customs revenue. The city's merchant guilds had become enormously wealthy too by ensuring that all business was conducted only in famously pure Chongqing silver. Traders from elsewhere across the empire had to sell their wares through the guilds in order to obtain the local silver ingots needed for making their own purchases.

Money was a nightmare for any traveller in nineteenth-century China. The only government-issued currency was "copper cash", small coins with a square central hole that allowed them to be tied together in strings. These were universally accepted but worth so little that you needed hundreds to buy the most trivial of household necessities; half a kilo of them only just equalled the value of an English shilling. All serious trade was carried out using palm-sized silver ingots, shaped something like a soft shoe and valued in "taels", or Chinese ounces, weighing approximately twenty-five grams. However, not only did the accepted weight of a tael differ from place to place, but the purity of silver varied between regions too, so in every town there were endless arguments with money-changers over the exchange rate between the ingots you had brought in from elsewhere and the local version. As a result, the actual quantity of silver required to buy something valued at "one silver tael" was almost impossible to predict; Mesny sometimes gave up even trying to exchange currency on his travels, and instead borrowed money from sympathetic local missionaries or government officials.

Chongqing's entire peninsula was surrounded by red sandstone walls, built during the 1840s to replace disintegrating medieval defences; though, as this "Mountain City" was constructed on high hillsides facing the water, Mesny noted that modern gunboats could fire shells over the walls easily enough. (During the Second World War, when eastern China was occupied by the Japanese and Chongqing served as the national capital, the walls were no defence either; the invaders simply bombed the city to rubble from the air.) Once inside, Chongqing's appearance fell well short of expectations: the narrow streets were crooked, filthy and blocked by hawkers, the houses were crammed tightly together and public buildings were in a shocking state of disrepair. A few handsome temples and brightly decorated mansions provided a break from the mess, but it was only the shops that impressed Mesny by their sheer range of products. These included foreign goods such as British cloth and French pornography – probably imported from colonial holdings in distant Burma, India and Vietnam.

Mesny and his companions docked amongst the vast fleet of junks moored at the eastern tip of the peninsula and climbed a steep flight of steps, alive with gangs of porters weighed down under vast bales of fabrics, to enter Chongqing's walls through the Chaotian gateway. They found lodgings nearby at the imposing Huguang Guildhall, run for the benefit of merchants and well-connected travellers from Hunan and Hubei provinces. Inside the yellow-walled complex was a temple, meeting rooms, shaded courtyards, wood-screened galleries, theatre stages and an inn, the beams and eaves ostentatiously carved with gilded illustrations of Confucian moral tales – which, ironically, promoted the virtues of restraint and self-sacrifice. Still standing today, the guildhall dates back to 1759, though the story of its foundation reaches back over a century earlier to the very start of the Qing dynasty, when Sichuan had been overrun by the bloodthirsty warlord "Yellow Tiger" Zhang Xianzhong. Having literally slaughtered millions, Zhang was defeated by the Manchus who then set about repopulating the devastated region with transmigrants from central and southern China. When trade picked up again, merchants from Hunan and Hubei provinces found communities of fellow-countrymen already living at Chongqing, and the guildhall was founded for their mutual benefit.

Rooms at the inn were comfortable but offered little privacy, and Mesny entertained a stream of curious visitors, including Chongqing's French Catholic bishop and a Chinese general who had never knowingly seen a foreigner before and was amazed to find that they had knee joints. Military contacts also informed Mesny that the Sichuan Army, a force of some seven thousand soldiers, had already departed for Guizhou to work with the Hunan Army in securing the north of the province. The campaign was apparently going well; several towns lost to the Chinese for over a decade had been recaptured, and a combination of overwhelming military might and magnanimity towards the defeated was encouraging rebels to defect en masse to the Imperial cause. Mesny was instructed to move south and join the Chinese forces at Zunyi, a garrison town around a week's journey from Chongqing in northern Guizhou.

Guizhou province is famous in China for three things: miserable weather, miserable terrain and miserable poverty. It was one of the country's forgotten corners, too poor to exploit, too mountainous to travel through easily, and inhabited by fractious ethnic minorities. Chinese garrisons first barged in as late as the Ming dynasty, founding military outposts – later Guizhou's main towns – along Imperial post roads. Wu Sangui had followed, bringing heavy-handed rule and eventual rebellion, turning the province into a battleground. Then came the Qing dynasty and an eighteenth-century influx of Han Chinese settlers, who by weight of numbers and debt manipulation pushed Guizhou's original inhabitants off the more productive lowlands and up into the hills, where farmers were often lucky to scrape a living from the undernourished, porous soil. Resentment at this intrusion had simmered away ever since, and by the time Mesny arrived there had hardly been a point in the previous two centuries when some part of Guizhou hadn't been in revolt against the government.

The situation was made worse by a vein of incompetence and corruption amongst the provincial authorities. Being remote and unproductive, Guizhou tended to get lumbered with lacklustre officials who didn't have the *guanxi* – professional connections – to help find themselves a more profitable posting. Badly paid and aware of their own shortcomings, they looked down on the locals, extorting them mercilessly and threatening slaughter at the least sign of dissent. But then the Taiping Rebellion erupted in eastern China, showing Qing authority to be something of a paper tiger. Inspired by the Taiping's example, in 1854 an impoverished Han Chinese named Yang Longxi began his own uprising, spreading the message of rebellion around the disgruntled province as he fled official retribution. By the late 1850s, almost the whole of Guizhou was up in arms: Chinese rebel militias, including ex-Taipings and "Red Flag" and "Yellow Flag" factions in northern and central Guizhou, Muslims along the western border, who had spilled over from another rebellion in adjacent Yunnan, and the peoples of Guizhou's southeast, a region marked on European maps of the time as being inhabited by *seng miause*, "Independent Miao".

Miao is a slippery word. During the early stages of the Chinese occupation it was used as an insulting, blanket term for all of Guizhou's inhabitants, some of whom were probably even of Han Chinese descent. But by the time of their nineteenth-century revolt, "Miao" was beginning to refer to a specific ethnic group, the Hmong. These people had originated thousands of years earlier in the regions between the Yangzi and Yellow rivers, slowly migrating southwards through Hunan and into Guizhou before most of them finally settled in the province's mountainous southeast. Here they built dark wooden villages, hunted, terraced the steep hillsides to farm rice, and dressed in richly embroidered jackets and heavy silver jewellery, the designs unique to specific villages. Mesny noted the Miao love of game meats and sticky rice – either cooked in leaves or fermented into wine – and the way they sacrificed water buffalo at funerals. They were divided up into dozens of clans, though inventing new ways to classify the Miao remains an ethnological pastime: an eighteenth-century Chinese manual lists eighty-two different tribes and today there are between two and 150 different Miao groups in Guizhou, depending on whether you sort them by language, region or dress.

Chinese accounts tend to portray the Miao as eternal troublemakers, never far from rebellion, but the Miao themselves had a very clear idea of why they went to war in 1855. The trouble began east from the provincial capital at Taijiang, the town whose Sisters' Meal festival had started me off along Mesny's trail. Taijiang had been founded in 1729 by the Chinese military, and as it developed into a permanent, walled town – whose officials began to collect taxes – the Miao decided they had been imposed on enough and launched an uprising. Huge numbers of Qing troops had to be drafted in to quell the unrest, which lasted for three years.

Now, in 1855, flooding and a plague of grasshoppers at Taijiang had destroyed crops, leaving widespread destitution in their wake. When a party of Miao leaders petitioned the courthouse to suspend taxation, Taijiang's unsympathetic Chinese magistrate drew his sword and demanded furiously that they paid their debts in full. Villagers were forced to sell their farm tools and pillage old graves for funerary silver. One Miao song describes how village hearths grew cold and their cooking utensils rusted from disuse, while Taijiang's officials became bloated from continually feasting in the town. So a call to war went out and all the chieftains gathered: Yang Daliu from Langde, Pang Laomo with his rebel Chinese followers, Guan Baoniu from Zhaitou, Zhang Xiumei from Bandeng, Zhu Song from Furong village, and the woman warrior E-Jiao from Huangpiao. They drank buffalo blood mixed with wine and swore to drive the Chinese from their lands.

At this point, accounts begin to fray. The modern version is that Zhang Xiumei was unanimously elected head of the rebellion, perhaps because he had already fought against the Chinese during Yang Longxi's short-lived rebellion of 1854. Contemporary reports, however, name Li Zaifu and Gao He as the "arch-rebel" leaders: like Zhang, Gao was a seasoned campaigner, having served in militias fighting the Taipings in eastern China. For his part, Mesny believed that the overall Miao chieftain was a man named Jin Dawu, with their military led by Bao Dadu ("Big-belly Bao"). Whichever of these accounts is correct, the Miao at Taijiang began their insurrection on 30 April, 1855.

The Miao homeland was perfect for waging guerrilla warfare – a crush of moody green, rugged mountains covered in rough undergrowth and thick pine forests. Miao forces descended from the hills, took Taijiang and ran riot across the southeast, slaughtering Chinese settlers and besieging the region's river-valley towns. Imperial forces fought back, recapturing a few settlements, but the Miao had caused so much damage that little more than ruins remained, hardly worth the effort of securing. Navigable rivers, essential in the rest of China for transportation, barely penetrated into the region, and the Chinese military were hard-pushed to keep supply lines open along the post roads. If defeated in pitched battles, the Miao simply withdrew to their hills and ambushed any traffic that passed through the narrow valleys below.

The Miao had another tactical advantage too: they were far more experienced with firearms than the Chinese. Cannon had been made and used in China since the thirteenth century but guns were still fairly rare, the Manchu fondness for skill in archery dominating the military exams. But somehow a practical knowledge of personal firearms had trickled down into rural Guizhou. Legend has it that, after Wu Sangui's death in 1678, one of his generals named Ma Sanbao retreated into southwest China with a large shipment of artillery and guns; either the Miao ambushed him along the way and captured the arms, or General Ma and his soldiers settled in Guizhou, married Miao women, and taught their descendants how to shoot. By the 1850s the Miao had become skilled gunsmiths and marksmen, hunting with short-stocked, long-barrelled matchlocks known as *niaoqiang* ("bird-guns"). These were single shot only and took ages to load – a short metal rod had to be dropped down the barrel and shaken to tamp down the charge – but made fine weapons for sniping. In close combat the Miao, like the Chinese, used swords and spears, the tough women fighting alongside men, babies strapped to their backs and dressed in their finest embroidery. Prisoners captured on the battlefield were taken as porters to carry spoils back to their villages, then beheaded or scalped for trophies. Describing Miao tactics, one contemporary Chinese source wrote: "When you attack the Miao they retreat, when you retreat they attack. Walking through their territory, you hear the women and children wailing and shouting, then you know the men are in ambush, waiting to attack".

During the summer of 1868, immediately prior to Mesny's arrival in Guizhou, the course of the Miao war had finally begun to turn in China's favour. Their first major victory was at Dingpatang, below a high ridge just north of Zhaitou village, where a leader named Guan Baoniu had marked out his territory with yellow clay walls and held the area unchallenged for eleven years. Then the Hunan Army invaded, but Guan Baoniu and his twenty thousand warriors drove them into hidden pits filled with poisoned bamboo stakes and the Chinese were beaten. The Hunan Army's commander-in-chief was dismissed and replaced by Xi Baotian, who resorted to deception, enlisting the help of a traitor called Wan Maogou. The heights at Dingpatang was impregnable, said Wan, but Zhaitou itself was vulnerable; attack here and Guan Baoniu would rush down to defend his home village. So the Hunan Army torched Zhaitou using fire arrows and ambushed the Miao forces as they descended onto the soggy green plain, fatally wounding Guan Baoniu. The fight must have been intense; older villagers in the area today still remember finding musket balls scattered all over the Dingpatang battlefield when they were children. A Miao lament recalls the tragedy of their defeat: "The Han Chinese came to Dragon's Pond. They arrived at Dingpatang. They came to the place called Liang Mo Xing and killed the hero Guan Baoniu. Everybody's heart sank down. All our hearts were broken. Even the chickens were silenced." That final phrase might sound comical, but for anyone who has spent the night in a Miao village, kept awake at all hours by the cluckings and gruntings of livestock, it is immensely poignant.

In the wake of this recent Chinese victory, Mesny and his companions were expecting an easy march along the well-worn post road between Chongqing and Zunyi. They passed banyan trees, shady focuses for villages all across southeast Asia, festooned with odd things related to local folk religions – sandals, bells, red ribbons – and at last crossed the border into Guizhou province. Almost immediately they encountered Miao for the first time, a clan whose jackets, heavily embroidered with bright geometric patterns, identified them as "Flowery" Miao. Both men and women wore silver collars and bracelets and Mesny found the girls very forward, flirting with him and keen to emphasize that they were not Han Chinese, or "Guests" as they called them.

The small fortified town of Zunyi, where Mesny expected to meet up with the Sichuan Army, looked south from mountainous foothills over a long, flat river plain. Outside the walls, Mesny saw the "famous rebel chief" Liu Yishun, who was on his way to execution at Chengdu. Liu, a Han Chinese, was 89 years old and the leader of an obscure but sizeable religious sect who had fomented rebellion across Guizhou for the previous decade. Mesny also found a Christian community established at Zunyi, whose French-built Catholic church, complete with cloisters and rose window, still stands at the heart of the old town. It was in a building nearby that Mao Zedong took over the leadership of the Chinese Communist Party during their Long March across China in 1935, while on the run from Nationalist militias.

By the time of Mesny's arrival the Sichuan Army had already moved on, advancing a good few days' march southeast from Zunyi to a new base at the market town of Niuchang, well inside Miao-held territory. There was no option but to pick up a military escort and follow them. Signs of recent conquest were everywhere: roadside towns lay in ruins, and there were freshly-built Miao stockades up in the hills – a worrying sight as Mesny's bodyguards were poorly armed with bamboo spears and old, ill-maintained matchlocks. And rebels weren't the only hazard. At their camp at the Wu River, an alarm one night turned everybody out of bed to find that one of the staff had lost an arm to a leopard. In the morning they discovered that the Miao had been busy too, setting adrift the ferries, but these were soon recovered. Heavy, soaking rain set in and

Mesny soon developed a cold; having dosed himself with quinine he wrote that, in Guizhou, "everybody eats chih-li pepper and garlic to keep their soul and body together, otherwise they would be shaken to pieces by the evil effects of fever and ague". Mesny couldn't stand garlic.

It's not always easy to identify historic locations in Guizhou. Some place names have changed completely since the 1860s, often in memory of the Chinese conquest at the end of the war: hence the Qingjiang ("Clear River") of Mesny's day has become Jianhe ("Sword River"). With Niuchang, the "Bull Market", the problem is that there are too many of them. Before the Western calendar was introduced to China, country markets traditionally rotated from place to place on a twelve-day circuit, each day named after one of the dozen zodiac animals – the dog, dragon, buffalo, snake and so on. But buffalo are also important creatures in the countryside, both as farm animals and in mythology, so "Niuchang" is an extremely common place name – there are said to be over eighty in Guizhou alone. As Mesny never specifies which one he wrote about, it's only by cross-checking his account with contemporary maps that it's possible to pinpoint his rendezvous, on the man road between Weng'an and Fuquan. Here he arrived in mid-September to find that stragglers in his party had been captured by hostile Miao, and that the Sichuan Army was encamped on a sugar-loaf hill, Bagua Shan, one of several isolated outcrops that overlook the little market town.

Mesny was met by the Sichuan Army's famously brave commander-in-chief, Tang Jiong, a Zunyi man who had gained military honours fighting the Taipings. Tang was about forty years old, and later photographs show him as lean and upright, bald on top but with a thick moustache. Mesny liked him, respecting his obvious sincerity, though he was unaware that the commander had private doubts about employing a foreigner. Tang was, however, keen to equip his men with modern firearms and have them drilled in the European manner, and introduced Mesny to the Sichuan Army's officers and some former rebel chiefs now fighting for the Chinese cause. Tang's forces comprised twenty-six battalions under four generals. Each battalion was supposedly made up of 500 soldiers and 150 porters, though the real numbers tended to be far fewer than this. It was widespread practice for generals to claim pay and supplies for "phantom" troops, who existed only on paper, and to pocket the balance.

Mesny impressed everyone with an arms shipment that he'd brought along from Hankou – which included rockets, mortars and field guns – and by snuffing out a candle at fifty yards with a rifle, at night. On 21 September 1868, he began his military career by being commissioned into the Sichuan Army with the brevet rank of *qianzong* (usually translated as lieutenant, though Mesny says captain), at a salary of 150 silver taels per month, and was appointed Armourer and Instructor of Gunnery and Musketry to General Liu Heling. Liu, an associate of Jean Dupuis – the Hankou arms merchant who had helped send Mesny to Guizhou – was taken by Mesny's fluency with the language and his skill with chopsticks, and the very next day set him to drill his men in modern warfare, despite having just 240 guns to share between his eight battalions. Mesny eventually persuaded Liu to fill the shortfall by ordering a further 2700 British naval rifles through his contacts in Hankou, but had to wait months for them to arrive. There were also problems in translating English technical terms into Chinese, though the ever-resourceful Mesny got around this obstacle by simply inventing his own phrases. But he had only just taught the troops to load and fire their weapons before Liu decided that this was good enough and took them all to the front, leaving Mesny behind. Boredom soon gave way to dysentery, malaria and the debilitating effects of a diet of rice, boiled cabbage and toasted chillies. Miserably, he catalogued a wealth of local produce – all sorts of beans, cabbages, gourds, roots, onions, grain and fruit – which seemed completely at odds with what was actually available.

As he convalesced, Mesny gradually made friends among the ordinary soldiers. Some were keen musicians and in the evenings he played flute to their *erhu* and *guqin*, the Chinese fiddle and zither. Though everyone was enlisted in the Sichuan Army, the men came from all over southwestern China. The Sichuanese themselves were considered fast learners, though General Liu felt that the Hunanese were more reliable in actual combat, and made fine sappers. Troops from Guizhou were lazy, careless at maintaining their firearms, refused to carry their own gear and neglected to build even basic fortifications at night, but they were good shots and skilled at skirmishing over rough terrain. The Yunnanese, though slow to advance, were stubborn fighters. Amongst these regular recruits were a handful of professional swordsmen who lived according to *wude*, the martial code of honour, and roamed the country righting wrongs, standing up for the weak and powerless, making girls swoon, fighting duels and staying true to their one true love back home (in spirit, anyway). Some of these badly scarred swashbucklers, such as the charismatically ugly colonel Xiang Chengqiu, had once been outlaws.

Mesny's description of his comrades provides a rare snapshot of the human side of the Chinese army; official records focus on commanders and campaigns, and common soldiers were mostly illiterate and didn't tend to write about their experiences. Other foreign accounts from the period invariably patronize Chinese soldiers as "braves" and stereotype them as displaying "a large share of the Oriental failing of cowardice", though any reluctance to fight was probably down to a lack of formal training, little faith in their commanders and being poorly armed. The soldiers' pay was atrocious and there was no honour in the profession, so there was little encouragement for them to lay down their lives for a wider cause.

Finally, the new arms shipment arrived at Niuchang. Along with the naval rifles were three field guns, which at first proved something of an embarrassment: not only did the accompanying artillerymen have no idea how to load or fire them, but the mountings broke during a demonstration in front of Tang Jiong and had to be repaired in the field by Mesny. All the same, Liu Heling's force was now decently equipped and so, wrote Mesny, "at the end of the year 1868 we were ready to do a little fighting with the Miao".

Having won an introductory scuffle that November, General Liu advanced a short way northeast to a new camp at Mapingba, a site now occupied by the two-street township of Shangtang. From here the Sichuan Army was planning an assault on the highlands town of Jiuzhou, which straddled the main post road between Guizhou and Hunan provinces.

Unusually, Jiuzhou was also accessible to shallow-draught sampans and bamboo rafts along the Wuyang river, and the town sat right on the edge of the largest piece of flat ground in all of Guizhou, its spread of broad, well-cultivated fields a unique sight in this mountainous province. The Miao had held Jiuzhou since 1856 and retaking it was a key step in Chinese plans for Guizhou's pacification, as it would allow Sichuan forces to co-ordinate with the Hunan Army, which was based a day's ride north of here. So while Mesny recuperated at Niuchang, Jiuzhou fell to Tang Jiong and Liu Heling after a tough fight. The Miao had been busy stockpiling provisions for winter and the Chinese found enough rice, pork and preserved vegetables to feed the army for months. But the victory was badly marred by the antics of General Liu's pet monkey, which somehow managed to set fire to some thatch; the flames spread and a large part of Jiuzhou was burned down. Ruins from the fire survive to this day.

Liu now sent for Mesny, who was eager to join in the fighting. The Miao had withdrawn into the hills above Jiuzhou and Mesny was lucky to get through alive from Shangtang: right outside town, he came across the remains of a whole convoy that had been ambushed and cut to pieces just hours earlier. There were trees felled across the narrow path and bodies strewn all over the place, many scalped.

Winter was in the air, bringing with it a light dusting of snow. Buoyed by their victory and the arrival of modern weaponry, the Chinese at Jiuzhou were growing overconfident. On one of his first nights at Jiuzhou, Mesny went around the outlying stockades and found the soldiers totally unprepared against an attack, clearly silhouetted as they huddled around large fires which blinded them to what was going on in the darkness beyond, and blandly certain that the Miao would be too scared to come out and fight. But the enemy had no intention of running away. Wandering over to what appeared to be a woodcutters camp, Mesny walked straight onto a party of armed warriors, but they were so startled by the sudden appearance of a foreigner that he escaped.

With Jiuzhou occupied, if not actually secured, the Sichuan Army began probing further south along the post road to where a strong detachment of Miao kept raiding a Chinese encampment at Tang Ai. A group of officers took Mesny out on his first foray along with a few hundred soldiers and a field gun; they arrived at Tang Ai in the aftermath of an attack to find another thirty casualties. Having discussed the terrain and Miao tactics, Mesny came up with a plan: he advised the commanders to lay two hundred men in the woods at the top of the valley, with a similar number amongst rocks down below, and then to ambush the Miao as they withdrew after their next attack. The Chinese would be outnumbered and outgunned, with just thirty rifles and a few hundred matchlocks between them, but Mesny felt that the shock of an ambush would push the battle their way, though the "young inexperienced foreign upstart" had a tough time convincing his superiors. But the plan worked: after a short, bloody fray the Chinese were victorious, capturing a thousand Miao guns and recovering stores which had been looted a few days earlier. Several hundred Miao were killed. The Chinese lost just twenty men.

But then shocking news arrived: Tang Ai had been a diversion, and now twenty thousand Miao had surrounded Jiuzhou, intent on recapturing both the town and their vital winter supplies. Mesny raced back with a battalion of riflemen and two field guns, scattering Miao before him as he went. An overwhelmed Liu Heling rallied at his arrival and harangued his men, promising ten pieces of silver for every Miao head and a bullet in the back for any Chinese deserter. Mesny was disgusted at this brutality but Liu maintained that this was no time for kindness: Guizhou had been in chaos for decades, tens of thousands had been killed and trade halted; they had to defeat the Miao and end the war.

Suddenly Jiuzhou was under heavy fire, the hills crawling with Miao snipers and bullets whistling everywhere. Mesny rushed to defend the ruined east wall; one of his companions was hit, and General Liu himself was shot through his trousers. The Miao warlord "Big Belly" Bao appeared at the head of a charge, urging his men forward, but the Chinese returned fire and Bao was badly wounded in the leg, stalling the attack. Meanwhile, Miao under Jin Dawu – the man whom Mesny believed to be the overall leader of the revolt – were busy storming the north gate, but became suddenly distracted by the unexpected appearance of a caravan bringing supplies for the Chinese. As the Miao turned to raid the caravan rather than push home their attack on the town, General Liu gathered a thousand soldiers and rushed out of Jiuzhou in a flanking movement. The Miao saw him coming and massed on a hilltop from where they had a clear run at both Jiuzhou and the caravan, waiting to see where best to attack. In what could have been a disastrous tactical blunder, Liu called up reinforcements, leaving the town virtually unoccupied. The Miao cottoned on and gathered for another charge, but Mesny grasped the situation in time and shelled the hilltop with cannon, driving the enemy from the battlefield.

Jiuzhou and the caravan were saved, but it wasn't much of a victory for the Chinese: five seasoned commanders and around two hundred men had been killed, with a thousand more seriously wounded. All the same, the Miao had been shaken at the failure to recapture the town with such an overwhelming force and vanished completely for several days, until one morning a group of five men, the heads of local clans, came in to offer their surrender. They told the Chinese that Jin Dawu's battered army had retreated southeast, and were gathering around the large Miao hamlet of Gulong. As the architect of the ambush at Tang Ai and the improvement in Chinese firepower, the Miao had also put a bounty of three thousand pieces of silver on Mesny's head, and so Tang Jiong decided to keep Mesny back in camp from now on, rather than risking him on the battlefield. But his given reason – to protect this valuable foreign asset – is not entirely believable. Mesny never seemed to grasp (or at least never wrote about) the politics of his presence in the Sichuan Army and the way that the Chinese officers might have seen him. Tang Jiong was certainly impressed by Mesny's worth as a drill instructor, his knowledge of arms and his bravery as a soldier, but while the others probably found Mesny useful enough, they wouldn't have wanted him to appear too successful in case this diminished their own achievements. It must have become very irksome to his employers if – as his accounts in the *Miscellany* suggest – Mesny saved the day as often as he claimed to do, though in newspaper articles written just two years after the events, Mesny took no credit for any victories during the campaign.

The peace turned out to be another bluff. The day after Chinese New Year 1869, on February 12, five thousand Miao once again descended on Jiuzhou, firing from a distance and trying to draw the Chinese out of town. Mesny suggested obliging them by dispatching a regiment of battle-hardened guards disguised as the "Right Wing," who had previously fought very poorly. The Miao took the bait and attacked what appeared to be an easy target, only to meet a devastating bayonet charge. They left hundreds dead on the battlefield and the Chinese soldiers returned to camp laden with enemy guns, heads and silver jewellery. Jiuzhou finally seemed secure and some fifty thousand Miao surrendered in the battle's aftermath – so many that the Chinese even considered forming a "native" battalion. But Liu Heling distrusted the Miao on principle, and nothing came of the idea.

Mesny offered to take the disgraced Right Wing in hand, promising to drill them into a competent force. General Liu appreciated the thought and promoted Mesny to be his official advisor on foreign affairs, though this proved to be a backhanded compliment – a title with no actual command – and Mesny was, in fact, ordered back to Shangtang "to rest". Shortly after his arrival, news came of an Imperial amnesty being offered to any Taiping soldiers still on the run. Mesny's travelling companions from Hankou now decided to give themselves up and, having fought bravely since their arrival in Guizhou, were offered official rank in the Sichuan Army. This pragmatic rewarding of former enemies was widely used by the Chinese, as it gave insurgents a reason to surrender – assuming, of course, that they were fighting only for personal gain and not for any moral cause. But then few rebellions in China have ever been about overturning the system as such; warlords might have their eyes on the throne, but there's never any suggestion that the throne itself should go. General Liu was probably right, however, to distrust the Miao, who were not likely to be bought off with official posts. They wanted the Chinese out of their lands.

Building on their successes, the Sichuan Army decided to advance on Chong'an, a busy post-road marketplace south of Jiuzhou. Brushing off an ineffectual ambush along the way, they arrived on March 19 to find that Chong'an occupied an open river valley, with flat-topped hills rising all around; it appeared to be an industrious, well-cultivated area. Villagers had fled at their approach, though a deputation of local Miao and Hua Gelao soon returned to offer their surrender. The Hua Gelao – also known as Gejia – were a distinct group who saw themselves as being completely separate from Miao; unmarried women wore a headpiece with an orange frill and tassel, and they were known less for embroidery than their unusual batik work. Gejia and Miao didn't get on – even today, the two groups won't intermarry – and it was perhaps no surprise to find them surrendering to the Chinese.

Not all Miao at Chong'an were friendly and the hills remained thick with rebel warriors continually sniping at the Chinese as they built their fortifications and dug themselves in. A bullet shattered Mesny's rifle stock and several Chinese were killed, but they returned fire and drove the Miao off. The situation was perilous, however: the Miao had built stockades high above the valley at Tiekuang Po, the Iron Mine Hills, shooting and scalping any foraging parties sent out by the Chinese and cutting off the road to Jiuzhou behind them. Food and ammunition threatened to run short and when the Miao raided a nearby village which had surrendered, a Chinese detachment sent to help out suffered heavy casualties.

Next morning, a huge Miao war party attacked Chong'an itself. Liu's main camp was in a strong defensive position on a slope, with a deep gully dropping off one side. As the Chinese were short of ammunition they held fire until the very last moment, turning the main Miao charge with heavy slaughter. An outlying Chinese encampment didn't fare so well, the rebels climbing a slope overlooking their position and shooting down on them. A third Miao detachment also attempted to take the town but were again soundly beaten. As the fighting ebbed, Tang Jiong arrived from Jiuzhou with reinforcements and extra ammunition, and the remaining Miao swiftly retreated. Taking in the situation, Tang relocated the Chinese defences to a more secure position in the hills on the north side of the river, with Chong'an town at their rear. There was no bridge, and it took ages to ferry the army across.

Despite the difficulties of simply holding on to Chong'an, Tang Jiong immediately ordered an ambitious assault on Lushan, a county town to the west that again had been in rebel hands for over a decade. Much to his irritation, Mesny was forbidden to go along and had to be content with sending a field gun and artillery officer in his place. The Miao had gotten wind of the Chinese plans and met them halfway along the road; Tang Jiong defeated them and then easily took the undefended town, again finding large stockpiles of winter grain. As at Jiuzhou, the Miao quickly regrouped in force and launched a fresh attack, but were laid low when Mesny's men loaded their howitzer to the muzzle with scrap iron and fired it directly into the mass of charging warriors, with devastating effect. The gun was blown apart too, but the Miao didn't know this and abandoned the field. After the victory, Tang returned to Chong'an leaving Lushan in the hands of General Chen Shuiqing – a decision which was to cause him much grief.

Many more Miao were now surrendering in light of the string of Chinese successes, and Mesny developed an eye for the women, who he describes as strong, with unbound feet and long, modest skirts. There was also a Han Chinese living among them named Miss Yang, the daughter of an official from Jiuzhou who had lost her family when the Miao captured the town in 1856. It's known that Jiuzhou's magistrate, Du Zhouzhang, had killed his entire household when the town fell, afraid that his wife and children would be raped or sold into slavery. But a maid escaped the carnage with Du's infant daughter and fled to Sichuan. The child became the mother of Guo Moruo, a famous twentieth-century romantic writer turned Marxist scholar. Mesny's account might suggest that this "Miss Yang" was, perhaps, another of Du Zhouzhang's children. At any rate, Tang Jiong adopted her and friends inevitably put Mesny's name forward as a potential son-in-law. He declined, writing in the *Miscellany* over two decades – and two marriages – later, "I am now sorry I did not take their advice".

Having cleared a corridor deep into Miao territory, Tang Jiong wrote to Xi Baotian, the Hunan Army commander-in-chief who had defeated

Guan Baoniu at Dingpatang. Xi was based northeast of Chong'an at Zhenyuan, an old garrison town sunk into a narrow valley along the aquamarine Wuyang River, very close to the Hunan border. Tang's plan was for Xi Baotian's men to sweep the area south from Zhenyuan, using the river as they had gunboats, while the Sichuan Army would tackle the troublesome Miao stockades at Tiekuang Po, the "Iron-mine Hills" above Chong'an, and then head north to meet up with Xi's advance. At the same time, the battalions stationed at Jiuzhou would move eastwards, trapping any fleeing Miao between the three armies.

At this point in the campaign there was no overall command for the Chinese military in Guizhou; both the Sichuan and Hunan armies were independent forces whose commanders were unwilling to work together unless each could find a personal advantage in doing so. Xi Baotian was obviously hard-pushed to see how Tang Jiong's plan benefited his career, and days passed while the Sichuan Army waited for a reply. Eventually, Tang decided to act out his end of the plan anyway and storm Tiekuang Po at the beginning of May 1869. At the last moment, the Hunan Army seems to have agreed to co-operate.

Nobody in the area today knows the location of the Tiekuang Po battlefield, or even remembers there being a battle nearby, but a likely candidate is the similar-sounding Tiechang Po – "Iron-factory Hills" – a distinctively pointy outcrop up on the plateau south of Chong'an, with a red scar at one corner marking the ore workings. Mesny accompanied General Liu's force in a multi-pronged dawn attack on Tiekuang's thirteen stockades; the Miao watchmen were knifed silently by advance parties, allowing the Chinese to climb right up to the fortifications undetected, despite encircling ditches filled with poisoned spikes. The Miao were taken completely unawares and thousands killed in hand-to-hand fighting, with Mesny setting the Chinese toll at a few hundred. The Miao leader Jin Dawu escaped, badly wounded, but much-needed provisions were looted by the Chinese and carried down to Chong'an in triumph. Mesny and the Sichuan Army commanders waited all day on the top of Tiekuang Po for the expected signal fires from the summit of nearby Ma'an Shan, the distinctly-shaped "Horse-saddle Mountain" to the north, indicating that the Hunan Army had captured Miao positions there in a similar action, but saw nothing.

They returned to Chong'an at dusk to find terrible news. "Big Belly" Bao's forces had ambushed and totally routed the Hunan Army at Huangpiao, a sheer-sided plateau east of Jiuzhou. Miao accounts tell how Bao Dadu and Zhang Xiumei gathered their armies on the ridge at Huangpiao, so that when the Chinese arrived they suddenly saw hundreds of rebel banners fringing the hills. The Miao attacked from two directions at once and pushed the Chinese to the top of the cliffs as if they were herding ducks. Trapped on the precipice, the Chinese had been massacred. For years after the battle, farmers at Huangpiao dug up arrowheads, scattered bones and even whole skeletons. When fresh Chinese forces arrived to revenge their defeat, the Miao all hid in a remote cave to the northeast, halfway up a cliff so that they couldn't be reached.

Official histories flesh out the story. Xi Baotian had been warned against trying to storm Huangpiao, as it was well-defended and the Chinese supply lines were already stretched. But General Long Weishan, a giant renowned for his bravery, laughed at Xi's timidity: the Miao would be easy to beat, and taking Huangpiao would be as simple as cutting bamboo with a sword. Impressed by his bravado, Xi Baotian dispatched Long's force to Huangpiao but then had second thoughts, belatedly ordering three other generals – Su Yuanchun, Deng Zihuan and Huang Runcang – to follow Long and ensure a victory.

Long Weishan reached Huangpiao on 3 May 1869, found the Miao forces encamped, and attacked immediately. The Miao sent out decoys who shammed defeat and ran away, luring the Chinese onto the plateau. Long Weishan fell for the bait just as Deng and Huang joined him with reinforcements; Su Yuanchun was in the rear. The Miao were packed up the hillside and encircled the Chinese several lines deep, firing cannon and rolling down rocks into their ranks. After the initial rout Long Weishan's forces attempted a retreat, so the Miao opened up a false trail to the cliff-top where the Chinese were slaughtered. Long Weishan, Deng and Huang were killed and their forces thrown into confusion; Su Yuanchun was injured by cannon but managed to break through the Miao lines with a few score of his men. In some versions of the story, Long Weishan survived the battle but was killed in a later skirmish when Su Yuanchun ordered him back to Huangpiao to collect the bodies.

The Hunan Army's dead are buried today outside the nearby village of Shidong, forgotten under an overgrown mound in a field of rape. The mass grave is known as *wanren keng*, the Pit of Ten Thousand Men, which may not be a poetic exaggeration. Out of the 18,500 Chinese that fought at Huangpiao, locals believe that 12,000 were killed, though official records put the body count at just 3000; Mesny, writing at the time, estimated 2000 dead and a similar number of modern arms captured by the Miao. The higher estimate is probably based on the number of battalions wiped out, whose actual personnel might not have been anywhere near their official complement. The lower figure is likely to have been closer to the number of bodies actually recovered, though it's plausible that this was under-stated by the Chinese in order to downplay the disaster. About nine hundred survivors made it through to Jiuzhou and Chong'an over the next few days – many had been shot through their feet as they ran away. It was a defeat which, as Mesny later wrote in the *Miscellany*, checked the Chinese advance into Guizhou for a further seventeen months.

The defeat at Huangpiao put new pressure on the surviving Chinese forces in southeast Guizhou. Buoyed by their victory, Miao now returned to fill the hills above Chong'an, sniping continuously into the Sichuan Army camp. Raids on the Imperial post road increased too, and it was again becoming increasingly difficult to maintain contact with Jiuzhou. The Chinese countered with regular skirmishes in which Mesny took part; he was nearly captured at one point but managed to shoot his way out. Friendly Miao, who were paid a bushel of rice for every head taken, also helped by launching frequent raids against the rebels. But it was all reactive, with no question of a further advance into hostile territory. Food was running short too. Some of the soldiers numbed their hunger pangs with opium, which seemed to make them immune to malaria and dysentery, though they suffered from piles. Others were reduced to eating bridles, boots and almost anything that wasn't actually poisonous. Many succumbed to disease and Mesny himself came down with a serious bout of malaria, nearly dying after he ran out of quinine. He was saved by the timely delivery of a fresh bottle, sent by friends in Hankou.

Then a large shipment of Enfield rifles unexpectedly turned up at the Chinese camp, along with a howitzer, ammunition and a mixed bag of British, German and French firearms. But instead of using this windfall to form a crack, well-armed unit, the weapons were distributed evenly, so that each battalion received only fifty guns for ten times this number of men. Even so, Chinese spirits were revived, and they built two guard posts overlooking the road to Jiuzhou, which reduced Miao raids on their supply lines. There was certainly plenty of game about and Mesny went out shooting fish, turtles, wild boar and deer to supplement the larder; he even woke one day to find an old male wolf in his tent. He bagged it with his revolver, and inevitably the soldiers ate the meat for its novelty. It tasted disgusting. Still, he was learning to enjoy garlic and gradually developed affection for the local cuisine: Mesny's favourite Guizhou dish was *lazi ji*, an eye-stingingly spicy stew made with an equal weight of chicken and dried chillies. He also appreciated dark red *pu'er* tea from Yunnan province, supplied by Tang Jiong, a musty brew that he infused with ginger.

Meanwhile, campaign honours and promotions arrived from Beijing. Tang received a jade trinket from the emperor, while Liu Heling was given a yellow riding jacket, a considerable honour. This went to his head somewhat and, feeling "that his battalions were too few for a man of his importance", he asked for ten more from Tang, or threatened to withdraw his troops. Tang, who had no men to spare, gave Liu permission to raise four battalions himself and asked the authorities at the Sichuanese capital, Chengdu, to supply the rest. However, Sichuan's penny-pinching viceroy, Wu Tang, seemed to show little interest in his army's Guizhou campaign, authorising an increase in General Liu's force by just three-and-a-half battalions. Much-needed back pay was also being withheld, along with sufficient food and ammunition. Indeed, there was such a shortage of lead for making bullets that Liu had to buy in supplies at his own expense.

Mesny characterised Wu Tang as "playing with... Peking pug-nosed dogs, and humming theatrical airs, amassing wealth from every possible source and neglecting his duty as Viceroy". This may not be entirely fair.

The Guizhou campaign was costing Sichuan 700,000 silver taels a year, and Wu Tang was under pressure from a cash-strapped Beijing court to save money by reducing the size of the army. In 1870, according to the *Peking Gazette*, which reported on Imperial edicts, it was "decided that Sichuan should send money to Guizhou instead of men, [and so] 20 battalions were disbanded". However, a succession of natural disasters had caused a sharp rise in the cost of food in Sichuan, the disgruntled population was rioting and, with his reduced military, Wu Tang was having trouble keeping the peace in his own province, let alone in neighbouring Guizhou. Unhelpfully, the memorial continued by suggesting that, as there was no possibility of funding enough troops, forces should be distributed so that they "occupy the more important places, and to retain near at hand a body of picked men ready for an emergency". Whatever Mesny might have thought of Wu Tang, the viceroy obviously couldn't spare anything like the ten battalions that General Liu had demanded.

Much to Tang Jiong's indignation, the powers at Beijing had overlooked Mesny for promotion, though the Imperial envoy did make a personal call to confirm that there was indeed a foreigner serving with the Chinese forces in Guizhou. It seemed like a good idea for Tang to travel to Sichuan, sort out the reinforcements and back pay issues with Wu Tang, and organize honours for Mesny at the same time. On his return, Mesny learned that Zuo Zongtang himself had already recommended him for the fourth degree of official rank, and so Tang Jiong had petitioned the viceroy to promote Mesny further, to the third rank: "Early the following year I received the rank and decoration I had been recommended for a year previously, but I had now earned more honours... [so Tang Jiong] sent me a present of an official winter hat, with a clear blue button, denoting the rank of brevet colonel, Tsang-chiang-hsien, and the Flowery Plume, Hua-ling."

The nine ranks of Chinese officialdom were identified by various belt buckles, buttons and badges. The "buttons" were actually a large bead made of glass or semi-precious stone and mounted on a metal spindle atop of the official's hat, with a different colour for each grade. Rank badges were an embroidered panel attached to the front and back of jackets, decorated with a specific animal identifying the degree: birds such as cranes, pheasant and geese for civil officials; tigers, bears or other fierce creatures for the military. Mesny's clear blue hat button marked him out as a third rank official, whose military badge depicted a leopard; the accompanying pension was 130 taels of silver. The "flowery plume" that Mesny mentions – a peacock feather with a single eye spot – really wasn't much of a prize, as they were handed out for almost anything. Much later, Mesny was also awarded the *bao xing* or "precious star" medal, which were issued solely to foreigners and shaped like a large gold coin with a sapphire mounted in the centre.

With the Sichuanese Army bogged down at Chong'an, news came of a further serious setback: on August 19 the Miao had overrun Duyun, an important town over to the west, capturing a large cache of modern firearms. This disaster was only slightly offset by the failure of a similar attempt to take the nearby settlement of Guiding, whose citizens, dissatisfied with Chinese rule, had decided to surrender to the Miao. Having secretly negotiated an agreement with local chieftains, Guiding's gates were opened to the rebels one moonless night; but a small detachment of Chinese soldiers, led by a crafty general named Yang, snuck in behind the Miao in the dark, suddenly raised the alarm, and slaughtered the intruders as they attempted to flee in the confusion. Even so, Duyun's capitulation further boosted Miao morale and made the Sichuan Army's position at Chong'an seem ever more isolated, given their tenuous grip on the supply road to Jiuzhou. With Xi Baotian's battered forces at Zhenyuan in no condition to help out in an emergency, fresh trouble was expected.

Sure enough, one morning the Miao began massing for a fresh attack outside Chong'an. Mesny set up a field gun in preparation, while General Liu – anticipating Miao tactics – had already led out a battalion to ambush the enemy from behind. Tang suggested engaging the enemy directly outside Chong'an to tie them down, but Mesny was dubious; without Liu's help they'd be hard pressed to tackle such a large force in the field.

As the Miao charged down towards the town, Mesny opened fire with his cannon, exploding their magazine with a lucky shot. The Chinese now poured out of Chong'an and soon had the Miao on the run, only to find General Liu under heavy fire in the next valley, having himself been drawn into a trap. The appearance of reinforcements turned the battle in his favour, but Liu's detachment had been badly mauled, with over half his men seriously wounded. Liu was furious and embarrassed at the failure of his ambush, and in a vindictive spat of revenge killing ordered his sole Miao prisoner to be dismembered, instigating a gruesome cannibalistic ritual amongst the Chinese troops: "the heart and liver were taken from the carcass and carved up in small portions for all who wanted a piece". Mesny often relished repeating grisly hearsay, but this story is unlikely to be an invention; similar cannibalism features throughout the Chinese outlaw classic *The Water Margin* and was even rumoured to have been practiced in neighbouring Guangxi province as recently as the 1960s, during the chaos of the Cultural Revolution.

Tang Jiong's visit to viceroy Wu Tang eventually bore fruit. In late January 1870, a detachment of fresh troops arrived at Chong'an, along with a consignment of much-needed provisions, allowing Tang to resume his reconquest of Guizhou. By this time, the bulk of Miao forces had assembled some way east of Chong'an around Gulong, a clutch of wooden houses, cobbles and muddy lanes facing out over a winding river plain. Their main base was up in the hills above at Jiaba Niuchang, which Tang now decided to occupy. Today, Jiaba is another small hamlet with a far-reaching view of brilliant green terraces and dusty blue ridges backsloping into an atmospheric haze – then, the Miao had occupied the very top of the hill, an almost impregnable position. Locals say that it was a Gejia man named Luo from Kaitang village who eventually led the Chinese up here, further proof of the lasting animosity between the Gejia and Miao.

Liu Heling now undertook to capture Jiaba, pointedly leaving Mesny behind at Chong'an – probably because he wanted to regain some respect after his recent near-defeat. But he failed again, winning an early skirmish only to have his men (weighed down with their battlefield trophies) beaten after the Miao regrouped and stormed his camp. Tang Jiong asked for advice and Mesny suggested launching phantom raids towards nearby Miao-held towns, which successfully drew the rebels away from Jiaba, giving Liu time to dig in. Tang, with no further troops of his own to spare, sent an urgent message to Xi Baotian at Zhenyuan, asking him to make a foray south with the Hunan Army to reinforce Liu's position, but was ignored.

As a last resort Mesny was packed off to Jiaba, where he found the Miao busy fortifying their stockades and advised Liu to attack directly, before the enemy had time to defend themselves properly. In a replay of Tiekuang Po, the Miao positions were taken at dawn after a fierce action in which almost all the Chinese were wounded, though great quantities of loot, guns, ammunition and provisions were captured. Almost two hundred Miao perished, including five chiefs, while the Chinese lost just seven men. Before the battle Liu had promised a bounty of ten taels for each Miao nose; one of the injured Chinese woke up to find he had lost his while lying unconscious, cut off by an over-enthusiastic comrade. In the aftermath, Mesny managed to save just two Miao prisoners from Liu's wrath – the rest were beheaded – who became his understudies. Years later one of them, Liu Chin-Hsiang, was to play a minor but heroic role in the Sino-French scuffle over Tungking, northern Vietnam.

So General Liu ended up victorious at Jiaba. But then, insanely, he abandoned the field and the entire Guizhou campaign, taking two hundred of his private guards and heading home to Hunan to visit his ageing mother, refusing to return unless Tang provided him with the extra battalions he had demanded. It was career suicide, but perhaps this second near-defeat – and being rescued yet again by Mesny – had simply proved too shameful. This, at least, is the impression given by the account published twenty-five years later in the *Miscellany*, but in a newspaper article written soon after these events, Mesny saw things differently. He believed that the Chinese victory at Jiaba Niuchang was decisive, and that little effort would have been needed to mop up the remaining Miao resistance and end the war in Guizhou. But Liu's staff, whose careers had blossomed during the campaign and would probably wither away at its conclusion, persuaded him to destabilise the peace by running off to Hunan. They reminded Liu that if Guizhou were pacified, he would lose his salary, not to mention the chance of skimming his men's wages and making useful contacts: "Even if [Liu's pay] remained as at present, he could not make *more* than Tls. 10,000 or 12,000 per month, whereas if he had 10 or 15 battalions more he could double the sum, and place many of his friends and relatives in remunerative posts, and [that having an] exalted position would give him a great influence near the throne".

Without General Liu, Tang Jiong lacked sufficient manpower to hold the Chong'an district. He again asked Xi Baotian to advance south from Zhenyuan to occupy Jiaba, freeing up the Sichuan Army to move west and recapture Duyun. This would consolidate the Chinese grip on the region and help draw increasingly bold raiding parties of Miao away from the provincial capital, Guiyang. But Xi rejected the plan: he would be reduced to simply caretaking territory captured by Tang Jiong rather than actively campaigning, and he desperately needed to attract some glory in order to restore his reputation after Huangpiao.

Undermanned, undersupplied, out-of-pocket, with confidence low and discipline collapsing, Tang Jiong therefore had little option but to plan a retreat. He made a final sortie southeast from Chong'an to Banghai, thrashed the Miao one last time, and then, in mid-August, withdrew northwest along the *gu yidao*, the old granite-flagstoned post road. Stretches of this were used by mule trains well into the 1960s and still survive intact, though were extremely slippery in wet weather (unshod horses had a firmer grip in the rain, but their hoofs split and rotted, while fully-shod ponies fell continually. Some muleteers shod just the front hoofs). The retreat took the Sichuan Army past its former, hard-won bases at Jiuzhou, Shangtang and Niuchang, and back halfway to Zunyi, to the partly ruined town of Weng'an at the very edge of Miao-held territory – an utter, bitter capitulation of their entire two-year campaign.

In October 1870, while Tang attempted to restore the Sichuan Army's morale by supporting them in relative comfort at Weng'an, General Liu reappeared, still demanding his promised battalions. Exasperated, Tang suggested that, given his own failure to convince Wu Tang of the need for extra men, Liu himself should head off to Chengdu and petition the viceroy personally. Liu had barely left for Sichuan when there was a sudden upheaval in the camp. Chen Shuiqing, the general whom Tang Jiong had left in charge at Lushan the previous year, had panicked at Tang's withdrawal from Chong'an and fled to safety at the provincial capital, Guiyang, abandoning all his military hardware along the way. This had been recovered before the Miao got their hands on it, but Chen had covered up his cowardice by shifting the blame: according to him, it was Tang who had run away in confusion, leaving Chen with no option but to retreat as quickly as possible. Incredibly, he was believed. Tang Jiong found himself abruptly stripped of rank and honours and ordered to Sichuan for a court martial; this after recapturing and securing territory held by the Miao for fifteen years and despite having to battle continual enemy hostility, a shortage of supplies, indifference from his superiors and a scheming pack of disloyal, self-interested generals.

As his troops were disbanded, Tang characteristically ensured that they were paid wages due, and personally handed out presents of clothing and padded quilts to every man. This left him virtually bankrupt, to widespread scorn amongst his former comrades that he hadn't used his position as commander-in-chief to enrich himself. (Tang was later pardoned and given further official appointments; Mesny was to meet him again.) Liu Heling's forces were demobbed too, but in his absence, Liu's staff claimed that there were only 150 men in each battalion – there were probably three times this number by now – and pocketed the balance of their salary for themselves. Soldiers accepting this shabby treatment were given about a third of their money, while those who complained were beaten and turned out of the camp, wages unpaid.

General Liu now returned from Chengdu, ridiculously expecting a promotion. Instead he found that Tang's dismissal had placed responsibility for the Guizhou campaign in the hands of the seasoned General Zhou Dawu, who owed Liu a huge gambling debt. Furious, Liu blamed General Chen's cowardice and Tang's withdrawal from Chong'an for giving the government an excuse to appoint Zhou, forgetting that it was his own flight to Hunan that had forced Tang to retreat. Liu refused to serve under Zhou and decided to head home for good, but found himself trapped in the camp by a large mob of angry, unpaid soldiers, loudly demanding their wages. Alarmed, Liu called in their officers, apologised for not having the cash available and offered them 2,000 taels each – an enormous sum – to escort him safely to Zunyi, where he would hand over the men's pay. Keen to make such easy money the officers agreed, but once at Zunyi Liu admitted that he had no funds there either, and he abandoned his bodyguard to make their own way back to Weng'an, humiliated by his duplicity. It also surfaced that Liu, after buying those naval rifles through Mensy earlier on in the campaign, had deducted the cost of the consignment from his men's wages and later sold the arms to Zhou Dawu at a huge profit. Once news of this got out, Zunyi's disgusted citizens kicked Liu through the streets if he dared to appear in public, and hounded his house day and night until he fled the city.

Before leaving Weng'an, Liu offered Mesny one of his daughters in marriage and promised to find him employment in Hunan. It was a tempting opportunity, despite Liu's character, but Zhou Dawu topped it by granting Mesny a substantial pay rise as Provincial Superintendent of Foreign Arms. Mesny proudly declared, "I had a seal of office with those characters on it": the one-time mercenary had become a Chinese official, a Mandarin. He had begun the campaign as a brash young adventurer, willing to run any risk to escape from boredom; exposure to war had given him the chance to prove he also had courage, resourcefulness and even common sympathy. In February 1871, a few days before Chinese New Year, he was ordered to the provincial capital, Guiyang, to take up his post.

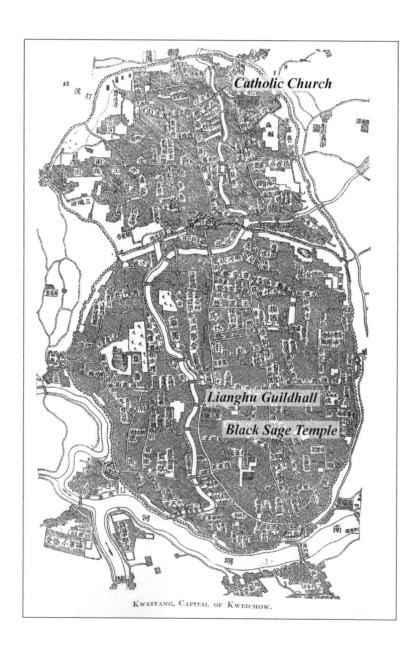

Catholic Church

Lianghu Guildhall

Black Sage Temple

KWEIYANG, CAPITAL OF KWEICHOW.

GUIZHOU IN THE SEVENTIES
1871–77

Mesny arrived at Guiyang on February 17 1871, two days before the Chinese New Year. As almost the only city in Guizhou to have come through the war without falling to rebels at some point, the lozenge-shaped capital was unusually orderly and attractive, a small and compact place surrounded on all sides by high limestone hills. The city's broad streets were lined with tidy buildings and packed with good-natured, jostling holiday crowds, amongst which Miao women were busy hawking festive goods, dressed in their distinctive embroidered jackets and pleated skirts.

Rooms were found for Mesny at the little Black Sage Temple on Zhonghua Road, built to honour a loyal Tang dynasty general who had since been deified as Guizhou's patron saint. But he decided not to stay: with the army's arrival, the temple had become a makeshift magazine, its wooden halls packed to the rafters with barrels of gunpowder, amongst which droves of New Year worshippers were busy setting off firecrackers and burning incense, completely oblivious to any danger. (The magazine was later shifted to a safer location outside Guiyang's south wall where, ironically, it was struck by lightning and exploded in May 1877, destroying eighty houses.) He eventually settled into new lodgings nearby at the Lianghu Guildhall, the clubhouse for travellers from Hunan and Hubei provinces – a suitable address for his new position as an official in the Hunan Army. He later founded a children's school here, employing an impoverished student as its teacher.

Mesny spent much of the next six years based at Guiyang, where he was touched by the friendly and quite genuine respect paid to him: "All classes of society, from the highest civil and military officials, literati and gentry, to the humblest Buddhist and Taoist priests, tradesmen and country peasants, have given me the heartiest welcome, when and wherever I have met them, not only on account of my official position, but because I am a stranger or guest". The city had a growing French Catholic community too, so Mesny at last had some foreign company and spent time with the fathers resurrecting his rusty French. Guizhou had seen some heavy-handed persecution of Christians in previous decades – five martyrs had been executed here during the 1860s – but now the church was enjoying official protection, and by the time Mesny left Guiyang in 1877 the congregation numbered perhaps two thousand. In 1874 they consecrated a splendid cathedral in the northeastern outskirts of the city, built in a blend of Chinese and European architectural styles and funded by the Chinese government as compensation for their earlier anti-Christian stance. Some of the French priests had led exciting lives and entertained Mesny with tales: one, petitioned by villagers to shoot a man-eating tiger in some remote corner of Guizhou, had bagged the cat but was almost killed by the ferocious recoil of his double-barrel shotgun.

According to his father's unreliable reminiscences, recorded over a decade later in Guernsey's *Star* newspaper, Mesny was kept busy in his official post at Guiyang's armoury, working with Chinese craftsmen to cast and bore cannon. But his day-to-day duties were probably light, leaving him at leisure to manage a farm at the tiny hamlet of Shuitian, some way northeast of the city, and to marry his first wife, nineteen-year-old Nien Suey Tsen. Mesny's father described Nien as "a Chinese lady of noble birth, who was a Taeping", but this is a romantic exaggeration. Her late father, Nien Pu Wan, had been a low-ranking official at Guiyang and her mother, refusing to remarry after being widowed, had her name inscribed on an ornate marble *pailou*, a large, rectangular memorial arch carved all over with "little figures of men, beasts and birds in bold relief", praising her Confucian virtue. These arches once lined the eastern highway into

Guiyang; only a single example survives today, but old photographs show a dozen or more straddling the white, winding gravel road. According to a local magistrate Nien Suey Tsen was something of a harridan and henpecked Mesny continually; more seriously, she also proved unable to have children. Failure to produce a son and heir before the age of thirty was justification for divorce in China, and Nien's family offered to buy Mesny a Miao woman as a concubine so that their first son could be adopted as Nien's child – a perfectly acceptable solution which would have guaranteed Nien domestic security. Mesny refused their proposal for "private and religious motives", but this decision may well have made his home life fractious.

There was also time enough for Mesny to indulge in business speculation. The magistrate at nearby Kaiyang town, named Long, sought Mesny's advice about draining a flooded mercury mine; gangs of labourers were already working around the clock with chain pumps, but they had made no impression on the water level and Long wanted help in purchasing modern machinery for the job. Mesny was impressed with the mine's prospects and persuaded the provincial treasurer to allow him to form a stock company, offering 20,000 taels in shares to raise money for the necessary equipment. However, as often seemed to happen, the machiavellian workings of *guanxi*, Chinese business relationships, undermined Mesny's plans: an official's relative underbid him for the job, claiming that he could buy the machinery for a fraction of the cost. Mesny withdrew scornfully from the project, and sure enough within three years the funds had been exhausted with nothing to show. However, the incident seems to have whetted Mesny's appetite for prospecting: from here on he routinely investigated any mineral deposits that he encountered on his travels, and was full of ideas for developing China's mining potential.

But perhaps the most important development during his stay at Guiyang was that Mesny, an almost uneducated jack-of-all-trades, now began writing regular dispatches for China's foreign-language press, his articles first appearing in the caustic *Shanghai Evening Courier*. Most of these were anonymous, but the style and content make it clear that Mesny was their author. Others were signed "W.M." or, oddly, "J.M." – perhaps letters about his adventures that Mesny had written to his brother John at Hankou, who then passed them on to the paper for publication. Within a year, English-speaking readers around the country knew that there was a foreign arms instructor serving with the Chinese military in Guizhou, and from here onwards Mesny's name appears in a growing number of external sources: newspapers, consular and missionary records, the journals and letters of other adventurers and old China hands. Often their comments are fleeting, but they sometimes fix elusive dates or throw light on his activities – and, occasionally, provide insights into how others saw him. Taken together, these contemporary records make a useful counter to Mesny's later version of events in the *Miscellany*, untainted as they are by thirty years' worth of faulty memory, personal grudges and altered points of view. They also include entirely new material, which Mesny never got around to writing up elsewhere, such as a record of his subsequent military career in Guizhou.

A photograph of Mesny survives from around this time, showing him as a young man of perhaps thirty years, moustached and broad-chested. He's seated bolt upright, dressed in official Chinese robes and thick-soled felt boots, holding a lozenge-shaped fan. On his head is a conical straw hat – an official's lightweight summer wear – with what would have been a broad red tassel spread at the front. Mesny's third-rank blue button is just visible at the apex of his hat, as is the "flowery plume", the single-spot peacock feather, drooping behind his head like a shadow. Around his neck is a long necklace of 108 "Buddha beads" (another sign of office), with a rank badge stitched across his chest, though the photograph is too faded to make out the leopard design. Standing behind Mesny to his right is a younger, slighter Chinese man wearing a similar military hat and jacket, but without any insignia. The fact that he is standing while Mesny sits suggests a student-teacher relationship: he is Mesny's protégé, not simply a servant. Though identification is impossible, it's tempting to think that this might be the Miao youth, Liu Chin-Hsiang, who Mesny had saved from execution after the slaughter at Jiaba Niuchang, and who seems to have stayed on with him for at least the following decade.

The photograph comes from an archive on Jersey and, while there is no supporting documentation, it's reasonable to speculate that it was taken while Mesny was at Guiyang during the 1870s and sent home to his family, to show that he was doing well.

Off in the countryside, the Miao war continued. Taijiang – where the rebellion had begun back in 1855 – fell to the Chinese whilst Mesny was still at Weng'an, and the first few days of 1872 saw Xi Baotian's revitalised Hunan Army restoring their honour by decisively defeating the Miao in a second confrontation at the site of their earlier humiliation, Huangpiao. Thousands of rebels were killed and their stockades burned, allowing the entire Imperial post road across northeastern Guizhou to be reopened after eighteen years of war. Xi Baotian had already recaptured the important county seats of Danjiang and Kaili – not that there was much left of either by the time fighting had finished – and an Imperial edict announced that western Guizhou was also well on the way to being pacified, with the bulk of the province north of the Pan River "restored to tranquillity".

The region southwest of Guiyang was another matter, where war had been flaring for as long as anyone could remember. Many of the local people were *tunpu*, "garrison folk", not exactly an ethnic group but descendants of the innumerable Chinese soldiers who had been sent down over the centuries to pacify this remote land. Wu Sangui, the Ming general turned Qing warlord, had also carved out his territory here, building an isolated hilltop fortress near the city of Anshun and violently oppressing the resident Bouyei – a Thai-speaking people who had settled the region in medieval times.

Now some ten thousand Miao warriors and assorted refugees had occupied the heights of Xianglu Shan, Incense-burner Mountain, west of Anshun in Guanling county. The flat-topped summit rose in three distinct tiers, connected by a narrow goat-track, and the Miao had ringed the middle one with almost impregnable stone fortifications. In early February 1872 Mesny was ordered here by Zhou Dawu, who was counting on his skill with field guns to pound the rebels into rapid submission. Sure enough, the day after his first bombardment a small party of Miao came in to the Imperial camp to arrange terms of surrender, offering to lay down their arms in return for safe passage off the mountain. But the Chinese officers wanted glory and rejected their proposals, making it clear that the siege would only end when all the Miao at Xianglu Shan had been slaughtered. Shelling continued until the Chinese ran out of ammunition a month later, at which point Mesny was recalled to Guiyang. He went gladly, writing in the *Courier* that "the faithless, cowardly and cruel tactics of the Imperialists are utterly disgusting to any one with one spark of honour left".

It took three more months for Xianglu Shan to fall. After the artillery failed to shift the defenders, the Chinese built a wooden battery around the mountain, moving it steadily higher up the slope until they were within storming range of the fortifications. But the Miao rolled rocks down the mountain sides, demolishing the wooden barriers and scattering the troops. So the siege dragged on until early June, by which time the Miao were utterly desperate for fuel, water and food. Several thousand warriors attempted to break out but, betrayed by spies, they were ambushed and cut down. The last die-hards retreated to Xianglu Shan's uppermost terrace, where most of them were killed during a sortie a few days later. On June 14, the Chinese scaled the terrace using ladders and chased the few survivors into a remote cave. Unable to reach the entrance, they walled it up until the last Miao inside had died of starvation. All male rebels captured during the campaign were tortured to death; the few children and female prisoners taken alive were sold to slave dealers from neighbouring Guangxi province, who had followed the army like vultures "on the lookout for such bargains".

As events unfolded at Xianglu Shan, another major detachment of Miao had regrouped southeast at Leigong Shan, Thunder-god Mountain. This gloomy, densely forested peak sits at the edge of an especially rugged stretch of countryside that reaches all the way down to the border with Guangxi province. It was an excellent place to mount a defence but was also something of a last stand, beyond which there was nowhere left to run. Sifting through the contradictory accounts of the campaign offered by oral histories, official reports and Mesny's newspaper articles, it seems likely that the Miao leaders here included Zhang Xiumei and Gao He, the "arch-rebel" whom the Chinese believed had led the uprising from the start. Short of food and weapons, the other chieftains wanted to attempt a retreat, but Zhang persuaded them to try breaking through the Chinese lines in a last desperate charge.

According to Chinese sources, in April 1872, divisions of the Hunan Army advanced to Leigong Shan's foothills at Wuyapo – the ominously-named "Crow Slope" – and laid siege to rebel positions. Their first attacks were repulsed, Gao He leading the Miao troops in person. But after seventeen days the Chinese rallied, attacking on two sides at once in a pincer movement, and the Miao were utterly overwhelmed. No quarter was given: thousands of prisoners were beheaded on the spot by the victorious Chinese, while Gao He and Zhang Xiumei were captured and carted off to Changsha, Hunan's provincial capital. Though Xianglu Shan had yet to fall and a few rebels escaped the carnage to carry their fight across the southeast during the following year, the battle at Leigong Shan marked, effectively, the end of the Miao Rebellion.

After a brief imprisonment, Gao and Zhang were executed, their bodies hacked to pieces and their heads put on public display. The *North China Herald* newspaper published a graphic account (possibly by Mesny) of Gao's appalling "death by 1000 cuts", the most cruel of all Chinese executions: "The Criminal Judge, attended by executioners, in the presence of the assembled armies, ordered [Gao He] to be stripped naked and wound round with strong iron wire... When this was done, and he was securely bound to a stake, the executioners began their work of slowly picking the flesh from the bones with sharp iron instruments something like a three pronged fork... To give a little variety to their amusement, the executioners beheaded several inferior rebel chiefs while Gao He was standing, and then, returning to him, they cut the head from the still living skeleton of bones".

Not all the Miao leaders were killed or captured at Leigong Shan, though few survived its aftermath for long. A group Chinese commanders, demoted for reporting ridiculous body counts from their campaigns amounting to more than the entire population of Guizhou, resorted to treachery to restore their careers. Having lured five of the fugitive chieftains out of hiding with favourable offers of surrender, they immediately handed them over to the higher authorities for execution. One of the betrayed men was "Big Belly" Bao Dadu, who had been shot through the thigh and badly wounded at Jiuzhou. He had hardly taken to the field since, though his followers had defeated the Hunan Army at Huangpiao. They were all tortured and beheaded.

Today, the roles played by Gao He, Bao Dadu and other Miao chieftains has largely been forgotten, but Zhang Xiumei's nominal leadership of the rebellion is commemorated by a huge granite statue of him in Taijiang's public square. Hand resting on sword hilt, Zhang gazes off into the distance, managing to look bold and heroic despite a backdrop of modern apartment blocks. The face was modelled on contemporary descriptions and a strong family resemblance in his descendants, though the light breastplate and studded belt are wrong; Zhang wore a home-made helmet and suit of banded armour, still preserved in the bowels of Guiyang's provincial museum. His home village, Bandeng, sits high up in the hills west of the town, a good four-hour hike along muddy country roads past wallowing water buffalos, scattered hamlets of timber houses, old trees hung with red ribbons and roadside family tombs. There's no obvious poverty or squalor, but life here clearly entails continuous physical labour for few material luxuries – pretty much as it has done throughout China's history. It's hard to believe that a country which seems to be single-handedly supporting a sagging consumer world still has villages like this, where the livestock live downstairs and the family above, their drinking water collected in buckets from wells or streams.

Just beneath the crest of the hills, Bandeng stands out amongst a patchwork of terraced fields as a little cluster of dark wooden buildings, their eaves hung with drying bunches of chillies. Villagers still remember how, after the final battle at Leigong Shan, the Chinese rampaged through the countryside burning down every settlement they could find and killing everyone who couldn't run away. Bandeng was virtually destroyed, though Zhang Xiumei's wife escaped, along with their son, Je. After Zhang's execution, somebody bravely stole back his head and returned it to Bandeng for proper burial, and his recently-restored tomb stands at the edge of the village, a small grassy mound ringed in grey brick, with the Chinese characters for "Zhang Xiumei" picked out in crimson on a headstone. The view down off the mountain from here is fabulous, the steep rice terraces and a succession of forested ridges dropping into hidden valleys, all blued by the distance. A good spot to spend eternity.

July 1872 saw Mesny returning to the field on the far side of southwestern Guizhou, this time fighting Muslim Hui insurgents who had spilled over the border from their ongoing revolt in adjacent Yunnan province. The campaign against them had been especially bloody, with the entire Muslim population of Xingyi – a town of around seven thousand people – massacred the previous December after surrendering to the combined Yunnan and Guizhou armies. The rebels were now making a final stand in the well-fortified town of Xincheng, and Mesny, once again bored and inactive at Guiyang, was allowed to head to the front and "see what could be done by way of bombarding the place". Chinese forces were being held back by heavy fire from Xincheng's rough stone defences; but Mesny saw that the town was closely overlooked by hills, bringing it well within the range of modern artillery. Sure enough, his twenty-pounder field guns had soon flattened a long stretch of Xincheng's walls, but the Chinese soldiers held back from storming the gap, terrified by the Muslims' ferocious reputation for hand-to-hand combat. When they finally picked up enough courage to launch a half-hearted attack two days later, the Hui – armed with three-pronged forks and rifles – mounted a brave resistance and sent the Chinese packing, leaving two hundred dead on the battlefield and twice this number injured, with no appreciable losses for themselves.

At this the Imperial forces withdrew to a safe distance and sat idle, firing about a dozen shells daily over Xincheng's walls in the vain hope of demoralising the rebels. Mesny reported a few vignettes of the siege: at one point the Hui had put a Chinese field gun out of action and then shot the men who were trying to repair it, so a captain Wang, immensely strong, picked up the gun himself and carried it back unaided, miraculously avoiding bullets. On another occasion, a frustrated Mesny successfully cajoled the commander-in-chief at Xincheng, General Zhong, into occupying some battered earthworks that the Hui had abandoned, but then had to watch in disgust as two battalions of Chinese turned tail and ran after the defenders fired a couple of shots in their direction. Once again, Mesny speculated whether such feeble tactics were, in fact, a deliberate attempt to prolong the fighting: "The whole thing put me in mind of dishonest workmen at home who, in cases where work is paid for by the day, do their utmost by laborious idleness to spin the work out for as long as possible".

Ultimately it was Xincheng's own authorities who took the initiative, negotiating a bloodless surrender of the town in November. Inevitably, having occupied Xincheng, the Chinese reneged on the deal and executed the leading Muslim cleric, Jin Wanzhao, along with six hundred of his followers. Reporting the event in the *Shanghai Courier*, Mesny believed that the Muslims would have held out to the bitter end and died fighting had they known how the Chinese would treat them; indeed, one group pulled out hidden knives whilst being bound for execution, killing four guards before they were overpowered.

By late 1873 virtually the whole of Guizhou was back in government hands and the province was declared pacified, though all but two of its major settlements had been reduced to rubble. It's impossible to give an accurate cost of the conflict in lives, as there's a wide discrepancy in official estimates, but it seems likely that at least half of Guizhou's pre-war population of seven million were either killed or displaced.

While the fighting might have ended, peace brought its own troubles. Guizhou's entrenched poverty meant that other provinces had always had to contribute to its upkeep, and the cost of Zhou Dawu's military campaigns had been borne by Sichuan. But now that the war was over, Sichuan – which had financial worries of its own – was no longer willing to continue subsidising its poorer neighbour. Without these funds, Zhou was unable to pay his battalions, some of which he needed to keep areas pacified, others which he wanted to disband. Mesny commented, "*One*

Million Taels would hardly suffice to pay off [Zhou Dawu's] braves, and that *another Million* is required by the [provincial treasurer] himself to pay up the arrears due to the Civil and Military Mandarins and the regular troops; all of whom have received little or no pay for the past twenty years and are anxiously awaiting the squaring up of their accounts, many of the Mandarins being reduced to actual beggary." Unpaid and with no career prospects ahead of them, there was the real risk that these men would turn bandit for a living, dragging a newly-pacified Guizhou back into lawlessness.

Having taken just two years to subdue a region which had been in open revolt for almost two decades, Zhou was justifiably furious at this treatment, the insult heightened by his superiors taking credit for his victories and barely mentioning him in their dispatches. Furthermore, Sichuan's treasurer accused Zhou of the old trick of lining his own pockets by claiming pay for "phantom" troops. Incensed, Zhou toyed with the idea of resigning his commission and travelling to Beijing to petition the emperor personally, though Mesny believed that even then he would find "that the Literati [at the capital] are too powerful to be made to acknowledge the rights of the Military, whom they have despised for so long a time".

The situation on the ground at Guiyang was certainly uncomfortable. While Zhou kept up a furious correspondence with Sichuan's bureaucrats, his men received their regular wages in rice instead of hard cash, if they were paid anything at all. Many were forced to sell off their possessions, leading to a sudden glut of guns and gunpowder being offered for next to nothing on Guiyang's streets. The governor tried to buy them up quickly before they fell into rebel hands, incidentally earning himself credit with the civil administration for purchasing military stores at such a remarkably low rate. But it was worrying how Guiyang was suddenly overrun by aggressive Hunanese beggars, whom many people suspected to in fact be members of the nebulous Gelao Hui, the anti-dynastic "Society of Older Brothers". Similar secret sects had plagued China's various ruling houses for millennia; they typically cloaked themselves in obscure religious rituals and thrived on channelling dissent, explaining the ingrained mistrust that Chinese governments have always displayed towards organizations that they don't control. Awash with cheap firearms and thousands of impoverished, resentful, battle-hardened veterans, post-war Guiyang was certainly a prime recruiting ground for the Gelao Hui; there were even rumours of a planned attack on the city, which was only defended by a civil militia. The society was later to play a major role in ruining Mesny's career.

In late November 1873, the need to secure further military funding became acute when fighting once again broke out in southern Guizhou. A large band of rebels, flushed out from their refuge along the Guangxi border, recaptured the towns of Bazhai and Danjiang, not far from the Leigong Shan battlefield, killing the magistrates and stirring up the local ethnic minorities against the government. Imperial troops soon had them on the run, but the incident showed how fragile Guizhou's peace really was.

At Guiyang, Mesny began a habit for collecting curios that lasted the rest of his life. He had also scooped up plenty of ethnic souvenirs during the war, and these he now bundled off to the museum at the Royal Asiatic Society at Shanghai. Two items in particular caught the Society's attention: a Miao chieftain's sword and a bronze drum of a type in use since ancient times throughout southern China and southeast Asia. All Miao villages needed them for festivals and they had been common enough when Mesny first arrived in Guizhou, but by the end of the war they had become rare, much sought-after by antique dealers and collectors from Sichuan and Hunan. The Chinese believed that they dated back to the third century, distributed by the master strategist Kongming during one of his forays into Guizhou.

The first few months of 1874 also saw Mesny designing what would become his lasting personal monument. During the Chong'an campaign, Tang Jiong had been repeatedly frustrated by the time it took to ferry his army over the river outside town, which ran through a deep, unbridged gorge. Mesny now undertook to construct a chain-link suspension bridge over the chasm, following the line of the post-road to Beijing, and was soon busily employed drawing up plans and costings estimates. "The bridge will have a span of 190 feet, with a width of 10 feet, and will be 56 feet (all Chinese measurements) above the level of the lowest water. The quantity of iron used will be about 60,000 catties, and will cost altogether less than Tls. 10,000. The cost will be paid by [Zhou Dawu], whose orders I am awaiting to commence the work, should he approve of the plans which are on a new principle of which your humble servant claims to be the inventor." Mesny never explained his "new principle", and in fact chain suspension bridges had already been used for centuries in southwestern China.

The initial plan had been to forge the iron for the chains at the Guiyang armoury from old military scrap and then cart it over the hills to Chong'an. However, by early March it was decided to set up a foundry on-site, and Mesny was off in the countryside studying traditional smelting techniques. But this marked the end of his involvement in the project. He left town shortly afterwards and never saw the completed bridge, which still crosses the lime-blue Chong'an river. A stone memorial tablet under plum trees on the north bank makes no mention of him, but does explain that the bridge ended up costing Zhou 12,000 taels, and that construction began in October and lasted until the following June. Locals confirm that the iron was mined up in the hills at Tiekuang Po, site of Tang Jiong's victory against the Miao, and that the twenty-four chains used to hang the bridge were forged right on the riverside. They were so well made that they have never rusted, even after nearly a century and a half in the open.

In April 1874 Mesny and his wife left Guiyang, accompanying Zhou Dawu on a journey north into Sichuan province. Mesny was probably going along for a change of scenery – he hadn't left Guizhou for six years – but Zhou was on a serious mission to confront the Sichuanese authorities directly about back pay for his troops. Travelling through Chongqing, they reached the provincial capital, Chengdu, at some time in May and settled down for a six-month stay.

If Chongqing was Sichuan's commercial centre then Chengdu was its cultural heart, a substantial walled city brimming with ornate temples and historic memorial gardens. But even here there was unrest. To the Chinese, unusual natural phenomena were a sign of impending chaos on earth, and Chengdu was suddenly overwhelmed with them: Coggia's comet appeared to the north, its tail appearing as "a narrow shower of sparks", a fire broke out at the courthouse and destroyed ninety homes, and the city was rocked by a sharp earthquake. There were reports of rebellion breaking out in Guangxi and Beijing, and the roads were said to be swarming with bandits and murderers – rumours Mesny rightly dismissed as entirely imaginary or greatly exaggerated. More tangible were the posters that appeared across the city abusing the viceroy, Wu Tang, for allowing the Chengdu currency to become so debased, "the cash being made of a mixture of zinc and sand, with the smallest possible amount of copper to keep the other ingredients together". Wu had the posters torn down but took the hint – spurred on perhaps by the bad omens – and reduced the price of rice. Chengdu was promptly ravaged by a storm, and citizens swore that they saw a dragon ascending to the skies after a lightning strike. Overshadowed by these dramatic events, nobody paid much attention to urgent appeals for help filtering into the city from northern Vietnam, a distant Chinese protectorate, which was feeling threatened by growing French expansionism in the south of the country.

By now the government owed Zhou Dawu more than 700,000 taels to cover his personal expenses from the Guizhou campaign, in addition to his troops' overdue wages. Wu Tang, knowing that Zhou was already extremely wealthy and didn't really need the money, had stalled payment in the hope that he would reduce his demands. After months of pointless bickering, an exhausted Zhou finally agreed to accept a settlement of 580,000 taels, with 300,000 paid immediately and the balance – earmarked for his men – due in one month's time. Wu Tang, however, then ordered the treasurer to pay Zhou only 200,000 up front, with the rest to be delivered in monthly instalments over the following year. Zhou was so angry at this further delay that it was only with difficulty that his staff again prevented him from appealing directly to the emperor, a disastrous tactic which would likely have ended with the demotion – or worse – of both himself and Wu Tang for daring to drag the throne into the whole sorry affair. Infuriated, he threatened to retire and leave Chengdu's civil authorities to settle the situation as best they could. Depressed at fresh reports arriving from Guiyang that the troops there were almost starving, Mesny wrote: "Altogether things do look gloomy – a miserable picture of misgovernment in a country having every possible physical element of prosperity and greatness".

Discharged soldiers now began rioting in southern Sichuan, and for a while it really looked as if civil war might break out again. Mesny felt that the only solution was for Chinese authorities to borrow several million taels from foreign banks to pay the men off. There were untapped copper, tin and mercury reserves across the region, and if these were responsibly worked using modern machinery, perhaps the loan could be repaid within a decade, besides keeping the demobbed soldiers busy in a profitable enterprise. His articles in the *Shanghai Courier* appealed to the British embassy at Beijing to set the process in motion, offering to provide them with accurate facts and figures about the situation.

Despairing that Zhou would ever manage to successfully settle his disputes, Mesny left Chengdu in early October and headed back east through the Three Gorges to his former stamping grounds at Hankou. Along the way he stopped at Wuxue, that nightmarish, whorish town on the Yangzi where he had arrived during his salt-smuggling days to see dogs being slaughtered. Here he sent off another collection of antiques and curios to the Royal Asiatic Society – musical instruments, an ancient bronze mirror, Tibetan religious icons, rare books and maps – and met the clergyman David Hill, who later became a family friend, at Wuxue's Methodist chapel. Hill described the encounter in a letter to his father, providing one of the earliest portraits of Mesny:

"The other day Mr William Mesny, a colonel in [His *Imperial Majesty's*] Service, spent an evening at my house. He has been for the last 6 years quite away from all formal society (except that now and then he has seen the R. C. missionaries) in the province of Kwei Chow. He speaks Chinese like a native and appears to be a true Christian; his parents are Methodists in Jersey or Guernsey and I doubt not follow their son with their prayers. Being a Mandarin he has access to a higher grade of society than we have, and in that sphere has borne testimony for the master. He tells of several officials with whom he has had conversations bearing on Christianity and personal Christian experience. Baptized with the spirit, he may be made of great service in the work of God in this country. He is now on his way to Shantung, the governor of which province has applied for his services. He is well up in the minutiae of Chinese etiquette which so few foreigners care to learn. He has married a Chinese lady and this gives him access to the families of officials. He threw out a suggestion which another friend of mine – I think I may say my nearest in China – Mr Foster has before given: the great influence that a man would have, who supports himself by trade in China."

Mesny was back at Hankou by late November. His friend Dupuis – the man who had sent him off to war in Guizhou six years previously – had left town on a private business venture, running a shipment of arms up into Yunnan through Vietnam, and was well on the way to precipitating the international incident which would drive France and China to war. But there was at least some good news about the soldiers' pay dispute in Sichuan: Wu Tang had decided to raise the necessary sum by ordering his subordinates across the province to dig into their own private funds. The money collected would be nothing like the million that Mesny had estimated was needed, but at least the troops would finally receive something for their years of hard service.

Just before Christmas, Mesny officially registered his marriage to Nien Suey Tsen at the British consulate, witnessed by his brother John – still employed in the customs service, and himself now married to a Chinese woman and busy raising a huge family. Nien's signature appears on the document only as a shaky cross, evidence of a surprising illiteracy. While only a small percentage of women in nineteenth-century China were able to read or write, the daughter of even a minor official should have at least been able to sign her name; middle-class women frequently handled their household's finances and some became fine calligraphers.

Back in 1873 Mesny's prestige had been bolstered by his promotion in rank to major-general and receiving the title of *batulu*, an award for bravery on active service. This entitled the bearer to considerable support when travelling on government business: county magistrates were obliged, if asked, to supply a *batulu* with food, fodder, twenty horses and eighty men. Mesny now decided to make use of this new-found privilege and spent the first part of 1875 on a trip north to Beijing, stopping off along the way at Ji'nan, capital of Shandong province, to meet the viceroy, Ding Baozhen. Ding was originally from Guizhou, where he had held a military command during the Taiping Rebellion and later been promoted to various civil posts; he was considered an upright, well-respected administrator. In 1869 he executed the arrogant palace eunuch An Dehai for making an outrageously pompous grand tour around Shandong. An had been a well-protected Imperial favourite, and Ding's actions were a measure of his political and moral clout. He was also one of several late Qing dynasty generals honoured by having a restaurant dish named after them: "kungpao chicken", a stir-fry with chillies and peanuts, was invented by his chef and named after Ding Baozhen's official title, *gongbao*, "Palace Guardian".

According to what he had told David Hill on his way to Hankou, Mesny was in Ji'nan at Ding's invitation, and now lobbied him about establishing a modern arsenal and surveying the Yellow River. The river, which allowed agriculture to thrive in Shandong's otherwise arid climate, was also popularly known as "China's Sorrow" for its habit of regularly shifting course, causing catastrophic floods. Mesny offered to design flood-proof embankments if Ding would only have him appointed Director General of River Works. Not surprisingly, the Imperial court declined the opportunity of promoting this precocious thirty-two-year-old foreigner to one of the country's most important civil posts. At Mesny's urging, Ding also wrote a memorial to the throne recommending that maths and geography should be added to the Imperial Examinations, which were otherwise wholly based on the Confucian Classics. Though the suggestion was again ignored and Ding seems not to have retained his services, this was the first of Mesny's repeated attempts over the next few decades to take an active role in China's development by serving regional authorities as an advisor on modernisation.

Beijing is essentially an alien construction – the city of invaders – founded by the Mongol Yuan dynasty during the thirteenth century and duly adopted as the Manchu capital in 1644. Then as now, Beijing was the seat of national government and its monumental bureaucracies, of foreign embassies and their stuffy, self-important staff, of grandiose architecture and portentous proclamations. The city's weather was terrible too, scorching in summer and appallingly cold in winter, with spring blighted by dust storms regularly blowing in from the Gobi desert to the northwest, engulfing the city in an abrasive yellow twilight. It was all somehow unreal and divorced in many ways from life in the rest of the country, whose distant population were content with the maxim, *shan gao huangdi yuan* – "The mountains are high, and the emperor is far away".

Mesny was probably in town to get his military rank, issued in the field, officially confirmed; the process would have involved paying out the necessary administration fees – bribes, really – to influential government staff, a practice he always despised. Even so, it seems wilfully perverse that Mesny, who was to write around a million words in the *Miscellany*, left almost no record of his impressions of China's Imperial capital; nothing of Beijing's vast, alienating scale, its warrens of narrow lanes known as *hutongs*, or its many gardens, palaces and temples. This is the first in a long list of missing descriptions of cities visited. In fact, his sole direct observation of the capital was on the appalling squalor of Beijing's streets, which disgusted even such a hardened traveller as himself: "Human excrement is everywhere, besides the droppings of many draught animals, mules, asses, ponies and oxen as well as camels. There is also the soil from every household, collected in cesspools anywhere in the road, and the foulest of drains, the sewerage from which is used to water the streets. Men are seen in every street and alley in broad day-light, and indecently exposing their dirty parts to the full gaze of passers bye. The lower classes of Peking inhabitants appear to be alike dead to shame, and filth, of every description."

It was at Beijing that Mesny first nurtured what was to become one of his major obsessions: pioneering new trade routes. Transporting goods any distance overland in China was both dangerous and prohibitively expensive. Banditry was rife, and it cost more than grain was worth to cart it more than fifty kilometres or so from the point of production. Rivers offered safer and cheaper travel, but where navigable rivers dried up – in much of southwestern China, for example – roads were the only option. At this point China had no railways, but foreign powers were desperate to introduce them, partly for the lucrative construction contracts they would have been able to wrangle from the Chinese government, but mostly because they would have opened the country up, making trade cheaper and increasing foreign profits. But there was great resistance to the idea from within China: powerful transport cartels knew that they would be priced out of business, and officials realised that they would lose their transport taxes, a major source of income.

Then in 1875, some rails and rolling stock were presented to the emperor. After some discussion, it was decided to showcase the benefits of railways by using them to construct a short line between Shanghai and its sea port, Wusong. The *Miscellany* claimed that this idea was Mesny's, though most contemporary accounts credit the Americans for secretly buying up land for the line and the trading giant, Jardine Matheson, for funding its construction. The first six-kilometre-long stretch opened the following year, an engine named the *Celestial Empire* completing the journey in seventeen minutes, and proved a huge popular success. But the Qing authorities were horrified, convinced that the foreigners would use the railway as a corridor to stretch their territorial claims from Shanghai city right out to Wusong. In a rare instance of forthright government action, Shanghai's governor bought up the line and had it dismantled and shipped to Taiwan. It was another thirty years before a commercial railway would open in China.

Towards the end of 1875, Mesny inexplicably turned down the post of Secretary to the Chinese Legation in London and returned to Guizhou despite a wave of anti-foreigner hostility spreading across China, much of it directed against Christian missionaries and their converts. This was nothing new. In popular imagination, the history of Christianity in China was entirely negative: the Jesuits had helped the Manchu invaders to cast cannon, which they had used to conquer the country; European Christians had forced their way into China through the Opium Wars and treaty ports; and the Taipings had been Christian, and had brought nothing but more devastation and chaos. Christianity had therefore become associated with invasion, and missionaries who ventured into previously unexplored corners of the country were believed to be spearheading further European expansionism. Worse yet, it was widely believed that church-run orphanages paid criminals to kidnap children, so that the nuns could sell their body parts for use in medicine. Chinese converts also had the habit of noisily clamouring for foreign protection in civil disputes with their non-Christian neighbours. In short, the alien religion divided communities and caused trouble.

There had been several bloody purges of European priests and their Chinese followers over the years; the worst, at Tianjin in 1870, saw sixty Christian converts massacred by a mob, along with a French Consul and two Chinese officials attempting to intervene. In Guizhou and Sichuan, the trouble which had begun with unpaid, rioting soldiers was now also assuming an anti-Christian aspect, which the *Shanghai Courier* attributed to the malevolence of "one General Ming, an old rebel chief," who was said to have powerful supporters in Beijing. The southern half of Guizhou was once again in open revolt, with several cities captured by rebels barely two years after the province was supposed to have been pacified, though Mesny doubted whether the insurgents had any firm convictions or could stand up against a disciplined force sent against them. Cynically, he suggested that the British should end the trouble by employing Chinese soldiers to restore order "and make use of them to conquer their native land; for they are not particular whom they serve as long as they get their rations and their pay."

Mesny was now offered another government posting, described vaguely in the Hong Kong *China Mail* as "a splendid position in Szechuan, which he may accept if peace is actually restored". Once again he failed to take up the offer and instead resumed his former work at Guiyang's arsenal, indulging in a little private enterprise by selling watches as an agent of a French jeweller at Hankou. He donated funds to the Catholic Church too, and helped the city's newly-opened Protestant mission by supplying them with religious texts translated into Chinese.

News was also filtering in from elsewhere around China. In the Muslim northwest, Zuo Zongtang had finally suppressed the Tungan Revolt – the commission he had undertaken just before meeting Mesny in Hankou almost a decade earlier. Then there had been the "Margary Affair" in Yunnan, involving the murder of a British consular official, Augustus Margary, who had been guiding a trade expedition travelling between Burma and China. Foreign outrage at Margary's death had forced the Chefoo Convention of 1876, in which the Chinese government apologised for the murder, promised to provide protection for British subjects and were required to make the treaty ports duty-free enclaves, freeing up the cost of importing and selling British goods. Details of the convention were now being posted in towns and cities around the country as the "Margary Proclamation" so that locals would know to leave foreign travellers alone.

Back at Guiyang, Mesny had been contacted by another explorer, Captain William Gill of the Royal Engineers, who in late 1876 had arrived at Shanghai from Britain looking for an interpreter and guide for an extended journey through western China. Gill had made plans to travel up through the Three Gorges to Chongqing and Chengdu, where he hoped Mesny could join him in early summer the following year. Unspecified events – perhaps that destructive lightning strike on Guiyang's magazine – delayed Mesny's departure, and it wasn't until 21 June 1877, the longest day of the year, that he and Gill met up in the Sichuanese capital. Mesny wouldn't return to Guizhou for over two years.

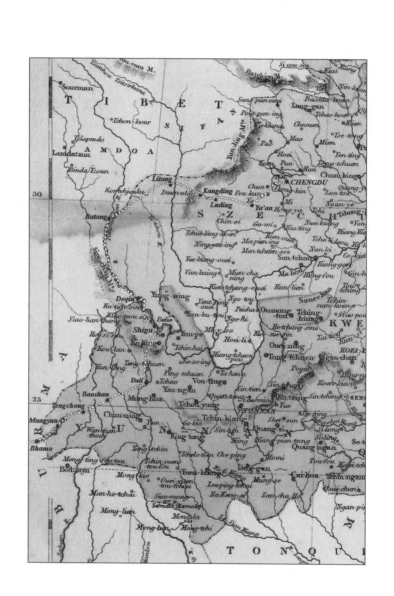

WITH GILL TO BURMA
JUNE–NOVEMBER 1877

Sandwiched between central China and Tibet, Sichuan was split by a range of mountains slanting southwest across the enormous province. East of this divide lay the warm, wet, fertile Red Basin, one of China's most densely-settled regions, a land of easy abundance where fruit and vegetables flourished and farmers harvested two crops of rice every year. With the metropolises of Chengdu and Chongqing facing each other across the basin, eastern Sichuan was also unusually cosmopolitan despite being cut off from the rest of China by the Three Gorges. The region had used its isolation to enjoy a comfortable independence from centralised rule, nurturing famous scholars, poets, statesmen and warriors. Towns were full of grand guildhalls and busy markets, and the garrulous population seemed to enjoy taking life slowly, spending their time eating, drinking and lounging around the many teahouses and restaurants that thronged the roads, even far out in the countryside.

Western Sichuan was another world entirely, full of ice-bound mountains overflowing from the Himalayan plateau, for the large part inhabited by Tibetans and other non-Han peoples. These nomads spent their lives in felt tents, herding yaks between seasonal high-altitude pasturage; a tough existence on a diet of thin air, harsh winters and few diversions. Settlements were widely spread, mostly comprising of trading depots and self-contained monastic complexes – fortress-like communities housing thousands of monks and lamas – strung along the caravan roads which crossed westwards over the ranges and into Yunnan province or Greater Tibet.

It was these lonely roads that were now attracting the attention of foreign powers. Britain was particularly nettled that, despite the Opium Wars and treaty ports, she was still unable to exploit markets in China's remote interior, home to the bulk of the country's vast population – somewhere in the region of four hundred million potential customers. With the Chinese still holding out against the introduction of railways, the British had been mulling over the notion of importing opium, cotton and cheap tea directly into southwestern China from their territories in adjacent Burma and India, avoiding the prohibitively high cost of shipping these goods to Shanghai and Hong Kong and then ferrying them overland across the country.

Routes between China and Tibet were collectively known as *chama dao*, or "tea-horse roads", after the goods trafficked along them. Tea wouldn't grow in the mountains but Tibetans were enthusiastic consumers, annually importing around three million kilos of leaves from eastern China and exporting their stocky, powerful horses in exchange – animals greatly valued by the Chinese military. But for the British, Tibet – technically a Chinese-administered protectorate – was a problem. The country had been closed to outsiders since the 1840s, the Tibetan theocracy keen to keep foreigners away in case they introduced Christianity and undermined their own influence over the population. The Chinese worried that British merchants would either sell arms to the Tibetans or muscle in on the profitable tea trade.

The alternative – crossing into southwestern China from adjoining countries – had, until recently, been almost impossible because of the Muslim Uprising in Yunnan province. But the Chinese government had now suppressed that rebellion, and even during the war Lagrée's mission had managed to visit the rebel capital, Dali, in 1868. The same year, Thomas Cooper – the man who had decided not to employ Mesny as an interpreter – nearly made it to Dali too, while the British Browne-Sladen expedition had crossed into southern Yunnan from Burma before being turned back. Their second attempt in 1875 was clouded by Margary's murder, which happened just inside the Chinese border. All these near-misses seem to have frustrated Mesny, living so close to the region at Guiyang, who now wrote a letter to the Royal Geographical Society in London about how he hoped that "the opening up of Western China to trade, and the vast mineral wealth of this province, will make it become more interesting to the British Public than it has been hitherto".

Captain William Gill was altogether a very different person from the brave but poorly-prepared Cooper. A lightly-built man with close-cropped hair and a freewheeling moustache, Gill was a professional soldier serving in the Royal Engineers who had been born into a military family at Madras in 1843. In what sounds like the plot of some Victorian melodrama, he unexpectedly inherited an enormous fortune from a distant relative; but instead of retiring into obscurity and frittering away his wealth, Gill decided to stay in the military and accept special commissions of exploration. He picked up the basics of surveying on a trip to Iran, where he helped to fix the exact line of the disputed border with Russia, then returned to Britain and stood unsuccessfully as a Conservative candidate at a London by-election, and was casting around for some fresh adventure when a friend suggested he explore China's western fringes.

Gill arrived at Shanghai in September 1876, where he discovered that there was a fellow countryman living in the interior who was fluent in Chinese and familiar with the region that he hoped to explore. He contacted Mesny, engaged his services and arranged to meet up with him the following summer in Sichuan, writing in his diaries that Mesny "in all probability knows more of China and understands the Chinese better than any man living not himself a 'celestial', and I am very fortunate in securing him as an interpreter – & all he wants is to have his expenses paid".

Travelling north, Gill visited the Great Wall and sought advice on possible routes across western China from seasoned hands at Beijing's British Legation, who liked "the idea of English officers travelling about to spy out the land" and offered him their full support. A paper in the British National Archives entitled "*China. Military Report on the Province of Cheh-Li, by Captain W Gill, RE*", proves that even at this early stage he wasn't simply playing the tourist. He returned to Shanghai in time to catch a boat up the Yangzi with Edward Colbourne Baber, a British diplomat who was also heading west on a special investigation into the state of trade in Sichuan. Back in 1862, the voyage between Shanghai and Hankou had taken Mesny six weeks aboard the heavily-armed *Rob Roy*; now, as a sign of how quickly communications were improving in China, the same trip took a luxurious modern paddle steamer just eight days. Gill arrived at Chengdu on May 10, and finding that Mesny was still on the road he decided to toughen himself up by making a short foray into the Tibetan areas of northern Sichuan.

Aside from scattered articles in the *Shanghai Courier* and a few notes in the *Miscellany*, Mesny never wrote about his journey west with Gill, so the record is largely culled from Gill's travelogue, *The River of Golden Sand*, named after the Chinese term for the Yangzi's upper reaches. Like the river, the book was extremely long – the original two-volume set had to be edited down for later editions – and was full of lively detail about almost everything Gill experienced, as witnessed by the enquiring eyes of a newcomer to the country. But it was strangely neutral towards Mesny himself, who hardly appears in the entire narrative and is described only once as "an officer in the service of the Chinese". Fortunately, Gill's private diaries – weighty, leather-bound volumes which were obviously never intended for publication – reveal far more about his personal feelings than it was politic to include in *The River of Golden Sand*. Written in pencil, in a cramped but legible hand, the daily entries pour out Gill's frequent irritation with Mesny's eccentricities, his frustration at the numerous delays and his true opinions of the Chinese staff and officials that he had to deal with. But the text never stoops to cynicism, and also emphasises how highly Gill valued his travelling companion's virtues as an interpreter and troubleshooter.

Following their meeting at his rooms on the evening of June 21, Gill used these diaries to record his candid first impressions of Mesny's impulsive, honest and frequently naive character:

"Mesny is an exceedingly fat man and a fearful talker who seems unable to keep his tongue quiet a moment. He told me his whole history in half an hour he regularly wears his heart on his coat sleeve – he was not in our army as I supposed but began life on board ships he had a taste for mechanics and used to carry a few tools about with him. He was taken prisoner by the Tai Pings who treated him very well and insisted on his repairing a musket one day, which he accomplished, and since then he has [so] improved his knowledge and his skill that he has been in charge of an arsenal and not only that but has acted as musketry and artillery drill instructor – He has always been well paid but he told me that all his savings were in Honduras and Turkish bonds [the value of which had recently collapsed; Mesny was never lucky with investments] – When he first heard from me (I only wrote to say that I was *thinking* of travelling and would like to hear from him whether it would suit him to accompany me *if* I should feel inclined to make use of his services) he was disputing a claim with the Chinese for 5000 Taels – he at once resigned his appointment, wrote to the British Legation at Peking that he was coming with me – sent a lot of muskets, pieces of copper and stones of many kinds that were his own private property to the arsenal and asked the Chinese Government to pay him for them, but came away without even a promise from them that they would do this and left 2 or 3 houses that he had bought as a speculation in Kwei Yang with no one to look after them, and all this because he is fond of travelling. He sent a lot of tea and satin to England but lost 50 per cent on the value and found out afterwards that he might have sold his goods in the province of Shantung at a profit of 100 percent – He is not a likely man to make a fortune amongst the Heathen Chinese – He has a round face, black hair, moustache and infernal dresses motié Europeanne et motié Chinoise; can apparently eat anything for on arrival here he was hungry and I had nothing to offer him but these beastly sugared cakes which he enjoyed, however, thoroughly. He always lives à la Chinoise and for years has neither eaten European food or used a knife or fork – He drinks no wine or spirits of any kind and does not smoke – One day when 18 years old he took to smoking opium because everyone else did and got so much with the habit of it that on one occasion when he had been deprived of it the usual symptoms of hunger without being able to touch food, irritability and blue devils generally came over him – he did not know what was the matter with him but some one told him all he wanted was a pipe of opium – But though so young he fortunately had the sense and strength of mind to resist the temptation was miserable for 3 days but never touched opium again."

The two travellers spent the next few days together, mulling over the choice of routes between China and India. Tibet was off-limits of course, and following in Cooper's footsteps towards Burma sounded too unadventurous, so Gill had his eyes on an ambitious third option: to head north from Sichuan into Gansu province, pick up the line of the historic Silk Road, and follow it northwest through the deserts of Chinese Turkestan to distant Kashgar, a Muslim oasis town on the frontier between China, Russia and Central Asia. But things weren't looking good in this direction either: northwestern China remained in chaos following the suppression of the Tungan Revolt, Kashgar had become the base of a rebel khan known as Yakub Beg and Britain and Russia were locked in "The Great Game" – a shadow-war over the very borderlands that Gill would have to cross before he could reach India. Now Mesny brought along the additionally unwelcome news that British diplomats at Beijing had changed their minds over Gill's mission and had decided to prevent him from travelling to Kashgar in case the visit was misinterpreted by China as support for Yakub Beg's cause.

Feeling hugely let down, Gill fumed at the "wretched people at Peking", but now had only one option left to him, that of linking Cooper's trail – which crossed western Sichuan to the Tibetan border, then followed it down into Yunnan – with Margary's route through Yunnan into Burma. In compensation, Gill would at least be making the first accurate maps of the region, and there was always the romance of being among the few

Europeans to have trodden these trails since Marco Polo's travels in the thirteenth century.

It took a couple of weeks to prepare for the journey. As always, there was a struggle to convert their taels into local currency at a fair rate of exchange, despite Gill having plenty of high-quality Chongqing silver. Mules and porters for routes west were scarce too, as there was an important Nepalese delegation due at their first destination, Kangding, and all available transport was either already reserved for them or unwilling to head that way in case they were pressed into the envoy's service for an indefinite period. Sichuan was also suffering a serious drought, and it looked as if supplies might be hard to find along the way. The dry weather brought the risk of fires breaking out in the city itself, so Chengdu's southern gates had been sealed up as Zhurong, the fire deity, was associated with this direction.

Mesny and Gill spent their spare time sightseeing. They thoroughly enjoyed the Sichuanese capital; Mesny went so far as to describe Chengdu as the finest city in the empire, while Gill found it well-designed and orderly, full of wealthy citizens and grand public buildings. The streets were clean and the shopfronts attractively lacquered and gilded – the merchandise ranging from foreign goods to an enormous variety of locally-grown fruit, vegetables and flowers. The markets were unusual in having large stone troughs full of running water for displaying live fresh fish instead of the usual foetid buckets and barrels seen elsewhere in China. Ten kilometres of walls encircled the city, but with several important temples now standing isolated in the surrounding countryside it was clear that Chengdu had once been far larger. The capital had never regained its former glory after having been sacked by the cruel despot "Yellow Tiger" Zhang Xianzhong during the 1640s, at the end of the Ming dynasty; indeed, Zhang's massacres had almost depopulated the whole of eastern Sichuan._

At Wenshu Yuan, one of the country's largest Zen Buddhist monasteries, they found vegetarian food, repulsive statues and polite monks. Across the city, the scruffy Taoist complex of Qingyang Gong claimed to be the birthplace of the religion's founding sage, Laozi, whose wiry priests dressed in dark blue robes with their long hair tied back into a tight bun. Beyond Chengdu's locked south gate was Wuhou Ci, the "Memorial Hall to the Minister of War", a large garden of ancient cypress trees and bamboo groves scattered with pavilions, where people came to picnic. It formed something of a shrine to the Three Kingdoms period, a turbulent time during the third century when Sichuan had enjoyed independence under the warlord Liu Bei, whose body lay buried beneath a wooded mound at the gardens' centre. Gill, however, was more interested in a large map of the world he found hanging in one of the halls, apparently made by French Jesuits during the seventeenth century. On it, two great bodies of water were marked in central Africa, seeming to prove that even back then the Jesuits had known about the existence of lakes Victoria and Tanganyika, which had only recently been discovered by British explorers. Mesny attempted, unsuccessfully, to buy the map from the temple's caretaker.

There was another ornamental garden further outside the city named "Du Fu's Thatched Cottage" after the soulful Tang dynasty poet who had lived here in poverty over a thousand years earlier. Having failed to achieve any significant government position or much critical acclaim during his career, Du Fu's poems were now greatly admired – the former viceroy, Wu Tang, had even helped publish a definitive collection in 1873 – and these nostalgically antique gardens were popular with Chengdu's upper classes, who came to stroll and socialise in lakeside teahouses. Mesny's Chinese friends invited them here for a banquet. Gill was impressed by the scale of the feast but found the food bland and was disgusted by Chinese table manners, which left the teahouse spattered in a mess of grease, dropped morsels, spilled sauces and discarded scraps: "the debris collects on the table more or less, though a person accustomed to these things... spits or throws it on the floor".

Mesny also renewed contact with Ding Baozhen, his former patron from Ji'nan, who had recently replaced Wu Tang as Sichuan's viceroy. Sichuan was unusual: provinces were generally paired with a neighbour as a joint administrative region – for instance Hunan and Hubei, which were collectively known as "Lianghu". A regional governor oversaw the activities of the two provincial viceroys under him, diluting their power; but Sichuan stood independent of any region, meaning that Ding could act on his own authority alone – further proof of how much this honest official was trusted by the Imperial court.

Ding was using his new appointment to cement his reputation as a reformer, renovating the two-thousand-year-old Dujiangyan irrigation scheme north of Chengdu – where a sandstone bust stands in his memory today – and overhauling the Sichuanese salt trade, which had become thoroughly corrupt. Salt accounted for almost half of the provincial revenue, and was tapped as brine from an enormous subterranean basin underneath Zigong in central Sichuan. Gill had passed through Zigong in his travels and described how the town was entirely covered in bamboo piping, its skyline pierced by the tall spires of drilling rigs. The government had previously granted monopolies whereby the salt was sold at a fixed price to approved dealers, who then transported it around the country and disposed of it at whatever the local market could stand. In good years they made a fortune – Zigong's wells brought in over six million taels a year, a tremendous sum – but when transport costs rose through graft or war, the merchants found themselves with a product that they couldn't shift at a profit. Ding Baozhen now decided that the Sichuanese government itself would be responsible for transporting salt, which standardized the distribution networks and increased the quantity sold – and so, despite the considerable financial outlay, also increased government revenue. One of the architects of the reforms was Mesny's military mentor, Tang Jiong, who had been pardoned for his record in Guizhou and was now working closely with Ding at Chengdu.

Eventually, all was ready for the road. As their baggage was sorted into piles it became obvious that the expedition would need a shocking number of staff: three overseers, sixteen men for the sedan chairs and thirty-nine porters for the luggage, besides two ponies to carry the heaviest loads. Ding Baozhen had given Mesny a generous present of 300 silver taels, adding to the weight; Gill hoped that they could exchange it for gold along the way, which was meant to be cheaply available.

The evening before their departure, Mesny visited Ding a final time to thank him for his gift. The viceroy asked where they were headed and Mesny sketched out their plans for reaching India via western Sichuan, Yunnan and Burma, skirting the Tibetan border for much of the journey. Ding was surprised:

> "But that is a very long and tedious journey. Why do you not go [directly through Tibet]?"
>
> "We don't know anything about that route – none of our countrymen ever travelled it and I always heard it was very bad."
>
> "Not at all. The road to Lassa is very good and much frequented, from there you can get to India in 20 days. I have been in these parts and I strongly advise you to go this way – the road is better and shorter."
>
> "Well, we shall certainly think over your advice, as my friend and I are both very anxious to get home quickly and if that is the better road we may change our plans".
>
> "Well wherever you go I shall send an order beforehand to have the officials on the lookout for you and order them to take every care of you".

When Mesny repeated the conversation, Gill was stunned: "The idea of going into Tibet I had abandoned as utterly beyond hope and here was the Governor General dangling the glorious prize before our eyes. I dare not believe he was in earnest for it appears to me too good to be finally true – Hitherto the Chinese have thrown every obstacle and every impediment in the way of travelling via Tibet and that the Governor General here should suggest it appears to me inexplicable – it has thrown me into a fever of excitement".

Gill would have to wait many weeks, until they reached the Tibetan border at Batang, before he would find out whether Ding had indeed been playing with them.

On July 10, Gill and Mesny headed west out of Chengdu, following the highway past the township of Shuangliu. Both men already had considerable experience of the rigours of travel in China, not least in the state of the roads and type of accommodation they were likely to encounter. In theory, a network of well-maintained highways criss-crossed the empire, linking together all the major settlements. The reality was that wide, smooth and orderly "roads" as such were rare outside the north China plains; local authorities were meant to draft in villagers to maintain them, but the scheme caused so much public resentment that officials usually let the roads degenerate into narrow, muddy tracks interspersed with erratic stretches of dangerously uneven, slippery granite flagstones. This made them totally impassable for any form of wheeled transport. All goods had to be carried by pack animals or on porters' backs; peasants went on foot and even for a wealthy traveller – who might ride a horse or be carried in a sedan chair – journeying long distances was inevitably slow, arduous and uncomfortable.

As with the voyage through the Yangzi Gorges, contemporary travel writing revelled in describing the horrors of Chinese accommodation. True, there was never a shortage of places to stay – Mesny and Gill rarely needed to sleep outside – but conditions were usually atrocious. City inns could be substantial, two-storied affairs built around a central courtyard, with the best beds upstairs, where there was at least a chance of catching some fresh air. Out in the countryside you could expect livestock to be penned in on the ground floor, making the rooms rank and malodorous; there would be little furniture and only an open, hopelessly smoky brazier for warmth. Either way, beds were guaranteed to be infested with vermin, something that Gill guarded against by dusting his sheets with carbolic powder every night. Mesny – who seemed to attract all manner of biting insects – jokingly complained that this drove Gill's fleas across the room and into his own bed. Gill privately thought it more likely that Mesny, being so fat, made "rare good feeding".

On top of this, the Chinese disliked quiet on principle, and inns were always noisy places where the guests whiled away their evenings by visiting each other to play rowdy drinking games, to conduct business or simply to argue. There also wasn't any concept of privacy, especially for foreigners, who were seen as curiosities and could expect a constant procession of visitors, from gruff and sometimes hostile soldiers through to throngs of loud, gawping sightseers. If crowds were let in for a closer look they tended to ransack luggage (often taking "souvenirs"), and if barred from the room would stare open-mouthed from doorways and poke holes in the paper window panes for a better view.

Gill was impressed by Mesny's sedan chair carriers, who he had brought with him from Guizhou and kept up a steady pace along the paths: "Carrying Mesny who weighs 15 stone, one time today they beat my chair coolies with an empty chair, doing 6 good miles with a bit of a hill 400 feet high in an hour and a half". He was less impressed with Mesny himself, out of condition after years of easy living at Guiyang, who found it hard going having to walk steeper sections of the road where it was impossible to be carried. Gill, freshly hardened from a month tramping around northern Sichuan, proved rather unsympathetic and privately hoped that the exercise would help Mesny, a chronic insomniac, to sleep.

These sedan chairs, wickerwork seats slung between two bamboo poles and carried by four bearers, were an essential part of travel in China, and not just for transport on the road. When visiting important officials along the way – perhaps for their help in arranging somewhere to stay – it was considered impolite to arrive at the courthouse on foot, or even on horseback; you needed to emphasise your own status by being carried in a chair. The inevitable crowds of ordinary Chinese that gathered to enjoy the spectacle were often so dense that court police had to beat people out of the way with cudgels, sometimes using their long "pig-tail" hair plaits as whips. Foreigners usually found the whole procedure excruciatingly embarrassing, not least for being carried by men so poor that they had to do such exhausting work for a living.

By the time they had reached Ya'an, around five days from Chengdu, the two men were growing to know each other. Ever optimistic, Mesny became increasingly certain that they would be able to enter Tibet. Gill, more the realist, wasn't so sure. Gill was warming to his companion though, writing, "I rather like having him about the place for I never take any notice of his chatter while I am writing and he now has given up talking unless he sees I want him to – and at and after dinner I get much amusement and information for [Mesny's] having a Chinese wife and having lived so many years amongst the Chinese". For his part, Mesny took note of Gill's purposeful, scientific approach to travel, and on future journeys always carried basic surveying equipment and kept a detailed journal.

Ya'an sat out on the edge of a plain right at the foot of Erlang Shan, an imposing range of mountains that marked the abrupt border with western Sichuan. Said to be one of the first places in China that tea had been introduced, little was actually grown at Ya'an itself but the town had become a major clearing house for the Tibetan trade. Factories here produced tea "bricks", compressed blocks of coarse twigs and third-rate leaves that the Chinese wouldn't touch, which were easy to transport and could be stored for years without losing their taste. Porters, weighted down with up to two hundred kilos of these bricks – more than even a mule could safely carry – took three weeks to haul their cargo westwards over the mountains to Kangding, from where yak teams ferried them deeper into Tibet. Despite taking a break every few steps to rest their heavy bamboo backpacks on an iron-shod crutch, the porters' backs were soon bent out of shape by the enormous weight of their loads and they rarely lived much into their thirties. Wages for the entire journey amounted to just a couple of silver pieces, and they could only afford a diet of plain steamed buns.

For their part, Gill and Mesny expected to reach Kangding in just ten days. Immediately outside town the road began to climb into Erlang Shan's densely cultivated foothills; this was the first real ascent of the trip and Gill was to describe the rest of the journey to Yunnan as "continually going up a staircase". They rested part-way up at a convenient wayside restaurant, all full of bustle and chatter, where the patrons lounged around eating roasted broad beans and the staff ladled out bowls of freshly-steamed rice from huge wooden tubs. Above here they passed horse teams led by a *mafu*, a head groom, the animals' necks hung with red ribbons and handfuls of little brass bells embossed with tigers' faces to ward off bad luck – and, pragmatically, to warn other road users of their approach. A definite traffic hierarchy became apparent: everyone got off the road for official sedan chairs, pedestrians stepped aside for horses, and the heavily-burdened tea porters were pushed or even whipped off the path by the expedition's unsympathetic Chinese staff.

The road grew increasingly rough as it left the farmed fields behind and climbed to a 2800m-high pass, where they paused at an isolated teahouse and admired the views of greener, gentler slopes on Erlang Shan's far side. Descending to an uninspiring township far below, they found the inns packed out by Tibetan emissaries; from here the road was appalling and it took them half a day to cover the next fifteen kilometres, past another team of unsmiling and emaciated tea porters. One final pass and they were down at Luding, a little town set in a deep, narrow gorge through which the Dadu River tore in a rough torrent. Luding was famous for its suspension bridge, designed by a blacksmith in 1701 and the only crossing for hundreds of miles in any direction. It was only safe to use in the morning; by the afternoon, fierce winds whipped up through the gorge, twisting and buckling the bridge's dangerously dilapidated wooden planking. In 1935, Mao Zedong and his communist army would find themselves cornered here by Nationalist forces during their Long March to safety in northern China, only managing to escape by climbing hand-over-hand along the bridge's iron chains.

Gill and Mesny's inn was comfortable enough, despite a ground-floor pigsty, but their northern Chinese servants continually found fault with the hostel's Sichuanese staff. A fight broke out between them, but it wasn't serious.

Kangding – Darzêdo to the Tibetans – turned out to be a bustling, squalid town of fortress-like houses crammed into a narrow river valley, all overshadowed by jagged, frosted peaks. The enormous, ethnically Tibetan region spreading west from here – Kham – had been annexed by China in 1792 and was now governed from Kangding by a Chinese resident, whose court staff and military, Mesny noticed, seemed "exceedingly oppressive and over-bearing towards the Tibetan people." The town was a nexus between worlds: out on the streets, Han shopkeepers and Muslim butchers rubbed up against tough, dreadlocked Khampa nomads who seemed impervious to the cold, the men's greasy leather jackets worn crosswise so that one arm was always bare to the shoulder. They all carried long knives with decorated scabbards tucked into their waistbands. Khampa women were tall and attractive, wearing high boots and draped in chunks of amber, coral and turquoise jewellery. Raw turquoise also came in useful for barter, though Kangding's traders favoured the Indian rupee and Gill was proud to find his queen's portrait on coins in this remote part of the world. Nobody paid the two foreigners much attention; Kangding was so full of non-Chinese "barbarians" from beyond the fringes of the empire that everyone assumed them to be merchants from India or Nepal.

The local diet took some getting used to. Given that only barley and maize would grow at this altitude, Tibetans, though Buddhist, pragmatically excused themselves from being strict vegetarians; while forbidden to kill animals, they did actually eat meat on occasion. Even so, most people lived almost entirely on *tsampa* – roasted barley meal – and butter tea. This dubious beverage was made by breaking a nugget of compressed leaves off a tea brick and churning it together with boiling water, a little salt and a blob of yak butter; Tibetans consumed it in vast quantities but Europeans found the rich, rancid flavour an acquired taste. Gill thought it "not such a repulsive drink as would be supposed", especially once you had mastered the technique of blowing any stray yak hairs off the surface of your bowl. But Han Chinese don't eat dairy products, and Mesny – who hadn't touched butter in a decade – suffered a "violent bilious attack" after indulging. He soon recovered by dosing himself with Holloway's Pills, a popular Victorian-era cure-all to which Gill found him virtually addicted.

Kangding's best inns had once again been reserved pending the arrival of the Nepalese ambassador, so Gill and Mesny rented an apartment overlooking a small public square where gamblers and idlers spent the day. Most of the town's guesthouses were run by Tibetan women; traditional polyandry was rife and their landlady, despite already having three husbands (two of whom were Chinese merchants), was open to the idea of adding a foreign man to her stable and sent them "a suitable present".

Unsure of how to proceed with their travel plans, they contacted Kangding's Catholic community, which included French fathers and a bishop who had been living in southwest China for decades and who had accumulated a mass of local knowledge. They had nobody else to share it with, however, as an imperial edict allowed them to preach Christianity only on the understanding that they never left the country. So priests in their early twenties arrived in China from France, only to vanish into the mountains of Sichuan, Yunnan and Eastern Tibet, perhaps never to see other foreigners again.

Bishop Chauveau welcomed the travellers warmly but warned them that organizing the next stage of their journey was likely to take a while. The biggest problem would be finding pack animals. As people of rank could freely requisition them for as long as they liked, owners were understandably reluctant to offer their beasts for hire. Gill put the word around that he was willing to pay, but nobody believed him. It was also widely understood that Gill and Mesny were hoping to cross into Tibet, perhaps even making an attempt to reach the capital, Lhasa, and Kangding's influential lamas had forbidden locals to help the travellers in any way. It was clear that they would need to solicit aid from the Chinese governor.

Seeking official assistance wasn't a question of simply turning up at the local courthouse and pleading your case. The first step in the process involved sending out visiting cards to the authorities, which gave them time to decide whether it was prudent to meet with you. Officials had many responsibilities towards important guests, but as the cost of providing transport and accommodation came out of their own pockets, there was great temptation to side-step requests for them. A high-ranking mandarin's wage was only a niggardly 185 taels per year, plus an allowance of 500 taels for expenses. Considering that a staff budget alone could easily exceed 1,000 taels, officials – honest ones, at least – were always short of funds. In fact, unless from a wealthy background, it was impossible for a government official to do their job properly without indulging in various money-raising schemes, and corruption, whether blatant or indirect, was inevitable. Kangding's magistrate was none too subtle in this regard: Gill believed that he made the equivalent of £10,000 a year, "all from squeezes or presents received, which ought more properly to be called bribes".

Foreigners were a further annoyance because of their general ignorance of correct protocol, their tendency to grow angry at delays, and their habit of making ridiculous demands – such as assurances of safety while travelling through countryside known to be infested with bandits. The life of a Chinese official continually teetered on the brink of disaster: as Tang Jiong's experiences in Guizhou had shown, previous success was no protection against any errors of judgement. So it's little wonder that, faced with the financial burden and unpredictable consequences of providing assistance, officials frequently resorted to tactical stalling, making visitors wait for days or even weeks for an audience while citing a heavy workload or ill-health as an excuse, hoping that the guest would eventually depart without involving them. As a man of rank, Mesny became increasingly sensitive to any social slights paid to him, real or imagined, and on later occasions was capable of causing his hosts considerable embarrassment by demanding what he considered to be his rights.

While their negotiations with officialdom slowly gathered momentum, Mesny and Gill explored a lamasery on Kangding's outskirts. The complex was guarded by fierce, woolly mastiff dogs and was full of red-robed clergy orbiting clockwise around the main courtyards, each monk spinning a hand-held prayer drum as he walked. The buildings were claustrophobic, poorly lit by sour-smelling butter-fat lamps and decorated with gruesome murals of hell; one hall was full of badly stuffed dogs, deer, bears and wolves, all leaking straw, spattered with either red paint or blood and fitted with oversized glass eyes. Tibetans might have been fervent Buddhists but their interpretation of the religion, which was steeped in elements of Bon, the country's original shamanistic faith, was far darker and less forgiving than versions practiced elsewhere in China.

Gill respected Tibetan beliefs as such but, in keeping with many European travellers of this period, had little time for their priests, the lamas, who he felt wielded tyrannical power over the ordinary people. Lamaseries owned most of the arable land through which they amassed huge wealth in rents. They employed slaves but paid no taxes and provided no labour themselves, and the lamas themselves were considered by some as "a curse to the country... detested by the people as much as they are feared". This was perhaps resentment on Gill's part as the lamas tried hard to make things difficult for the expedition, though the travellers accepted their hostility as part of the adventure. Gill, however, caved in to insistent rumours of extreme cold on the road ahead and had a set of padded furs made up, which proved totally unnecessary.

There were two roads west from Kangding to the Tibetan border. Mesny and Gill planned on taking the shorter southern highway via the monastery towns of Litang and Batang, a distance of around six hundred kilometres. Officials had initially tried to dupe them by arranging a team of yaks as baggage animals; these were cheap enough but so slow that the trip would have taken a month. Yaks were also notoriously difficult to manage, liable to panic for the slightest reason and career off into the hills, scattering baggage and taking hours to round up. After the necessary outrage at this duplicity had been expressed, mules and horses were made available at a higher price but also with a written contract, extracted from the head of the caravan, that the journey would take no longer than twenty days.

Now came the question of whether to buy horses for their personal use or rent them at each stage along the way through local officials. Gill sent Mesny off to seek advice from the magistrate, but was frustrated by the way Mesny allowed himself to be fobbed off with vague promises: "Mesny is by no means a good man of business; when he gets amongst his Chinese friends he talks upon every topic except the one important one. He laughs and jokes and forgets all about the information we all are seeking. I never heard a man talk at such a pace as when he talks Chinese or French; I cannot judge for the Chinese but French he speaks so incredibly fast that neither the missionaries nor myself understand half he says. English he does not jabber so much. I think he is afraid of making mistakes and his English is not very good, he is rather rough on the aspirates".

Fortunately, the French fathers helped smooth the matter out and also found a Tibetan interpreter to accompany the expedition. Goodwill now abounded, Kangding's magistrate presented Gill with a pair of valuable porcelain cups and invited them to a lavish farewell meal at which the dish "Happy Family" was served – a huge mixed stew of pork, duck, chicken, seafood and vegetables.

Today, the journey between Kangding and Litang takes around eight hours by bus. Travelling on foot, Mesny and Gill managed it in ten days, villagers along the way hospitably providing food and drink despite the lamas' prohibition on helping the expedition. The road continued to steadily gain in overall height; between rocky passes strung with fluttering, brightly coloured prayer flags, they descended through thick pine forests into flower-filled meadows, discovering that some of the plants had the valuable property of killing lice. For the first time they saw, posted at an inn, a copy of the Margary Proclamation, the official edict ordering officials to protect foreign travellers in the wake of Margary's murder.

On August 17 they reached the top of a 4000m-high pass and found Litang spread out on the dry plain below, hemmed in to the south by a range of stunningly serrated, snow-capped peaks. The town is one of the highest in the world and all but Gill were feeling the effects of the increasingly thin air, which made negotiating even gentle slopes surprisingly exhausting: "I don't know who is most grateful [to arrive], Mesny or the muleteers; the former would I think like to halt 2 days out of 3, and the muleteers get a day's halt without it counting against them".

There were perhaps a thousand families at Litang, with three times this number of monks living in the great gold-roofed monasteries perched high on the slopes above. The Khampa of eastern Tibet are not known for being a peaceable people, and Litang's lamas were openly hostile to Chinese rule, clearly resenting any outside interference in their affairs. On one occasion they had even tried to secede from Greater Tibet and had only decided to surrender when the regent at Lhasa sent an army of specially trained leopards and tigers against them.

Now a tiny Chinese garrison was stationed here to enforce the peace, and the travellers found nothing of interest to keep them in town. Litang's inhabitants were sullen and poor, the climate was arid and cold, and the altitude meant that no crops at all could be raised; with no trees growing nearby, the only available fuel was dried yak dung, which made their rooms insufferably smoky. Nor did Litang manufacture anything worthwhile, though it was a seasonal marketplace for the bizarre caterpillar fungus, known as *yertzu gumbu*, or "winter-worm, summer-grass", sold to the Chinese as a medicine. They did find some fine saddles, horses and weapons for sale, but these had all been imported from the Manigange district, ten days' travel to the north.

The road to Batang was clearly marked but dismal, carpeted in the remains of dead pack animals as it traversed a bleak, 5000m-high gravel plateau dotted with pale blue tarns. On the far side, their depression was lifted by the magnificent sight of Nenda peak glowing in the afternoon sun as it rose a further thousand metres above them. Not much further on they crossed a bridge, which people claimed had been built back in the seventeenth century by Wu Sangui, the man who had betrayed both the Ming dynasty and the Manchus. Beyond here grew an ancient forest of straight-trunked oaks, bushy rhododendrons and gnarled pines; the area was notorious for bandits but the only trouble came from a bear, which killed and ate one of the mules. As they dropped into the fertile valley at the end of their journey, the climate began to warm.

They reached Batang on August 25, two days ahead of schedule. Surrounded by fields it was a small, pleasant town, recently rebuilt after having been totally destroyed in an earthquake – a Biblical-style retribution, wrote Mesny, "because there was not a chaste woman in the place". The Tibetan border, marked by the path of a youthful Yangzi – here called the *jinsha jiang*, Gill's "River of Golden Sand" – lay ten kilometres away to the southwest. Batang's monastery housed over a thousand monks and five hundred lamas, far outstripping the town's diminutive population, but this was the case with even the smallest settlements, as Tibetans habitually sent most of their sons to the nearest lamasery to study.

The travellers received a welcome present of bread and wine from Batang's French Catholic community and were greeted respectfully by the town's joint Chinese and Tibetan governors, though local politics were obviously frosty. The Chinese declared themselves willing to help the expedition but made it clear that the explorers would have a fight on their hands if they attempted to cross the border into Tibet; forces were already massing to oppose them all along the road to Lhasa. Cooper had faced the same resistance nine years earlier, when only Batang's Catholics had offered him any assistance. But Cooper realised that even the Frenchmen had a hidden agenda: if he was killed trying to enter Tibet, Britain would possibly invade, opening the country up for all foreigners, and if he succeeded, the lamas would no longer be able to deny the church access. Cooper eventually abandoned his plans, and instead followed the course of the Yangzi southwest along the Tibetan border to Yunnan. Gill and Mesny eventually convinced everybody at Batang that this was their intention as well, and the tense atmosphere eased. They paid off their Chinese porters from Kangding who, having completed the journey in less than the agreed time, were presented with an unexpected bonus. Half of them immediately asked to be re-employed for the next stage down to Deqin, Yunnan's most northerly town.

When the expedition departed Batang, it was politely accompanied for a way by both the Tibetan and Chinese authorities. Incredulous villagers came to stare too, not at the foreigners but at their sedan chairs; ordinary Tibetans didn't use furniture and few people had seen such extraordinary objects before. The road passed unusually rich meadows which should have provided good grazing for livestock but lay empty and dotted with abandoned farmsteads; villagers had either been chased away by the recent earthquake or, insinuated Mesny, by the constant demands from passing Chinese officials to provide porters and pack animals.

On a map, borders appear to be bold and clearly defined. In reality they are vague and uncertain places marking the furthermost limit of national authority, where wider rules of law are likely to be negotiable. The region ahead, where Sichuan, Tibet and Yunnan rubbed up against each other, was no exception: roads were even worse than usual and there were rumours of bandits lying in wait along the way – indeed, Cooper himself had been mugged here. Not wanting to be held responsible for any disasters, Batang's officials provided the expedition with a military escort which steadily grew in size as they marched along until they were accompanied by no less than two hundred soldiers mounted on sturdy Tibetan ponies, most of them armed with swords and matchlocks. And for a moment it seemed as if they might need them: rounding a corner, they found the road ahead blocked by a sizeable Khampa war party, sent to prevent Gill and Mesny from crossing into Tibet. A few warning shots were fired but tempers cooled after the Khampas understood that the foreigners were heading southwest into Yunnan, and let them pass unmolested.

The next few days dragged by in a succession of desperately miserable lodgings, awful mountain trails and incessant, soaking rain, until the expedition found themselves wobbling along the razor-edged ridge dividing Sichuan from Yunnan province. The ludicrously dramatic view westwards took in a whole series of narrow ranges, thousands of metres high, between which three of Asia's major rivers – the Yangzi, Lancang and Nu – flowed south in a tightly-grouped, parallel band. The escort was supposed to head back to Batang at this point, but had nothing good to say about Deqin's administration and felt it was their duty to make sure the foreigners arrived safely at their destination. During the steep, slippery descent along a "villainous" road they lost one of their horses over the edge, but otherwise made it down off the mountain intact and so entered Deqin, as the rain continued to pour down, on September 5.

Most of Deqin's population spoke Tibetan and the town sported the inevitable lamasery and even a Catholic church, but there were clear signs of Chinese influence too – not the least of which was in the sudden luxury of household furniture. Deqin was yet another marketplace for that ever-important commodity, salt, which was panned from springs over the mountains to the northwest; there was a high incidence of goitre in town, though the Chinese had known since the seventh century how to treat the disease with iodine. Mesny emphatically disliked Deqin, prudishly dismissing its inhabitants as shockingly immoral, men, women, Chinese, Tibetans, half-castes and all. This might have been a misunderstanding of Tibetan polyandry, where the women formed sleeping arrangements with several men; fatherhood counted for very little and children were brought up by their mothers, who also ran the households – all completely contrary to Confucian beliefs, in which Mesny was immersed.

As they were now leaving the Tibetan regions, Gill tried to buy a few cultural souvenirs. He had an especially tough time finding anybody willing to part with one of the wooden alms bowls typically carried by most Tibetans, as it was widely believed that selling a food bowl to a foreigner would foreshadow the country being conquered by outsiders. There was also a new complication in arranging porters, something that was to dog the rest of their journey. In this part of Yunnan, porters were not professionals but peasants hired through local chieftains; they worked for set stages, sometimes covering only a few miles to the next village, and then had to be replaced. Once again, help was always scarce because nobody expected to be paid for their labour, and the struggle to round up workers and pack animals caused daily delays.

By September 9 they had everything ready and looked forward to an early start on their journey south towards Dali. "But", wrote an exasperated Gill, "we were now in Yun-Nan, the province of China in which more opium is smoked than in any other." The porters arrived late, befuddled and disorganised, and then demanded breakfast. It took until dark to reach the hospitable hamlet of Dong Zhulin where, in the 1850s, the pioneering French priest Father Alexis Renou – disguised as a Chinese merchant – had studied Tibetan with the abbot in exchange for a telescope. Over the next few days the party traversed low, multiple ridges to reach the Jiuka river valley, which they found planted with groves of walnut and persimmon trees. Small hamlets and cultivated fields began to appear and in one place, to the Chinese staff's delight, they discovered a tiny patch of rice, the first they had seen growing since leaving Ya'an in mid-July. A week later found them descending through monkey-infested forests to Tacheng, whose thirty families all turned out to get a glimpse of the strangers. Tacheng's magistrate, an unusually talkative and helpful official named Sun, had already organised porters for their next stage.

Since leaving Deqin they had been crossing largely unknown territory. Cooper had passed through the area back in 1868 but had followed the parallel Nujiang valley down to Weixi town, one range further west from Tacheng. It was terrible timing: the Muslim Uprising was in full swing and Weixi had already been sacked twice by rebels, some of them former Chinese soldiers who had turned bandit after two years without pay in this remote posting. Weixi's obviously hostile governor proved suspiciously helpful, issuing Cooper with a visa to cross into Muslim territory; it was only later that Cooper discovered the man had spread rumours ahead that he was a spy, surveying the way for a vast Chinese invasion. Pro-Islamist villages that had been harassing Weixi hurriedly switched sides to avoid retribution, but Cooper now realised that attempting to continue to the Muslim capital at Dali would be suicide. He returned to Weixi where the governor – fearing for his life should the Englishman reappear in eastern China and denounce him to the higher authorities – attempted to assassinate him. Fortunately, Cooper managed to break out of the town with the help of a friendly Tibetan warlord, and so escaped back into Sichuan.

The landscape was becoming ever-more cultivated. Gone were the prayer flags, lamas, yaks and other symbols of the spartan Tibetan regions, replaced by Chinese scenes of water buffalo ploughing fields, pumpkin vines growing on trellises and porters shouldering burdens about on carry-poles. They rejoined the path of the Yangzi and followed it out of the mountains to little Shigu town where the river, having flowed southwards for over a thousand kilometres in a virtually uninterrupted arc, was deflected sharply northeast. Shigu – literally "Stone Drum" – took its name from a large marble disc covered in weathered text, which recalled a bloody victory won by the ruling Naxi armies over an attempted invasion centuries earlier by either the Tibetans or Chinese. The town was in high spirits: it was the Mid-Autumn Festival, celebrating a thirteenth-century uprising against the Mongols, and soon the expedition's porters were all drunk. Shigu's magistrate met the party and escorted them with much pomp to their accommodation, a tumble-down temple on top of a hill. Nothing else had been arranged for their stay and Mesny suspected that the official, a self-important Han Chinese, was despised by the townsfolk. The magistrate heartily agreed and condemned his subjects as a pack of savages who would do nothing for him.

The next day brought scenes of a bewildering mass deforestation, tree trunks felled haphazardly across the road, before they left the mountains behind at last in one steep, abrupt descent. Ahead lay a gentler landscape of rolling hills with rich red earth; there were suddenly people everywhere, Chinese-style arched bridges and their first proper inn since leaving Batang. But they were also entering lands ravaged by the Muslim Uprising and its violent suppression: the district was under the thumb of overbearing Chinese officials and poverty-stricken villagers were refusing point-blank to hire themselves out as porters, suspecting that their wages would be withheld. Even after long negotiations, Gill could only get the men moving by threatening them with a choice between either shouldering their bundles or having to carry Mesny, who – even after months of hard travel – still weighed about fourteen stone.

At Jianchuan, a formerly wealthy caravan town, they found decrepit houses, a rotten inn and district officials mired in some obscure dispute with each other. But the evening was brightened by a conversation with their host. Asked what life had been like during the Muslim Uprising, he replied bashfully that he had kept his head down and done nothing. "'Don't you believe it,' said his wife, who was standing at the top of the stairs. 'He went over to the [Muslim rebels]; like a fool, he was always fighting, and of course got wounded all over his body for his pains.'"

For once, the next morning found a crowd of willing porters gathered outside the inn, though they refused to start before their opium-addled headmen arrived. It began to rain again. Yunnan – literally "South of the Clouds" – was known throughout China for its pleasant climate but this autumn was proving unusually wet, a strange contrast to the drought they had left behind in Sichuan. The road became irritatingly difficult too, erratically paved in rubble and slaloming all over the flat, heavily-settled plain for no apparent reason. Their horses grew skittish and troublesome, slipping on the wet flagstones if they stayed on the road and getting stuck in mud if they strayed off it.

Every town they passed had been utterly wrecked during the war and the resident Bai population – who, despised by the Chinese, had largely sided with the Muslim cause – massacred. Evening found them at the village of Niu Jie, where the accommodation proved typically dismal and whose magistrate refused to help them in any way. The following day was similarly drab and ended at Eryuan, another thoroughly dispirited settlement whose gateway was the only part of the town wall left standing. Eryuan's authorities were away on business, but Mesny and Gill were taken in hand by a civil innkeeper who helped them prepare for the final stage to Dali, just a day's journey to the south. Gill was much amused by their landlord, who stood in the doorway of his establishment issuing a running commentary to bystanders on everything that the two foreigners did, such as carrying pen and ink in their pockets, and sharpening their pencils with knives. Mesny also took a fancy to an antique plate, one of an otherwise uninteresting mismatched set of four, and entertained Gill with his bargaining skills: "He told the old man he wanted 4 plates and asked the price of the lot – this price he said was too high unless he could have all 4 alike but the old man could not accommodate him. Then he asked how much 2 would be, ultimately he decided to take one of each kind, getting the 2 for 300 cash (about a shilling); one of the plates was mere rubbish but the other, though ugly, was old".

The sodden climate was getting to Gill: "Weather as before Rain Rain Rain". But up ahead in the distance rose three pagodas, and beyond them, Dali. They had been on the road for three months.

Neatly walled and nearly square, Dali guarded a corridor of flat fields between the narrow, blue spread of Er Hai Lake and the forested slopes of the isolated Cang Shan range. In any other province the town would have been little more than a rustic backwater, but Yunnan wasn't much like the rest of China: it shared borders with Tibet, Burma, Laos and Vietnam, and the ethnic "minority" population far exceeded the province's Han Chinese. Dali's strategic location, right at the crossroads of trade routes running well beyond China's frontiers, was first recognised during the eighth century by an aspiring warlord named Piluoge, who invited his rivals to a dinner, burned down the banqueting hall with them inside and then took their lands, thereby becoming the first ruler of the Nanzhao Kingdom. With Dali as their capital, Piluoge's successors expanded their rule deep into southeast Asia before the Nanzhao imploded during the tenth century, replaced by the smaller Dali Kingdom. This survived until 1253, when Genghis Khan's Mongol armies stormed through on their way to conquer all of China.

Mongol rule, though brief, had a lasting effect on Yunnan. The invaders brought with them large numbers of Muslims from central Asia, known as Hui, who settled down across the province as merchants, shopkeepers and muleteers. By the seventeenth century, relations between these Muslims and their Han Chinese neighbours were beginning to fray. Part of the problem was that the Hui were businessmen amongst a sea of farmers; they accumulated steady wealth whilst the fortunes of the resident Chinese rose and fell with erratic harvests, droughts and floods. The Hui also practiced an alien religion, avoided intermarriage with the Han and had strange dietary habits, refusing to eat pork, the meat of choice elsewhere in China. Worse yet, they did eat beef and lamb, both traditionally avoided by many Chinese: cattle were seen as workmates in the fields, not food, while lambs were considered to be virtuous, filial creatures because they knelt down to suckle. A final source of friction was the Hui practice of adopting Chinese orphans in order to increase the Muslim population, a deliberate attempt to counter escalating Han migration into Yunnan during the eighteenth century.

These ingrained tensions eventually erupted into open violence between Han and Hui communities, which swept steadily eastwards across Yunnan towards Kunming, the provincial capital. Following a spat of race riots in nearby townships, the city's governor issued a stern but poorly-worded proclamation against further unrest, which Han vigilantes interpreted as a license to deliver retribution. On May 19 1856, Kunming's gates were locked and the city's Hui population was butchered by the mob.

When word of the massacre got out, Muslims across Yunnan rose in a furious rebellion. Kunming was stormed and its outlying suburbs – almost the entire city – were totally destroyed. Buoyed by this easy victory and burning with years of resentment, Hui armies fanned out across the province. Their anger was focused entirely against the Han Chinese; minority ethnic groups were ignored or allowed to pillage in the wake of the rebel onslaught. In September the fighting reached Dali, where the town's Hui, aided by a band of mercenaries led by the Muslim scholar Du Wenxiu, overthrew the Chinese governor. On looting the arsenal, Du found himself in command of a well-equipped army, the equal of any provincial Chinese force. Dali had been the capital of an independent kingdom twice before, so why not again? He declared the foundation of an Islamic state in western Yunnan named "The Pacified South" and took Dali's courthouse as his palace, thumbing his nose at the Chinese emperor by having the building roofed in yellow tiles – a colour symbolic of heaven, strictly reserved for the Imperial household. Du also adopted a grand title which translated into something like "Ruler and Generalissimo", though he was known to the British as Suleiman, Sultan of Panthay.

The Qing government, tied down by foreign invasions and civil wars in eastern China, had few military resources to spare on distant Yunnan. A badly-planned attempt to retake Dali failed, though Kunming's obstinate city walls continued to hold off the insurgents for a full five years. But in 1861, the Hui general Ma Julong – who had carved out his own independent fief in central Yunnan – redoubled his efforts to capture the capital, forcing the Chinese government to send in a young official named Cen Yuying to broker a ceasefire. Cen was from an impoverished but once-powerful family; he had been serving as a magistrate in Yunnan when the war broke out and soon displayed a natural talent for military affairs, raising a local militia to fight the rebels. Western commentators described Cen as a cruel man, ambitious, sly and staunchly anti-foreign, but he and Ma Julong struck up a friendship and soon reached an agreement for ending the war. In return for handing back captured towns, Muslims would be pardoned for their past offences and their commanders would be given official posts. In March 1862, Ma raised his siege of Kunming, "surrendered" to Cen Yuying and peaceably entered the city as its new governor.

While Ma Julong was busy switching sides, Du Wenxiu expanded his own influence across western Yunnan and into Burma. To strengthen his position he began to look further afield for allies, sending his son Hassam to London to seek British approval for his rule. In 1868 he beat off another Chinese attempt to take Dali and chased the defeated army all the way back to Kunming. This time it was Ma Julong who had to defend the capital, holding out until Cen Yuying returned with reinforcements from Guizhou, where he had been fighting the Miao.

For saving Kunming, Cen was promoted to Viceroy of Yunnan and launched a systematic reconquest of the province. A disgraced Ma Julong was packed off to pacify the south while Cen co-ordinated Chinese forces in a steady advance westwards, picking off rebel towns one at a time as they went. Dali surrendered in January 1873 following a two-week siege: Du Wenxiu was captured alive but committed suicide by taking an opium overdose on his way to the execution ground, where his corpse was beheaded anyway. A few days later a jubilant Cen Yuying invited Dali's surviving Muslim hierarchy to a banquet and, as Piluoge had done centuries earlier, had them murdered as they sat eating. Thousands of unarmed citizens were cut down as they attempted to flee the subsequent carnage, many of them chased right into Er Hai Lake by triumphant Chinese soldiers. Mesny, who was later to have close dealings with Cen, never forgave him for authorising this butchery, perhaps remembering the similar scenes he'd witnessed at Xincheng in Guizhou.

Along the final stretch of the road to Dali, Gill and Mesny fell in with groups of hopeful military candidates, all heading to town to take part in the provincial examinations. Like the civil exams, these were open to all Chinese as a pathway to official rank, though as passing them was mostly down to physical prowess rather than intellect – the written part of the test was extremely superficial – military officials enjoyed little of the social status or respect given to their civil counterparts. Each of the candidates toted a bow and, despite the advent of modern weapons, none of them would be tested on much beyond their proficiency as archers.

Up ahead rose Dali's three pagodas, their distinctively layered, tapered towers dating back to the Nanzhao Kingdom and still standing despite a millennium of warfare and earthquakes. Then they were amongst the ruins of Dali's former suburbs, trying to find a way in to the town. While Chengdu's south gates had been closed off through their association with drought and fire, here, due to the heavy rain, Dali's northern gateway had been sealed in honour of Beidi, the flood-protecting God of the North. The expedition made its weary way around to the eastern entrance, where they found further mess and disorder. Many of Dali's mud-brick houses were collapsing in the unseasonal deluge and the town's run-down main streets were awash with exam candidates, who had occupied almost all the accommodation. The travellers had to threaten an unsympathetic landlord with imprisonment before he finally agreed to rent out what seemed to be Dali's last available room. They unpacked to find half of their belongings were rotten with damp and mould.

Finally settled in, the room full of smoky charcoal braziers and drying clothes, Dali turned out to be a friendly enough place whose authorities welcomed them with gifts of geese and fresh pomegranates. The townsfolk were a varied bunch: there were Bai, the dominant local ethnic group who lived in villages all around the lakeshore; Tibetans on pilgrimage to nearby Jizu Shan, a holy mountain to the west; and –surprisingly – a substantial population of white-turbaned Muslims, who had returned to live here despite the town's recent history. Gill and Mesny also met with Father Leguilcher, a French priest who had interpreted for the Lagrée Expedition during their brief visit to Dali during the Muslim Uprising back in 1868. Leguilcher recounted his three-hour audience with Du Wenxiu, admitting to having been terrified; Gill thought him very timid but felt sorry for the elderly, isolated missionary, and on leaving presented him with a bottle of wine and a pocket watch. In fact Leguilcher seemed perfectly happy at Dali, and was still living there in 1900.

As a military man, Gill was far more interested in being introduced to General Yang Yuke, an energetic, hunchbacked soldier affectionately known to his troops as "The Monkey", after the bold and mischievous Monkey King in the Chinese classic *Journey to the West*. It was Yang's forces who had actually captured Dali from the Muslim insurgents; he was an ethnic Bai and kept a private army, which made the Chinese government deeply suspicious of him, though he seemed quite content to serve the Qing and showed no sign of starting his own rebellion. Despite enormous wealth and unquestionable bravery – he always led his men into battle on horseback, totally unafraid of enemy fire – Yang's violent temper and Bai heritage counted against him, and he had been unable to find a well-bred Chinese woman to marry. He was busy when Gill and Mesny called but had some delicious mutton delivered to their inn as a welcoming gift, and later amazed Gill by humbly walking across town to see them – a thing no Han Chinese of his status would ever have done.

Reaching Dali marked the end of Gill and Mesny's pioneering adventure; from here on they were following a well-worn trade route westwards into Burma. But considering how few Europeans had travelled it before, Gill's account of the final few weeks of their expedition seems surprisingly superficial and disinterested in the people and places they found along the way. Perhaps it was because the region was increasingly less "Chinese", and Mesny wasn't able to communicate with the locals as easily or explain what they were seeing, but by this point they simply must have been eager to reach the end of what had been a long and exhausting journey.

The road ahead also held particular dangers. During the war these borderlands had been violently contested by Chinese, Muslim and Burmese militias, not all of whom had dispersed in the aftermath – many had now gone freelance as bandits, protected from government retribution by local chiefs. The very route that Gill and Mesny were now planning to take had been the one followed by the ill-fated British consular official Augustus Margary, when he had been killed close to the Burmese frontier just two years earlier in 1875. His murderers had never been brought to justice and, for all anyone knew, were still lurking in the forests, hoping to add to their tally of foreign heads. While *The River of Golden Sand* continues its account of their travels at a steady pace, Gill's diaries – written on the spot – become increasingly tense as the expedition geared up for the final stage of their journey.

By October 4 they were ready to leave Dali. They paid off most of their staff, some of whom had come with them all the way from Chengdu, hired fresh pack animals, bid farewell to Leguilcher and set off south between the lake and mountains. At the crossroads town of Xiaguan – today a busy transport hub overlooked by wind farms, but then in a predictable state of decay – they turned west, following an increasingly poor road. The next few days were far more enjoyable than expected: they were treated politely and drew very little untoward attention, as Westerners were again simply bundled into the plentiful "not Han" category in this diverse border region. The rain stopped and the climate warmed steadily, nurturing lemon trees, rainforest, rich grasslands and a welcome abundance of fresh food.

But then came an ugly scene. Having nearly been gassed by clouds of acrid smoke one night at their inn, after their neighbours had decided to roast their entire annual chilli-pepper crop, the expedition ran into trouble outside the township of Yang Pi. The officer leading a welcome committee took Gill for one of Mesny's porters and physically barged him off the path, refusing to acknowledge his presence. Furious, Gill rode into town to find that his servant, Chin Tai, had been unable to find them a room for the night and was now complaining about having to move on to the next village. After a heated argument, Chin Tai jumped angrily on his mule and was promptly bucked off; he pretended to be badly hurt but when this won him no sympathy he grabbed a pickaxe and, had Gill not stopped him, would have hacked the poor animal to death. Chin Tai had been with Gill since he first arrived in China the previous year; he was a decent cook and had been good-natured at first, but since leaving Chengdu had grown increasingly familiar, temperamental and grasping. Gill, by now in a filthy temper, decided to dismiss him.

Mesny advised him not to. He felt that a resentful Chin Tai would go straight to the nearest magistrate and denounce Gill as a British spy plotting an invasion of China, producing Gill's diaries and carefully-surveyed maps as proof. At the very least, Mesny believed that the authorities would refuse to let them continue to Burma and might even imprison them. Gill thought this very unlikely, but knew enough of his companion's situation to understand his fears: "it might be absolute ruin to the unfortunate Mesny who depends for his livelihood on the good will of the Chinese government and on this account I determined I would eat my words, though it is most abominable to be in the hands of this disreputable fellow". Chin Tai kept his job and Gill tactfully left the incident out of *The River of Golden Sand*, though he did sneak in a mention that Yang Pi's official was "a frightful tyrant".

At last the road descended to a suspension bridge over the Lancang, the upper reaches of the Mekong River. Margary, armed only with a light gun, had gone game hunting here to find that the three deer he was stalking closely up the hillside were, in fact, tigers (fortunately, they took off without noticing him). On the far side of the river was Baoshan, a formerly rich town left in "a sad spectacle of ruin and devastation" by the war, though a rebuilt quarter of busy shops and markets hinted at a rapidly returning prosperity. Better yet, there was a bright new inn and, for once, a surplus of pack animals for hire. Mesny went out shopping and came back loaded with uncut gems; years of war and plunder had left them in the hands of people who had no idea of their real value. Among a good deal of rubbish were some bright, unflawed and strongly-coloured stones, and Gill felt that Mesny was doing good business. The only blight to their stay came when an army general, disgruntled at finding foreigners occupying the inn's best rooms, complained loudly until their landlord found him accommodation elsewhere.

Beyond Baoshan lay another major river, the Nu, and a tiring hike over the Gaoligong Ranges' high line of forested ridges. Then came the Longchuan valley, whose broad, emerald-green plain was dotted with busy villages;

locals welcomed the travellers by firing off guns and exploding strings of firecrackers, causing the horses to buck and bolt.

Tengchong, the final outpost of Chinese rule in this direction, was reached on October 17. The city was completely surrounded by paddy fields and defended by crenellated basalt-block walls and heavy gates, plated in iron. Inside were the usual scenes of post-war ruin and decrepitude. Despite the defences, Muslim armies had captured Tengchong and held the city for ten years; all the Chinese temples had been defaced, walls were pitted with bullet holes and the streets remained unnaturally quiet and deserted. Like Baoshan, Tengchong had once been a marketplace for gemstones; Margary had heard that villagers dug them up in handfuls from the loose volcanic soil and sold them for a song. Now merchants lamented the run-down state of trade, though the town's jade cutters were back in business, working pieces of the hard, dark-green Burmese rock into rings and bangles, which were so valued across China for their supposed ability to impart longevity.

Gill was expecting to find a letter waiting for him from the British resident at Bhamo, their destination in Burma, but it hadn't arrived and he was beginning to fret. Tengchong's officials – one of whom was a friend of Mesny's – were hospitable enough but there were unsettling rumours of a band of outlaws roaming the road ahead, estimated at being anything between ten and three hundred strong. Gill was keen to set off directly, before news of the expedition's presence ran on ahead of them, and the city's muleteers, detecting his urgency, were asking outrageous prices for the use of their animals. Gill was tempted to accept their offers anyway, but knew that to do this without haggling would only make them raise their prices even further. "It is really enough to break one's heart and everybody about me is so pleased at the delay that their delight that beams on all their countenances only irritates me the more".

Despite Gill's pessimism, the expedition was back on the road within three days, expecting trouble but receiving nothing but kindness from Shan Burmese villagers along their route, who welcomed the party with more pork and vegetables than they could eat. The Shan superficially resembled Chinese except that the men tattooed their legs and bound them in rattan gaiters while the women wore distinctive turbans; people also chewed betel nut, a very southeast Asian habit, which turned their teeth black. Sadly, the expedition's Chinese porters treated the Shan with utter contempt, denouncing them all – men, women and even high-ranking village headmen – as savages only fit for extermination. One retorted that he had lived at the Burmese capital, Rangoon, where he found that life under British rule was far preferable to the Chinese experience – hinting, thought Gill, that locals would be happy for Britain to annex this corner of Yunnan. To make matters worse, the obnoxious Chin Tai began quarrelling with Mesny's servant.

At last they reached Mangyun, the infamous frontier town where Margary had met his end. Surrounded by mud-brick fortifications, it had the predatory feel of a lawless backwater, full of shifty fugitives. The population of seven hundred was divided between a Chinese quarter of grubby streets and roaming livestock, and a neater Shan district, whose homes had tidy gardens and where the animals were kept penned. As a sign of how distant they were from mainstream China, Mangyun was governed by a princess, a "stout little woman of fifty summers, of quiet, self-possessed carriage", who had been given the town as a wedding present and held court within a Chinese-style palace. Gill and Mesny were put up at a temple which doubled as the magistrate's residence, where crowds gathered daily at mealtimes to watch them eat. This close to Burma there were even a few "English" products for sale at Mangyun's markets, though here Gill sounds slightly ridiculous proudly listing cotton, buttons and thread as proof of his nation's commercial acumen.

The two men were soon paid a visit by Li Xietai, a former bandit who had supported the Chinese cause during the Muslim Uprising. Gill – and most Western authorities – believed that it was Li Xietai himself who had most probably killed Margary, cutting him down while he was on his way to visit hot springs outside the town. Margary had been guiding the Browne-Sladen expedition into China from Burma, and had found Li deferential and helpful at first. But he also knew that many people at Mangyun were hostile to his presence, fearing that the expedition was a spearhead for British expansionism, and that Li himself might not have been entirely free from enmity. Margary had been warned about a possible ambush but thought it unlikely and went on ahead of the main party. On February 22 1875, deep in the forest on the final stage to Mangyun, the Browne-Sladen expedition was attacked by a large, well-armed force of bandits. They managed to drive them off after a hard fight, but then news arrived that Margary had been killed at Mangyun on the previous day.

Not surprisingly, given how distant Mangyun was from any government authority, Chinese investigations into the incident were perfunctory and inconclusive; no witnesses came forward and nobody was tried for the affair. The British suspected Li Xietai of carrying out the actual murder, but weren't so sure about who had sponsored him or why. One candidate was the Burmese king, who was known to oppose the British forging independent trade deals with China in case they undermined his own profitable monopolies. Many others – including a few Chinese officials – believed that Cen Yuying, as the viceroy of Yunnan, was at least legally responsible for the incident and should be held accountable. Mesny went further than this: for reasons left unexplained, he was absolutely certain that Cen had personally ordered Margary's killing and added it to the grudge he already held against him for the unnecessary slaughter of civilians at Dali.

Only fifteen kilometres separated Mangyun from the border. Li Xietai thought that Gill and Mesny should easily cover the distance within two days and that there would be no danger along the way. Others advised them to take gifts of opium for local chiefs, to carry firearms in case of an attack by "wild men" and to dismount before passing any houses, as villagers believed that to ride past on horseback was disrespectful. This last suggestion annoyed Gill, who felt that bowing to native superstition was beneath his dignity. As if to remind them for one final time that they were still in China, pack animals were mysteriously unavailable until Mangyun's Chinese magistrate became involved in negotiations for them; he had, of course, been preventing anyone else from striking a private deal with the travellers in order to take a cut of the profit. But then he had also fed and housed Gill and Mesny at his own expense, so perhaps this was a way of recouping his costs without the vulgarity of openly demanding payment.

At last they set off on the final stage to the frontier, and soon reached the place of Margary's death. Gill paused to pontificate on "the right of Englishmen to travel unmolested" and talked about erecting a monument. Perhaps he would have approved of the stone tablet which stands there today, inscribed in Chinese characters with the simple statement "Site of the Margary Incident". He would have been less happy with the modern Chinese view that Margary was a spy, and that his murder and the attack on the Sladen-Browne expedition was a co-ordinated attempt by local powers to repel a British invasion from sovereign Chinese territory.

The trail entered a thick forest of lianas, tall bamboos and butterflies, where they paused in a clearing for breakfast. The two men were on edge, expecting trouble before crossing the border, and for the first time on their entire journey were carrying weapons at the ready. Suddenly there were shots from the undergrowth, a flurry of activity, cartridges rammed into guns and bolts driven home, but their would-be-assailants melted away into the jungle, leaving them startled but unhurt. The next day it was their turn to launch hostilities. Gill, who had fallen behind the party after being savagely bitten by red ants, rounded a corner to find Mesny squabbling with a man for not having dismounted as he rode past his house. At Gill's appearance, the usually diplomatic Mesny cowed the villagers by pulling out his pistol, an unpleasant scene the British tried to justify later by pretending they would have been robbed otherwise. The previous day's scare, Margary's fate and their proximity to British territory seems to have stirred up an unusual nervous arrogance.

A final day brought them safely over the border to Mamou, a small township on a tributary of the Irrawaddy River. Here, Cooper – the man who had pioneered the route along the Tibetan border into Yunnan, and who was now the British resident at their destination, Bhamo – had arranged a house and sent guides bearing bundles of long-missed luxuries: newspapers, provisions and cigars. On November 1 they set off downriver, arriving at Bhamo at three o'clock in the afternoon to be greeted by Cooper with "a hearty British shake of the hand". It had taken Gill and Mesny nearly four months to travel from Chengdu, making them the first foreigners to have surveyed the whole of this potentially promising route across southwestern China.

From Bhamo it was a matter of a few days to catch a boat down the Irrawaddy River to Mandalay and the Burmese capital, Rangoon, where notions of order and civilization began to reassert themselves – to Mesny's immediate disadvantage. Here it wasn't enough to have spent a decade boldly exploring foreign lands along unknown trails; you had to look as if the experience, however monumental its consequences, had in no way diluted your essential "Britishness". Mesny, who had been raised in the francophile Channel Islands and had spent most of his adult life overseas, must have fallen well short of the social standards expected by Rangoon's colonial set. Gill wrote, "Mesny has no English clothes, but I believe has hitherto flattered himself that he is dressed à l'Engliénne in a shirt without a collar and much of which shows below his coat (for he wears it like other people do a waistcoat); his coat of brown silk, also without collar, single breasted and loose with 5 brass buttons down the front (in shape for all the world like a sleeping coat); Black cloth trousers tricked with Black velvet [and] Chinese boots which come up to the knee. His appearance is comical [but] I have never ventured to say a word to him on the subject for he is a little touchy on those matters but now I am afraid for the fellow that after having been such an almighty swell for the last 10 years amongst the Chinese he begins to feel that there is a slight difference between Chinese and English society."

The two men soon embarked for Calcutta, where Gill decided to stay for a while – he had been born in India, after all – but Mesny, despite suffering a bad fever, caught a passenger liner to Britain in late November.

The rest of the tale can be wrapped up in a few lines. Cooper was assassinated by his own bodyguard at Bhamo just five months after Gill and Mesny's departure, another Margary-like martyr to the unstable Burmese borderlands. Back in Britain, Gill was awarded the Royal Geographical Society's Founders' Medal and published *The River of Golden Sand*. Mesny's contribution to the mission was almost completely overlooked; the *Pall Mall Gazette* got his name wrong and described him as "a French gentleman in the Chinese service".

Gill was later employed as a troubleshooter for the British government. In August 1882, while on a foray to secure the Suez Canal during an anti-European uprising, he and his travelling companions were killed by Bedouins in Egypt.

BACK IN BRITAIN
1878

Arriving back in Britain on 8 January 1878, Mesny spent a night ashore at the lavish South Western Hotel, close to the Southampton docks and railway station, and then most likely caught the first available ship to Alderney. He had been out of the country for almost eighteen years, his brother John had followed him to China and his invalid mother was dead, so his father – a sturdy but gentle-looking man with a square-cut white beard, also named William – must have been overjoyed to have him back home again. It was William senior who had given his son permission to go to sea in the first place, and Mesny had always felt ashamed at having deserted his ship at Shanghai in 1860 without his parent's consent. Now, in a thoroughly Confucian display of filial humility, he prostrated himself at his father's feet to ask forgiveness.

Once the theatrics of the homecoming were over, Mesny settled down for a few months' stay on Alderney. He had brought along a wealth of cultural curiosities from China, enough to found a small museum – antique manuscripts, a comprehensive collection of Miao silver jewellery, weapons and ornaments from the Tibetan and Burmese borderlands – which he put on public display at his father's house. Twenty years later, the *Miscellany* mentioned that this "Mesny Collection" was still available for viewing at the Jersey home of his cousin Charles Mesny. Whether they were dispersed on Charles' death in the 1930s or vanished during the German occupation of the Channel Islands during World War II, there is no record of their whereabouts today.

It's unclear whether Mesny planned to remain in Britain indefinitely, but he certainly made a few attempts to set up in business as an agent for importing Chinese-style wares. Besides antiques, he had loaded down his luggage with trade samples, which must have accompanied him all the way from Guiyang – perhaps explaining why the expedition had needed so many porters. His original plan had been to exhibit these goods at the Paris World Fair of 1878, where there was a lavish traditional Chinese garden and a full-sized replica temple. But he arrived too late to get them entered and so "took them to Manchester and Birmingham at great expense, and hired premises wherein I exhibited them on my own account, but entirely failed to get any one to take an interest in them. I was told that no sensible Englishman would ever be found foolish enough to change any of his machinery in order to produce such articles."

Undaunted, he spent his spare time applying for a patent on a new type of life belt, and designed a breech-loading rifle whose bullet split into four fragments on firing, causing terrible wounds. The Russian ambassador to Britain showed some interest in developing the gun, but Mesny's pacifist father – a Methodist lay preacher – objected to his son profiting from an invention of this kind, and so he dropped the project (which makes you wonder how much he told his father about his arms-dealing activities). Mesny also spent some time in London, where his given postal address was "Great Portland Street" – just a stone's throw away from the Chinese embassy at 49 Portland Place – and where he commented that "food is dear, raiment is dear, fuel is dear, and rents are very high."

Meanwhile, a storm was brewing. The Chinese embassy in London was barely two years old but there were already concerns back in Beijing that exposure to foreign culture was turning the ambassador, Guo Songtao, too pro-Western. Guo had become profoundly impressed with British technology, showing open admiration for the rail network and heavy industry, being presented to Queen Victoria at Buckingham Palace and having his portrait painted in oils by the artist Walter Goodman. He had also dared to argue the British viewpoint that Cen Yuying, brutal conqueror of Dali, should be investigated over his possible role in

Margary's death. Worse yet, Guo had published extracts from his diaries which "described everything in England as greatly superior to China" and directly blamed corrupt and uncaring Chinese provincial officials back home for driving ordinary people into the arms of the hated Christian missionaries, who offered them aid and sympathy.

But the most immediate problem was that Guo had fallen out with his former assistant, Liu Xihong, who – in order to get him out the way – had been shuffled over to Europe as the Chinese ambassador to Berlin. Liu was totally unsuited to a diplomatic career: he was openly xenophobic, smoked opium, displayed coarse table manners and spat continuously – not in itself an offensive trait at the time, but Liu's expectorations were unpleasantly noisy and prolonged. The Chinese government decided to have him retired, and Guo now asked Mesny to chaperone Liu back across the globe. Whether Mesny felt that he had exhausted all the avenues open to him in Britain, he jumped at this unexpected chance to return to China, packing up and fleeing Alderney within three days. He reached France, caught a train to Marseilles and "embarked with [Liu Xihong and his retinue] on the Messageries Maritimes steamer *Irrawaddy* to Hongkong... Minister Liu was very indiscreet as well as much prejudiced against all foreign innovations... [He] was subsequently degraded and died at Peking in disgrace about the year 1881". Guo Songtao fared little better: he was recalled to China the following October where, fearing official retribution for his pro-Western sympathies, he retreated into academic obscurity.

And so, after an absence of just over a year, Mesny returned to the Chinese world on 26 December 1878. He disembarked at Hong Kong to find that a terrible fire had just swept through the colony, but the Governor nevertheless managed to throw Liu's party an official banquet. John Mesny was still working for the Maritime Customs Service and had been posted to Xiamen, not far up the coast, where William joined him early on in the new year, doubtless bringing the latest news from home. Here the *Foochow Herald* reported on Mesny's meeting with the provincial military commander, dressed – as Gill had noted the year before – in a slightly ludicrous confusion of Western and Chinese clothing, combining the thick-soled felt boots of a Chinese official with a "foreign hat", on top of which balanced his Mandarin rank button. The paper also questioned his correct military title; since leaving China he had been styling himself as "General Mesny", but the *Herald* pointed out that his actual rank was that of a more lowly *fujiang*, variously translated as either brigadier-general or colonel.

By early March 1879 Mesny had relocated to Guangzhou, partly in preparation for heading back to Guizhou or, as one paper grandly put it, "to return to his post in the interior". Guangzhou had undergone a social transformation since its conservative, anti-foreign days at the height of the Opium Wars, now enthusiastically embracing such Western innovations as mirrors, kerosene lamps, motorized river craft and schools for women. Even the city's literati – traditionally staunch Confucians, opposed to any sort of change – were finding benefits in having foreigners around: the British had built three new lighthouses to guide ships along the river, which the scholars believed had improved Guangzhou's *feng shui* and had been responsible for a string of recent Cantonese successes in the Imperial Examinations. With all these changes afoot, perhaps an entrepreneur could find work.

Mesny approached the high official Liu Kunyi to suggest that he should open up the West River to steam navigation. Liu was governor of the Liangguang region, incorporating the two provinces of Guangdong and Guangxi: the West River ran through both of them from its source in distant Yunnan to feed into the Pearl, on which Guangzhou was sited, and it had immense potential as a trade conduit. The river would require considerable dredging to make it reliably navigable to large vessels but, if it could be opened up, the profitable trade with inland China that now travelled along the Yangzi and into Shanghai's coffers might instead flow down the West River to Guangzhou and Hong Kong. Liu, whose interests centred on politics and the military rather than in developing business, rejected the plan, but he admired Mesny's drive and offered him a lucrative post supervising naval defences, with money for the project – and handsome wages, set at 12,000 taels a year – to be funded by a lottery.

It seemed the perfect outlet for Mesny's talents, combining his experience of war with a sound knowledge of the sea and maritime fortifications, dating right back to his childhood on Alderney. But in a misplaced blaze of morality, Mesny disparaged Liu's lottery scheme as encouraging the sin of gambling and was promptly dismissed, to his staff's incredulous dismay; they would have made a fortune in commissions.

So, with no further employment opportunities on the horizon at Guangzhou, on 9 March 1879, Mesny boarded a junk and set off up the West River, heading back to his wife and home at Guiyang.

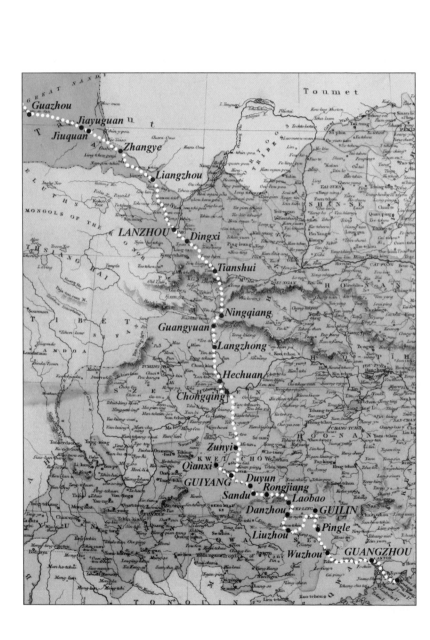

ACROSS CHINA TO TURKESTAN
1879–81

As Mesny's junk sailed away from Guangzhou, there was little sense that he was setting off on a four-year circuit around China, a monumental expedition that would take him to the borders of central Asia, Tibet and Vietnam, and involve him – indirectly – in the country's first serious conflict with a foreign power since the Opium Wars. This long immersion in China's provincial backblocks as a traveller, entrepreneur, plant collector and reporter was to have immense repercussions, and not just for Mesny: it would help crystallize his plans for the country's modernisation, plans he would try to sell, along with his services, to two influential Imperial ministers. One of these would later employ him as an advisor and use his schemes to alter China's entire economic landscape, and the other would be closely involved in ruining his career.

The journey didn't begin well. Just eight days into his travels, Mesny found himself detained at Wuzhou, a busy port at the junction of the West and Gui rivers. The city was a minor Chongqing of the south, its back lane markets packed with goods from all across southern China, which meant that it was also swarming with officious bureaucrats eager to "squeeze" travellers – and Wuzhou's many wealthy local merchants – for everything they had. In the first of many similar mishaps he was to suffer in Guangxi province, Mesny was pulled up for having neglected to obtain the necessary permits for his journey. He might be a *batulu*, with all the privileges that the title entailed, but he was also a foreigner and, as far as the authorities were concerned, foreigners needed a passport to travel through China. The situation could probably have been cleared up with a discreet gift in the appropriate quarters, but this was never Mesny's style, so the city magistrate held him under house arrest for a few days while he fumed and argued his case, then packed him back off downstream to sort the matter out at Guangzhou. It took him another six weeks to organise the proper paperwork and return to Wuzhou.

Given that the Taipings and their alien, Christian-inspired rebellion had kicked off in Guangxi, it was hardly surprising to find the authorities here deeply mistrustful of Westerners and their foreign ideas. The province was a difficult place to police, being mountainous and sandwiched between Vietnam and the equally unruly provinces of Guizhou and Yunnan; there were few towns of any size and communications between them were slow and irregular. Yet for a seasoned China traveller such as Mesny, two aspects of Guangxi's infrastructure would have been all too familiar: the appalling state of the roads, which were considered to be largely impassable and plagued by bandits, and the province's filthy inns, bluntly dismissed in the *Miscellany* as "extremely dirty and miserable, tumble-down-like hovels in which an English farmer would object to keep his cows or pigs". All this goes some way to explaining why Mesny chose to travel through the region by house boat, responsible for his own accommodation and minimising contact with any potentially hostile authorities. And there's little doubt that, by personally investigating the river system, Mesny also wanted to prove that Liu Kunyi had been wrong to dismiss his idea of opening up Guangxi's waterways to navigation.

On May 10 Mesny left Wuzhou and the West River behind, heading north up the smaller Gui towards the provincial capital, Guilin. Enthusiastic moderniser though he was, even Mesny conceded that the Gui was far too shallow and broken by rapids to ever be accessible to large vessels; the current was so strong that it took a full two weeks to complete the journey up from Wuzhou, but only four days for his boatmen to make their return trip downstream. The river changed its name at the tiny market town of Pingle, becoming the Li before passing Yangshuo – today a tourist blackspot – and a difficult patch of shoals. Above here, it curled through a picturesque corridor of closely-packed limestone pinnacles, each of the jagged grey peaks wisped by low cloud and rank vegetation and riddled with strangely-shaped caves. Little hollows between the hills – not quite valleys – were planted with sugar cane and thick groves of bamboo; placid water buffalo wallowed in the shallows and villagers poled along the river on almost-submerged bamboo rafts, fishing with specially-trained cormorants. People could be seen foraging in the hills for timber and herbs, dressed in dark blue homespun cotton and wearing enormous conical bamboo hats as protection against the tropical heat and rain. At the thinly-stretched township of Daxu there were argumentative, piratical locals and an unusually fine stone bridge dating back to the Ming dynasty, arched and guarded by a pair of carved lions at either end, beyond which the landscape opened out again as they followed the Li upstream to Guilin.

For a capital city, Guilin was unassuming. Its houses were single-storey, whitewashed and rectangular with dark tile roofs, all arranged in geometric blocks; a few grander buildings sported elaborate entrances or high, fire-baffle end walls but the general effect was sober and plain. What rescued the city from mediocrity was another scattering of weathered peaks rising all about, topped by temples and ornamental pavilions, which had made the city a place of scenic wonder since ancient times. During the Ming dynasty, half of southern China had been ruled from here by a now-extinct line of Imperial aristocrats; their citadel still formed the core of the city and their tombs dotted a plain east of town.

Not that Mesny found much of a welcome. Guilin's authorities were openly xenophobic, and the previous year had demolished a private house where two French priests had stayed as a warning to anyone else thinking of harbouring foreigners. A deputation of nervous officials met Mesny at the docks, earnestly advising him to turn back; they left only partly mollified when he promised to sleep aboard his boat. Guilin's prefect decided it was better to offend an anonymous foreigner than his fellow citizens and rudely refused to grant Mesny an interview, despite his military rank, but Mesny went ashore all the same and explored the city until chivvied back to the dock by a mildly hostile crowd. There was just enough time ashore to register that Guilin's population were unusually fond of meat – a rare festival luxury in rural communities elsewhere across China – consuming everything from pork through to beef, dogs, ducks and fish on an almost daily basis.

A well-maintained post-road ran north from Guilin, but Mesny decided to continue his journey by water, first drifting back downstream along the Li before bearing southwest onto what is still marked on maps as the "Ancient Gui-Liu Canal". This dated back to the seventh-century reign of China's only acknowledged empress, Wu Zetian, and had been comprehensively restored in 1729 in an attempt to improve trade routes within the province. Navigating the canal through its twenty-eight locks – fifteen ascending and thirteen descending – was a tedious, exacting business, and Mesny's junk proved almost too beamy to pass in places. The landscape was a continuation of Guilin's, with hills rising in every direction above the soggy, grassy plains, but they finally wore through to meet the Liu River and complete their run up to Liuzhou. For once the city's officials proved friendly, but Liuzhou was sadly ruinous and depopulated in the wake of the recent rebellions. In earlier times, the city had won fame for the quality of its timber: "Marry in Hangzhou, Eat in Guangzhou, Die in Liuzhou" went the saying, Hangzhou being renowned for its beautiful women, Guangzhou for the quality of its food and Liuzhou for its splendid pine trees, used for making coffins. Now cotton was the mainstay of agriculture, and Mesny – not for the last time – mused on how easing taxes and improving navigation along Guangxi's river systems might restore healthy trade.

By now it was late June, and the weather was becoming increasingly humid. North up the river lay Rongshui, a prosperous little township on the edge of Miao territory, whose polite but curious population swarmed along the riverbanks to glimpse the foreign traveller. It seemed to Mesny that Rongshui would make an ideal terminus for a rail line south from Guiyang, from where steamers could be taken down to Liuzhou and so, via the Liu and West rivers, to Wuzhou, Guangzhou and Hong Kong. As late as 1899 he was still badgering provincial authorities about the scheme, but he was well ahead of his time: it would be another fifty years before both Liuzhou and Rongshui were connected to China's rail network.

The next stop was Rong'an, where Mesny unexpectedly bumped into his troublesome superior from the Miao wars, General Liu Heling. Forested limestone hills began to pop up again, home to local groups of Miao and Yao who were portrayed by more aspiring folk in town as rustic savages, happy to own just a knife and a home-made gun. The river now ran increasingly low and rough, and Mesny had to exchange his wide, comfortable junk for a shallower-draft Miao vessel reminiscent of a long canoe, just one person wide. On the last day of the month they reached a mid-stream island on which stood the "dull little country town" of Danzhou, a walled trading post founded during the sixteenth century where Miao and Yao came down from the mountains to shop for necessities and sell their wares at market. Nowadays the island is half-covered by groves of pomelo trees, whose yellow, heavy fruit is a springtime market staple right across southern China; it also produces tung oil, traditionally used for waterproofing ships' hulls. Mesny's attention was fully occupied by the female hill-dwellers in town who went about half-naked, dressed only in silver jewellery and short skirts, and from here on began an almost daily commentary about how little clothing local women wore. To be fair, he'd been away from his wife for almost two years.

A day later they reached the tiny military outpost of Laobao, set in amongst steep outcrops of rock at the junction between the Rong and Duliu rivers. The Chinese garrison here were a rough lot, badly paid and surly, but Mesny managed to get away without mishap, his vessel bearing westwards up the Duliu. That night they found lodgings at the Sanwang Temple, dedicated to a local folk hero, the Bamboo King, and his two sons. The whitewashed halls were large, spacious and romantically mildewed with age, and he shared rooms with an interesting company of itinerant actors and wandering scholars; the temple still stands, exactly as Mesny described it. A pause upstream on the following day inspired a rare self-portrait: Mesny, who had clearly taken to heart that scornful newspaper report of his habit of mixing Chinese and Western dress, was now wearing a proper colonial explorer's kit – pith helmet, long-sleeved shirt, tight white trousers and black leather shoes – and the sight of a blacksmith, draped in nothing but leopard skins as he hammered away at his forge, left him feeling very alien indeed.

Expecting a storm, they pulled ashore at Yangxi. This sat on the edge of Dong territory, a hill people superficially similar to the Miao but with a distinct history and language, who had joined in the general struggle against Chinese rule during the 1860s. Like the Miao they were expert carpenters and built two-storey wooden houses, with the family living upstairs and the livestock penned in below. Dong settlements always featured at least one tall wooden drum tower and a covered "wind-and-rain" bridge, which besides serving as focal points for village life were also connected to their folk religion. With all this timberwork, fire was a terrible hazard, and families took turns in serving as fire-wardens for the community, but even so Yangxi had only recently been rebuilt after burning to the ground. Mesny found that the Dong enjoyed glutinous rice and pork, and drank a strange, oily, bitter tea made from fried leaves and rice crisps. The women of the village watched with undisguised curiosity as he combed and brushed his hair; he enjoyed their attention and reciprocated with another long passage about their shapely legs, short skirts and revealingly loose jackets.

Up ahead lay the provincial border and the last town in Guangxi, Meilin, a customs post where Mesny was excused paying duty because of his military rank. Meilin's officials greeted him politely but apologised for being unable to accompany him to the border as they ought to have done. A tough stretch of rapids here slowed progress and Mesny put ashore for the night at a hamlet where many of his boatmen had been born, still just inside Guangxi. Needing to cool off after a scorchingly hot day (the temperature in his cabin had reached 33ºC), Mesny gravitated towards a spring where several young women were drawing water and dressing their hair, commenting uncharitably – and extremely unconvincingly – that they were "very ugly indeed". He was entertained by somebody's uncle, a trader along the river all his life, who recalled the bad old days when Miao warriors had regularly raided the village during their rebellion, reducing everyone to poverty.

On the next day, July 5, they finally crossed back into Guizhou.

Congjiang was a sad ruin. There was little left of the town beyond overgrown rubble, and the place was so blatantly poor that Mesny was embarrassed at lumbering the magistrate with his sizeable party. This region, at Guizhou's southeastern extremity, had for centuries been the source of superlative fir and camphor trees, whose fine-grained, long-lasting timber was in great demand for building palaces and temples. In 1889, when the Hall of Supreme Harmony at Beijing's Forbidden City burned down, the government sent timber-getters to the region who logged over fifty huge trunks for replacement pillars. But now the riverbanks around Congjiang had been stripped bare, the trees probably cut down for firewood by soldiers during the Miao war or rapaciously harvested by Chinese settlers afterwards, as the Miao were very careful about conserving their supply.

The desolation continued upstream, with undisturbed animal tracks all along the shore and little sign of human habitation aside from the occasional sight of stone indigo vats, stained purple from use, standing abandoned on little shingle beaches. Post-war, the Miao chieftains had been stripped of their authority and the population had decamped into the hills to avoid persecution and to guard their precious timber; but now retired Hunanese soldiers and recently-arrived traders from Guangdong and Fujian were colonising the lowlands. In general there was little love lost between the Miao and these interlopers, though as always a few intermarried.

Xiajiang, another one-time military post torn apart by the war, was now only really populated on market days. It wasn't a happy town; three years earlier, the former magistrate had been murdered and "pounded to jelly in a rice mortar", and a vengeful Chinese army had afterwards slaughtered most of Xiajiang's inhabitants. The sympathetic regional governor, Yi Fushan, had since banned forced labour, which he believed had caused the uprising; he also eased taxes, destroyed the formerly ubiquitous opium fields and urged people to plant safflower as a cash crop instead. Mesny was impressed but couldn't let someone else take the credit for such enlightened views, claiming that Yi – whom he had once met briefly – had borrowed his own progressive notions. At any rate, Xiajiang's new magistrate made him welcome and Mesny spent the evening chewing over past times with Colonel Liao, an old friend.

At Rongjiang, a substantial town for these parts with several streets, there was another change of boats for the final stretch up to Sandu, beyond which the river ran too shallow for navigation. It was Rongjiang's Miao who had first mastered the art of musketry and introduced guns to rural Guizhou after capturing a horde from the remnants of Wu Sangui's army during the 1670s. Indeed, they grew so bold and rebellious with their new-found skills that a military outpost had to be built here in the eighteenth century to keep the area quiet. Like every other town along the river, Rongjiang had changed hands so many times and with such violence during the Miao war that there had been little worth recovering afterwards. The town's female Miao wore piled hair and distinctively embroidered jackets but no silver jewellery; Mesny wondered if this was to reduce their chances of being robbed and raped by Chinese soldiers. Wandering the streets that evening, he bumped into Captain Wang, another former comrade-in-arms, who was smartly dressed but rather depressed, with no money or chance of further advancement now that the war was over.

The next few days passed in a repeat of rapids and dilapidated outposts. At Dujiang the entire Miao population had fled into the hills, and there were so few people about that usually secretive wild pheasants could be seen fearlessly wandering around the town's outskirts. A final rough stretch of water brought them to the dock at Sandu, from where overland routes continued to Guiyang. Mesny spent a few days here organising porters, strolling in the countryside, visiting markets, worrying about his wife, drooling over young Miao women, espousing Christianity and chatting to scholars and a rare female actor – their roles were usually played by men on stage. He also took note of Sandu's rich coal deposits, which are still being mined today. He was interested in everything.

In the end it took another fortnight to reach Guiyang, twice as long as Mesny had hoped. All went well until he reached Duyun around a third of the way into the journey, where his porters staged a strike in an attempt to renegotiate their contract. Duyun's magistrate refused to get involved in the affair, leaving Mesny to moan rhetorically – as many travellers have done since – "When shall this overcharging of strangers cease in China?" Fortunately, given that the negotiations stretched out over several days, Mesny's inn proved to be the best of the journey so far, run by a helpful Hunanese landlord. Duyun itself had played a pivotal role in the later stages of the Miao Rebellion, when rebels had captured the city and found the armoury full of modern weapons, allowing them to continue their fight for a further eighteen months. Now the citizens appeared to be Han Chinese, but Mesny suspected that many were actually Miao, dressing and speaking like their conquerors to avoid trouble. He approached some to make notes on the local Miao dialect, but nobody would admit to being able to speak the language.

And so on 4 August 1879, after an absence of two years, Mesny returned to his home near Guiyang's courthouse to find that his wife Nien Suey Tsen "was the only one who manifested any joy at my arrival". Cen Yuying, the man he was known to despise as being bloodthirsty and anti-foreign, had just been appointed as Guizhou's new governor, and now former friends cold-shouldered Mesny in case they risked Cen's displeasure: "even my wife and her relations trembled with fear, lest they should suffer on account of their relationship with me".

But Cen didn't seem to share Mesny's antipathy and in fact offered him employment at 100 taels a month – presumably handing him back his former position as head of Guiyang's armoury – though he wasn't interested in pursuing Mesny's schemes for modernising the province, such as building a railway between Guiyang and Rongshui. Shortly after the Chinese New Year in February 1880, Mesny wrote that business at Guiyang had slumped and the city's only foreign trading house, "Sheng Hou" (in fact, his own company, whose name translated as "Abounding Generosity") had been forced to close indefinitely through want of customers. He presented his grievances to Cen, who retorted that there was not even enough money in the treasury to pay the government troops, let alone sponsor development. Mesny suggested raising revenue by investing in Guizhou's mining potential but Cen dismissed the idea as being too long-winded and unreliable.

The *Shanghai Courier* shortly afterwards translated an anonymous article which had appeared in the Chinese press – almost certainly written by a frustrated Mesny, keen to champion his hobby-horse in the face of official indifference – in which the author "strenuously advocates the opening up of the mineral resources of Kwei-chow, which are, it says, thought to be of a very valuable description... Of course to achieve any great success in that direction, the mines in Kwei-chow would have to be worked scientifically with modern machinery, and foreign experts would have to be employed... But if the development of the mines of Kwei-chow is to be left to the officials, there will be little done." Sure enough, a memorial from Cen soon appeared in the *Peking Gazette*, outlining a scheme to replenish the provincial treasury by working Guizhou's reserves of lead ore, so perhaps he did eventually listen to Mesny's advice.

In Cen's defence it must be said that he had far more important issues to deal with besides involving himself in Mesny's schemes. Firstly, there had been a revolutionary scare at Guiyang itself that November, in which a military official named Yang Haitai had attempted a coup, planning to assassinate Cen and his colleagues during a banquet. But the authorities were forewarned: Yang and his accomplices were captured and executed and their families sold into slavery. Cen was now busy reorganising the provincial army. He was about to be promoted to Viceroy of Yungui – the combined territories of Yunnan and Guizhou provinces – which meant that he would have to look into the increasingly unstable situation in northern Vietnam and deal with an ongoing revolt in eastern Yunnan led by a Taoist priest, who had already defeated Imperial troops sent against him.

So with business stagnant at Guiyang, Mesny began casting around for new opportunities. The first hint of his long-term plans appeared in a letter to Gill (who had yet to depart on his fatal trip to Egypt), written in late February 1880:

"I have just received a passport available for 6 provinces, viz [Yunnan, Sichuan, Gansu, Shaanxi, Shanxi and Zhili] all of which

I intend to visit if possible. I have sold some of my property here, and am taking the little stock in trade of foreign goods. I had these here there being no demand for them just now business being at a standstill owing to the scarcity of money.

I will write you at least one letter from each province if it is possible to forward correspondence from any Treaty Port therefrom, and I intend to keep a special itinerary for you, with a few readings of the barometer and thermometer added under the name of each place.

Trusting this will reach you safely, and that it will find you in the enjoyment of good health and much Happiness

I remain dear Sir and friend
    Yours very much obliged
    W. Mesny"

Aside from showing that Mesny and Gill had remained on good terms after their travels, the letter proves that, even at this stage, Mesny was contemplating a major expedition around China. The area covered by his permits was vast, stretching from Beijing to the empire's westernmost boundaries; it's noteworthy that Shaanxi and Gansu provinces had been on Gill's original itinerary, before a revolt there had forced him to choose his final route to Burma in 1877. The mention of carrying merchandise shows that Mesny was also following the advice he had given to Reverend David Hill six years earlier, of "the great influence that a man would have, who supports himself by trade in China."

The property that Mesny sold was part of his farm at Shuitian, about twenty kilometres northeast of Guiyang. Mesny had originally hoped to set up a mill here, but the land had such favourable *feng shui* – a hill to the north, flowing water to the south – that several rich officials approached him with generous offers to buy it for their grave sites. With typical perversity – and kindness – he instead made over the land at cost price to Tang Jiong, his disgraced commander from the Miao war, who was looking for somewhere auspicious to bury his recently deceased stepmother and spent a huge amount beautifying the plot with trees and walkways. It was in consequence of this filial act, says Mesny, that Tang was forgiven his perceived military failures against the Miao and restored to official favour (though in fact by this time he was already working with Ding Baozhen at Chengdu).

All this aside, missing from the letter to Gill is any mention of *why* Mesny was travelling. According to the *Miscellany*, his main purpose was to petition General Zuo Zongtang to accept a loan from France on behalf of the Imperial treasury. At this point, the Chinese government was tied down in a confusion of debts to Western powers at varying levels of interest; the French now offered to consolidate all these into a single package at a fixed rate. In the most detailed, circumstantial version of the story (he produced several conflicting accounts), Mesny was approached on his return voyage to China in 1878 by a Mr Hardcastle, one of the directors of the Comptoir d'Escompte in Paris, who "sought my assistance for the proposition of a loan to the Chinese government of seventeen million Taels at the uniform rate of 6 ½ per cent. for the consolidation of all the then existing loans... one condition of the said consolidation loan was that it should be made in silver dollars coined at the French government mint in Paris for the Chinese government at a cost of half per cent. for mintage... Mr Hardcastle and his friend then asked me if I knew [Zuo Zongtang]. I assured them that I did, and they then asked me if I would like to undertake a journey to his camp in the north-west to make this proposition to him, and they promised me a very fine commission on the transaction if I succeeded".

Zuo was then in Turkestan, in China's northwestern extremity, where he had been fighting Muslim separatists. Now that these had been suppressed, Zuo was squaring up to take on Russia, which had opportunistically annexed a corner of these distant borderlands whilst China's attention was elsewhere. But so far Mesny's travels hadn't shown much definite sense of purpose beyond returning to Guiyang. In a separate letter to Gill, Mesny spoke of making a broad sweep of Yunnan province before heading back east to Chengdu, never mentioning northwest China at all; while a letter to his brother, written a few months later, stated that he wanted to reach Beijing before the winter, and so was undecided on whether to travel through the northwest or simply to proceed to

Hankou and catch a steamer to the capital. So for a while at least, Mesny seems to have been making up his itinerary as he went along, despite a retrospectively purposeful account in the *Miscellany*, where he asserts that he "volunteered for service" in northwestern China. This is stretching the truth: at this stage there's no indication that he was serving anything but his own interests.

It's also plausible that after his previous trip across China – and Gill's successes with his book and medal from the Royal Geographical Society – that this new journey was an attempt by Mesny to be taken seriously as an explorer. In support of the notion, not only was there the promise to provide Gill with regular updates and basic scientific information, but Mesny had also begun to collect plants for Henry Fletcher Hance, the acting British Consul at Guangzhou. Plant collecting was becoming a very big business back in Britain, with eager competition between nurseries, private gardens and scientific institutions, and since the 1840s a succession of dedicated plant-hunters had been scouring China for colourful new blooms to take home. There was also a less attractive side to their activities: one of the earliest of these collectors, Robert Fortune, had successfully smuggled tea plants out of China for the British East India Company, allowing them to establish the first tea plantations in India. Clearly, it hadn't been enough for the Company to undermine the entire Chinese state by flooding it with cheap opium; they had to rob the country of one of her major exports too.

Hance himself had been in China since 1844, botanising in his spare time and encouraging other travellers to add to his collection. Mesny was one of his protégés, and the specimens he sent back – their mummified, fragile remains now stored in the British Museum of Natural History – look professionally collected and pressed, for which he must have been carrying some fairly bulky equipment. Despite finding the whole business something of a chore, and frankly admitting in the *Miscellany* that "I am not a botanist, and indeed do not know anything of that useful science," Mesny managed to collect around seventy-five species on his travels, eight of which turned out to be new. These included the pretty yellow-flowering *Jasminum mesnyi* and *Salix mesnyi*, a small, spear-leafed willow shrub, both named in his honour.

How far he had planned the extent of his future travels isn't clear then, but with business at Guiyang stagnant for the foreseeable future, Mesny set out for Chongqing in March 1880, perhaps tempted by the possibilities that the larger city offered. Doubtless glad to be rid of him, Cen Yuying generously sent Mesny on his way with 1,000 taels for travelling expenses, a letter of introduction to the authorities at Beijing and a copy of a memorial to the throne recommending him for further promotion.

All went well for the first few days, with the party of about thirty – comprising Mesny's staff, porters and a military escort – heading northwest on what should have been an easy two-week journey. Then, on 15 March, a slightly disturbing entry appeared in Mesny's journal: "At 2.56 entered city up fine large street, no accommodation all inns full of soldiers, put up at a wretched place... The city is called [Qianxi], and is noted for the anti-foreign feeling of its people." This was because a French missionary had been roughed up and driven out of town by an angry crowd a few years previously. The entry is followed by a four-day blank, resuming with a laconic "Arrived back at Guiyang"; there was no mention of an incident which had nearly cost Mesny his life and which within weeks was the subject of wild speculation in both the Chinese and foreign press. The earliest of these slightly garbled reports had him involved in a firefight with bandits who were trying to steal his luggage; Mesny had either shot his way out or been taken prisoner, but at any rate he was now under military protection, perhaps at Hankou or Chongqing.

The rumours weren't so far from the truth. During the late afternoon of March 15, a mob at Qianxi – ordinary citizens led by some soldiers from the city's battalions – made a "furious and murderous attack" on Mesny's inn for reasons which were never explained. Perhaps there were none beyond his being a foreigner. Mesny fired off a revolver into the crowd, killing four of his attackers and wounding several others, but had no time to reload and would certainly have been killed had he not picked up a lance dropped by one of the fallen Chinese and used it to fight his way clear. Just in time a detachment of soldiers from the Hunan Army, his old force who were billeted at Qianxi for a review, came to his rescue and battled with the rioters until after midnight, resulting in a "terrible carnage". During a lull in the fracas, Mesny and his party escaped through the back streets to the courthouse, from where three hundred soldiers escorted them secretly out of the city and back to Guiyang.

In a letter to his brother, later published in the *China Mail*, Mesny was fairly matter-of-fact about the affair, though he had lost all his baggage and several hundred taels in cash at the inn. He'd had the foresight to leave the rest of his valuables – which he valued at 25,000 taels – with Qianxi's magistrate before the assault, and was shortly expecting them to be delivered back to Guiyang. But it must have come as an unwelcome shock to realise that, despite all his years of service in China and his marriage to a Chinese woman, people were still capable of identifying Mesny simply as one of the hated foreign invaders, and of turning against him without further provocation.

The incident also ended Mesny's uneasy relationship with Cen Yuying. By the time of the *Miscellany*'s publication fifteen years later, Mesny had become convinced that the assault at Qianxi was a plot engineered by Cen to murder him, in the same way that he believed that Cen had been behind Margary's death in Yunnan. From this perspective, the gifts of travelling expenses and congratulatory letters were acts of cynical favouritism, intended to anger Guiyang's anti-foreign elements and spur them on towards violence against Mesny. The obvious flaw in this argument is that these same agitators would surely have been even more tempted to murder Cen himself for displaying pro-foreign leanings. But Mesny's suspicions may not have been pure paranoia, and it's possible that he had information about the affray at Qianxi which he never wrote down; at any rate, he afterwards became relentlessly hostile towards Cen and never missed an opportunity to vilify him in print.

Mesny rested up at Guiyang for the best part of three weeks. Much to his annoyance, Cen sensibly forbade him from attempting the same route again, so he followed a more direct road north and gave the entire Qianxi district a wide berth. It was on this stage of the trip, at the hamlet of Meizhu near Wujiang town, that Mesny collected the new species of jasmine now named after him. He finally reached Chongqing on April 25.

Mesny spent eight months at Chongqing making up his mind on what to do next, scouting for business opportunities, promoting the idea of building steamships to run through the Three Gorges and trying to stir up interest in the construction of another rail line, this time between Chongqing and Chengdu. In his spare time he made forays into the hills outside the city collecting plants and visiting "Manzi" cave tombs – sculpted crypts left by a culture which vanished during the third century BC. He also wrote copious articles on politics, gossip and local customs under the pen-name "Pioneer" for the four-page *China Mail* newspaper in Hong Kong, some of which were reprinted in Shanghai's influential *North China Herald.*

Since Mesny's first visit in 1869 a tiny foreign community had established itself at Chongqing, though it withered to almost nothing during his stay. First to leave was the Reverend Samuel Clarke of the China Inland Mission, who later authored *Among the Tribes in South-West China*, the first comprehensive English-language account of the Miao. He was followed by the British consul at Chongqing, Edward Colborne Baber, who had shared a river steamer with Gill back in 1877. Baber had been on "special service" in Sichuan and Yunnan for four years, travelling almost as widely as Mesny himself while ostensibly reporting on the opium trade. Despite declining health his presence had lent moral support to the city's foreign enclave, which was now reduced to Mesny, a handful of missionaries, and the Catholic bishop Père Vinçot, who had been here for decades. Mesny spent a good deal of time with Mr & Mrs Nicoll of the China Inland Mission; like all members of their organisation, the Nicolls lived as locals and had adopted Chinese dress in order to blend in. Despite being occasionally heckled in the street by hostile Chinese, Mesny himself still wore European clothing at all times.

Mesny had been unable to recover most of his baggage after the assault at Qianxi, so was angered when a Shanghai paper reported that the government had paid him 1,000 taels in compensation. He rebuffed the claims, asserting that he had received nothing and was being supported at Chongqing by donations sent by friends in Guizhou. But his staff – who had also lost everything – believed the newspapers and began pressuring Mesny for their share of the payout. On top of this, the families of the four men he shot in self-defence were threatening legal action; not over the deaths themselves but the funeral expenses (though the case was swiftly thrown out by local magistrates). Disgusted by the way Chongqing's authorities were handling the matter, Mesny toyed with the idea of retiring from the Chinese military and claiming 60,000 taels in back pay, plus the same sum for having rescued himself at Qianxi – thus saving the Chinese government from British wrath had he been murdered. Others advised him to stay in the army but to demand 200,000 taels in compensation, plus promotion to a higher rank.

News arrived from Guiyang: Cen Yuying was looking for skilled engineers to cast mortars and field guns, and there was speculation in the press that Mesny might return to oversee the project. But he wasn't tempted, and later heard that the cannon had been so badly made that several exploded on use, killing their crews. Cen had meanwhile successfully suppressed the Taoist rebellion in Yunnan and was busy executing members of the outlawed secret society, the Gelao Hui – though Mesny couldn't help repeating the popular rumour that the charges were false and the victims were in fact members of a wealthy family whom Cen had accused of being rebels in order to extort money.

Mesny now set up shop under the name "Mesny & Co", hoping to sell off a stock of pocket watches to Chongqing's elite. However, business here was no livelier than at Guiyang and the city's merchants, rather than buying luxury items such as watches, were busy collecting unpaid debts to make ends meet. Mesny & Co's profits were also being threatened by underhand competition. In exchange for paying a set tax direct to the Chinese government, British trading firms were eligible for Transit Passes, which allowed their agents to move goods through the country without paying the unpredictable *lijin* taxes. It now transpired that a batch of these passes had been obtained by dubious methods and sold to the highest bidders, allowing the Chinese merchants who bought them – none of whom had any actual connection to the British companies named on the passes – to trade tax-free under a foreign name. This naturally outraged Mesny, who was having trouble obtaining legitimate passes for his own company and was simultaneously being "squeezed" for bribes. In the end, the whole Transit Pass scam was brought to a neat close by the Sichuanese viceroy and Mesny's former employer, Ding Baozhen, who simply banned the use of foreign company names at Chongqing. Mesny had to resurrect his Chinese one, "Sheng Hou".

Though Mesny respected Ding Baozhen as an unusually honest and industrious official, Ding had a way of continually frustrating his plans. A complaint against him by "Pioneer" now appeared in the *China Mail*: Ding had ordered in a large consignment of arms from either Shanghai or Hong Kong instead of buying them locally through "Mesny & Co" because, wrote the author, he didn't want foreign traders setting up shop in the interior. In fact, Ding was simply adhering to the letter of the Chefoo Convention, which China had been forced to sign following Margary's murder and whose primary aim was to ensure the safety of foreigners travelling in China's interior. But in an unusual concession to Chinese protectionism, the convention also expressly stated that "British merchants will not be allowed to reside at Chung King, or to open establishments or warehouses there, so long as no steamers have access to the port". As it was impossible at this stage for ordinary steamers to navigate through the treacherous Three Gorges – a feat not achieved until 1898 – Mesny, part of the Chinese service but still British, was breaking the law by even living in Chongqing as a merchant, let alone actually conducting trade there.

Outmanoeuvred in the arms business, Mesny now discovered that the silver taels used as currency at Chongqing contained tiny traces of gold, and asked permission to extract it from the provincial treasury's horde. But he was again turned down. Firstly, Ding Baozhen considered the whole scheme nothing better than alchemy – gold was gold, silver was silver, and to talk of extracting one from the other was ludicrous. Secondly, even if it were possible, Ding would refuse permission because he believed that the silver would be devalued in the process. Mesny argued unsuccessfully that Ding would be left with both the gold and the silver, and bemoaned the similar failure of his earlier offers to extract kerosene from rock oil owing to official incredulity that the process was possible – "and yet a few days ago I saw more than one thousand gallons of American kerosine oil landed at this port".

Ding Baozhen was soon running into official difficulties of his own. Following the success of his salt trade reforms, which had considerably increased provincial revenue, Ding had donated 400,000 taels towards Zuo Zongtang's military campaign in northwestern China. This had drawn the unwelcome attention of the Beijing government: if Sichuan was so wealthy, surely the province could contribute a million taels to the Imperial treasury? Ding was now desperately trying to raise the necessary funds but, coming on top of a bad year for business in which many merchant vessels had been wrecked in the Three Gorges, cash was in short supply. His attempts to introduce a pork tax led to an aggravated protest by Chongqing's butchers, who barricaded themselves into their guildhall and took a government inspector hostage until their demands for exemption from the tax were met, tying the poor man to a pillar and almost drowning him in excrement. Mesny felt that this was all part of a rising wave of popular discontent against the government, one that was playing into the hands of anti-foreign and anti-dynastic societies; unless foreign troops were called in to enforce order, trouble would soon break out right across the southwest. He reported that several Yunnanese merchant guilds in the city were of a similar opinion, and were busy transferring their assets to Hong Kong, Hankou and Shanghai for safekeeping.

While all this was going on, Mesny was busy ferreting out current news about China's northwestern extremity, Xinjiang. More evocatively known at the time as "Chinese Turkestan", Xinjiang comprised of a pair of vast desert basins spreading for 1500 kilometres from the far edge of Gansu province to China's blurry frontiers with Russia and Central Asia. The western tail of the Great Wall petered out amongst the sand dunes here, and the Silk Road, that ancient caravan route between China and Europe, had once threaded across Xinjiang's searing plains via a string of oasis towns. Despite the name – Xinjiang means "New Territories" – this ethnically diverse region had been claimed by China as early as the Han dynasty, though it was only formally incorporated into the nation during the eighteenth century and had been invaded by others or split by civil war on numerous occasions. Indeed, Zuo Zongtang was campaigning up there now and Mesny, mindful of the profitable bank loan that it was in his power to negotiate, decided to make the journey to meet him.

Since they had last seen each other at Hankou in 1867, Zuo had been battling a succession of rebel groups across northern China. His main campaign had been against a disunited but widespread insurgency across Shaanxi and Gansu provinces amongst the Tungans, Hui Muslims who – like the Taipings – had seen in a weakening Chinese government the chance to throw off outside rule. Zuo put the origins of these troubles down to sectarian fighting over interpretation of Islam's "New Teachings", which had been imported from central Asia during the eighteenth century. Government forces had been sent to quell the disturbances, leading to the usual atrocities on both sides, after which the Chinese military were settled in the region to enforce the peace. Inevitably, when these troops were withdrawn from the northwest to help fight the Taipings during the 1850s, the friction between local Muslim and Han Chinese communities soon erupted into full-scale fighting.

At the height of the rebellion, Muslim forces actually besieged the great walled city and former Chinese capital, Xi'an, but by 1873 Zuo's systematic use of German-made cannon had cleared the rebel groups from Shaanxi and Gansu provinces and ended the Tungan Revolt. While reasonably humane in the early stages of the war, Zuo's final campaign against the warlord Ma Wenlu was unremittingly bloody, culminating in mass executions and the transplanting of Muslim survivors out of the region. It's possible that fourteen million people, both Han Chinese and Hui, were killed in the rebellion's suppression.

With the fighting over, Zuo based himself at Gansu's capital, Lanzhou, where he banned opium production in favour of cotton, established textile mills, employed his otherwise idle troops in farming and revegetation projects and turned his attention north towards Xinjiang. Since 1864 the region had been in upheaval under Yakub Beg, a Muslim of the dominant Uighur ethnic group – a Turkic-speaking people who had migrated into Xinjiang from central Asia. As a youth, Yakub had fought the Russians and then become embroiled in the politics of his native Uzbekistan. In order to get rid of the fiery young man, the Uzbeks had sent him to support an anti-Chinese revolt at the border town of Kashgar, where he soon took over the rebellion. By 1873 Yakub Beg was in control of much of Xinjiang and had declared himself, with the Sultan of Turkey's blessing, as Khan of Kashgar.

China found its military finances stretched to their limits. In Beijing, Li Hongzhang – the man who had fallen out with Gordon over the sack of Suzhou during the Taiping Rebellion, now a rising statesman – was pushing for the modernisation of China's navy, to prevent any further attempts by Western powers to force their way into China from the sea. Facing the loss of all Xinjiang, however, a landlocked Zuo Zongtang favoured beefing up the army and appealed to the throne for a loan of ten million taels to be raised through foreign banks. After much debate as to the value of securing this remote, troublesome territory, which even in peacetime had proved a huge financial drain on the Imperial treasury, Zuo won the argument and the loan was approved in 1875. The following year he began contemplating a new threat to the region: Russian expansionism.

In fact, both Russia and rival British India were eyeing up Xinjiang's strategic potential and had already begun probing covertly towards Kashgar. There had been official approaches too: in 1873, Britain sent the Forsyth Mission to meet Yakub Beg, while the Russians conducted a trade expedition through northwestern China the following year under Colonel Sosnowski. In the meantime, the Russian military had opportunistically occupied Chinese territory along the fertile Ili valley in order, they said, to preserve law and order in the absence of Chinese authority. Russia now sent its own embassy to Yakub Beg to negotiate mutual borders, assess his military capabilities and to see how closely, if at all, he had in fact allied himself with Britain. The mission found the khan to be a capable and energetic man who lived simply, though heavy taxation to support the war against the Chinese was making his rule unpopular. Yakub ultimately covered himself by signing trade agreements with both Russia and Britain; neither, however, was prepared to support him militarily against China.

In the end, Yakub Beg's fall was rapid and unspectacular. Zuo Zongtang warned the foreign powers not to take sides in an internal Chinese matter (a phrase still trotted out today by Chinese politicians), and, following his strategy of "seizing the north then taking the south", reconquered Xinjiang with little effort. Yakub Beg committed suicide, died or was murdered in May 1877; his children were variously executed or castrated and sold as slaves, and a year later virtually all of Xinjiang was back under Chinese control. (It was at this point that Gill had been refused permission to cross Turkestan.)

China now demanded that Russia return the Ili valley. Russia, stalling, proposed the insulting Treaty of Livadia, which shifted the mutual Russian-Chinese borders in her favour and demanded a five million rouble indemnity to be paid for the cost of the Russian occupation of Ili. For approving these terms, Beijing's ambassador to Russia, Chong Hou, was sentenced to death by an irate Imperial Court, though he was later released after a two-year incarceration. (The British press, which followed Chong Hou's story, believed that Queen Victoria personally interceded on his behalf, but in fact Chong bought his freedom with a substantial donation to the Board of War's coffers; he died in retirement in 1893.) The *Shanghai Courier* couldn't see what China was making a fuss about: five million was a perfectly reasonable sum given the expense that Russia must have gone to in occupying Ili – implying that China ought to be grateful for the unwanted occupation of her territory by foreign forces. Chinese indignation was fanned by a violently anti-Russian memorial to the throne written by an obscure scholar-official named Zhang Zhidong, and China began to make war-like noises.

But what would happen should the two countries actually go to war? An anonymous but very Mesny-esque report in the Shanghai press doubted China's military abilities, which, the author believed, had been greatly exaggerated by other foreign commentators. As Mesny was the only foreign drill instructor currently employed by the Chinese, the report continued, the majority of their troops were therefore not trained in modern warfare. The Tungans had been overwhelmed not because China's military was itself an efficient or skilled fighting force, but because the Tungans' antiquated weaponry was unable to deal with the sheer numbers of Chinese soldiers sent against them. China was now reducing armament production, although Russian forces along their common border were armed with "500 Lowell battery guns and 50 millions of cartridges with which her generals could sweep the army of [Zuo Zongtang] off the face of the earth; besides five batteries of fifteen centimetres Krupp guns, and an enormous supply of ammunition."

A party of Russians witnessing Zuo's army on manoeuvres back in 1875 had been equally unimpressed: these front-line forces had been armed only with rickety old British guns with spring-loaded triggers and no stocks, and the poor men had to fire their weapons while holding onto the barrels with their bare hands, burning them badly. Unsurprisingly, few of these marksmen came near to even hitting their targets, though they stood just five paces away.

Ready or not, in June 1880 Zuo shifted his headquarters to Hami, just inside the Xinjiang border, and began planning a campaign against Ili – at which point Russia softened its stance and began negotiating a new treaty. But then on 11 August came a disheartening anti-climax to the whole affair – at least from Mesny's point of view – when the court at Beijing recalled Zuo from his thirteen year mission to pacify Xinjiang. Though Mesny asserts several times in the *Miscellany* that he was shocked to find on arriving at Hami the following April that Zuo had left just weeks earlier, his recall would have been announced at the time in official gazettes and Mesny must have known that Zuo had departed Xinjiang long before he set out from Chongqing. But there was still a fair chance that Zuo's replacement at Hami – or any other high-placed official Mesny might meet along the way – would still accept the loan; and there was also the attraction for Mesny in exploring the route to central Asia that Gill had so badly wanted to follow back in 1878.

So in early December 1880, and despite his wife and mother-in-law having recently joined him at Chongqing, Mesny finally decided to depart for Xinjiang. The only explanation he provided for this poor timing was an ambiguous comment in the *China Mail*: "Dispatches received last night have decided me to take this step without delay"; most likely, Mesny had heard that Zuo had been recalled from Hami and planned to race north in order to catch him as he passed through Lanzhou on his way back to Beijing. He paid the necessary farewell visits to the city's officials, who seemed relieved to see the back of this demanding, anomalous foreigner but were still surprised to find him leaving before the arrival of Chongqing's new British representative, a Mr Parker. Fortunately, given Mesny's lack of mercantile success in the city and the unwillingness of the authorities to compensate him for the affair at Qianxi, friends in Guizhou had promised to loan him a further thousand taels in travel expenses.

But preparations for departure could never run smoothly. Chongqing's officials now suddenly decided against his leaving, worried that if Mesny were killed on the road by bandits or bad luck then they would be held responsible. They begged him to at least adopt inconspicuous Chinese clothing and travel hidden in a sedan chair or on horseback, to which he agreed if they would pay for it: the chair would cost 200 taels for the first stage of his journey alone, and "A suitable winter outfit is not cheap, as several fur garments are necessary." A magistrate donated a pony but, being lame and far too small to carry Mesny's fourteen stone, he sent it back. On top of this, his promised funds had not yet materialised from Guizhou. But with unusual speed, the authorities came up with an effective solution, ordering a wealthy Chinese Christian to loan Mesny his travel expenses. Not only could Mesny now afford to depart, but all responsibility for the expedition was transferred to his benefactor: Chongqing's officials could no longer be held accountable for any future disaster.

Mesny's regular articles for the *China Mail* dry up at this point, but fortunately a bare account of the rest of his expedition has survived in the form of log books and "daily observations" written on loose foolscap leaves, now squirreled away in the archives of the Royal Geographical Society in London. Most likely these are duplicates sent back to Gill, neatly laid out on lined paper in Mesny's tidy handwriting with Chinese place names marked in red ink; there are no signs of the weather-staining, coffee spills, dog-eared corners and crossings-out that scar most notebooks brought back from a gruelling research trip. They cover not only the missing part of Mesny's journey from Guiyang to Chongqing and then on to Hami in

Xinjiang, but also his later travels between Xinjiang and Beijing, ending with his arrival at the Chinese capital in February 1882. Entries are dry and factual, giving distances covered, barometric readings, temperature, road conditions, and bare sketches of settlements and landscape; there are also brief notes on trade, industry and the possibility of river navigation. There are some lengthy gaps too – Mesny tended to make entries only while travelling, so that whole months spent in cities are left almost blank – but the journal's precise dates are invaluable: those in the *Miscellany* are all over the place, sometimes out by a whole year. Admittedly, the *Miscellany* was written decades later and mostly from memory, but at times it's hard not to suspect deliberate fudging of the schedule in order to bolster Mesny's role in events.

On 21 December, Mesny and his party set off westwards to Futu Guan at the neck of the Chongqing peninsula, well within the modern city's suburbs but then a separately walled clifftop settlement under its own military authority. Here they turned north along the Jialing River to Hechuan, recently rebuilt after a flood had swept the old city away, whose shipyards turned out the sturdy, shallow-draft wooden transport barges used by the salt trade. Just outside Hechuan was the hilltop citadel of Diayou Cheng and one of the world's greatest forgotten battlefields, where Mongke Khan, leader of the Mongols, died in August 1259 during a campaign against China's Song dynasty, either from disease or a poisoned arrow. Mongke's death almost certainly changed the entire course of European history, when Kublai was elected Khan in his place and abandoned the Mongols' conquest of Egypt and the Mediterranean in order to consolidate his already enormous empire in Asia.

From Hechuan the road wound over increasingly high hills to the prosperous market town of Nanchong and a succession of small, salt-producing hamlets where brine was tapped from subterranean artesian basins. As Gill had seen at Zigong, miners sank narrow wells using percussion drills, where a heavy iron bit was winched to the top of a derrick and then dropped down the shaft to shatter any obstructing rocks. It could take decades to dig down deep enough to reach the brine, which was then piped to the surface and evaporated in shallow ponds.

Nine days into the journey they crossed a long pontoon bridge over the Jialing River and reached Langzhong, a rectangular collection of grey-tiled roofs, antique watch towers, wooden-fronted shops and inward looking *siheyuan* courtyard houses. Mesny unfairly dismissed the town as being of "no great commercial importance" (its most famous product was smoked beef), though he believed that this could change if small steamers began operating between here and Chongqing. In fact Langzhong had a long history, even serving as the Sichuanese capital for a couple of decades after "Yellow Tiger" Zhang Xianzhong had razed Chongqing and Chengdu to the ground at the end of the Ming dynasty.

There was a sizeable military garrison stationed here, a *gongyuan* hall where government candidates sat for their provincial examinations (despite its small size, Langzhong had produced several ranking civil servants) and plentiful, inexpensive inns – Mesny paid just 120 copper cash for two rooms, and his porters were each accommodated for a third of this price, including their bedding and a meal. Some of these inns were quite famous; one claimed to have been in business long enough to have played host to the eighth-century statesman and poet Su Dongpo. Mesny also made a special visit to the tomb of Zhang Fei, a loyal but violent Three Kingdoms general who was assassinated while campaigning at Langzhong by two of his underlings. He had since been deified, appropriately enough, as the patron saint of pork butchers.

A few days further up the Jialing River from Langzhong lay Guangyuan, the last major walled town in northeastern Sichuan. Even by his log book's sparse standards, Mesny's mention of Guangyuan is brief – just that he stopped at an inn on the main road – and notable for being the first of many occasions that he forgot to describe the many monumental Buddhist grottoes which lay across his route. Guangyuan's were especially unusual in that they commemorated the Tang-dynasty empress Wu Zetian, a great patron of Buddhism who, in Mesny's words, "is said to have invented women's' rights in China". As second wife to emperor Gaozong (she had also been his father's concubine), Wu Zetian skilfully charmed, manipulated and murdered her way to the throne, finally deposing her own son and founding a short-lived dynasty in 690. Though many other Chinese rulers have done far worse, Wu Zetian's reign contradicted Confucian sensibilities which placed women down towards the lower end of the social scale, and she was vilified by later historians. So it's feasible that vandalism and neglect at Guangyuan's grottoes had left little for Mesny to comment on, though photographs from the early twentieth century show the painted cliff sculptures here partly intact.

Departing Guangyuan just after New Year 1881, Mesny caught a boat to Chaotian town then turned north over the high, barren Chipan Pass, crossing from Sichuan into Shaanxi province. On the far side, Ningqiang was a disappointingly dull and expensive place, whose magistrate attempted to arrest him for impersonating a military officer and had to be threatened with a pistol. This disturbing near-repeat of the events at Qianxi escaped mention in Mesny's log books, which instead blandly noted that the increasingly cooler, drier climate favoured wheat and potatoes and that noodles, a northern Chinese staple, were replacing rice. Beyond here he regained the Jialing valley and followed it up past Lueyang, another dismal salt transport town. Then it was up and over the icy Minshan range, thick with dripping bamboo forests, and into Gansu province. Mesny had two fingers frostbitten in the mountains but it might have cheered him to know that on the same day, 15 January, the *China Mail* published a short version of his "Notes on a journey from Canton to Kwei-yang Fu up the Canton River", which had been rejected by British newspapers and which he later expanded for the *Miscellany*.

Two days later the party reached Tianshui, a prosperous, double-walled town where the old Silk Road between China and Central Asia intersected routes to Sichuan and Tibet. It was here that Zuo Zongtang had defeated the Hui warlord Ma Hualong in 1871, executing most of his family and thousands of his followers in the aftermath. Ma, considered by the Chinese to be one of the main instigators of the Tungan Revolt, had previously surrendered but refused to disband his troops, and Zuo suspected they had been covertly aiding lesser rebel leaders. Mesny's journal described the numerous mud-brick forts from this period still standing on surrounding hills and the ruins of the war-ravaged "old" Tianshui, but again omitted the monumental Buddhist art carved into a sandstone rock face at nearby Maji Shan, Wheatstack Mountain, which dated back to the fifth century.

Lanzhou, Mesny's initial target, lay north of Tianshui along the main highway, but Mesny decided to follow a lesser-known route via Qin'an county town. It seemed a popular detour, however; there were *lijin* customs posts at regular intervals and frequent encounters with mule teams laden with salt. Mesny's horses bolted at the sight of their first camel train, a string of over sixty double-humped Bactrians carting cut tobacco from Lanzhou; the clonking sounds of their wooden bells helped keep their handlers awake when they travelled at night. But it proved to be a dismal, bitterly cold journey: inns were unheated and there was nothing to eat beyond noodles and potatoes, or a type of flat bread moistened with hemp oil. The suppression of the Tungans had left former Muslim settlements utterly deserted, which added to the sense of desolation. By the time his party rejoined the main road at Dingxi six days later, Mesny was again suffering from frostbite. The town, strangely undamaged by the war, was prosperous and the highway here lined by a European-like avenue of trees, part of a greening project instigated by Zuo Zongtang during the 1870s. Zuo, who had been a gentleman farmer before becoming a soldier in middle age, liked the idea of European avenues and ordered a belt of trees to be planted along the main road between Henan in central China and Anxi, on the way to Hami – a distance of over 2500 kilometres. In 1881, a memorial by Zuo to the throne reported that "the elms and willows that had been planted along the sides of the roads have now grown into woods, and from [Jiayuguan] to the provincial capital [Lanzhou], there is an unbroken line of trees". A few hardy specimens survive to this day, often adorned in red ribbons and still known to locals as *zuogong liu*, "Lord Zuo's Willows".

Supplies remained scarce until they descended into a fertile valley at Gancao Dian – literally "Hay Store", an appropriate name for a caravan town – where snow had been carted down off the mountains for agriculture and drinking water. A few days later, on 28 January 1881, they reached the broad plain outside Lanzhou, passing a military camp and memorial temple to the recent conflict in the outer suburbs, and so entered under the city's east gate.

Mesny stayed twenty-five days at Lanzhou, the capital of Gansu province, celebrating the Chinese New Year. If he hadn't already known about Zuo Zongtang's recall he certainly learned of it now, as Zuo had passed through the city just three weeks earlier on his way to Beijing. So, with such a potentially huge reward in sight, why didn't Mesny follow him? His explanation was that Zuo was already too far ahead and travelling with great speed to Beijing, and that it would have been impossible to catch up before he arrived at the capital, but why this would have been a problem isn't clear. Instead, he put his case for the French loan to Gansu's acting viceroy, Yang Changchun, who kept him waiting for a reply.

Lanzhou filled the narrow neck of a valley where the clay-coloured Yellow River cut between high, crumbly hills. These ranges were part of the loess formation, a dry plateau covering a huge swathe of northern China, laid down over millions of years by the ever-shifting river. Loess was typically prone to deep vertical fracturing, the gritty, eroded landscape all shades of brown, yellow and grey and continually being sculpted and reshaped by an abrasive wind. The soil was fertile in itself, but Gansu's climate was of hot summers and icy winters with low rainfall, so the region tended towards arid semi-desert. Lanzhou was the only city in China actually located on the Yellow River, which despite being the country's second longest was barely suitable for navigation anywhere along its entire five thousand kilometres. At Lanzhou it was some 500 metres across, bridged through the summer by an unstable pontoon made of boats and iron chains; in winter, when the river froze solid, the western highway out of town crossed straight over the ice. At ground level the Yellow River appeared strikingly flat, the only level landmark in a bowl of rough brown peaks.

The city itself formed an irregular rectangle on the south bank, with a central commercial district flanked by separately-walled suburbs and a military quarter housing five battalions. It didn't look especially large but Mesny estimated the noisy, jostling population at 100,000 souls, most of them apparently recent migrants from Hunan. Lanzhou was yet another of China's cultural crossroads: westwards was the great Kumbum Lamasery at Xining and the fringes of the Tibetan world; to the north was Mongolia; Turkic Xinjiang lay northwest; while Han China sprawled eastwards. Arriving from the south, Mesny is likely to have been struck by how comparatively tall and solid the northwestern Chinese were; people here were also harder-faced and less openly friendly, the products of a harsher, less lavishly supplied land, one prone to extremes of climate and with settlements separated by vast distances.

Lanzhou's commercial reputation rested on its excellent tobacco, grown and processed in small-scale home industries. Mesny was impressed with the state of the city streets and also by the presence of handsome carts with heavy, studded wheels, on which everything was shifted about. Provisions were inexpensive and plentiful, and though few trees grew anywhere nearby, good-quality coal was available.

On the far side of the river was a hilly park offering good views over the city, whose coloured temple roofs stood out alongside the spires of accompanying pagodas. One of these, attached to a ruined temple in the south of Lanzhou, was a *bai gu ta* or "White Bone Tower", a memorial to soldiers killed during the foundation of the Han dynasty over two thousand years previously, and Mesny offered the plausible suggestion that *bai gu ta* might be the origin of the English word "pagoda". Renovations at the temple in 1987 uncovered a Ming dynasty noblewoman's tomb which was packed with gold, silver and jade ornaments: Lanzhou, despite the desolate setting, aftermath of war and apparent isolation, had once been a cultured place on the Silk Road, not in fact so distant from China's ancient capital, Xi'an.

Six years before Mesny's visit, a Russian "trade mission" had passed through Lanzhou on the last leg of a journey that had seen them circling around eastern China before heading up through the northwest and back home via Kazakhstan. It's difficult to see any real commercial aspect to the expedition, which was led by Colonel Sosnowski and was doubtless more interested in mapping out China's military strengths.

At Lanzhou they met Zuo Zongtang, by now in his early sixties, who was busy restoring the region to some semblance of order after his victory against the Tungans. Sosnowski described Zuo as "an excellent old man, very clever and well educated", though others in his team were less convinced of his qualities. Doctor Pavel Piasetski, the scientific officer (he also collected plants and authored *Journey to China*, a two-volume account of the expedition's progress), found Zuo polite but unimpressive: "He was small and stout, [with] barely three hairs in his beard, but his moustache was rather thicker. His movements were full of affectation and perhaps intended to produce a strong impression. I fear that in this he did not succeed."

Piasetski was also nettled that the Viceroy seemed oblivious to the Russians' status as ambassadors, though it appears that initially Zuo had no idea who these strange foreigners were. Later, when things had been explained, he received the Russians with great courtesy, loaded them with presents and invited them to several splendid banquets, where they were served German wine and questioned closely about European politics. Zuo was clearly adept at playing foreigners off against each other, and must have known that Russia and Britain were economic rivals, if not actually at war. He flattered his guests, confiding that he thought the British devious and untrustworthy compared with themselves, and railed against modernisations: "We do not require telegraphs and railways; the first would corrupt the people and the second bring them loss of work and consequent starvation". But the Russians repaid his efforts at hospitality with bluntness, sarcasm and criminal neglect – they only invited Zuo to dine on one occasion – and when they departed neither Zuo nor any other Chinese official put in an appearance to accompany them to Lanzhou's outskirts, as they would normally have done.

Whatever the Russians' opinions of him, Zuo had spent his three years at Lanzhou attempting to improve the city's infrastructure and industry. Alongside the city's outer wall stood a vast wooden water wheel, whose twelve buckets scooped water up out of the Yellow River and fed it into a series of oblong cisterns beside Zuo's mansion. Once the mud had settled out, the water was piped off to a public supply through a dragon-headed spout. Mesny seems to have believed that the entire apparatus was built by Zuo, though information at the site today credits the project to a Ming-dynasty engineer named Duan Xu; so perhaps Zuo just restored and improved its function. During the winter, or when the river periodically ran too low to operate the wheel, water was brought up using a steam-powered pump of foreign design: this inevitably broke down after a few years and, with nobody at Lanzhou capable of repairing the mechanism, Zuo had oxen-driven pumps installed instead.

Another of Zuo's inventions was the issuing of silver coins as a bridge between the necessarily large bunches of almost worthless copper cash and equally unwieldy tael ingots. These new coins, stamped in Chinese and Turkic as being worth one *qian* or a hundred copper cash, were used to pay soldiers' wages and, in the absence of a proper mint at Lanzhou, were struck at the city's arsenal using cartridge-making machinery. It's hard to appreciate just how huge an innovation the production of a moderately valuable currency for daily use was at the time in China, and the coins were such a success that not enough could be minted to keep up with demand. As often happened when a Chinese official displayed initiative, Mesny later asserted that the idea had originally been his, one he had recommended to Zuo during their meeting in Hankou in 1867 but which Zuo had rejected at the time as being unnecessary.

Lanzhou also had a steam-driven iron foundry for casting cannon, but the city's industrial showpiece was its woollen mill. This was yet again one of Zuo's projects, though not completed until long after he had left town. Thanks to the Muslim population's dietary restrictions and the arid, semi-desert conditions which prohibited other livestock, China's northwest was full of sheep, so fleeces were easy to procure and the mill had been set up by a German team: Theodore Ancke, a builder, and Franz Strom, a cloth manufacturer from Aachen, who had imported the modern looms and carding machinery. Despite Lanzhou being a three-month's journey from Shanghai's port and foreign community, the consortium funding the project had somehow been convinced that it would be cheaper and more efficient to site their factory here than transporting fleeces to the coast for manufacture.

Mensy was given a tour of the mill by the German management, who indulged him with excellent home-made beer. But the project's Chinese backers turned up late and then carelessly sent two low-ranking officers to show him around; Mesny felt slighted, and his article in the *China Mail* described a modern, efficiently-managed project headed by an "honest and intelligent foreign director" undermined by inefficient workers, official indifference and second-rate raw wool, the best of which was only fit for making the coarsest rugs and flannel. This sparked an angry rebuttal by the mill's managers, who admitted the poor quality of their product but protested that the mill had been operational for barely two years and that Mesny's criticism "appears to be not so much his desire to make correct statements as to give vent to his ill-feelings towards the mandarins and us foreigners, both parties not having treated him as he might have expected". They also wondered how Mesny's position as a drill instructor in the Chinese military qualified him as an expert on the woollen industry, especially given the brevity of his stay at Lanzhou.

While Mesny rarely had anything good to say about Germans, on this occasion he seems to have been fair enough, as within ten years "carelessness and rascality" had brought woollen manufacture at Lanzhou to a close.

Having managed to offend the city's tiny foreign contingent and with no encouragement from Governor Yang regarding his loan, Mesny decided to proceed northwest to Hami and talk directly with Zuo Zongtang's successor there, Liu Jintang. He headed west out of Lanzhou on 22 February, crossing the frozen Yellow River over the ice. The first stretch of road was barren and stony, scattered with devastated settlements and little temples to the Horse and Ox deities, along with a row of Tibetan prayer wheels and a curious pavilion with a domed roof and cruciform design, the only one Mesny had ever seen in China. At Pingfan there were two towns, one Chinese and one Muslim, then they were caught in a sandstorm. It began snowing and the road grew worse, but there was nowhere to shelter.

Travel beyond Lanzhou has always been an endurance test. Even today, comfortably cocooned inside modern, heated transport, it's a twenty-hour run to Hami by road or rail, and the same journey was to take Mesny seven weeks on foot across an increasingly bleak, hostile landscape. In this light, it's not difficult to sympathise with Mesny's growing obsession with developing China's transport infrastructure, but not everybody has felt the same way. During the 1920s, local warlords battled the Nationalist Government's attempts to lay rail lines through northwestern China, which would have made the region more accessible to centralised authority and so threatened their own power. It took until the 1990s for the track into Xinjiang to be completed.

And so they trudged on. Temples appeared in the middle of nowhere, simple grey boxes perched on ochre hilltops, and despite occasional villages there was little sign of cultivation; perhaps it was too early on in the year. Then, after Yongdang, they crossed over a ridge and suddenly descended into a large, well-irrigated valley, its seasonal waterways lined with poplars and willows. This was the entrance to the Hexi Corridor, a thousand-kilometre-long ribbon of gravel squeezed between parallel, snow-streaked mountain ranges – the Qilian to the south, the Bei Shan to the north – which stretched northwest into the distant haze. The location of towns within the corridor echoed where there was permanent snow on the mountain tops; in summer, meltwater was channelled down across the plains into irrigation canals, some of them run underground to minimize evaporation. Houses, each with bales of hay piled outside as winter fodder for their livestock, were excavated into sunken courtyards so that only the upper third of each building showed above ground – and that surrounded by a wall – as protection against extremes of temperature and the abrasive, ever-present wind. The ground was still frozen but at last there were fields and farmers ploughing them, and flocks of grubby sheep looking like brown tumbleweeds. They passed the Liangzhou White Pagodas, a group of 108 stupas marking the site where Tibetan officials submitted to the rule of the Mongol Yuan dynasty during the thirteenth century, one of the foundations for China's current claims over Tibet.

Mesny's route followed the flanks of the Qilian Mountains along what appeared to be a dry river bed, to where the twin pagodas of Wuwei rose out of the horizon. The town was neatly laid out on a cross pattern and mostly Chinese, with a smaller Manchu quarter, and there was a welcome supply of inexpensive goods. Even so, they nearly ran out of food on their next stage, arriving exhausted at Yongchang – a dusty few streets of mud-brick and timber buildings – after a forced march of nearly fifty kilometres through more atrocious weather.

Beyond Yongchang the view took in a brilliant rugged mountain range with birds of prey circling overhead, where their progress was slowed by farmers having deliberately breached dykes along the river to irrigate their fields after two years of drought. It was here that they first encountered substantial remnants of the Great Wall, scoured and raked for two thousand years of desert winds into a discontinuous, irregular line. Much of it stood less than two metres high, little more than an embankment, the former watchtowers and guard posts reduced to rectangular stumps. But it grew steadily in stature as they travelled westwards alongside it, rising ever more emphatically to a steady four metres, so that the wall's method of construction – by ramming the yellow loess soil into forms until it was concrete-hard – could be seen like tidemarks in its layered formation. Then the road itself cut right through the wall, leaving it to spin off southwest, running straight and clear into the distance.

Ahead lay a dusty prairie, home to semi-wild horses which had been bred for the Chinese military since the Han dynasty, and the market town of Shandan. It was here that Mesny finally took note of one of the many giant Buddha sculptures which lay across his route. Both Buddhism and monumental rock-carving skills had arrived along the Hexi Corridor from India at some point during the first century, leaving northwestern China awash in religious art, some of which covered entire cliff-faces in gigantic images of the Buddha and his acolytes in all their various incarnations. Shandan's were up against a cliff some way outside the town, protected from the elements inside a seven-storey gallery. At fifteen metres tall, the main statue was fairly modest in scale – China's largest is nearly five times its size – with painted robes and a gilded head, all seemingly carved from free-standing stone embellished with plaster.

At last came a proper town, Zhangye. Sandwiched between the long, snow-capped ranges, the solid walls formed a regular square, six kilometres in circumference, surrounded by faint traces of dried-up moat, all plopped down at the narrowest point in the Hexi Corridor. Three separate strands of the Silk Road converged here: the border with Mongolia was just sixteen kilometres north and camel trains continually lumbered through town, bringing in salt and exporting Zhangye's surplus grain, melons and vegetables. Street names echoed the faiths which had brought travellers safely through the deserts – Confucius Temple Alley, Horse God Road, Guildhall Lane, Xilai Temple Street – and the city was peppered with pagodas of all shapes and styles; round, square, Indian, Tibetan and even Burmese. One, a four-storeyed wooden affair which dated back over a thousand years, towered over Zhangye's low-set houses; it says something about China's immense sense of history that this pagoda was *first* rebuilt during the sixth century. Another ancient survival was a temple, built in 1098, whose main hall – its doors decorated with painted phoenixes, nearly sandblasted off with age – housed an attractively stylised reclining giant Buddha with enormous, individually sculpted toes.

Mesny paused at Zhangye for just two days on this occasion – he spent a month here on his way back from Hami – perhaps staying at the Shanxi Merchants' Guildhall which still stands on the east side of town, its wooden eaves a spray of interlocking beams carved as dragon heads. He set off again on 12 March, crossing the Hei River and an isolated patch of sand dunes which had buried two towns; antique archways could be seen emerging from the shifting mounds, constructed from small bricks which dovetailed into each other. Beyond the peaceable settlement of Gaotai, their carter told Mesny that the sandy plain ahead was Ko Pi Tan – the fabled Gobi Desert – and the next few days were spent skirting around its fringes on a badly potholed, difficult road. There wasn't much of a living to be made along the way, and many of the people they met suffered from goitres, but isolated patches of pasture somehow supported small villages and their livestock; they also saw wild deer, wolves and a few birds. The landscape was layered in dust, inches deep in places, and it must have been frustrating to struggle through such desiccation within constant sight of snow on the distant mountaintops.

Finally they picked up another avenue of Zuo Zongtang's trees and followed it into Jiuquan, at that time the last large town in provincial China. Jiuquan had been a Tungan stronghold, retaken by Zuo after a three month siege in 1872, which ended when German-made heavy artillery pounded their own way in through the city walls. Much was already in ruins, the insurgents having destroyed all the Chinese temples and slaughtered Jiuquan's citizens; Zuo returned the favour and had seven thousand Hui prisoners executed. Nine years after this mutual butchery, Mesny found Jiuquan recovered to some extent, the main street full of good-natured, bustling crowds. At the central crossroads stood a squat, grey brick drum tower – a common feature of Chinese towns, used to herald the dawn and dusk – whose labelled arches faced each point of the compass: "East lies Hua Mountain", "North through the desert", "South rise the Qilian mountains", "Head west for Hami". In fact it was impossible to head directly west from Jiuquan: marauders had always attacked from this direction and so the western gate had been bricked up years before.

Mesny doesn't mention him, but a Belgian named Paul Splingaerd – Lin Fuchen in Chinese – also arrived at Jiuquan later on in 1881. Splingaerd led a parallel, if far more successful life to Mesny: he was born in the same year and had accompanied the German explorer Ferdinand von Richthofen on his journey around China between 1868 and 1872; now the veteran statesman Li Hongzhang had appointed him customs inspector at this remote desert outpost. Splingaerd remained in the northwest for fifteen years, and later played an important role in securing Belgium's contract to build the train line between Beijing and Hankou, China's first major passenger railway, for which he was knighted by the Belgian king. In direct contrast to Mesny, Splingaerd's career is an example of how much a foreigner could achieve in China if he served in the civil administration instead of the military, and was prepared to progress slowly and selflessly court the goodwill of his superiors – things that Mesny was temperamentally ill-equipped to do.

From Jiuquan it was only thirty kilometres across another dreary gravel plain to Jiayuguan, a service town for a gigantic fortress built like a full stop at the westernmost tail of the Great Wall: in the Chinese mind this was the nation's final civilized frontier beyond which lay nothing worthwhile, only barbarity and Xinjiang's endless, searing deserts. The town proved relentlessly ordinary, stretched out along wide streets that were far too spacious for its scanty population, and Mesny, arriving late and exhausted after a long day's travel, barely mentioned the place. He left before dawn and at sunrise found himself beneath the fort's massive, tan-coloured adobe walls, their flat faces and crisp angles providing a comforting geometry against the surrounding, immense desolation.

Today, Jiayuguan's museum has its own take on local history, proclaiming that, since the earliest times, "Hexi was a land which had been open to the outside world and welcomed every nation." Which rather beggars the question of the fort's very existence, attached to the world's longest defensive wall. The current rectangular fortress was built during the Ming dynasty to guard a five-kilometre-wide pass between the snowy ridges of the Qilian Mountains to the south and the far lower, rugged Mazong Range. The defences comprised two layers of ribbed walls, the higher inner layer around ten metres tall and topped by substantial battlements, lookout posts and gate towers. Coming from the south, as Mesny did, you entered through iron-plated gateways into a square "quarantine" area between the inner and outer walls, where passports were inspected by red-cloaked guards and goods were checked for weapons and contraband while archers looked down from above. Assuming everything was in order, the inner gates were opened allowing access to the fort itself; fully manned, this might have been a bustling little hub, full of tents, people, livestock and noise. But nowhere does the Great Wall appear more imposing close-up and totally ineffectual at a distance, utterly dwarfed by the scenery. Mesny didn't leave much of a description but Major Clarence Dalrymple Bruce, travelling overland between India and Beijing in 1905, was unimpressed: after all, there was nothing to stop marauders simply riding around it.

The fort's most elaborate structure was its northern gate-tower, a three-storey wooden construction topped by a tablet reading *tianxia diyi xiongguan*, "The Foremost Toughest Pass in the World", the calligraphy supplied by Zuo Zongtang. Travellers heading northwest passed through a cobbled passageway underneath the tower, emerging into blinding sun: beyond the dust-hazed horizon lay Xinjiang, the "New Territories" of Chinese Turkestan. It had yet to become a proper province at the time of Mesny's journey, appearing on contemporary maps as an 1800 kilometre-broad *terra incognita* between Gansu and the Indian and Russian frontiers.

For exiled officials – such as the Opium War precipitator, Lin Zexu, who is commemorated at Jiayuguan with a statue – this was an infinitely bleak place to exchange China, with its teeming cities and refined culture, for a life of solitude and loneliness.

With the fort's gate at his back and a bitterly cold wind tearing down through the pass, Mesny now faced a nineteen-day slog across the desert to Hami; regularly-spaced shingle cairns marked the line of the road, which had otherwise been obliterated by dust and sand. He passed the future site of Yumen, a short-lived oil boom town during the 1990s and today the site of two enormous wind farms, whose forest of white towers and blades now fill the plain. Off to the south were small lakes and a patch of marshland but no greenery, the grass around the shoreline withering to straw as it grew.

The first proper settlement was Guazhou, a town that had been almost totally destroyed during the campaign against Yakub Beg, whose garrison was now a losing a second battle against the mobile sand dunes which threatened to engulf the city's walls. Southwest of Guazhou lay the former caravan town of Dunhuang: Mesny didn't mention the ancient Buddhist grottoes here because they had long-since been forgotten about; not until a couple of years after Mesny had finished publishing the *Miscellany* would Aurel Stein and Paul Pelliot uncover – and cart off to Europe – a treasure trove of Tang-dynasty manuscripts and paintings which had lain perfectly preserved for over a thousand years in Dunhuang's dry, sealed caves.

On the outskirts of Guazhou they paused at the eighteenth-century Longwang temple, where travellers prayed to the Dragon King for protection before crossing the difficult stretch of road ahead. Again it was freezing cold, Mesny envying the carters, who were sensibly dressed in heavy sheepskins against the incessant, cutting wind. Slowed by a sandstorm and a cart falling through a patch of thin ice into a bog, they pressed on through the night. Their reward the next morning was a dingy inn whose *kang* – a heated brick sleeping platform designed for the northern Chinese winters – was cold for want of fuel. A few more days of this rough, waterless terrain brought them to the rocky Xingxing pass, the modern border between Gansu and Xinjiang, where folklore held that the monkey deity Sun Wu Kong, cheeky hero of *Journey to the West*, was born from a stone egg. Here they negotiated an extinct volcano crater, seventy metres across, where the carts had to be lowered carefully down the steep sides on ropes.

It is a sad fact that there are times when travel can be a numbingly dull endurance test with little sense of striving towards a worthy goal. Moments of purpose and drama tend to be added later, when mental notes have been sorted through and it becomes clear which experiences led somewhere and which were dead ends – the times when you were, in fact, simply spending a day in discomfort for no good reason. But for Mesny, there were at last signs that his party was nearing their destination: other travellers on the road, busy inns and an increasing amount of fresh food. On 12 April 1881 they sighted a customs post – sure evidence of a Chinese presence – and an elaborately tiled Islamic mausoleum "of a green colour and shaped like a round tower with a dome." Having spent more than two years on his journey from Guangzhou, Mesny had arrived at Hami.

Hami was technically independent. The line of its khans dated back to 1697, when the Qing emperor Jiajing granted hereditary rule to the local warlord Erbedula. But at the time of Mesny's visit, Hami was effectively under Chinese martial law, an unconvincing city whose separately walled districts lacked any unifying purpose or focus. At the centre was a Chinese area confusingly known as the "Old Town", founded during the early eighteenth century and now occupied by a barefoot and badly-equipped military; the original settlement lay to the south of here, an entirely Muslim maze of irregular lanes and mud-brick houses. To the north was a growing "New Town" full of traders and, north again, the satellite residence of the Manchu Imperial Commissioner. The Old Town and Muslim districts had been virtually destroyed during Yakub Beg's rebellion and were still recovering; despite well-cultivated farmland planted with grain, maize, melons and fruit trees, all provisions were expensive, and manual labour even more so.

In the Muslim area, survivors from the pre-war days told of Hami's former glories when "everyone lived like a king" on the back of the town's silk farms. The Uighur population spoke and wrote a Turkic language similar to Kirghiz and were generally polite and obliging to foreigners, though the Han Chinese viewed them as untrustworthy and violent, a people whose constant belligerence had lost China control of the Silk Road and its rich trade. All Uighurs wore turbans but the women went unveiled and were "prettier than the Chinese, and not shy". At one of Hami's many mosques, brick-paved affairs of courtyards and galleries, Mesny met Yussuf Akchun, the former Governor of Kashgar who had been deposed by Yakub Beg. Yussuf, whom Mesny described as an intelligent, intellectual and hospitable gentleman, was being detained at Hami in disgrace rather than being reinstated to his former position at Kashgar, because he had earlier aided the British Forsyth Mission.

The domed mausoleum that Mesny had passed on his approach to the city contained the tombs of Hami's khans, including that of Muhammad Bixir, Hami's seventh ruler, who died in 1867 during Yakub Beg's revolt and was succeeded by his son Wulamidin. A mosque stood nearby, its simple whitewashed walls with upswept eaves and cupola a successful fusion of Chinese and Islamic themes. Today, a notice at the site reads: "All the princes of Hami played positive roles in stabilizing Xinjiang, putting down rebellion and defending the unification of the country" – again, at odds with why the Chinese military was here in the 1880s, asking for money to subdue the region.

After enduring several nights at an obnoxious inn, Mesny met with Zuo's replacement and understudy, Liu Jintang, who was gearing up to kick the Russians out of the Ili valley and thought that the French loan was a splendid scheme. There was still a shortfall of funds: the Chinese government believed that, in the event of war, Russia would immediately annex the strategic Zhoushan islands off the coast near Shanghai and take control of the lower Yangzi basin; so military efforts were being directed in that direction, with little money earmarked for the Ili campaign. Liu made Mesny thoroughly welcome, suggested raising the loan to twenty million dollars, offered to use his position to bring the matter to Zuo Zongtang's attention and promised Mesny a commission to purchase all the modern guns and artillery his army would need. Indeed, Liu was so enthusiastic that it's difficult not to believe that he was making fun of this eager foreigner – or at least keeping his options open by encouraging him to stick around – though at the time Mesny himself was convinced of Liu's sincerity.

So Mesny settled down for two months at Hami, waiting for Liu to confirm the deal, studying the local version of Turkish and compiling a comprehensive journal – later lost – on Chinese Turkestan. Then news arrived of the Treaty of St Petersburg, signed on the 24 February 1881 – six weeks before Mesny had even arrived at Hami and on the very day that Zuo Zongtang had reached Beijing. The Russians now agreed to vacate Ili in return for trading rights, new consulates in Xinjiang and an indemnity of nine million roubles.

It seemed at first that these terms were even worse than the original Treaty of Livadia for which Chong Hou had been sentenced to death – Russia had then demanded only five million roubles, and no consulates – but the new version was held to be a triumph because China was no longer required to cede any territory. The very time that it had taken for the news to arrive at Hami proved how isolated Xinjiang was, and why there were doubts about the value of defending it given the more immediate threats that the empire was facing in eastern China. But as far as Mesny was concerned, St Petersburg was a disaster: the Russians were clearing out of Xinjiang without a fight and all Chinese forces in the region were to be disbanded. There was no longer any need for the loan.

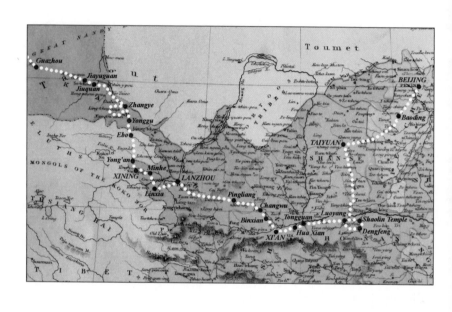

ROAMING THE NORTH: HAMI TO BEIJING
JULY 1881 – 4 FEB 1882

Crushed, Mesny considered his options. Returning to central China was the least of them: ahead lay caravan routes running for well over a thousand kilometres across Xinjiang's two desert basins to the borders of Central Asia, India and Russia; the very territory that Gill had so badly wanted to explore. There was no doubt that had Mesny successfully completed this journey his reputation would have been made, but again his plans were foiled.

Months later, having tramped the 800 kilometres back south to Zhangye in defeat, Mesny wrote to the *China Mail* complaining that he had been unable to get beyond Hami "for the want of a special permit or passport. [Liu Jintang], the Commander-in-Chief of the Chinese army in Turkestan, gave me permission to go [to Ili], but when I was ready to start, he withdrew his permission on the plea that the roads in that quarter were not safe for travellers etc, and advised me to return the way I came, giving me money for my travelling expenses (carts, fuel, food and forage for myself and attendants) all the way back to Lan-chou."

In the *Miscellany*, Mesny adds: "I also offered to travel across the Chinese frontiers to Afghanistan in one direction and to Kashmir in another, in order to ascertain the feelings of China's neighbours in those directions, but Liu would not listen to my counsel, so I resigned [my position as advisor to him] and returned to China". Bitter at the collapse of his financial and travel prospects, Mesny became spiteful towards the man who stood in his way: "Liu is rather young for the position he holds; and the Central Government will do well to send an experienced politician to take supreme control of the affairs in the new territory... his disregard and ignorance concerning the Mighty Powers in Central Asia unfit him for the post." The Imperial court thought otherwise and, when Xinjiang was granted full provincial status in 1884, appointed the forty-year-old Liu as its first viceroy.

And so, in mid-July 1881, Mesny found himself back amongst Zhangye's temples and pagodas. Having sped through the town on his way north to Hami, he now decided to linger for a couple of weeks and investigate the arid Qinghai plateau to the west, where he had heard that there were gold mines. The plateau sat on the fringes of the Tibetan world and it wasn't long before Mesny stumbled across a black-tented encampment of nomadic Fanzi – a derogatory term which he assumed simply meant "Tibetans". The women fed him *tsampa* and gossiped that a prospective husband had to give "at least a mare, 5 cows, 50 sheep and 4 pieces of calico or serge" to the bride's relatives – a complete reversal of mainstream Chinese notions, where it was the woman's family who paid the dowry.

Gold was, in fact, fairly scarce in the area, but a workable pocket was being panned in a dry riverbed by fifty Chinese. Mesny was "shown handsfull of gold nuggets varying in size from a turnip seed to a pea and I was told that lumps of several taels in weight were occasionally unearthed". He had a search around himself and found traces of platinum, though local miners were at a loss how to work it because of the extremely high temperatures required.

Returning once again to Zhangye, Mesny decided not to retrace any more of his outward route and on 18 August set out on a lengthy detour south towards the Tibetan monastery town of Xining. He was diverted by flooding along the Dasha River, but otherwise made good time past the usual run of small walled settlements, patches of gravel desert and scattered valleys planted with corn and poppies. Yonggu, at the foot of the Qilian ranges, had been badly mauled during the Muslim rebellion, though trade was picking up again in rhubarb, spirits and especially deer antler, valued as a strengthening tonic in Chinese medicine. Here Mesny collected an armed military escort for a trek over the mountains to the rat-infested, mud-brick fortifications of Ebo, beyond which were more mountains, gold diggings, outlandish Tibetans, yaks and huge flocks of small-tailed sheep guarded by mastiffs. Both the escort and their pack animals became frisky as the convoy approached Yong'an, a bustling garrison town founded in 1725 during a war with Tibet; today Yong'an has been abandoned and its crumbling outer wall stands empty amongst an undulating patchwork of barley fields.

Three more days at this steady pace – hardly slowing even to cross the Datong River on an inflated ox-hide raft – brought Mesny to Xining at the start of September. Xining's small size – barely a kilometre across – belied its nominal function as the capital of Qinghai province, which sprawled westwards in a blaze of infinite horizons, grey-brown gravel plains and enormous, shimmering salt lakes. The city centre formed a torpid collection of government buildings housing the Chinese and Manchu administration, and most of Xining's citizens lived outside the walls in a lively jumble of lanes full of butchers, bakers and restaurants. Alongside a floating mass of Tibetans, Salars and Mongols, perhaps three-quarters of the city's permanent residents were Muslim, and veiled women were a common sight on the streets. Though infinitely remote from eastern China, a posting here could be profitable: Xining's authorities issued passes to merchants crossing Qinghai into Mongolia and Tibet, but as these were valid for only forty days and inevitably expired long before the merchants could complete their journeys, officials made a good living by collecting fines and bribes. This was countered by a healthy smuggling industry, especially in tea.

Much to the annoyance of Xining's Chinese officials, who regarded Tibetans as little more than troublesome savages, a deputation of lamas appeared shortly after Mesny's arrival and coaxed him away to stay at Kumbum. This monastery, which lay twenty kilometres southwest of the town, was one of Tibet's great religious hubs: Tsongkhapa, founder of the dominant yellow-hat Gelugpa sect, had been born nearby in 1357, and the monastery itself was built beside a sandalwood tree said to have sprung from drops of blood scattered from his umbilical cord. At his death in 1419, Tsongkhapa left behind two continually reincarnating disciples who became the heads of the Gelugpa order: the Dalai Lama, considered to be the earthly embodiment of the Bodhisatva of compassion, Avalokitesvara; and the Panchen Lama, that of the spiritually wise Bodhisatva Manjusri. As "joint popes", they shared temporal and spiritual authority until the aggressive fifth Dalai Lama, Lobsang Gyatso, made himself effective sovereign of all Tibet during the seventeenth century.

Set at the foot of a flat-topped hill, Kumbum formed a sizeable community of between two and three thousand lamas. There was a whitewashed shanty-town of monks' quarters, a clutch of double-roofed halls capped in brilliant gold tiles off to one side, bulbous chortens, the smell of yak butter, the clunking rattle of prayer wheels being spun by pilgrims, red-beaked choughs nesting under the temple eaves and monks prostrating themselves full-length in the main hall before a solid gold statue of Tsongkhapa. In one small courtyard, a stump of the original holy tree still struggled to put out spindly branches, the leaves mysteriously decorated with Tsongkhapa's image. Mesny was surprised to find that Kumbum's monks looked to the Panchen Lama, rather than Dalai Lama, as head of the Tibetan church (a division exploited during the 1940s by the local Muslim warlord Ma Bufang, who consolidated his hold over Qinghai by allowing the Panchen Lama to set up a self-governing state at Kumbum, independent of his religious rival's authority at Lhasa).

Mesny was not the first European to visit Kumbum; the determined French missionary Abbé Huc had lived here for several months in 1845, learning Tibetan and waiting to join a caravan to Lhasa. He succeeded only to be expelled by the Chinese the following year, becoming the last European to reach the Tibetan capital for nearly sixty years. Mesny now made some hopeful enquiries of his own about routes into Tibet, but the lamas told him that war and banditry had made the journey impossible. Several years previously, two pilgrims had actually reached Lhasa along the old road from Kumbum, but their trip had been so fraught with dangers that they had been forced to return the long way around through western Sichuan, and nobody had even attempted the journey since.

Leaving Xining on 6 September, Mesny and a fresh but poorly-armed escort followed the Huangshui southeast along the main Xining–Lanzhou road, occasionally encountering mule trains weighted down with coal, pepper and cloth. Three days brought the party to Minhe from where – perhaps to avoid paying duty at inter-provincial customs posts – they made another long detour by dropping south and inland, well away from main roads. At Guanting town Mesny spent a sleepless night being devoured by vermin and the next day crossed the Yellow River, here running wide and very fast, in a tiny ferry which was pushed over by the boatman swimming behind. Then came Muslim-dominated Linxia, a Sufi town famous for its mosques and abrasive population. In eastern China, most temples – Taoist, Muslim, Buddhist, Confucian – tend to follow the same basic architectural patterns and can be difficult to tell apart, but in this part of the country mosques sported minarets and distinctively pointed domes, capped in green tiling. Mesny was now as distant from Lanzhou as when he left the main road at Minhe, and his party took a further ten days to complete their journey.

Thanks to his ill-advised opinions on the woollen mill, there was no friendly welcome waiting for Mesny at Lanzhou. Within two days of his arrival on 27 September, "receiving no encouragement to stay there", he was on his way again with his luggage loaded aboard three mule carts, heading southeast towards Xi'an, China's great inland metropolis and former Imperial capital. Yet again, he avoided the obvious highway in favour of a less-travelled route through the dry valleys of Ningxia and eastern Gansu, where cave houses could be seen cut into the fractured loess landscape. These dwellings were dug into suitable cliffsides as a single-chambered arched tunnel lined with bricks; at night you slept on a heated brick *kang*, scorched on one side and frozen on the other, which in this treeless region was fuelled with dried dung. Mesny spent at least one unhappy night lodged underground, half-suffocated by fumes.

Across the border in Shaanxi province, the town of Changwu had been ransacked by the Nian rebels in 1868 and still lay ruinous and dirty, but beyond lay the intriguing Jing He valley, which Mesny followed down towards Binxian. Here was more cave architecture but on a monumental scale, with an entire temple complex excavated from a prominent sandstone bluff. "In all directions are the doors and windows of the cave dwellings, one tier communicating with another above by means of stairways formed in the face of the cliff. Here also is the entrance to the temple. A long corridor conducts to a semicircular hall which receives its light through openings in the roof overhead. In this semicircle are three gigantic figures of Buddha cut, like all others here, from the red sandstone. The central and largest figure faces the entrance to the corridor, the lesser images [of Guanyin and Dashizhi, representing compassion and intelligence] being erected, one either side, in the semicircle. The central figure is about 90 feet high and is seated in the pose usually represented, with the legs crossed, the hands resting on the knees, and the face expressive of deep reflection." The temple dated back a millennium to a great flowering of Buddhism under the Tang dynasty and was being restored after suffering vandalism during the Muslim revolt; in fact the sculptures – which survive today – are only around sixty feet tall but, thickly gilded, looming, impassive and beatific in the gloom, they make a powerful impression. Further down the valley, a similar temple dedicated to the Monkey King had been excavated at this deity's fabled home, Huaguo Shan – "The Mountain of Fruit and Flowers".

After Binxian it was a straightforward journey south to Qianling and the imposing mausoleum of Wu Zetian, the Tang dynasty empress whose hometown, Guangyuan in northern Sichuan, Mesny had passed back in January. Her tomb consisted of two large artificial hills guarded by an avenue of stone animals and officials, many of them now sadly decapitated, but the wonder of the site was the "Wordless Stele", a huge square-sided pillar standing out in the open on its own. These steles were usually carved with salutary accounts of the monarch's reign but Wu Zetian's had been left blank and mute on her own orders, perhaps because the empress wasn't proud of her achievements – which had included overthrowing an emperor, having half her own family executed and disguising her lover as a monk. But given that she had also been a fervent patron of Buddhism, had overseen an efficient administration, encouraged the education of women and hadn't involved the nation in any costly wars, Wu Zetian was perhaps more deserving of praise than many of her male counterparts.

From Qianling, the final eighty kilometres of road to Xi'an passed more tomb mounds, far smaller than Wu Zetian's but still impressive in quantity, which lay clustered in the fields surrounding the comfortable, old-fashioned town of Xianyang – curiously dismissed by Mesny as "producing nothing but ancient relics and giddy women". Locals believed these to be the graves of other Tang emperors but they were in fact far older, dating back to before 220 B.C. when Xianyang had been the capital of the Qin, China's first imperial dynasty.

What makes Mesny's time at Xi'an unusual is how little his travel log says about the place: the entry for 22 October reads simply "Arrived Si-Ngan", followed by a ten-day blank. Whilst dynastic archaeology didn't pick up here for almost another century, with the discovery of the unnervingly realistic Terracotta Army guarding the tomb of China's despotic first emperor, Xi'an was certainly no backwater in 1881. An imperial capital for over a thousand years and the one-time eastern terminus of that cultural conduit, the Silk Road, the city still covered some fifteen square kilometres and was capable of reminding visitors of a second Beijing, with its equally imposing Ming dynasty walls, abundant ancient architecture, thriving markets and broad streets. The enterprise and wealth of its well-travelled merchants were legendary; with guildhalls in almost every city in China, Xi'an's businessmen owned most of the tea factories at Ya'an in Sichuan and similarly controlled Lanzhou's tobacco industry. But, as usual, Mesny's journal fails utterly when it comes to providing a description. Some historians have accused Marco Polo (whose ghost-written *Travels* omitted to include such essentially Chinese subjects as the Great Wall, chopsticks and bound feet) of never visiting China and merely spinning tales from gossip he'd picked up from merchants in Central Asia. By the same standards, Mesny – whose journals were written on the spot and yet are full of the most glaring and obvious gaps – might have never left Britain.

The highway east of Xi'an was relatively good, shaded by Zuo Zongtang's willows and with sturdy stone bridges crossing numerous streams along the way. Known since antiquity as the "Luoyang Road", it followed the Yellow River basin through the cradle of Chinese civilization, a route thick with historic and cultural monuments.

At Lintong, Mensy passed another artificial hill marking the subterranean tomb of Qin Shi Huang Di, China's first emperor, a mound which remains unexcavated to this day despite rumours of its jewelled magnificence – rivers of mercury, a bronze mausoleum the size of a miniature city, the "sky" a firmament of pearls and precious stones – being written up as early as the first century. Next came Hua Xian, the town where the Tungan Revolt had begun as an argument over the price of bamboo poles, which was being rebuilt from scratch after its utter destruction at the start of the rebellion. Hua Xian was also notorious for its prostitutes but Mesny stayed at an unusually excellent inn and visited a lavish temple dedicated to the deities of Hua Shan, the bald granite ranges rising immediately to the south. The mountains were holy to Taoism and their precipitous peaks were dotted with tiny temples, all connected by alarmingly basic ladders and iron chains bolted onto the sheer cliff faces. A popular tale held that the mountain had been staked in a game of chess between the Taoist mystic Chen Tuan, and Taizu, founder of the Song dynasty, who wanted to build a fort here. Chen Tuan won – he could see into the future and anticipated the emperor's every move – and the mountain remained in Taoist hands.

From Hua Xian it was half a day's journey to Tongguan, where the Yellow River, here relatively shallow and about 500m wide, was deflected sharply eastwards by the tail end of the Hua Shan range. Though Tongguan town itself was entirely insignificant, enormous fortifications on the hill above guarded what was seen as the gateway to eastern China; ingeniously constructed from interlocking blocks and reputedly "stronger than iron", the walls and their monumentally huge gates had stood here since long before the wandering poet Du Fu described them back in the eighth century. Passing an elegant pagoda of enamelled yellow and green bricks, the road then followed the south bank and the rest of the journey was memorable only for trains of unusually large mules, able to carry heavy loads of salt, sweet dates and fighting quails, and an oppressive poverty. The region was still recovering from a ghastly famine a decade earlier, when times had been so desperate that Mesny was told how mothers had been forced to eat their children "and human flesh was publicly on sale in the markets".

In mid-November the party arrived at Luoyang, another one of China's former imperial capitals and site of two famous places of pilgrimage: Guanlin Temple, where the loyal Three Kingdoms general Guan Yu was buried; and a procession of thousand-year-old Buddhist statues flanking a riverside rock face at the nearby Longmen gorge. Neither of these renowned sights are described by Mesny, who instead spent his time interviewing a party of Jews from the declining community at Kaifeng, a large city some 150 kilometres further east. Nobody was too sure whether the Kaifeng Jews had arrived in China as early as the Tang dynasty or as late as the Yuan, but now their dilapidated synagogue had been demolished by a flood and the small congregation were scattered, unable to read their remaining Hebrew texts and visually indistinguishable from other Chinese. Mesny remembered having seen one of the last surviving Kaifeng Torahs at Hong Kong during one of his visits; another had been collected by missionaries and presented to the British Museum in 1851.

Mesny spent the following week on a circuit from Luoyang that took him up into the rambling Song Shan range to the Shaolin Temple, "a monastery of 40 monks famous for their skill in fencing and for the good table they keep". The temple was one of the earliest homes of Chan (Zen) Buddhism, a school which used meditation to achieve spontaneous enlightenment. Chan was brought to the temple by the sixth-century Indian monk Da Mo, who, according to legend, also taught Shaolin's monks exercises based on animal movements to counter their lengthy bouts of inert introspection. Like many isolated communities in China, Shaolin needed to defend itself against bandit raids and the monks developed Da Mo's calisthenics into a fighting system, which became famous across China after Shaolin's warrior priests aided Li Shimin – the future Tang emperor Taizong – in his rise to power. They repeated the favour a thousand years later for the Qing emperor Kangxi, who donated examples of his calligraphy extolling their deeds – "First in Bravery; Matchless Heroes" – after Shaolin's abbot humbly refused all other rewards. The monks encouraged Mesny to settle down with them for a year or two, and though he declined their offer, he took time to look around. "The walls of the various halls of this monastery are covered with pictures representing the various historical battle scenes, in which the monks bore a conspicuous part. Their weapons are of various kinds, but their exercises are usually performed with single sticks, quarter-staves and clubs". Having been burned down by another warlord during the 1920s, today a resurrected Shaolin has become a commercial shrine to the modern Chinese cult of kung fu, swamped in tourists and surrounded by martial arts schools founded by former monks. The temple's battle murals and the "grand old trees" that Mesny mentions are still there, the latter scarred from generations of fighters using them to toughen their fingers by tearing bare-handed at the bark.

An hour's walk through the hills behind Shaolin brought Mesny to the red-walled Yongtai temple, another Zen establishment with an accompanying pagoda nestled amongst trees at foot of the Song Shan escarpment; Yongtai's nuns were famed for their immorality and had abandoned the temple because of the recent famine. Then it was on to the small town of Dengfeng and the Zhongyue temple – Taoist this time – where annual sacrifices were made in the emperor's name. The halls were grandly scaled and adorned with life-sized, cast iron statues of warrior guardians, but an air of neglect hung over everything and Mesny noted that "the people about here seem an idle and dissolute lot".

Rounding off his religious excursion, Mesny returned to Luoyang via the Baima Temple, said to be where Buddhism was introduced to China from India during the first century. Baima was also, according to the *Miscellany*, where the future Tang empress Wu Zetian withdrew in retirement as a nun after the death of her first patron, the emperor Taizong, and from where she scandalously ensnared the affections of his son and successor, Gaozong.

On November 24 Mesny finally left the Yellow River valley behind, bearing north from Luoyang in a three-week journey to Taiyuan, capital of coal-rich Shanxi province. The highway, though initially in poor condition, was extremely busy: inns along the way piled high with bales of goods and village streets almost impassable with slow-moving camel trains and other traffic. An icy wind tore down from the north, the winter countryside was dreary and a feeling of imminent unrest lay over the land; Mesny witnessed a brawl between a party of muleteers and some "rough looking characters" attempting to extort an ad-hoc toll for using a bare-plank bridge. Travellers along the road were supposedly protected by a string of regularly-spaced guard posts, though many were closed up and the few soldiers that were on duty seemed young and ineffectual.

Taiyuan, like many large settlements in northern China, was surrounded by suburbs, tombs, and temples in varying stages of decay. The city proper was laid out on the eastern bank of the river Fen, nominally protected from flooding by statues of mythical *qilin* (a blend of dragon, tiger and deer) and a pair of cast-iron rhinoceros. Yet despite its status as a provincial capital, Taiyuan had the air of some long-declining outpost: parts of the city had been abandoned – the southern and western districts were a quagmire of ponds and slippery muddy embankments which resisted all attempts to drain them – and the overall population was relatively small. The twenty-kilometre-long string of walls were visibly falling apart, the near-useless gates guarded by pairs of antique cannon; and a couple of *feng shui* pagodas, dilapidated with age and neglect, leant at rakish angles against the city's skyline.

Threading his way through Taiyuan's southern suburbs in the mid-afternoon of 11 December, Mesny had installed himself at the poorly-furnished Fu Yuan Lang inn, when he was shocked to discover that his bag, containing mineral samples and gems, along with a 650-page journal of his travels through the northwest, had gone missing. According to an article Mesny wrote at the time for the *China Mail*, the authorities were not sympathetic to his loss: "I called on the Governor [Wei Rongguang] yesterday, but he declined to receive me, and on hearing the account of my lost baggage, asked for a list of the contents, which I quickly furnished to the best of my recollection, but it is very difficult to get him to believe that my baggage comprised such a valuable amount of Precious Stones and Jewelry, such as my lost bag actually contained. If, say the Officials, your baggage was only worth a few hundred taels the matter could easily be settled, but the settlement of several tens of thousands is quite another affair."

Shanxi had suffered a large turnover of governors during the previous few years; Wei Rongguang, a thrifty, unpretentious man, was himself expecting to be replaced in the immediate future and was doubtless unwilling to cloud his final weeks in office by admitting responsibility – and paying out a substantial sum – for a lost bag containing a wealth that nobody had ever seen.

While waiting for the authorities to act, Mesny visited Taiyuan's various Christian missions: the Protestants were running hospitals and orphanages, while the Catholics had "a respectable looking cathedral in the Corinthian style" and claimed ten thousand converts throughout Shanxi province, a priest asserting that one of their earliest bishops in China had met Marco Polo. Shanxi's dry climate favoured grapes and the Catholics made their own wine; Mesny found their claret "undistinguishable from Bordeaux wine". Many of these foreign missionaries and their Chinese converts were later killed during the "Taiyuan Massacre" of 1900, one of the sadder chapters of the xenophobic Boxer Rebellion.

Meanwhile, Taiyuan's treasurer became hostile towards Mesny and questioned his right to even be in the city, let alone claim such outrageous reparations. Keeping his temper, Mesny retorted that as a decorated officer in the Chinese military he had every right to travel from one end of China to the other if he felt like it. But it was clear that the authorities were more interested in avoiding blame and milking the situation rather than actively searching for his property: Mesny learned that his carter, whom he had sent to the courthouse to give evidence, had instead been stripped of his fur coat and fined 3,000 cash by the court staff. After contradictory rumours of his bag's whereabouts fizzled out, the search was called off on Christmas day and Taiyuan's authorities, while offering to provide Mesny with travelling expenses, refused to accept responsibility or pay out any compensation over the incident.

Leaving Taiyuan on 9 January 1882, Mesny headed northeast towards the national capital, Beijing, still 400 kilometres away across the frozen, featureless north China plains. Although he didn't realise it, this unprepossessing stage was to mark a watershed in Mesny's travels, one where he would encounter the two men who were to influence the remainder of his working life. Up until now he had been a footloose adventurer; afterwards, he would be searching for a career, attempting to establish himself as an authority on modernisation.

Thirteen days into his journey, Mesny arrived at Baoding, the densely crowded capital of now-defunct Zhili province. Its viceroy was Li Hongzhang, the scholar-turned-general who had offended Gordon and wrangled with Zuo Zongtang over military funding for the northwest. Li had since risen to become one of the most powerful men in China: in 1874 he had raised a private army in support of the Empress Dowager Cixi during a palace coup, which successfully overthrew a faction which wanted to depose the child emperor Guangxu. The aftermath saw Cixi become China's effective ruler, and as a reward Li was appointed Senior Grand Secretary; his post at Zhili – the province which surrounded and protected Beijing – was a further sign of how deeply he was trusted by the Imperial court.

Whilst Li Hongzhang and Cixi were both utterly convinced of China's cultural superiority, Li was, unlike the Empress Dowager, also keen to introduce foreign technology: he was a great advocate of railways and steamships and only a month before Mesny's arrival at Baoding had overseen the construction of China's first long-distance telegraph line. However, a famous statement by Li made it clear that China's reform faction was not necessarily pro-Western, simply pro-modernisation: "In order to transform China into a strong nation we must acquire the use of modern weapons, and for this we must install machinery for making those weapons. By learning foreign methods, we shall no longer depend on the foreigners' services." Li's diplomatic career was to develop into a delicate balancing act between foreign powers and Chinese political factions. In the process he became a figurehead in the Western mind for all that was grand but devious in Chinese bureaucracy, the subject of several English-language biographies, and a fictional set of memoirs.

Mesny now secured an interview with Li, proposing a raft of schemes for introducing railways, mining and communications to China's interior. But Li, perhaps feeling that he already knew more about these subjects than Mesny did himself, seemed disinterested. And so Mesny continued on his way to Zhouzhou, a few days short of Beijing, where he arrived on 2 February 1882. Here he found Zhang Zhidong, a highly-ranked classical scholar who had successfully filled various important civil posts but would doubtless have led an unspectacular, if distinguished, career had he not submitted a memorial to the throne in 1880 which severely criticised Russia's occupation of Ili. At a time when craven submission to foreign threats was the norm, Zhang Zhidong's outspoken patriotic fervour drew praise from the powers in Beijing, and he was now on his way to Taiyuan to replace Wei Rongguang – the official who had failed to find Mesny's missing luggage – as Shanxi's governor.

During a long interview that evening, Zhang showed considerable interest in Mesny's progressive schemes and offered him a position as an advisor on foreign affairs. Mesny, who was desperate to reach Beijing, replace his travel-stained wardrobe and collect long-awaited mail – and perhaps even enjoy some foreign company – agreed, promising to rejoin Zhang at Taiyuan in mid-February, after the Chinese New Year.

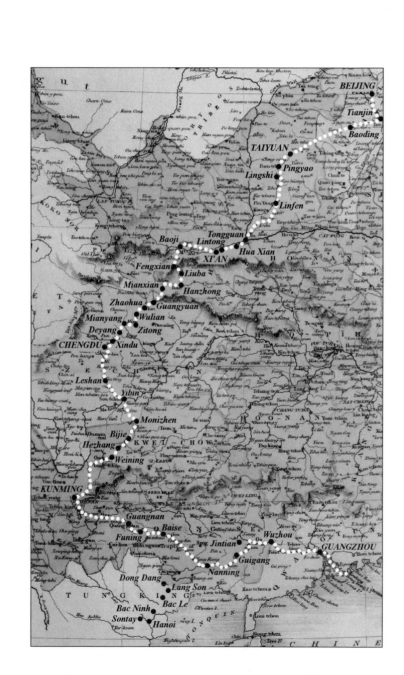

BEIJING
Tianjin
Baoding
TAIYUAN
Pingyao
Lingshi
Linfen
Baoji
Tongguan
Lintong
Hua Xian
XI'AN
Fengxian
Liuba
Mianxian
Hanzhong
Zhaohua
Guangyuan
Mianyang
Wulian
Deyang
Zitong
CHENGDU
Xindu
Leshan
Yibin
Monizhen
Bijie
Hezhang
Weining
KUNMING
Guangnan
Baise
Funing
Jintian
Wuzhou
Guigang
GUANGZHOU
Nanning
Dong Dang
Lang Son
Bac Ninh
Bac Le
Sontay
Hanoi

TUNGKING
1882–85

On 4 February 1882, Mesny entered Beijing over the stone arches of the twelfth-century Lugou bridge, which he describes grandiosely as the "Highway for all Nations" but was better-known amongst British expatriates as the Marco Polo bridge. Here his log books end, but the following months are sketched out in the *Miscellany* and new articles that Mesny wrote for the Shanghai-based *North China Herald*, the country's most respected English-language newspaper. These pieces were initially unsigned (though internal evidence proves that Mesny was their author), but later appeared under his old pen-name, "Pioneer".

At Beijing, Mesny had probably hoped to catch up at last with Zuo Zongtang, but would have been disappointed once again: Zuo had already left the capital for a visit to his home province, Hunan, on his way to take up a governorship in southern China. The battle-hardened campaigner was by now seventy years old, blind in one eye and in poor health; he had felt uncomfortable at Beijing, where his down-to-earth manners were unappreciated by the palace's grasping, self-important courtiers. But, if he hadn't known already, Mesny now discovered that he had been awarded the right to wear a second-rank red button on his hat (even though he technically retained his third-level, blue-buttoned status), and that his ancestors for three generations had been posthumously canonised. He also managed to wrangle an interview with the British Minister to China, Sir Thomas Wade, and Sir Robert Hart, who headed up China's largely British-run Maritime Customs Service – and so, indirectly, had been Mesny's employer during his days as a "tide waiter" at Hankou.

The authoritative old China hands showed polite interest in Mesny's travels, but declined to offer any financial support for his schemes to develop mining, telegraphs and railways across China's remote hinterland; in fact, they advised Mesny to settle down and build a career for himself at one of the treaty ports. While this was being realistic enough – foreign financiers had no intention of risking direct, large-scale investments in such an unstable country – their patronising brush-off must have been galling. Unlike most of his contemporaries, Mesny saw so much potential in China's interior.

Intriguingly, Mesny's entry in *Who's Who in the Far East 1906* also claimed that he was offered the post of "special attaché to H.B.M. Legation" at Beijing, but declined the appointment. At any rate, within a week or two he had departed for the nearby port of Tianjin, a considerable city in its own right and one whose population of merchants and businessmen were perhaps more amenable to ideas for improving trade than Beijing's stuffy bureaucrats.

It was a good move: almost immediately, Mesny was approached by Sichuanese firms wanting to invest in the Transit Pass system, the pre-paid transport tax scheme which three years earlier had undermined his own business at Chongqing. The plan was for Mesny's company to represent the Sichuanese firms, making their merchandise "foreign" and so eligible for the favourable tax rate, thus allowing them to undercut their rivals' prices. Mesny failed to take up this offer too, but it reawoke his interest in funnelling British goods directly into China's southwestern provinces, as he wrote in the *North China Herald*: "I firmly believe, as I told you before, that Guangxi, part of Yunnan and part of Guizhou could be supplied with foreign merchandise much better from Hong Kong than from anywhere else. The French, you may notice, are now endeavouring to do business in these parts". This was a considerable understatement: France was, in fact, just about to go to war with China over control of Tungking, northern Vietnam, right on the border with Yunnan, a conflict that Mesny was soon to become an authority on. The paper continued, "The "Pioneer" concludes his note by an expression of regret that the Colonial merchants should not encourage the trade from Hong Kong to Yunnan via Canton [Guangzhou]" – in other words, along the West River system that he had begun to explore back in 1878, right at the beginning of his travels. The idea of pioneering a viable Yunnan–Guangzhou–Hong Kong trade route was to fill pages of the *Miscellany*.

Mail collected, wardrobe replaced and with some fresh travel plans to consider, Mesny turned back towards Taiyuan and the promised posting with Zhang Zhidong. Along the way he stopped at Baoding and was granted a second interview with Li Hongzhang, who just a few weeks earlier had dismissed Mesny's grand plans for China's future. But now Li – perhaps spurred on by the thought of losing this eager foreigner's services to a political rival – assured Mesny that his talents would be wasted out in the provinces, and instead proposed that he take up a military command at Beijing with one of his own Huai Army battalions. This was an extraordinary opportunity: the patronage of China's most powerful statesman would have set Mesny up for life and it's excruciating to read of him casually turning Li down, explaining with naive candour that he had already given his word to work for Zhang. For somebody who had spent so long in China, Mesny seems to have had a poor appreciation of "face", the need to publicly honour an individual's self-respect. Li Hongzhang was seriously offended by Mesny's tactless rejection, especially as it was made in favour of accepting a vague post with an unknown, first-time provincial governor of no proven ability. The decision was to blight Mesny's later career, and it's no comfort to realise that his promise to Zhang probably had little to do with it; more likely, Mesny simply wanted to continue his adventures and wasn't prepared to be tied down indefinitely at Beijing.

The middle of March found Mesny back at Taiyuan, where he settled in for a nine months' stay. On arrival, he found Zhang – who was alarming his staff by talking of suppressing corruption and the opium trade, cancelling outdated taxes and reforming the army – strangely distant, and suspected an angry Li Hongzhang of putting out a rumour that he was not to be trusted. "I was not allowed to go to Yün-nan, as I might be a French spy, and Governor [Zhang] was thus undecided whether to receive and employ me or not ... I then went rambling about the province for a couple of months".

From June 1882 onwards the *North China Herald* published an outpouring of letters and articles from "a Correspondent at T'ai-yuen". In a foretaste of the *Miscellany*, these sketched out current affairs in Shanxi's capital through an entertaining, gossipy, random range of subjects, reflecting Mesny's startling inability to focus: in just one article, he managed to cram in an earthquake, advice on learning Chinese, the state of the weather, ways the local women dressed their hair, the history of vaccinations against smallpox, the market price for grapes and the results of the recent provincial examinations. Other issues included an exposé of poor-quality "British" firearms that had appeared in the city, widespread panic caused by the appearance of a comet, news of a wolf shot by his neighbour, the subject of tree worship, reports of a warlike Tibetan lama at Ili defending the territory against fresh Russian incursions, coverage of the mid-winter festival and an unusually snobby, knowing commentary on the poor quality of ponies being sold at a horse fair.

Yet several coherent themes do emerge from this tangle of serendipity. Mesny clearly spent some time with Taiyuan's missionaries and sketched out a history of Christianity in the province, which he believed dated right back to the thirteenth century. He indulged his interest in antiques too, admiring – and later acquiring – some fine porcelain, a Ming-dynasty bronze incense burner and a horde of coins from distant Kashgar, inscribed with Chinese and Turkic characters. Coincidentally, he also mentioned how a local official had just been robbed and the thieves "traced to the inn I occupied before moving here... The Innkeeper, a lazy, ill-natured, and incapable man has been taken up, with his guests, whose names were not entered on the register, as required that they should be by law. The Innkeeper's wife has been at my place all day trying to persuade me to intercede with the authorities on behalf of her lord; but I have steadfastly declined to have any thing to do in the matter."

July saw bespectacled scholars from all over northern China descending on Taiyuan to sit for the provincial examinations, muttering to themselves in regional accents as they paced the streets reciting classical texts. The military exams were being held too: Mesny was unimpressed with the candidates' speed and accuracy with a bow, even over relatively short distances, but admired their fencing skills and strength, especially one man who nimbly spun a huge, two-handed sword around with seemingly little effort. Only one in twenty competitors passed, gaining a promotion which would require them – as Mesny himself had been required – to visit the Board of War at Beijing the following year and pay out heavily in "presents" to have their new rank officially confirmed. On top of this expense, an officer's wages remained as low as ever: "The Military Officials are so wretchedly paid when employed that they cannot borrow money if they wish to do so, when unemployed, and the consequence is that they are, as a rule, exceedingly miserable. If they were paid at the same rate as the civil officers of corresponding rank, a better class of men might be persuaded to serve in the army, in place of the poor dejected creatures now serving."

Amongst the distraction of the Mid-Autumn Festival, with its visits to temples and the handing-out of mooncakes amongst friends, a prolonged drought – followed by the inevitable floods, which submerged the southern part of the city – caused a food shortage and raised the price of grain. Mesny was now introduced to a "Miss Kuo", who charmed him with her elegant manners, soft hands and finely-made clothing. Her father, either a well-to-do farmer or merchant, claimed to have been ruined by the famine and needed to sell her, blatantly offering Mesny first refusal: "I answered that I did not want a companion, but Niu and his wife exclaimed together 'You are forty years old, and have no children; this young woman will bear them for you, she is healthy and strong, as well as young and willing' … [Miss Kuo] is quite a mystery. It is my belief that she has been indiscreet and cannot be married in the ordinary way; otherwise such a fine young woman could easily find a wealthy husband".

Zhang Zhidong, meanwhile, surfaces from the *North China Herald* articles as a sincere, upright official, keen to learn the ropes of governance and undaunted by his inexperience. Despite being given the run-around by his staff – who were clearly testing the new governor's boundaries – Zhang had soon acquired "no small fame as a reformer… Useless officers are being removed and inefficient ones replaced, public buildings which had been allowed to crumble away into masses of debris are being rebuilt, the revenue is being looked after, and the treasury has been inspected; punishments are being inflicted for past misconduct, and warnings are being issued for the benefit of the future."

Indeed, Zhang was soon bombarding the throne with memorials about restructuring Shanxi's civil service, which was in a mess. His obstructive treasurer refused to release funds for development projects, while many of the government staff smoked opium and were, to say the least, untrustworthy. In one instance it turned out that several million taels earmarked for famine relief had been embezzled; Zhang ordered the accounts to be checked and the offending officials forced to repay the money they had stolen. His staff were now forbidden to accept bribes or presents, though petitioners still had to pay "fees" to court officials to ensure that their pleas were presented or to get documents stamped. Unsurprisingly, Mesny commented that "The Governor is not very popular [with his staff], in spite of his integrity, and I am continually hearing murmurs against his rule and meddlesomeness, and yet I am sure he has the best intentions towards everyone, excepting of course the embezzlers of public money."

Zhang still seemed to have little need of his services, but Mesny's free time wasn't wasted: August found him surveying coal and iron deposits in hills outside Taiyuan, and when Zhang finally asked his advice on how to increase provincial revenue, Mesny could report that he should improve the roads, introduce railways and exploit Shanxi's mineral wealth. "This province has very extensive fields of the finest coal known, easily got at and worked. It is found in all directions and is extensively used for domestic purposes, where the mines are not more than a day's journey off... Iron is the most important product of this Province, and it abounds in various places where the necessary fuel, coal, is also found. The iron is of the very best quality and can be converted into anything, from a monster cannon to a cambric needle, or a modern armour-plate to a tin cup. What is required is capital, and the most modern scientific abilities to use that to the best advantage." He was soon drawing up specific plans: "I am told that [Zhang] is well pleased with a proposal I have made to him for the erection of gasworks near the coal mines. If he only lets me do the thing properly for him I will give him a good supply of electricity also. There is good soft coal to be had a few *li* west of the Fên River, and fine, smokeless coal is also plentiful within a distance of ten or fifteen miles."

Another interview saw the two men discussing the opium trade. Zhang was particularly frustrated to find that almost all his court officers – the minor officials in charge of policing, running errands and secretarial matters – were to some extent addicted. Mesny suggested ways to cure the habit, though glumly noted that "opium pipes are however exposed for sale everywhere, as well as lamps and all the other necessary instruments for smoking. Sellers of anti-opium medicines, I imagine, make less money than sellers of opium." He pointed out that, with Britain still importing the drug, and almost all arable land in Guizhou and Yunnan being used to grow this valuable cash crop, what was needed was a gradual suppression of both trafficking and cultivation, co-ordinated by the British Anti-Opium Society. Zhang, however, thought it grotesque to seek foreign assistance for a problem wholly caused by foreigners, declared it despicable that Britain continued the trade, and suggested that India instead make its profits by growing cotton or tea. Mesny, ashamed by Zhang's sincerity, found himself completely unable to defend his country's attitude.

They also considered national defence. "I was compelled to tell His Excellency plainly that bows and arrows, and such like antiquated weapons, were simply useless ... at present there was not a foreign nation in Europe who feared China ... The whole army ought to be reorganized speedily, and one million of the very best arms procured without delay. The drilling of troops in a proper manner ought, I said, to be commenced at once ... A powerful navy armed with one-hundred-ton guns ought to be created and maintained; and the coast should be defended by cannon throwing projectiles a ton in weight ... The rifles can be purchased at once; machinery can be imported to make the necessary ammunition; iron-clad ships, of small size, to carry two very large guns, can be ordered and built speedily. At least one hundred such ought to be got without delay. Heavy guns for shore batteries can be made, wherever required, along the coast; and ammunition stored up wherever it is considered necessary. All the material is on the spot, or rather in the Empire; all that is required is machinery, and the ability to use such to the best advantage. China ought to be in a position to dictate terms to the world, instead of being at the mercy of every little state that wishes to dispute with her". A rousing speech, and one which Zhang Zhidong, judging by his future actions, took to heart.

Towards the end of his stay at Taiyuan, the threads of Mesny's discussions with Zhang began to coalesce, and the *North China Herald* of 21 March 1883 published the first version of what became, by the time of the *Miscellany*, Mesny's "Nineteen-Point Plan" for China's salvation: "What we want now is a modern She Huang-ti [China's first emperor, whose tomb outside of Xi'an is guarded by the famous Terracotta Army], who will break through the bonds of red tape that bind the present with the past, and let the future go free; cause every temple in the Empire to be turned into a school for the training of the young in modern arts and sciences; connect every town in the Empire by telegraph wires; join every city by railroad with its provincial capital, and every provincial capital with the great city, Peking; establish Military Academies in every province, and Naval Academies in every large seaport; substitute for the present tests at the examinations something more in accordance with the requirements of the age, and more in accordance with the duties likely to be performed by the successful competitors, whether civil or military, such as the reading and answering of a dispatch on ordinary topics of government, simple arithmetical calculation, the hitting with a rifle-shot a target 18 inches in diameter 100 yards off, the saddling, mounting and riding of a horse in a given time, and other light and easy exercises. Other things ought to be performed by the aspirants to civil honours. Ordinary reading, writing, arithmetic, and reflections on a case on trial in some Court, etc., would doubtless answer much better than elegantly composed essays on the writings of the ancients."

Mesny was no great visionary; it was obvious to most of his contemporaries – and not just foreigners either, but reform-minded Chinese as well – that China needed to do all these things, and more, in order to drag itself into the modern age. But in terms of Zhang Zhidong's career it's worth noting the timing of Mesny's manifesto, delivered in a backwards province to an obscure, inexperienced governor who, up to this point, was known only for an outspoken nationalist. Within a decade Zhang would burst out of rustication to become a driving force behind the "Self-Strengthening Movement" which swept China in the late nineteenth century; a man who employed over two hundred foreign advisors on his staff, built

China's first modern mint at Guangzhou, instigated the country's first long-distance railway and founded China's first major industrial project, the Hanyang Iron and Steel works at Wuhan. It's credible, therefore, that Mesny's proposal at Taiyuan – or at the very least, Mesny's fervent conviction that modernisation was essential to China's future – actually influenced the course of Chinese history. Mesny himself firmly believed so, and never forgave Zhang for not mentioning his role to the authorities at Beijing, "though as I had high Chinese rank he might have done so conveniently". In later years he also suspected a malevolent Li Hongzhang of deliberately suppressing his name.

As winter settled in across the plains, Mesny hardened himself against the lowering temperatures with frugal meals and taking cold baths every morning, his one concession to the weather being a daily bowlful of hot, sweetened water with ginger. With typical contrariness, and despite the apparent success of his talks with Zhang Zhidong and the various engineering projects and employment opportunities that seemed to be materialising, he was now gearing up to leave Taiyuan. Once again he gave no firm reason for wanting to move on, though it was clear that he had planned to revisit Yunnan since obtaining a passport for the province back in 1880. Zhang was paying him a retainer of 50 taels per month, which perhaps wasn't enough to secure Mesny's long-term loyalty (though a provincial magistrate's annual salary was only 80 taels). But it is also feasible – as both the *North China Herald* and the Hong Kong press reported – that Zhang himself was sending Mesny to Yunnan to report on France's increasingly aggressive antics in northern Vietnam. As he had done before with Russia over Ili, Zhang was agitating loudly against France's actions, a stance which was soon to see him promoted to take charge of the problem, and it would have made good sense in having a reliable, French-speaking foreign military advisor on hand. And yet, years later in the *Miscellany*, Mesny claimed he had gone to Yunnan at "the invitation of [Tang Jiong] to assist in the development of the natural resources of that distant and little known Chinese province". While it's true that Tang, Mesny's old mentor from the Miao War, had been recently promoted commander-in-chief of the Chinese military in Vietnam, it seems extremely unlikely that he would have been interested in advice on mining and railways during what was to prove an extremely bloody campaign.

And so, behind all these official-sounding orders and "invitations" to proceed to Yunnan, it's more likely that Mesny was simply bored with his settled position and was, once again, growing restless for adventure. In the *North China Herald* that winter, he let slip an unusually personal insight: "I have often been told that rolling stones gather no moss, but I have a weakness for travelling, having contracted the habit when I was only nine years old. If all goes well and the wind blows fair I shall soon be off westwards – moss or no moss. ... I shall adhere to my motto, and keep pioneering as long as I am able."

If the winds did indeed blow him to Yunnan, perhaps he could gather information about the Vietnam situation, look for a new patron willing to fund his modernisation projects, or find new markets for Western goods. And, if all else failed, there was always the prospect of exploring unknown trade routes back across southwest China and down to British merchants in Hong Kong.

On 2 December 1882, Mesny and twelve Chinese companions, along with the necessary carts and horses, left Taiyuan for Xi'an. The highway ran exposed on an embankment high above the waterlogged plains, making travellers an easy target for banditry. Despite regularly-spaced guardhouses painted with protective images of tigers, even the huddled groups of peasants they met along the way had armed themselves with rustic weapons. Two days brought them to the prosperous banking centre of Pingyao, whose enormous defensive walls enclosed a grid of tidy streets, still laid out along their Song-dynasty plan. Shanxi people were famous across China for their sound financial sense: the country's first cheques had been issued at Pingyao in the 1820s and the scent of money had spawned a host of bodyguard agencies, staffed by professional martial artists who protected caravans moving into and out of the city. There were also scores of jewellers in town, much favoured by dealers from Beijing looking for pearls and antiques to sell to foreigners back in the capital. Unfortunately, the manager of Mesny's inn proved a little too thrifty, offering them poor-quality provisions and refusing to let the porters cook their own food – presumably in order to charge them for a hot meal. Mesny had him marched off to court where the man was "pumped of his superfluous cash... to be taught better manners towards his guests in the future".

On from Pingyao they reached the river Fen and followed it southwest through a dusty landscape, all shades of brown; with a bitterly cold wind driving into them, travel became a cheerless, gritty experience. During a pause at Lingshi, "a small city with dilapidated or rather crumbling mud walls, and three gates only, the size of a private cart-house door", Mesny witnessed a punch-up between a military official's retinue and the court staff, who had been withholding promised carts in the hope of a bribe. Lingshi was more or less run by the influential Wang family, whose fortress-like mansion on the hills above town was a maze of interlocking courtyards and halls, all decked out in splendid taste; the Empress Dowager Cixi was to stay here in 1900, on the run from foreign vengeance after her support for the Boxer Rebellion. Mesny was intrigued by what looked like an iron meteorite, which sat under its own pavilion in a temple dedicated to Taoist patriarch Luzi.

The next few days involved a tough ascent into the hills, passing caravans loaded down with tobacco, wheat and dates. They spent one cheerful day accompanied by a wedding party, the bride hidden inside a covered carriage gaily decked out in red, the groom on a horse, but that evening Mesny's dinner was accidentally eaten by dogs. The following night found them installed at the comfortable Gaosheng Inn in Hongtong town, "where the walls are ornamented with Thibetan and Manchurian characters, this being one of the regular halting places of the Thibetan Embassies". Then came Linfen, an oasis town renowned today for its astounding industrial pollution but then mostly in ruins, the aftermath of Zuo Zongtang's suppression of the Nian rebels some fifteen years earlier. Here Mesny unexpectedly discovered a tiny community of Wesleyan missionaries, whose founding father, he believed, had been his old friend David Hill. It was threatening to snow and they pushed on to Shi Cun, whose inhabitants proved irritatingly intrusive but where provisions were inexpensive. "Small travelling dealers and traders pay only 40 cash for a dinner and a night's lodging... a breakfast will not cost more than 30 cash, and so 70 cash will do very well for those who desire to travel economically". But Chinese breakfasts were no slap-up meal: Mesny started his days with steamed buns and a bowl of rice porridge flavoured with Chinese dates, which set him back sixteen cash.

At Wenxi, a salt-mining town, there was an evening's entertainment at the theatre and Mesny was impressed to see a proclamation by Zhang Zhidong posted up outside the courthouse banning the growing of opium for any reasons whatsoever, on pain of severe punishments. The weather remained miserably cold, with gales bringing the season's first snow as the party pressed on south. Beyond tiny Kaolao they passed "some ancient tombs and monumental stone rams, and tigers, as well as posts; two of each forming a row on each side; that is, the grave appeared to have faced the south, and to have had a stone tablet before it; then came the two stone men some nine or ten feet high... then a ram on each side; then a tiger on each side; then two stone pillars like two immense candles with a flaming head". On December 17 they breakfasted at Kehe and finally crossed the half-frozen Yellow River in a fragile-looking punt whose crew worked stark naked despite the intense cold, their bodies steaming with the effort of steering the ferry between broken slabs of ice. On the far shore lay Tongguan, the border fortress which Mesny had passed through the previous year, where a minor disagreement with the bad-tempered magistrate escalated into a fist-fight between the court staff and one of Mesny's travelling companions. Tongguan's governor had to be called in to settle the matter, and they left town under a heavy cloud of animosity.

From here the party retraced Mesny's earlier route, passing ornamental gateway *paifangs* buried almost up to their tops after flooding over the years had laid down thick deposits of silt. Overnighting at Hua Xian, they found the streets "crowded with carts full of silk and satin from Shanghai, and camlets, cloth and serge from Europe, which, I am told, is the material necessary for the manufacture of clothing and flags for the Chinese army of occupation at Kashgar", a city away on the empire's distant northwestern fringes. The provincial examiners had converged here too, on their way back to their headquarters at Beijing, so there was little choice of accommodation and they wound up at yet another "wretched inn". There was no fuel available and, with the thermometer well below zero, Mesny's moustache froze solid as he wrote up his journal.

Next came Weinan, whose authorities furnished them with unusually comfortable, warm lodgings, beds smothered with padded quilts and walls tastefully hung with scrolls of fine calligraphy. The final stage before Xi'an ended at Lintong, now famous as the site of the Terracotta Army but then decidedly unprepossessing – "small and miserable, stuck close under the mountains, and having only a few wretched inns, with no accommodation for preparing food [and so, having taken rooms at one of these places,] our food was cooked at a tea-shop opposite". Lintong's saving grace was its renowned hot springs, where Mesny's party enjoyed the luxury of a good soak. "Lots of men and women were there, the latter in a separate inclosure and rooms. I got the men to open the official part, and had a private room to myself, with a good bath in it. It is called the Kuei-fei Tang, or Bath of the Noble Concubine [whose charms had made her the favourite of Tang-dynasty playboy emperor Xuanzong]... the water came up to my waist, and was just the thing, neither too hot nor too cold; it had a slight sulphorous smell, but not an unpleasant one, as some hot springs have. The water flows in through a dragon's mouth, the spout being about two inches in diameter... The building is like a palace garden, having ponds, with fish and lotus plants. Tea parties might be given in it very nicely, and probably are when the place is not occupied by high passing officials. Small fry, like myself, are usually entertained at a common inn, within the city, for everyone's convenience; but when a Governor or the Lamas pass they are entertained in the regular bungalow, which is really an elegant edifice".

Refreshed, the next morning they met a caravan from Sichuan transporting the province's annual tribute of local produce – tea, incense, medicinal herbs and cosmetics – to the emperor at Beijing. Escorting the tribute had once been a much sought-after perk (even though "volunteers" had to pay heavily in bribes to secure the post), as the guards were allowed to carry their own goods duty-free and requisition more supplies and pack animals than they actually needed, and then sell everything at a vast profit. But now the upstanding viceroy of Sichuan, Ding Baozhen, had withdrawn the escorts' privileges and told them to take a fee from magistrates along the way, who usually managed to weasel their way out of paying the men anything.

On December 22, the weather sunny but very cold, they finally sighted the metropolis of Xi'an, "and in less than an hour we entered the eastern suburb, through which it was difficult to pass, owing to the many mules and carts, and the general traffic. We then passed through the Manchu city, the gate-keepers asking for my card and papers, and halted in Ma-fang Kai, near our old inn. [But, as it was full, we lodged at another hostel] in the great street, which runs from the east to the west gate; San Chiao Kai is the name of it, and the inn is called the Chang-sen Kuan-tian, and is kept by a Szechuan man named Fang. We were fortunate to find it, as the city is full of officials and troops returning from Turkestan [now that the Russians have pulled out of Ili and the Chinese forces there have been withdrawn]."

As if to make up for his previously flimsy coverage, Mesny filled columns of the *North China Herald* with a lively sketch of Xi'an. This had been one of the earliest centres of Chinese civilisation, continually settled since the Stone Age and chosen by successive dynasties as the national capital. By the eighth century there were perhaps a million people living here, making Tang-dynasty Xi'an one of the largest cities in the world. It was also unusually cosmopolitan, thanks to its position at the eastern terminus of the Silk Road, down which all manner of cultural influences trickled in from Central Asia.

People arrived too, amongst them the great romantic poet Li Bai, who was born in China's northwestern borderlands and whose couch Mesny saw preserved at the Dongxing Lou restaurant. Central Asia became a useful recruiting ground for the Chinese military, leaving Tang art rich in glaze-dribbled clay statues of hook-nosed, bearded soldiers but also laying the groundwork for the dynasty's collapse. Infatuated by the charms of his concubine Yang Guifei, the emperor Xuanzong lost interest in governance and allowed power to slip into the hands of one of his foreign generals, An Lushan – an "ungrateful Turk", according to Mesny – who launched a coup in 756. The Silk Road also saw Xi'an hosting the first appearance of Christianity in China, which was "introduced [from Iran] by Nestorian Missionaries, whose memory and deeds are still recorded on a stone tablet beyond the west gate, in good preservation." The missionaries' efforts saw a handful of churches established before the tenth century and the tablet itself, dated to 781, has survived and is now housed in a museum by Xi'an's old south gate.

Over a millennium later, and centuries after the Silk Road itself had been abandoned and the Chinese capital had drifted eastwards to Beijing, Mesny found that Xi'an still retained the atmosphere of a great cultural melting-pot. "At present a continual buzz is going on in its streets, and strangers from all parts abound. Here are Mongols going on pilgrimage to Thibet, and Thibetans going on official business to Peking; Coreans selling ginseng, Hunan men, and many others, going to the great camp in Turkestan; and Turks selling their famous Turfan raisins. ... The city is extremely large and populous, and the streets are so full of people and vehicles of various kinds that it is not an easy matter to get along. All kinds of things are exposed for sale, from the richest sable furs to the commonest sheepskins, and silks and satins of all kinds made up into clothing. Almost everything procurable in the Treaty Ports is to be had here, and some are especial products of these North-western provinces – fruit and vegetables of all sorts, excellent beef and mutton, fish and game of various kinds, and poultry in abundance; so we will make ourselves comfortable for a few days."

Having paid his respects to the provincial governor and assorted military officials, Mesny spent Christmas day visiting Xi'an's missionaries; the Catholics claimed around 200 followers, whilst Protestant converts numbered just two, the owners of a small pharmacy. He spent the rest of his holiday shopping for yet more antiques to add to his collection – coins, jade and porcelain – though prices were high and he doubted the authenticity of the roof tiles being offered as Han dynasty relics, though these were much sought-after by scholars for use as ink palettes.

Beyond Xi'an the roads became impassable for vehicles and Mesny would need to abandon his carts and employ some seventy carriers – at the cost of ten taels each – to reach the Yunnanese capital, Kunming. There followed a rant at the discrepancy between this vast expense and the 180 taels in total it would have cost to rent three carts for the same journey. What the country needed were trains! "The next line of railroad I recommended to [Zuo Zongtang], some sixteen or seventeen years ago, when he was on his way to his post in these parts, was a line from Peking to Pao-ting Fu, thence to Tai-yuan Fu, and so on to this place [Xi'an] *via* Ping-yang Fu and Tung-kuan. The line could be easily and economically built, and maintained. Labour is cheap and plentiful, coal and iron are to be found everywhere in the Shansi Province and right along the line of route, and there are no serious mountain obstacles to be overcome... The Yellow River can be spanned over with a substantial iron bridge for about Tls. 25,000, and any other bridges or culverts necessary along the route can be made of native bricks or stones, or even native iron... The line would most assuredly be a very profitable one."

Having walked the whole way between Beijing and Xi'an, Mesny knew what he was talking about: the modern rail line follows his proposed route almost exactly.

In the end, Xi'an's governor supplied two carts for Mesny to use as long as the roads held out, along with twenty-six carriers: two teams of four men to carry Mesny in a sedan chair; six men for another two chairs (presumably he had two lighter friends with him); "one head coolie to do nothing and another to help him", and four others to carry bedding and suchlike. The heaviest baggage went in the carts, and the plan was to hire eight more men as needed to help carry the chairs up hills. On December 30, in a cold and confused start, the party headed west out of Xi'an into a snow flurry, the head groom insisting on walking in front of the train bearing a large red umbrella as a sign of Mesny's status.

The first few days of the journey worked out well, despite the excruciating cold; the carriers covered up as much exposed flesh as possible, while Mesny's face and hands cracked and bled in the severe chill. But the road was good, and sympathetic magistrates along the route provided cosy accommodation and fine food – sea-slug, shark fin, seaweed, dried prawns and oysters – all valuable delicacies this far inland. Some of Mesny's men, used only to cobbled or beaten earth floors, had never experienced the luxury of floorboards before and trod gingerly indoors, expecting to fall through the planking. Out on the plains, a farmer sold Mesny a black mare for a very reasonable two hundred strings of copper cash, which he added to his growing stable: he already owned two horses named Pasha and Speedwell – a frisky beast which had a habit of bucking off unwary riders – along with a white mule, Silvertail. A flock of wild geese flew across the winter sky as they passed Mawei, where the Tang emperor Xuanzong, chased out of Xi'an during the An Lushan rebellion, was forced to have his concubine Yang Guifei executed to appease his mutinous army. The soldiers blamed her for distracting the doting emperor, securing lucrative posts for her relatives and generally undermining imperial power. After the execution, a grief-stricken Xuanzong had Yang buried in a modest tomb (closed when Mesny visited), then fled south with his army along *shudao*, the historic "Sichuan Road" to Chengdu that the party was now following.

Passing a tiny clutch of cave houses at Yen-wa Ko – one of which, improbably, proved to be a Catholic church – they reached Qishan, whose honest magistrate drew praise from everyone they spoke to. On meeting him Mesny recognised his old friend Hu Shenyao, a former paymaster to the Sichuan Army during the campaign in Guizhou, who had reached a contented middle age after a respectable military career. A delighted Hu kept them at Qishan for several days, showering everyone with goodwill and chatting with Mesny about their hard year together fighting the Miao at Chong'an. He finally sent them off in style after a fine breakfast, presenting Mesny with food for the journey, an antique incense burner and another young mule, but also warned him that rumours were being spread about that Mesny was a fraud and that he might be cold-shouldered by officials further along the road. Mesny suspected that Tongguan's hostile magistrate was behind the story.

A solid day's march brought them to semi-ruinous Fengxiang, whose authorities initially treated the party well despite having received an official-looking letter warning them not to trust Mesny. A check through the accounts revealed that costs were rising; not only was the local exchange rate poor, but Mesny's sizeable retinue was costing him dear. "But of course if one wishes to travel as a gentleman he must also be prepared to pay as a gentleman, and that means in English, I believe, to be very liberal." The next morning he woke to find that his staff had been given a hard time overnight, the petty officials refusing them firewood and demanding gratuities, so Mesny hustled everyone out of Fengxiang at dawn, partly to prevent his disgruntled men from causing trouble.

At Baoji, a cattle auction was in full swing; suitably enough, the city claimed to be the birthplace of Shennong, the mythical "Divine Agriculturalist" credited in China with the invention of the plough, country markets and the use of medicinal plants. The magistrate, named Wang, was open and welcoming, and for the time being they seemed to have outrun malicious rumours concerning Mesny's status. But bad feelings were later stirred up after his head groom neglected to distribute the necessary "wine money" amongst Wang's staff, hoping to pocket it for himself.

Baoji marked the end of the good road: from here on their route climbed southwest into the crumpled Qin Ling, part of the huge Zhongnan Mountain range which split China's arid northern plains from the more humid, sub-tropical south. To get through, the carts would have to be abandoned and everything portered by servants or pack animal. The track, paved in the usual rough-edged granite slabs, was worn smooth by millennia of use and slippery with ice; in places there were treacherous "plank roads", wooden galleries mortised straight across the cliff-sides. These had been rebuilt since being torn down in antiquity at the orders of Zhang Liang, advisor to the warlord Liu Bang. Liu was retreating into Sichuan and, with the road behind him destroyed, gave the impression that there was no chance of his ever returning from exile to challenge the rule of his powerful, larger-than-life rival, Xiang Yu. The ruse succeeded: ignored in Sichuan, Zhang Liang and Liu Bang built up alliances, gathered an army and in 202 B.C. headed back through the passes to defeat Xiang Yu and found the Han dynasty. Mesny passed a splendid memorial temple to Zhang at Liuhou town.

Some of the Chinese hired small, wiry hill-ponies to negotiate the road's tricker stretches and Mesny spent a good deal of the journey walking just to keep warm, much to the relief of his bearers, who had found carrying him uphill in a chair an exhausting prospect. The scattering of hamlets turned out to be surprisingly well-stocked – pheasants for the pot were on sale everywhere, and they feasted one evening on roast chicken, salt mutton, and pickles, washed down with the local firewater – though horseshoes were unknown and it proved impossible to get Speedwell and Pasha properly shod for the mountain trails.

Descending towards Sichuan, they crossed the invisible culinary boundary which divides northern and southern China: "We have now entered a country where rice is generally eaten by all human beings, and where the other cereals are left to cattle". It was here that things began to unravel. At Fengxian (one-time home of Zhang Guo Lao, an eccentric Tang-dynasty Taoist mystic, chess-player and hard drinker), they endured "poor quarters" and a rude reception from the magistrate, who refused to meet Mesny or supply even basic hospitality. He openly accused Mesny of being an impostor and demanded to see his travel permits, and only grudgingly backed down when these were produced. Mesny was unimpressed. "I am told the stingy creature, whose name is Hsiao, is a native of Hu-nan... He shirks his duty on every possible occasion, pleading poverty as an excuse, whereas this is considered a lucrative post... He has also tried to treat me as he would a Christian missionary, with as much contempt and insolence as possible".

Worse awaited them at Liuba, whose tight-fisted magistrate found the party a comfortable inn but otherwise refused to assist in any way – not from hostility but simply so that he could keep the allowance given him by the government for entertaining passing officials. His staff were obstructive too, stalling over the necessary paperwork as they pressed for bribes, but what rankled most was discovering that their inn belonged to one of Liuba's officials, who was thereby profiting from every day that their departure was delayed. All this was further eroding Mesny's finances, as by now his retinue – which he had to pay wages to, feed and accommodate – comprised "50 odd persons with me, besides the baggage bearers supplied by the officials at each stage of our journey instead of the carts we had". At least potatoes were cheap, he declared sourly, so they wouldn't starve. Not for the last time, he looked forward to the day that railways would make travel through China straightforward.

Despite implying that he was being held against his will, Mesny's articles hint that he was refusing to leave until his presence had embarrassed Liuba's magistrate into making an apology. But when the ruse failed, Mesny announced that he would visit the prefectural hub, Hanzhong, and petition the higher authorities there about his treatment. This brought a flurry of activity from Liuba's junior ministers, who begged permission to arrange a compromise with their employer. "I answered that there was no negotiating about the affair, as the magistrate had offered me nothing but contempt and given me nothing but vain answers which did not answer my purpose nor advance me on my journey. ... I would now have all my dues, and my inn expenses paid; while the coolies must have each at least 100 cash a day for the time they had been detained." But the next morning, hearing that Liuba's magistrate was still refusing to recompense him and dithering even over the number of bearers he was prepared to provide for the next stage of their travels, Mesny stormed off to Hanzhong, speeding his journey by abandoning his luggage and most of his camp-followers at Liuba.

Two days later, having crossed another flurry of hills and followed the Baohe River south, he arrived at Hanzhong in a thick fog. This crowded, historic city sat astride the main Xi'an-Chengdu road and on occasion had served as a regional capital; Mesny saw people worshipping a stone lion which had once guarded the Imperial palace and, in common with many antiquities of an indeterminate age, was said to date back to the Han dynasty.

An interview was soon secured with the affable magistrate, another old acquaintance from Guizhou, who sympathised with Mesny's troubles but excused his colleague at Liuba on the grounds of inexperience; however, he arranged comfortable quarters and promised to have Mesny's baggage, which was now being held hostage at Liuba against his return, sent on directly. In the meantime Mesny explored Hanzhong, unearthing three English missionaries who ran a small dispensary and had converted some eighty locals and a young widow "of distinguished literary attainments" who turned out to be fairly attractive too, and well-spoken. Inevitably, her mother collared Mesny and bluntly proposed that he take her daughter as a second wife: "my daughter is young, and requires a husband. You have an excellent constitution and require a son. You are adapted to each other in size and intellect; she is sure to become a mother if you consent to be a father". Mesny begged off, unswayed by her pragmatic arguments and citing the renowned poverty of military men.

With luggage and entourage restored, the party set out for Mianxian, a county town thirty kilometres west of Hanzhong at the foot of Dingjun Mountain. It was here that Kongming, the master strategist of the Three Kingdoms period, had been laid to rest in 243 A.D., having spent decades in the service of the warlord and pretender to the Han throne, Liu Bei. Kongming's most celebrated ploy was his "Empty City Stratagem": having no troops to defend the key city of Xicheng from an invading army, Kongming opened the gates and sat in surrender on the battlements; but the enemy general, knowing of his vast cunning, suspected some elaborate trap and so fled. Kongming's alleged tomb had been restored by Mesny's paymaster friend Hu Shenyao, but there were scores of grave mounds in the cemetery and locals admitted that nobody really knew under which one Kongming was actually buried. And once again there were official troubles when Mianxian's magistrate, new to his post, prevaricated over expenses and accused Mesny of carrying false papers. This was too much for Mesny, who exploded in righteous anger and threatened to bring down the wrath of Hanzhong's authorities on the magistrate's head. The man apologised unreservedly at this barrage and provided all that was required, though Mesny refused to give him "face" by meeting with him again.

Despite a sudden and remarkable improvement in the quality of food available along the road, there were further irritations at Ningqiang, whose former magistrate Mesny had threatened with a pistol two years earlier. The current incumbent, a Muslim named Ma, proved more welcoming but again tried to underpay Mesny's carriers, causing yet more delay and bad feeling. Beyond was the Sichuanese border at Chaotian; the baggage carriers, by now heartily sick of mountains, elected to cover the next stage by boat but Mesny continued overland in order to cross the steep

Chaotianmen Pass, which he had missed on his way north. He descended onto a plain, past rockfaces carved with thousands of Buddha sculptures, and so returned to Guangyuan, Empress Wu Zetian's hometown. Here the magistrate, whom Mesny remembered from his previous visit as an honest and forthright official, paid his men without any fuss and provided lodgings and food.

Next came Zhaohua, where Mesny visited a memorial arch to a Ming-dynasty governor killed here by that notorious rebel, "Yellow Tiger" Zhang Xianzhong. But another troublesome night ensued, Zhaohua's magistrate proving to be old and insane, and none of his subordinates willing to take responsibility for hosting Mesny's party. As Chinese New Year was approaching – before which, by tradition, all debts needed to be settled – Mesny's carriers became fractious, demanding an advance on their wages for the final stages to Chengdu. At first they were dissatisfied with the amount he offered and refused to move on, but by mid-afternoon, with no money and no food, they relented and accepted his terms. Abandoning Zhaohua and its mad magistrate, they followed an old post-road up into the hills, the track flagged in sandstone slabs and flanked – as it still is today in places – by an avenue of ancient cedar trees, said to have been planted back in the third century by the Three Kingdoms' general Zhang Fei. Each tree was numbered, with the local authorities responsible for looking after them and planting replacement saplings as required. The party halted for a day's relaxation at the village of Ta-mu-shu; Mesny gave his carriers a New Year's present of money which they pooled to buy pork, chicken and eggs for a feast.

Festivities out the way, they descended past the tiny Liangshan temple and down a narrow, slippery track to Jianmenguan, the celebrated "Sword Pass" which forms a narrow slash in the barrier-like rage of granite hills slanting northeast across Sichuan. Jiange's magistrate once again pleaded an inability to fund their travels, so they pushed on across some beautifully wooded hills to Wulian, a large country town whose families produced the fine-quality silk for making the brocades for which Sichuan was once famed. It was by now the third day of the New Year, considered auspicious for visiting friends and relatives, and the streets were busy with people sociably orbiting between each other's houses despite the cold, clammy weather. Passing under a substantial *paifang* they entered Zitong county, the road slaloming all the while as it undulated to where a cluster of three large, red-walled temples sat on the forested slopes of Qiqu Mountain. One hall here was dedicated to the third-century Taoist philosopher Zhang Yazi, a local man later deified as Wenchang and "now worshipped by all the literati throughout the empire as the God of Literature". Shrines to Wenchang were often paired with ones honouring the complimentary deity of martial virtue, Guandi, showing that – in theory at least – the arts of learning and warfare were equally respected in China.

More trouble awaited them in the valley below at Zitong town, whose authorities had received an official letter describing Mesny as a "foreigner pretending to be in the Chinese service, dressed in Chinese clothes, wearing a queue and accompanied by a number of Chinese of various kinds". He once again showed his passport but, after considering the matter for a couple of hours, Zitong's magistrate decided not to supply the required number of porters. A cash-strapped Mesny was forced to send to Chengdu for more money so that he could afford to hire the carriers himself.

Relief from bureaucratic hostility came a couple of days later at Mianyang, a city set like a miniature Chongqing on a peninsula at the confluence of the Fu and Anchang rivers. Having just settled down to breakfast at an inn, the travellers were greatly surprised when a runner from the magistrate appeared with orders to escort them to official quarters, where Mesny's papers were cleared and they were promised everything his rank entitled them to. It turned out that Mianyang's magistrate was a friend of Tang Jiong, Mesny's former commander-in-chief in Guizhou, who had recently finished a posting at Mianyang and had left behind a reputation for integrity and valour.

West of Mianyang lay a broad, fertile plain awash with flooded paddy fields and wallowing water buffalo, where they rejoined the main highway to Chengdu; as the weather warmed dramatically, the carriers stripped down to their loincloths. At Baimaguan they passed a memorial hall to yet another loyal Three Kingdoms minister, Pang Tong, who had dressed himself up in his ruler's clothes to decoy the enemy, and so was killed.

Across the Mianyang River, Deyang was a handsome city with noxious sewers, where they found a school in the grounds of the local Guandi temple whose scholars were forbidden to smoke that pernicious "foreign mud", opium. In contrast, only three of Mesny's party – which now totalled eighty travelling companions, porters and hangers-on – didn't smoke the drug. Deyang's officials again fell short of expectations and Mesny's men staged a sit-down strike for their wages; fortunately, at this point his runner arrived from Chengdu with fresh funds.

Their final halt was at Xindu, a market town just twenty kilometres short of Chengdu, whose magistrate attended to all their needs and honoured them with a personal visit. Mesny toured the pleasantly-proportioned Baoguang temple with its tilted Tang-dynasty pagoda and splendid *luohan* hall, where five hundred statues of Buddhist worthies "are all elevated about four feet from the ground, placed in various attitudes, and gilded all over with gold-leaf. The grounds appear to be nicely kept by over a hundred monks, and most strangers travelling this way pay the monastery a visit... The place is famed far and wide throughout the Empire for the strictness of its discipline". Departing on the morning of February 18, they passed through Tianhui and, as they approached the Sichuanese capital, the traffic along the heavily rutted road increased considerably: "on we went, however, pushing, shoving, shouting and yelling to those ahead to get out of the way – altogether making such a noise that it was very difficult to know if you were being spoken to or not". At last they passed inside Chengdu's city walls and put up in an inn on little Mianhua Jie, Cotton Street, not far from the south gate. "Thus ended the second great important stage of our journey to Yunnan, and a troublesome one it has been so far".

Mesny stayed in Chengdu for two weeks, touring the sights, catching up with friends and, as always, spending time with the city's missionaries. There had been a few fires and an anti-Christian riot, and prices had risen considerably thanks to increased *lijin*, but overall Chengdu was much as he remembered it. Most of his energies were directed towards arranging the next stage of his travels: he planned to hire a junk and cruise south down the Jin river to the Yangzi port of Yibin, then head overland along a minor road to Bijie in northern Guizhou from where he could pick up the highway to Yunnan's capital, Kunming. The initial problem was finding a junk-master willing to captain a vessel to Yibin, anything up to a week away, for less than 28 taels – not counting the cost of additional transports for the animals and men. Fending off enquiries as to the reasons behind his journey, he reported coyly in the *North China Herald*: "It is now becoming known that I am here on my way to Yunnan. Friends call to pay their respects, and the curious to know my business in the west. All sorts of rumours are afloat, and all sorts of people offer me their services which I am of course forced to decline".

Shortly after his arrival, Mesny ran into Alexander Hosie, "Her Britannic Majesty's worthy representative in Western China", who was pausing briefly in town on his way between Chongqing and Dali in Yunnan. Hosie had begun his China career in 1876 as an interpreter and later filled various consular roles, travelling around the country to report on trade, transport and industry for the Foreign Office. He was presently juggling an acting consulship at Chongqing with investigating opium production in southwestern China; the British were concerned that the increasingly low cost of the widely-grown domestic product was undercutting their own higher-quality imports from India, lessening their profits. The two men had been in touch since Mesny's stay at Taiyuan and now met up over dinner, presumably to swap notes over their respective travel plans. Hosie had arranged an ambitious excursion southwest into Yunnan, through the territory of the much-feared Yi or Lolo, "a remnant of the aboriginal population who have remained unsubdued to this day... they often sally down to the Chinese lowlands and carry off men and women, cattle and horses, or anything else they can get hold of... They sell the Chinese whom they catch to the pastoral people of their mountainous fastness, and the latter make shepherds and herdsmen of them". Mesny, who at some point had acquired a Yi manuscript written in their distinctive pictorial characters (now in the Royal Geographical Society's archive in London), told Hosie of two Chinese slaves he'd once met, and how they had managed to escape from their captivity amongst the Yi.

Mesny also attempted to secure another interview with the long-serving viceroy, Ding Baozhen, whom he had met on previous visits to Sichuan. His first efforts were foiled by Ding's finance minister, who took a dislike to the idea of a foreigner roaming around the country at will and had Mesny questioned over his authority for doing so. Being hardened to this sort of thing by now, Mesny produced his official travel documents and forced an apology, but his meeting with Ding wasn't very successful. Ding looked exhausted and old; his second son had just died and his various hard-won reforms were unravelling. Restorations of the antique irrigation system north of Chengdu had gone well, but Mesny was unimpressed with Ding's new arsenal, which, despite employing over two hundred people, turned out only "one very poorly and clumsily made rifle per day... Yet I am told that there are sixty thousand taels-worth of foreign machinery in the establishment". Ding's shake-up of the salt industry had also failed to end endemic corruption, with salt bureau officials still soliciting fortunes in bribes from merchants who wanted a licence: "One year's service [at one of the salt-producing towns] was considered sufficient to provide for the life-time of an ordinary official. A hundred thousand taels was quite a small matter with salt commissioners in those days. I have myself known one to receive presents amounting to over forty thousand taels on the very day his appointment was posted up at the Fu-tai's yamen. Another batch awaited him on arrival at his post, and then the silver stream would incessantly flow into his spacious coffers during the whole term of his office".

Mesny estimated that salt cost about one copper cash per pound to produce, but sold at Chengdu – after corruption and transport costs were factored in – for at least forty times this price.

It was time to move on: the longer Mesny stayed at Chengdu the more he was harassed by mothers wanting him to take them or their unmarried daughters on as wives, servants or concubines. This prompted a diatribe against Chinese women, whom he portrayed as "very tender-hearted and charitably disposed towards all men – excepting their husbands... I would prefer a good English girl with a sound education and an amiable temper, to any woman I have yet seen in China. If Chinese women were educated even moderately, say just enough to read ordinary books, they might be much better; but those capable of reading or writing even a homely family letter are very few indeed". This might explain his reluctance to return to his own wife at Guiyang, despite plans to cut down through Guizhou on his way to Yunnan.

With the help of a Roman Catholic convert, Mesny finalised his travel plans on March 6, but not before spending 20 taels to buy the bond of a twelve-year-old girl who was about to be sold into prostitution and adding her to his entourage. He admitted in the *Miscellany* to buying several girls over the years, including "two in Szü-chuan for a few taels each, less than fifteen dollars. One I released in Tientsin, another died in Hong Kong; the other I gave in marriage to a faithful servant of mine". He also tried to take leave of Ding Baozhen, but the viceroy was busy with his son's funeral arrangements and the two men never met again; Ding died three years later, still in office at Chengdu. Quitting his lodgings, Mesny pushed his way down through the bustling city streets and out through the south gate to where his junk, captained by a cheerful woman, awaited on the clear-flowing river Jin (today a concrete channel full of vile slush). An uncomfortable night was spent in dock, where Mesny was kept awake by the noisy antics of opium smokers and again regretted how so many of his men had become addicts, beggaring themselves in the process. He rose grumpily at dawn to find that the pack animals had refused to get aboard their junk and, while stabled overnight at an onshore inn, had run riot and kicked down a partition. He added the cost of repairs to the expense of his stay in Chengdu and went ashore to coax the animals onto their vessel.

Mid-morning, the skipper announced that they were ready to leave and the excited crew set off strings of noisy, good-luck fireworks – though, in deference to Mesny, they refrained from killing the customary rooster. The junk's hull scraped and bumped over the shallow bottom as they dodged through the crowd of vessels – a collision, not serious, drew torrents of abuse from the other crew – but eventually they broke free of the suburbs, drifting out across the Chengdu plain's rural patchwork of green and yellow fields, where whitewashed houses could be seen half-hidden amongst clumps of bamboo. Soon the junk picked up pace, the river flowing faster and deeper as they passed Huayang and continued down past the temple village of Huanglong Xi to join the larger Min river above Meishan, hometown of the renowned Song-dynasty poet and administrator Su Dongpo.

They put ashore amongst a crush of huge junks at Leshan, where the Min converged with the murky waters of the Qingyi and Dadu rivers. Mesny strolled around the markets but was disappointed to find few British products on sale – only matches, in fact – amongst bolts of excellent Chinese silk and piles of fresh fish and vegetables. There was, apparently, a resident French missionary in the city, but Mesny decided not to visit him; after his recent experiences with officialdom, he also avoided having anything to do with Leshan's magistrate. (The crew, meanwhile, took advantage of his absence to sacrifice the rooster they had withheld at the start of the journey). Leshan is home to one of the largest Buddha sculptures in the world, a seventy-one-metre-high seated figure carved into the red sandstone cliffs diagonally opposite town, but despite sailing right underneath on the following day, Mesny gave it only the barest of mentions: "One colossal idol I saw is rather the worse for wear, although it is plainly discernable as a work of art". At least Mesny was not alone here; no real descriptions of the Buddha appear in English until a 1925 *National Geographic* article by the eccentric botanist and China traveller Joseph Rock, which shows a photograph of the head almost lost amongst wild vegetation. The statue dated back almost a thousand years to the Tang dynasty's embracing of Buddhism as the state religion, which also saw nearby Emei Mountain covered in temples.

An increasingly powerful current carried them past the salt wells at Wutongqiao, through the Cha-yu rapids and down to Qianwei, where twin pagodas and a nine-gated wall faced the water. With holiday decorations still plastered up everywhere, Mesny noted the Chinese affection for the auspicious colour red, used to tint sweet pastries, hard-boiled eggs and other festival treats. Even white livestock got a cheerful dab of red at the New Year (white being the traditional colour of mourning). Business cards – an essential social accessory for anyone of importance, sent in advance to officials when arriving at a town – also always had at least a strip of red on them.

Yibin, marking where the Min joined the Yangzi at a point where it became known as Da Jiang, the "Great River", was reached in the early afternoon of March 13, after a good run of under a week from Chengdu. Here Mesny was welcomed by the Catholic mission and confirmed his plan to follow an obscure route overland to Bijie in northern Guizhou; a deliberately difficult cross-country journey, with none of the historical attractions that had enlivened the march between Xi'an and Chengdu. Carriers were soon hired for the eleven-day trip – Mesny paid half their wages up-front, with half the remainder due at the mid-way stop and the balance on arrival at Bijie – then the party rode a ferry down the Yangzi to Nanguang, changing here for a shallow-draft junk heading south along a minor tributary. There was a moment of excitement when Mesny's vessel was sunk by a submerged rock, but they saved themselves and all the luggage and spent the night drying out ashore.

At Nanguang they left the boats and followed a dangerously slippery track to Shahe town, crowded to bursting on market day; there were men carting indigo from nearby Gongxian, and Mesny – forgetting his recent diatribe against wives – used a good deal of ink describing the charms of three peasant women who sat staring at him, mute with astonishment at the sight of a foreigner. Having slept at a house whose lower floor comprised a distillery, a pigsty and latrine, "without as much as a partition between them", Mesny was amused the next morning when two soldiers appeared, his official escort for the stage already completed from Yibin; he sent them packing without their travelling expenses, much to their surprise.

The following days were spent roaming to all points of the compass through the rugged, densely forested hills along the Guizhou border. There were minor delays – a day was wasted when the porters found a plentiful supply of spirits and decided to halt, despite it being just mid-morning; and all the pack animals fell off the narrow mountain trails at one time or another – but eventually they struck a proper, flagstoned road and followed it to the halfway town of Yuanning, where they were the first ever guests at a new inn. Yuanning's magistrate turned out to be the brother of a friend of Mesny's, and helped them get the horses re-shod and their ragged, travel-battered baggage repacked; another friend, a General Ho, had left for Guizhou just a few days earlier and Mesny suspected that his mission was to keep an eye on the population of Qianxi, where he had been attacked in 1880. In fact, Qianxi lay well off Mesny's eventual route, but it did sit on the direct road to Guiyang – suggesting that, at this stage at least, he might have been considering a return home.

The next few days passed in a blur of faint tracks and heavy rain, Mesny daydreaming longingly about railways all the while. The road improved slightly at the market town of Monizhen, where a stream of salt carriers and coal merchants passed between stalls selling rice and fried buns. Mesny spent the evening eyeing up the innkeeper's five daughters but one of his staff, a local man, heard the unpleasant news that his uncle had recently committed suicide in a drunken fit. There followed a descent to the russet Chishui river and the Guizhou border, which they crossed with little trouble after Mesny found that yet another old friend was the chief customs inspector. With luck, Bijie was now just a tiring three days distance, the undulating ranges in between inhabited by shy groups of Miao and a further acquaintance of Mesny named "Pluto" whose family, originally from Taiyuan, plied him with beer and gifts and begged him to rest up for a day at their expense. But Mesny pushed on, slowed only by trouble over his Sichuanese silver. A standard ingot would have exchanged for fifteen thousand strings of copper cash, weighing an impossible seventy kilos, so on the backroads Mesny carried smaller silver slugs worth considerably less. By now he had only one of these left and for some reason the local moneychanger wouldn't accept it. Fortunately, his innkeeper lent him funds to pay his bills. "It is high time a good mint was established for the manufacture of good useful coins of one tael, half a tael and a tenth of a tael in weight".

Bijie came into view in the early afternoon, a walled city sunk into a valley basin all ringed by hills and temples. The magistrate, though barely two weeks in office, had already won widespread approval by suppressing gambling and banditry, and he gained Mesny's affections by supplying a bodyguard and a good dinner. Unfortunately, there was a heavy downpour that night and Bijie's best inn turned out to have a roof which leaked badly, soaking the carriers' bedding and rubbing in the fact that they were back in China's wettest province; outside, people were grumbling that they had seen the sun only twice that year.

The recent passage of officials and opium merchants, each demanding large numbers of porters, had made carriers for their next stage to Weining city scarce and expensive. And in fact the local "highway" proved to be little more than a rough gravel track lined in tough, thorny bushes which tore their clothing; the carriers frequently lost their footing on the wet, slippery surface, spilling Mesny, chair and all across the road. There was a little rice growing in the valleys and a few stumpy tea bushes with dirty yellow flowers up in the hills, and the area had once been famous for its honey, but now almost all available farmland was given over to opium poppies and the bees had disappeared. Farmers also complained that wild animals – boars especially – caused havoc with their remaining crops. Still, there were some high points along the way: Mesny, flirting again with another likely young woman, was embarrassed when she respectfully called him "grandfather".

At the large village of Gaoshan Pu, the whole party were impressed with the dedication of an old schoolmaster and his pupils, who worked hard despite the condition of their classroom, sandwiched between a pigsty and an open sewer. Then there was Hezhang, whose district magistrate – a Yunnanese man named Qian Beiya, whom Mesny knew slightly – was in town investigating a murder and called at their lodgings, dressed incognito in peasant clothing. The two shared a meal that evening, chewing over old times and current policy: one mutual friend had been promoted to provincial governor but at a very insecure post, with plenty of responsibility and little chance of reward, military pay throughout the province was still in arrears, and there were growing demands that racial discrimination between Han and Miao should be abolished.

On April 1 – following a fight with the manageress of their inn, who had tried to overcharge them – they set off before dawn and, as the rising sun burnt off lingering fog, sighted the large, marshy spread of Caohai Lake in the distance, "created naturally upon the site of the old city of Wei-ning". By mid-afternoon they were down off the plateau at Weining itself, where yet another friend from the Miao war, General

Zhong, invited Mesny to stay at his headquarters. Zhong, a lively man now posted to this distant outpost as the military governor, had done well for himself, with six sons and the likelihood of further promotion ahead. Zhong insisted that they dine together daily during his stay, and plied Mesny with news of former army comrades: out of five fellow veterans of Zhou Dawu's campaigns, three had died and one had retired, leaving only Zhong on active service.

The *North China Herald* travelogue ends at Weining, abandoning Mesny close to the Yunnanese border, but from a follow-up article it's clear that within just two weeks, on 14 April 1883, he was safely installed at the provincial capital, Kunming, having completed the whole trying journey from Taiyuan in under five months. The question now, of course, was what to do next. Events were certainly heating up in Tungking, northern Vietnam, whose frontier was just a week away to the south, and Mesny was well-placed if he had indeed come to town to report on French activities in the region.

China's claims over Vietnam dated right back to a brief invasion in 218 B.C., though the country wasn't fully annexed for another century. After direct Chinese rule ended in 938, they continued to meddle in Vietnam's fractious internal politics by sending in military aid from time to time. By the seventeenth century, Vietnam had split into a southern kingdom with its court at Hue, and the northern state of Tungking, focused on the Red River delta surrounding Hanoi. Tungking's borders butted up against Yunnan and Guangxi provinces, and the peoples on both sides shared a common language, culture and history.

It was at this point that French Jesuits arrived in southern Vietnam to establish Christianity, encountering, as in China, strong opposition from a conservative, Confucian aristocracy. This inspired the missionaries themselves to become radically active in Vietnamese politics, and they raised a militia in support of the southern ruler, Nguyen Anh. Nguyen gathered his forces, stormed north into Tungking and, despite Chinese opposition, unified the country in 1802. Astutely, he then immediately apologised to China and – in return for paying an annual tribute as a vassal state – received Beijing's stamp of legitimacy for his rule. Nguyen maintained a friendship with France until his death in 1820, but this relationship deteriorated under his son and successor, Minh Mang. When a revolt against Minh broke out in the south, the rebels asked both Vietnamese Christians and neighbouring Thailand for support; Minh Mang defeated the Thais, captured the southern city of Saigon and took his anger out on a French priest, Father Marchand, by having him slowly dismembered. As the country rose in revolt, Minh Mang banned Christianity in no uncertain terms: native converts were to be cut in two, while "its European teachers, who are most to blame, will be thrown into the sea, with a stone around their neck".

France, meanwhile, was growing increasingly imperialistic. In 1857, partly in retaliation for the continuing persecution of Christians, a French naval expedition captured Saigon, and by 1870 France had annexed southern Vietnam. But Tungking remained independent and unsettled, awash with rebel factions fighting amongst themselves and, occasionally, Vietnamese forces sent against them. This worried China, who wanted a stable Tungking to act as a buffer against the threat of further French expansion towards her borders. Looking around for the strongest faction they found the Black Flags, led by an illiterate warlord named Liu Yongfu. Born in 1837 into a peasant family which had been ruined by gambling debts, Liu turned bandit aged just fifteen, gradually carving himself out a territory along the Guangxi-Tungking border. Having taken on the troublesome Yellow Flags – a rebel Chinese force which had fled into Tungking to avoid government retribution – the Black Flags' stabilising presence had already received tacit acceptance from the Vietnamese authorities, and now the Chinese appointed Liu Yongfu the brevet rank of Major General. Liu subsequently based himself at Lao Cai, the district bordering Yunnan, from where he promised to keep Tungking quiet and pro-Chinese.

While all this was going on, the French Lagrée Expedition, ultimately led by Francis Garnier, was weaving its way through Laos and into China. Arriving in Hankou in 1868, they met up with Mesny and his gun-running associate Jean Dupuis. Inspired by Garnier's tales, Dupuis himself left Hankou and headed west to Yunnan, where the Muslim

Uprising was in full swing. Here he was introduced to Ma Julong, the former Muslim warlord who had switched sides and been appointed governor of Kunming. Dupuis was soon supplying Ma with modern firearms but wondered if there wasn't a quicker, cheaper alternative to shipping everything up the coast from Hong Kong to Shanghai, along the Yangzi to Chongqing, and then carting it overland from Sichuan to Kunming.

In late 1872 Dupuis caught a steamship from Hong Kong to Hanoi in Tungking, accompanying a large consignment of French-made armaments. The Chinese had given him permission to blaze a new trail through northern Vietnam and into Yunnan, but the Vietnamese – having seen what France had done to the south of their country – had no desire to let a Frenchman roam around Tungking at will. Refusing to lend the expedition any sense of legitimacy they stalled Dupuis at Hanoi, where the river became too shallow for his steamship to continue. But a cartel of Cantonese merchants, eager to promote a new trade route with China, lent Dupuis a fleet of shallow-draft junks, allowing him to complete his journey to Kunming. He arrived there in early March 1873 to find that the war was already over – Du Wenxiu was dead and Dali had fallen – but the Chinese were delighted with the success of his mission and provided Dupuis with a large military escort for his return to Hanoi. By this time the Vietnamese authorities, outraged that Dupuis had made the journey without their permission, had arrested the merchants who had rented him the junks. Brandishing his Chinese papers, Dupuis – supported by a band of foreign mercenaries – bullied them into releasing the prisoners, seized a convoy of salt transports, thumbed his nose at threats of armed retaliation and, insultingly, raised the French flag in downtown Hanoi, refusing to leave until the Vietnamese paid him off.

The French government was appalled. Already suffering from the ruinously expensive consequences of the Franco-Prussian War in Europe, they wanted no further involvement in Vietnam and packed off their regional expert, Francis Garnier, to evict Dupuis from Hanoi and calm the situation down. But Garnier decided to support Dupuis. In desperation, the Vietnamese authorities called on Liu Yongfu and his Black Flags, who descended on Hanoi and managed to kill Garnier in a skirmish outside the city walls. A new French envoy now appeared, dragged Dupuis out of the country and somehow managed to convince the Vietnamese that he and Garnier had acted completely independently of French foreign policy. Dupuis, who had to pay his men out of his own pocket, was declared bankrupt and shipped off to France. (He later wrote several books about the war that he helped foster, faded into obscurity and died, aged 82, in 1912.)

Tensions between France and Vietnam were apparently resolved in March 1874 by the Treaty of Saigon. In return for recognition of Vietnam as a sovereign country – north and south – the Vietnamese would abide by French foreign policy, allow French merchants to navigate the Red River and call on France for military aid in times of need. It has never been clear whether the implications of this – that Vietnam was agreeing to become a French protectorate – was understood at the time by the Vietnamese. Mesny believed that, given the long-term persecution of Christians in Vietnam, the treaty was carefully engineered by the Catholic Church in order to give France a reason to re-invade Tungking at a later date.

More important, perhaps, was the fact that China already considered the Tungking region, if not all Vietnam, as its own vassal state, and refused to acknowledge the treaty. In 1878, a former Chinese army officer named Li decided to set up his own fief in Tungking and defected with several thousand followers. The Chinese government sent troops in after him while the Vietnamese – believing that Li might be after their throne – again called on the Black Flags for assistance. Li was soon defeated, but France was nettled that, contrary to the Treaty of Saigon, Vietnam had turned to others for help, and now decided that military intervention in Tungking was the only way to preserve their interests in the region. However, in order to avoid confronting the Chinese or Vietnamese directly, France chose to demonise the Black Flags instead – they had, after all, killed Garnier – using a campaign against them as an excuse for sending troops into Tungking.

Not that China was fooled. She reminded France that Vietnam had long been under Chinese protection: the Vietnamese king had, indeed, just sent his annual tribute to Beijing. France retorted that the Treaty of Saigon made Tungking a French protectorate which they had every right to defend against invaders. In March 1882, they sent a naval officer named Henri Rivière on a military expedition to Hanoi, ostensibly to support the garrison there. However, the Vietnamese believed that Rivière was spearheading a French invasion of Tungking, an impression he did nothing to dispel by repeating Garnier's ploy of taking over the city. The call again went out for Liu Yongfu's help, but Liu had, for the time being, fallen out with his paymasters and withheld the Black Flags from combat. As tensions rose, Li Hongzhang met with the French ambassador in Tianjin to discuss the situation, and – certain that China could never defeat France if it came to war – proposed dividing Tungking between them, the northern part remaining as a Chinese protectorate, the southern part becoming French. The Chinese military commander for Tungking, Tang Jingsong, was outraged by Li's plan and sent a memorial to Beijing advising that the only thing a treaty should recognise was China's historic claim to the whole of Tungking. The Vietnamese government too, indignant at the thought of being abandoned, appealed directly to Beijing for protection.

The French were also angry at Li Hongzhang, as, from their perspective, his proposals seemed too favourable towards China. They reinforced their position by sending more troops to Rivière at Hanoi, who now captured first the port of Hongay and then Nam Dinh, a strategic town on the southern channel of the Red River between Hanoi and the sea. Chinese mercenaries, recruited by the Vietnamese in lieu of the recalcitrant Black Flags, put up a stiff fight at Nam Dinh, and after the battle Rivière cruelly hanged them from his flagship. Liu Yongfu, taken aback by the fall of Nam Dinh and realising that the French could now move upriver to his stronghold at Sontay, decided to meet with Tang Jingsong about leading the Black Flags in a covert war against France on China's behalf. Accounts of their meeting differ, but it seems that Liu was encouraged to believe that, if he took power in Tungking, Beijing would recognise his regime; this would strengthen Chinese claims over the region and make it politically difficult for France to advance her territorial ambitions. Liu himself believed that the Chinese wanted the Black Flags to first occupy Tungking, and for him to then overthrow the Vietnamese throne and set himself up as king.

And so, with the Black Flags poised to engage French forces on China's behalf, Mesny arrived at Kunming in mid-April 1883. The city appeared wealthy enough but plain and unpretentious, with the ruins of former suburbs destroyed during the Muslim Uprising still surrounding the walls and its citizens pleasantly indifferent to the sight of a foreign face. Mesny spent the next month petitioning the governor with plans to construct a telegraph line to Beijing (only to be rebuffed by the assertion that "China did not require such things") and also caught up with Alexander Hosie, who had survived his mission through the heartlands of the Yi slavers and was now heading back east. In his travelogue *Three Years in Western China*, Hosie described their reunion: "In Yun-nan Fu [Kunming] I met Mr Mesny, of the Chinese Military Service, whom I had met eleven weeks before in Ch'eng-tu. He had now made up his mind to proceed to Canton by way of the West River, and he was good enough to give me the first offer of his horse and mule, which he could easily have disposed of to a Chinese".

Hosie's comments make it difficult to take Mesny's stated claims for coming to Yunnan seriously: one moment he was undertaking a difficult four-month journey to Kunming, "to assist the Viceroy [in gathering reports on Tungking] in consequence of his perfect knowledge of the French language", the next, within a few days of his arrival, he had already abandoned this plan and decided to head off on yet another voyage of exploration. In Mesny's defence, political forces were clearly working against him. In a letter written the following July to the eminent French sinologist Henri Cordier, Mesny explained that the Yunnan viceroy had refused him permission to travel to Vietnam, though "two of my men visited Liu Erh [Liu Yongfu], leader of the Black Flags, and were well received by him". The *Miscellany* also states that "the French Authorities in Tung-king having insisted that I should withdraw from Yün-nan I was obliged to leave the province". But given these versions of events, and Mesny's extremely brief stay in Yunnan, it's impossible to credit later reports by a Hong Kong newspaper that Mesny himself crossed the Vietnamese border and met with Liu Yongfu.

Though something of a fall-back plan, Mesny's renewed interest in the West River was not simply a frivolous way of concluding his four-year jaunt around China. As Dupuis had shown, the present routes for shipping Western goods into the Chinese interior were long-winded and expensive, and alternatives were needed – especially if these would also allow the profitable exploitation of the country's mineral deposits.

Indeed, one explanation of France's interest in Vietnam was that it was seeking a back door into Yunnan, which was wealthy in copper; surely Britain should look for their own shortcut into the province? Suggestions were already being floated around of building a railway from British-held Burma to Dali, but this might take years and the West River was already there: the system rose in Yunnan and cut diagonally across Guangxi and Guangdong provinces, finally intertwining with the Pearl River at Guangzhou and flowing into the sea near Hong Kong. It certainly wasn't all plain sailing – the upper reaches ran fast and shallow, while siltation lower down had made lengthy stretches difficult to navigate – but Mesny believed, perfectly reasonably, that if Tungking fell to France, trade currently conducted in and out of Yunnan along the Red River would be deflected along the West River instead.

Mesny left town around 21 May, having engaged a fresh battalion of pack animals and carriers "to convey myself and baggage to a frontier town called Po-ai... The muleteers are a rough looking and hardy set of small men, all scantily clad and heavily armed. They all have horse pistols and short swords stuck into their girdles, or slung on their back, ready for immediate use, as if they were bound to fight their way right through to their destinations". For their part, the carriers' sole weapon "appears to be their tongue, which they wag incessantly in praise or slander of everything and everybody".

The first three weeks was spent travelling overland to the headwaters of the West River system. Beyond the city of Guangnan, with its curious crowds, hot springs and friendly military, the difficult road climbed through a thick belt of cypress forest and into the mountains at Yangliujing village, a miserable prospect where, in the absence of an inn, visitors were put up at an old temple. Crossing the broad but shallow Xiyang River, there was a market attended by Miao toting stone weapons, a few Yi and a party of very shy Yao, each ethnic group distinguished by their own particular clothing and hairstyles. The township of Funing seemed to have suffered some natural disaster, with ruinous bridges and buildings; overall it proved "a wretched little place, with no trade or importance of any sort", not even a pawnshop. The trail continued up and down the hills, awkwardly paved but busy with lengthy mule trains; the first two animals always sported plumes and red tassels to chase bad luck off the road ahead, in much the same way that buses in China now hang Buddhist charms and pictures of Chairman Mao on their rear-vision mirrors.

At the end of the overland stage was Po'ai, a small port set on a sharp bend in the You River, whose houses were raised above flood levels on wooden piles or stone foundations. From here it was a swift, fifty-kilometre run downstream through a corridor of rapids and limestone cliffs to Baise in Guangxi. Baise itself, reached on June 21, was a prosperous trading centre favoured by Cantonese firms, with the usual array of merchants' guildhalls and a substantial military presence under the command of Li Xingu, a veteran of the Muslim wars in Yunnan. Mesny believed that the river here was just deep enough year-round to make it a viable terminus for steamers coming up from Guangzhou, which he thought could manage the nine-hundred kilometre journey in just five days. At present, a junk took anywhere between a month and six weeks to pull and pole against the currents. Once at Baise, there were in fact two routes to Kunming: the direct one Mesny had just followed, and a busier but longer option, entirely overland, via the northwesterly town of Xingyi.

Mesny now "engaged two junks to carry myself, baggage and retinue numbering about thirty persons" down to Guangzhou; he was again accumulating followers and possessions. He left no record of the next few days, but the You would have carried the party down past Nanning, now Guangxi's provincial capital but then just another sizeable port, where a year earlier the seasoned traveller, Archibald Colquhoun, had been prevented from landing due to the citizens' hostility. Beyond Nanning the river broadened and slowed down as it wriggled steadily eastwards through central Guangxi's hillocks and rice paddies; an easy, trouble-free journey on Mesny's well-equipped vessels, but one which was brought to a rude halt on July 6 outside the walled town of Guigang, where a disorderly mob in gunboats boarded his ship looking for contraband salt.

Not finding any, a landlord named Cheng Shouchun dragged off two of the crew as hostages. Mesny wrote immediately to Guigang's magistrate and demanded their release, but was blandly informed that the men were criminals and had already been fitted with cangues, weighty wooden boards attached like a yoke to their necks. A bribe to secure their release was clearly being solicited, but instead of paying up, Mesny moored outside Guigang's south gate and fired off protests to various authorities. Ten days later dispatches arrived from the provincial capital, Guilin, ordering the crew's immediate release; Mesny was, however, furious to discover that this was only because Guigang's magistrate had portrayed him as a dangerous bully who, caught in the act of smuggling salt, had abused and threatened the city's gentry. So as a matter of principle – or, as Mesny put it, "as a pioneer of commerce and Western civilization" – he refused to depart until he had been offered a full apology.

While he waited, Mesny busied himself by translating notes on Tungking from Chinese histories of Vietnam and making some original investigations into the origins of the Taiping Rebellion. This had started barely fifty kilometres northeast from Guigang at the village of Jintian, and Mesny tracked down former pupils of the Taiping leader, Hong Xiuquan, along with an ancient man, one of the original members of Hong's prototype Heavenly Kingdom. Sadly, Mesny never seems to have written up this unique source material; there are a couple of entries on Hong and his uprising in the *Miscellany*, but nothing beyond what any general history could have provided. The remains of an earthwork "fort" and a heroic red sandstone statue of Hong Xiuquan turned Jintian into a place of pilgrimage during the 1980s, when it seemed ideologically apt to make a hero of the man who nearly overthrew the Qing dynasty, but today – with a government not keen to glamourise revolution – the site, hidden amongst pine trees, has become run-down and neglected.

It took three months before Guigang's officials, by now hugely embarrassed at having an irate foreigner moored up indefinitely outside the city walls, managed to persuade Mesny to set sail again for Guangzhou and Hong Kong. He arrived there in mid-October 1883, proving the viability of the

West River route from Yunnan and having travelled over ten thousand kilometres around China since departing upstream four years previously. Triumphantly, he wrote to Henri Cordier: "So my Grand Tour is almost completed. I've travelled the eighteen provinces!" – perhaps revealing, after all, his main motivation.

Mesny's initial reception was underwhelming – the Hong Kong Chamber of Commerce rejected the offer to publish his travel journals – but he was soon being interviewed by the *China Mail*, who reported that he now habitually wore Chinese clothes with a false plait, in complete contrast to the earlier stages of his travels. The paper also built him up as something of an authority on the Tungking situation. Mesny's refusal to comment on Chinese troop deployment in Vietnam was variously interpreted: either he knew nothing about it or, as a member of the Chinese military, he was unable to say anything given that they might soon be fighting a European power. The *Mail* also pumped Mesny for details of the Black Flag's rumoured cannibalism, and he graphically confirmed that the soldiers habitually ate the heart and liver of those they killed, and "even eat their own people who die by accident".

By November, according to the rival *Foochow Herald*, Mesny had moved east along the coast to Fuzhou, the capital of Fujian province, where he claimed to be busy inspecting troops (or, as some Europeans suspected, raising them for the forthcoming Tungking campaign) at the direct orders of Li Hongzhang – though given Li's antipathy towards Mesny, this seems extremely unlikely. The *China Mail*'s belief that he was, in fact, at Fuzhou to take charge of the naval arsenal is more plausible, an explanation expanded on in the *Miscellany*: "In 1883 when offered the superintendence of the coast defence works in Fu-kien by Viceroy Ho Ching I accepted the offer, on condition that he would recommend me for brevet rank of governor of Formosa [Taiwan], as that was then part of Fu-kien province. Viceroy Ho said that no such rank had ever been bestowed on military officers, and he declined to recommend me for such, so I declined his offer. Subsequently, however, General Liu Ming-chuan was given the same post I had declined and with the very brevet rank I had asked for... He was subsequently given full rank of governor".

Later on in the month, Mesny returned to Hong Kong and – spurred on, as he put it, by the general "ignorance of the public" – settled down to write *Tungking*, his own take on Vietnam's past, French interventionism and the Black Flags. This fairly short work is heavy on history (Mesny takes over a hundred pages, some two-thirds of the book, to reach the 1850s) and stops short of an actual account of the hostilities between France and China, whose opening shots had yet to be fired. The bulk of the content was distilled from Chinese sources, or fed to Mesny by the Vietnamese diplomat Nguyen Thuat, whose diaries mention meeting Mesny in Hong Kong in late December 1883. But there was also some original material, including a colourful account of the Black Flags which, Mesny explained rather grandiosely, was "based upon knowledge acquired from two of my military pupils who were sent upon an Imperial Mission to the Headquarters of the band at Lao Kai". It's likely that one of these was Liu Chin-Hsiang, the Miao youth he had saved from execution after the battle at Jiaba Niuchang way back in 1870, and who possibly appears in the photograph of Mesny taken a couple of years later. Mesny contradicts this in *Tungking* by claiming that both these military pupils were locals from Guangxi, but clearly states in the *Miscellany* that Liu Chin-Hsiang visited Tungking and "was adopted by Liu Yung-fu, the Black Flag chief, as a brother".

Tungking was published in early 1884 in both London and Hong Kong, and received favourable reviews – except, predictably, in France, where *Le Rappel* described Mesny as "a rabid gallophobe". The book was straightforward and well-written, though completely uncritical of both its sources – part legend, part oral history, part fact – and the legality behind China's claims over Vietnam.

By far the most interesting section was about the Black Flags, whom Mesny was almost unique in taking seriously, portraying them as a professional fighting force, valiantly defending their country against a pretentious colonist (although his stance of moral outrage conveniently overlooked what Britain had done in China, and what it was then up to in Burma). The French, on the other hand, suffered "ridiculous irritability", were engaged in "criminal blundering" and – astutely seen, given the following century – were stirring up "a powerful and quietly inveterate enemy, who will spare no exertion till she has put herself in a position to retaliate". Not that the book was completely biased against France: Mesny believed that there would never have been a war if China hadn't covertly provided money, men and munitions to the Vietnamese in order to fan the flames of a conflict that promised the chance of taking on a European power by proxy, in a territory safely outside of China's actual borders.

The situation in Tungking had now begun to worsen. Back in May 1883, just as Mesny was departing Kunming for Baise, Rivière and fifty French mercenaries were killed by the Black Flags during a sortie outside Hanoi; Rivière's body was beheaded and hacked to pieces. The French minister at Beijing warned China against taking advantage of their loss, but the Chinese government, believing that France would now back down, beefed up their forces along the Vietnamese border and even occupied key towns in the north of Tungking. Tang Jiong, Mesny's superior from the Miao wars, was promoted to regional viceroy and head of military operations.

Mesny now broke his silence on troop deployment, commenting in the Hong Kong press that "the Chinese force on the Yunnan frontier two months ago consisted of eighteen battalions of 500 men each, all armed with modern weapons, but there were only two of the regiments drilled in the modern system. At [the strategic city of] Bac-Nindh, again, there were at least 5,000 Chinese". The article concluded with an eerily prophetic editorial take on the likely progress of the war: "It is very probable that the French will shortly succeed in driving the Chinese out of Tonquin, but the real conflict only commences when the frontier is reached".

France was in no way cowed by China's sabre-rattling, responding to Rivière's death with an emphatic recapitulation of its rights in Vietnam. They sent in gunboats to blockade Vietnamese ports and captured the southern capital, Hue, forcing a new treaty on its hapless king: Vietnam was unambiguously declared a French protectorate, subject to taxes; all international communications were to be made through French representatives; and all Vietnamese troops were to leave Tungking immediately.

The French military now arrived to battle the Black Flags, and after a few inconclusive skirmishes, drove them back to their defences at Sontay, west of Hanoi. Meanwhile, France demanded that the Chinese create a buffer zone along the China-Tungking frontier and open up the Yunnanese border town of Menghao as a treaty port. In the face of all this bellicose posturing, the Chinese government – nervous of rejecting these demands outright but angry at being pushed around – declared that Tungking must remain a vassal state of China, though conceded that there might be room for opening Vietnamese ports to foreign trade. The pragmatic Li Hongzhang was less equivocal, and again voiced his opinion that it was pointless going to war over a "useless tract of land" in a vassal state, and that China had neither the moral nor military power to dislodge the French from Vietnam.

On 14 December 1883, French forces closed in on Sontay, a well-fortified, moated town. A strong contingent of Liu Yongfu's Black Flags were holed up here – including Mesny's Miao understudy, Liu Chin-Hsiang – discreetly backed by Chinese troops.

After fierce fighting, the French captured a dyke outside the walls and then brought up artillery to bombard the relatively weak western gates. The barrage proved overwhelming and the defenders, having held Sontay's citadel for two days, fled under cover of darkness. They lost about a thousand men, while French fatalities numbered just seventy-five. Amongst the dead, Mesny later implied in the *Miscellany*, was Liu Chin-Hsiang, killed as he mounted a spirited defence of the gate during the final assault; "It was he who defended Son Tay so valiantly". An eye-witness account in *France and Tongking* by the British journalist James George Scott mentions a lone Black Flag soldier who held to his post as the French stormed in, continuing to fire until he was bayoneted to death, his finger still on the trigger of his Winchester rifle. Impressed by his bravery, the French buried Liu where he fell, inside the gate.

Although not quite admitting that its forces had been involved, China looked around for someone to blame for Sontay and picked Tang Jiong, who had taken a brief but unofficial leave at Kunming a few months earlier. He was now accused of causing morale to drop by his absence and sentenced to death. On February 4 the following year, Mesny published an eloquent plea for clemency in the *North China Herald*, praising his former commander's loyalty, integrity and military achievements: aside from his campaign against the Miao, Tang had fought rebels in Sichuan and at Xi'an, and had provided a stout defence at Sontay, holding out for several days against superior French firepower. "It would certainly be hard to find an official in the Empire possessed of so many virtues, and so few vices, as H. E. T'ang Chiung... [I implore] all the high officials of the Empire, to memorialize the Throne for another mark of the Imperial clemency, in pardoning a loyal and pure official, and a faithful servant of the Ta Tsing dynasty".

In fact, many of these high officials had already put in a good word for Tang, and suffered the consequences of speaking out against Imperial will: the day before Mesny's appeal was published, the Chinese-language *Shen Bao* reported that the no lesser men than Li Hongzhang, Zuo Zongtang and Ding Baozhen had been demoted for daring to request Tang's acquittal. Their joint pleas were successful, however, and Tang, one of the few Chinese officials that Mesny unreservedly admired, was once again pardoned. He later returned to public service, was appointed Junior Guardian to the Throne and died in 1909, his thankless career a roadmap of the hazards that awaited an honest official serving under the late Qing administration.

The Guangxi Army now openly crossed the Chinese border into Tungking to support Liu Yongfu and the Black Flags at Bac Ninh, northeast of Hanoi, the obvious next target for the French advance. In a decree, emperor Guangxu issued an ultimatum: "The fact that Anam [Vietnam] is a vassal state of China is universally known, yet France has actually dared not only to attack it in times past, but at the present moment is invading it with the purpose of usurpation, and has thrown the country into disorder. By doing so she has placed herself in the wrong. Moreover, the city of Bacninh, with its environs, constitutes one of the gates of the Celestial Realm itself, and in former times was guarded by numbers of our soldiers. Yet France has, on repeated occasions, sought to encroach upon this territory, in complete defiance of justice and propriety. We have, therefore, issued our express commands to the [Ministry of Foreign Affairs] to tell the Envoy of France that if his country should dare to make any further encroachment on Bacninh, China will immediately despatch a large army to give battle to the French." The decree went on to say that China considered the Red River to be the border, and that if the French crossed it to attack Bac Ninh they would be declaring war.

On the ground at Bac Ninh itself, Liu Yongfu was dismayed to find that the Chinese reinforcements were hopelessly disorganised; they barely seemed to understand how to use their field guns and ignored even such basic strategy as occupying the heights overlooking the town. His fears proved well-grounded: on 12 March 1884, the Guangxi Army fled in panic at the French approach, abandoning their weaponry without firing a shot, while the Black Flags, outnumbered and unable to offer battle alone, watched in incredulous disgust from the surrounding hills.

Flushed with such an easy victory, the French now threatened that, unless China relinquished all claims to Tungking, their navy would capture a Chinese port and hold it as security until a treaty was drawn up. The Qing government, humiliated by the cowardice of its troops, had little choice but to negotiate for what became the Tianjin Accord: China would withdraw her forces from Tungking, would recognize Tungking as a French protectorate, and would open Yunnan and Guangxi to French trade. For brokering this arrangement Li Hongzhang outraged his more bullish contemporaries, including Zhang Zhidong, who wanted to launch an all-out war. Even the Imperial court was dismayed by the scale of the submission and forbade the Chinese military from withdrawing from Tungking until the accord was actually signed.

That June a French force, on a mission to occupy the town of Lang Son on the Tungking-Guangxi border and struggling north through appallingly humid weather, ran across the Guangxi Army in a valley at Bac Le. A firefight broke out, with fatalities on both sides. In the ensuing diplomatic uproar, France claimed a breach of the Tianjin Accord while China reiterated her belief that the accord was invalid until signed. Mesny wrote that "the French have declared that it is their intention to demand satisfaction from China for this affair", provisionally amounting to payment of an indemnity of 250 million francs and, as security, the temporary handing over to French control of both the naval arsenal at Fuzhou and the port of Keelung in Taiwan. But this was pushing China too far: there was no way that even moderates could have agreed to cede sovereign territory. The ultimatum was rejected. The French Chargé d'Affaires shut up their legation in Beijing but, having no approval from Paris for a formal declaration of war, described the forthcoming hostilities as "reprisals" against China for the Bac Le incident.

China had expected the war to kick off in Tungking, where the French military were clearly at a disadvantage, with supply lines stretched and their troops unused to the torrid summer climate. And so they were caught by surprise when France opened hostilities on 23 August with a naval attack on the Fuzhou Arsenal, two thousand kilometres away along the south China coast. The arsenal had, ironically, been designed back in the 1860s by Frenchman Prosper Giquel and included a European-style shipyard, a naval academy and docks for the South China Fleet. The first of its kind in China, the complex was much admired by progressive-minded officials and was, in fact, where Mesny had just turned down a posting.

Despite numerous warnings – and even a letter from the French commander announcing the commencement of hostilities – the Chinese navy at Fuzhou appeared unprepared for battle. Cruising upriver, the French fleet comprised nine modern warships and two "torpedo" boats, which were designed to ram mines up against the sides of enemy vessels. They faced eleven Chinese gunboats, all armed with German-made cannon but otherwise, as one anonymous British observer put it, "more like ill-kept steam yachts than men-of-war". Within ten minutes of the opening salvo being fired at 2pm, the Chinese had lost three vessels and the French cruiser *Triomphante* was steaming inshore to shell the corvette *Yangwu*, whose midshipmen were American-trained. Returning fire despite being heavily raked and sinking, the *Yangwu* was finally dispatched by a torpedo. The rest of the Chinese fleet suffered a similar fate; only two vessels managed to escape upstream, though even these ran aground. At some point in the battle the Chinese set loose a flotilla of fire hulks, which proved of little concern to the French warships but caused havoc amongst the crowd of neutral vessels that had turned up to watch the fighting. By late afternoon the waters were littered with wreckage and Chinese corpses as the French pressed home their attack by shelling Fuzhou's coastal batteries. The arsenal was destroyed the next day. At least three thousand Chinese are believed to have been killed against just seven French casualties.

Initial Chinese reports announced a great victory, but when the truth reached Beijing the court issued an outraged and wholly unnecessary declaration of war, urging "the subjects of the Emperor to resist, capture or drive away the invaders". The Black Flag leader Liu Yongfu was openly made a general in the Chinese army and charged with recovering Tungking, while Zuo Zongtang, having been appointed as a special Commissioner to Fujian province, returned to a badly battered Fuzhou after a twenty year absence. The French navy, meanwhile, cruising east from Fuzhou to invade Taiwan, experienced an unexpectedly tough resistance to their landing and began an ineffectual blockade.

Back in Tungking, France launched a land offensive at Lang Son and captured the city in February 1885 after a difficult ten-day campaign. A second assault at Dong Dang saw the Chinese beaten right out of Vietnam and back into Guangxi through the narrow Zhennan Pass, whose crenulated stone wall had marked out the Sino-Vietnamese frontier since the Ming dynasty. The battle claimed the life of General Yang Yuke, the energetic, hunchbacked warlord from Dali who had so impressed Gill.

Despite these victories, the French government was rapidly tiring of the conflict, which was proving expensive, unpopular at home, and pointless – defeating China was only going to win them a distant territory of no proven value. They suggested peace negotiations. But before Beijing had time to react to this proposal, incredible news arrived from Tungking: the Guangxi Army under Feng Zicai, a veteran recalled from retirement in his seventies, had routed the French at the Battle of Bang Bo. His forces had faltered in their follow-up efforts to retake Lang Son but the French commander, de Négrier, had been badly wounded and his troops, believing that the Chinese were massing for a final, overwhelming assault, had abandoned the city.

It wasn't much of a victory – China had lost over two thousand men in this single battle alone – but the defeat toppled the French government in Paris. France's new leaders rapidly negotiated a peace deal based around the original Tianjin Accord; the demanded indemnity over the Bac Le incident was dropped and Chinese forces withdrew from Tungking. The Black Flags disbanded and Liu Yongfu was discreetly taken up by the Chinese government, who later made him an official in Guangdong.

On June 11 1885, Li Hongzhang – forced once again to be the official face of defeat – signed a treaty with France which recognized Tungking as a French protectorate. It must have been an especially dour occasion for Li, who had always been convinced of the futility of coming to blows, but he used the disaster at Fuzhou to strengthen his arguments for funding a modern navy. France duly occupied all of Vietnam and later, laying the groundwork for an advance into China, financed a railway between Hanoi and the Yunnanese capital, Kunming (where their former train station is now a restaurant, the *Gar du Sud*).

Not to be outdone by French expansionism in the region, Britain made Burma a province of India in 1885. From here they finally surveyed their own railway into Yunnan but never got around to building it. Sadly the West River, always too dependent on dredging, seasonal water levels and the whims of customs inspectors, failed to catch on as a transport artery, despite – just as Mesny had predicted – the French occupation of Vietnam displacing the Red River trade between Hanoi and Yunnan.

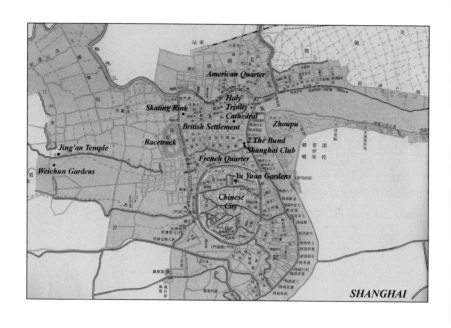

American Quarter

Holy
Trinity
Cathedral

Skating Rink

British Settlement

Zhoupu

Racetrack

2 The Bund
Shanghai Club

Jing'an Temple

French Quarter

Weichun Gardens

Yu Yuan Gardens

Chinese
City

SHANGHAI

THE MISCELLANY
1884–1919

As events in Tungking boiled over, Mesny was in his early forties, with almost a quarter of a century's worth of China experiences under his belt. He had fought in wars, visited every province in the land, built up potentially useful contacts with a few highly-placed officials and evolved plans for exploiting China's vast interior, full of untapped markets and raw materials. The question now was how to turn all this knowledge to his advantage.

There was no conscious sense of settling down yet and certainly no signs of returning to his wife at Guiyang; perhaps he felt that he had outgrown such a backwater. For much of the rest of 1884 Mesny was on the move: mid-June saw him in Beijing, reporting for the *Shanghai Courier* on the court struggle between Li Hongzhang's foreign appeasement faction and the pro-war lobby led by the outspoken Chen Baoshen and Zhang Zhidong. A few weeks later he turned up at Wuhan, discussing the Tungking situation with Chinese officials, who at that point – and despite their recent defeats at Sontay and Bac Ninh – seemed to believe that China could still easily defeat the French. Mesny wryly noted that soldiers at Wuhan seemed to be armed with little more than rusty old French muskets and (correctly, as it turned out) doubted the entirely fictitious report that the Chinese navy had just sunk several French warships off the south coast – the very cruisers that next month were to destroy the Fuzhou shipyards.

At Wuhan, Mesny also wrote to Jardine Matheson, a company whose wealth had been founded on the opium trade, touting for a loan of the kind that the Comptoir d'Escompte de Paris had given him permission to negotiate with Zuo Zongtang five years previously. As usual, the exact details of the affair are muddied by his various accounts of it. According to one version in the *Miscellany*, Jardine "placed two millions pound sterling at our disposal in 1883 for the purpose of assisting the Chinese government to build railways and other progressive works". In an earlier volume, however, Mesny says that Sir Thomas Wade made this offer at Shanghai in November 1875: "I called to see him at Jardine, Matheson's and he then told me that Robert Jardine had two million pounds sterling to invest at a reasonable rate of interest, and if I ever saw an opportunity of investing such a sum, more or less, on good security, I might write and let him know." And now, Mesny's letter to Jardine's gave the story yet another spin: "About five years ago whilst on a voyage from Europe to Ceylon, I was instructed by Sir Thomas Wade, on behalf of your firm, to offer the Chinese Government a loan of two millions sterling, for the building of Railways, Telegraphs, and other such progressive works". Presumably Mesny was hoping to get clearance for the loan, offer his services to Zhang Zhidong or some similarly progressive official, and then launch some of his modernisation projects. In the letter, Mesny went on to outline his valuable Chinese connections and linguistic skills, and suggested that Jardine's employ him full-time as an agent for their company. His *instructed by Sir Thomas Wade* sounds very definite, but Jardines replied with a polite, brief rejection of his loan scheme, though they were willing to consider his services as an interpreter and troubleshooter.

Disappointed, Mesny caught a steamer downriver to Shanghai in mid-July. Much to his annoyance, the captain dug him out of the Chinese section of the ship and forced him to upgrade to the first-class saloon alongside the other European passengers, at a greater expense. He was still at Shanghai that October, attending the first winter meeting of the Royal Asiatic Society.

This period of Mesny's life is marked by a sense of change, only partly fuelled by approaching middle age and the realisation that the days of his wider travels were probably behind him. In April 1884, in the first of a string of bereavements, Mesny's younger brother John died at Wuhan, aged just thirty-nine. He had been in China for around twenty years, working his way up through the ranks of the Imperial Maritime Customs; Mesny rarely mentions him in his writings, but from a few published letters the brothers seem to have been fairly close. John left behind "Elizabeth" Liao Chang, his Caribbean-born Chinese wife (who soon remarried), and at least seven children. None of the family enjoyed longevity: Elizabeth herself died in her early fifties, and only one of their many offspring seems to have survived into old age.

Just over a year later Mesny's own father died back home in the Channel Islands, at the age of seventy-three. Though William senior may have been disappointed that his son never became, like him, an "active and zealous member of the Methodist church", he had given his blessing to Mesny becoming a sailor at the start of his career and William had always stayed in touch, sending money home on a regular basis and even furnishing the small, comfortable villa on Alderney where his father spent his later years.

Not everything was bleak, however. March 1885 saw the birth of Mesny's son Husheng Pin at Shanghai – *husheng* means "Shanghai Born" – though not, as it turned out, to Mesny's wife Nien Suey Tsen, whom he had last seen five years before at Chongqing. The *Miscellany* never directly mentions the matter, nor what happened to the first Mrs Mesny, but from consular records it's clear that Husheng's mother was eighteen-year-old Han Fenglan, whose father had been a salt manufacturer. And the *Miscellany* does provide a convincing explanation, which neatly fits the circumstantial details of Mesny's life, in the form of a story about an unnamed "man" and his marriage woes. This man, aged forty and whose wife was barren, bought a sixteen-year-old concubine whose contract he then destroyed, leaving her free to stay with him or go as she chose. She stayed, and two years later they had a son, "still living and in good health". When his wife – who just happened to be from Guizhou – heard about this, she hurried down to Shanghai, keen to adopt the child as her own. Being rejected she became so bitter and vengeful that the man decided to divorce her, Chinese law allowing this if a wife had either reached thirty without bearing a son, or if she was shrewish and inclined to quarrel. The *Miscellany* also catalogues divorce procedures, one of which involved the humiliating process of driving the woman out of the house and then following her through the streets whilst banging a gong, so that everyone would know what had happened. Ominously, Mesny admitted that "I have seen one such case in Shanghai in 1884".

The fact that Mesny habitually bought girls out of prostitution lends further weight to the notion that this story is indeed autobiographical. If so, the rest of the article paints a troubled portrait of his life with Han Fenglan, culminating in her leaving him and running back home to her father around 1904. From the very little he wrote about her elsewhere, they didn't have a particularly happy life together.

As war with France escalated through 1884, Zhang Zhidong was promoted and sent south to Guangzhou as Viceroy of Liangguang, the twin provinces of Guangdong and Guangxi: Guangxi shared a border with Tungking, Zhang had spoken out against the French, and the Chinese government needed a hardliner in the region. Mesny found himself recalled to Guangzhou as Superintendent of Arsenals – the very post he had turned down in 1879 under Liu Kunyi – and was soon busy sourcing armaments for Zhang. In June 1885, he again wrote to Jardine's ordering five thousand magazine rifles and five million cartridges, six lightweight howitzers plus carriages and accessories, ten field guns, one thousand rounds of ammunition (including fuses and tubes for each gun) and ten machine guns, preferably four-barrelled, along with 500,000 rounds of ammunition. The commission on such a huge order must have been substantial; even so, Mesny went on to ask whether he was entitled to a discount.

Zhang had lost none of the reformist drive which had so frightened his staff at Taiyuan: with Liangguang's rich resources at his disposal he founded China's first modern mint, set up a publishing house, bought warships and, having little need for it, donated his salary back to the treasury. His more conservative-minded colleagues, concerned that Zhang's immense energy was making them look lazy and ineffectual, accused him of bankrupting his administration to fund these costly projects, but his accounts were examined and found to be in good order.

The viceroy frustrated Mesny in other ways. According to *Miscellany*, Zhang "retained me [at Guangzhou] one year and ten months, and when on the very point of ordering ten new cruizers for his new squadron he changed his mind and did something else, with the result that millions of taels have been squandered". Mesny had the right to be upset by Zhang's irresolution; he himself had been the middleman for the contract with "one of the largest and most respectable firms of shipbuilders in the whole world", and presumably when the deal fell through so did the fee he would have received.

Then came further unhappy news. By now Zuo Zongtang had arrived at Fuzhou to pick up the pieces of his naval yard in the wake of the French bombardment. From here he wrote to Mesny, inviting him to visit "with a view of undertaking some of the progressive works I had recommended years before, including telegraphs, railways and mining. Being then engaged in transacting some business at Shanghai for [Zhang Zhidong], I replied that I would call at Foochow on my return from Canton". But Mesny – having spent four years chasing the seasoned statesman halfway across China – had finally left it too late: Zuo, worn out after decades of continual hard service, died at Fuzhou in December 1885, aged seventy-three.

A year earlier, Mesny had praised Zuo in the *North China Herald* as "the most advanced and progressive statesman now living in China. Although he does not court the friendship of foreign nations, I believe him to be very justly inclined towards all. He was the first to establish an arsenal, and he also founded the great dockyard at Fu-chou, which he then intended to be a first-class one; and had he been left alone in his Governor-Generalship of the [southern] provinces, he would doubtless have done a great deal more. I have seen some of his private or secret memorials to the Throne in which [the joint designers of the Fuzhou naval yards] Messrs. Giquel and D'Aiguebelle were highly praised to His Majesty, as upright and very capable foreign officers".

Mesny rather spoiled the eulogy by continuing, clearly with reference to himself: "It is a pity that [Zuo lacked] the benefit of an intelligent foreign advisor near him during his north-western campaign. He might then have accomplished useful works, and conferred a lasting boon on these provinces".

Mourning for Zuo even reached the Imperial court, which donated a huge coffin and 2,000 taels towards his funeral expenses. Crowds lined the six-kilometre route to Fuzhou's port, where a steamer awaited to ferry Zuo's body up the coast and then inland to Hunan, his home province, for burial. His funeral procession included life-sized models of elephants, swirling dragons and lions made out of coloured silks and paper, soldiers carrying placards proclaiming Zuo's achievements and titles, a band of cymbals, crashing drums and wailing, clarinet-like *shawms* whose racket chased away bad luck, ranks of official mourners dressed in white robes, and a wealth of gold paper, scattered about like confetti. Zuo was honoured with the posthumous title *wenxiang* ("Cultured and Accomplished") and a modest memorial temple was built at his birthplace southeast of the Hunanese capital, Changsha.

It's an open question as to whether Mesny's fine opinion of Zuo would have survived actually being employed by him – he managed to fall out with almost every other Chinese official that he knew – but there's no doubt that the two men thought highly of each other. Shortly before he died, Zuo, a famous calligrapher, sent Mesny a pair of large hanging scrolls on which he had written the characters for *neng jiang wan ren wu zao qi, bu tong fan pin zai xu huai*: "Able to command many without impatience; Outstandingly modest in nature". Mesny treasured these scrolls for the rest of his life and used their laudatory inscription on the frontispiece of each volume of the *Miscellany*. A photograph taken at Shanghai in 1895 shows Mesny with his young son, Husheng, proudly seated between them.

With *Tungking* released to general interest it seemed that Mesny, despite his work for Zhang, might have found time to release an account of his adventures. Back in 1879, just before he had set off around China, he had approached George Bain, editor of Hong Kong's *China Mail*, with the hope of publishing a book – perhaps the earliest stirrings of what was to become the *Miscellany* – and Bain had suggested first whipping up interest by serialising Mesny's forthcoming travels in the paper. Mesny had duly sent him a few articles from the road which Bain had printed but neglected to pay for, as they had no written contract. Now Mesny was suing Bain for a thousand dollars; the jury decided in Mesny's favour but felt that the amount being claimed for only twenty-five columns of print was excessive, and awarded him just $126.25.

Tungking's preface had mentioned that Mesny had begun writing another book, "*The Chinese Empire*, now in course of preparation, which will contain an account of my travels, experiences, and observations". This work never materialised, but there were also the log books covering his journey from Guangzhou to Hami and Beijing, which Mesny had sent to Gill in London around 1882. Gill had done his best to get them published and now, following his death, they were being worked into a manuscript by Henry Holt of the Royal Geographical Society. Holt drew up detailed maps for the book with Mesny's route across China marked in coloured ink, and even went as far as collecting a mass of extra material to be woven into the threadbare text when word came from China not to proceed with the project: "After long delay a portion of Mr Holt's MS was printed and sent in proof to Mr Mesny, who made very serious objections to the compilation and the work was therefore not proceeded with." Perhaps Mesny was worried that the book would compete with his plans for *The Chinese Empire*, but it's a shame that, instead of simply rejecting Holt's attempt out of hand, Mesny never rewrote the work to his own satisfaction, leaving behind a successor to Gill's *The River of Golden Sand*.

And so, with his life story on hold for the present, from January 1886 Mesny satisfied his literary itch by writing a series of lengthy new articles for the "Outports" section of the *North China Herald* – which, given that they were highly critical of Chinese officials and their policies, he once again neglected to sign. The first few pieces focused on how Zhang was dealing with the responsibilities of his new posting, which included overseeing China's military withdrawal from Tungking. France was gradually consolidating her hold on the region but the end of the war had created a power vacuum, and to prevent the border being overrun by rebel militias Zhang assembled a peace-keeping force under the Miao war veteran Su Yuanchun, the sole Hunan Army commander to have survived the ambush at Huangpiao. Closer to home, Guangdong's roads and maze of waterways were awash with bandits and buccaneers, whose activities Zhang tried to deter with summary executions; Mesny suggested that the British navy should survey the West River, as the sight of their warships might drive off the infestation of pirates and allow trade along the route to blossom. On top of this Zhang was facing rebellion amongst his underlings, who complained that the viceroy's refusal to delegate was diluting their own powers; a local paper even whipped up a public demonstration against him, and Zhang's refusal to execute this hired rabble of prostitutes and idlers was seen as a great weakness. More seriously, an armed uprising had broken out on Hainan, the large island off China's southernmost coast, led by a mix of rebel Chinese and the indigenous Li population. Zhang spent much of his first few months in office scrabbling for funds to deal with these problems.

The former Black Flag leader, Liu Yongfu, now arrived at Guangzhou with remnants of his army, and was accommodated at the government offices until an official position could be found for him. Mesny met him at his lodgings, describing the famous guerrilla leader as "about 50 years old, with anything but an intelligent countenance, a smooth face, and might have a moustache if he allowed it to grow. He is very respectably dressed in fine furs, and has a few attendants only with him at the Yamen. He tells me however that he has brought several thousand with him, who are afloat [outside the city walls in junks]". Chinese descriptions of Liu were scathing, focusing on his scrawny frame and pinched features and deriding him as a "thieving Guangxi eunuch".

After some delay, Zhang granted Liu an audience and then returned the visit. This unusual honour (the viceroy was notorious for his offhand manners in keeping underlings waiting months for an interview) drew down further ridicule on Zhang, whose enemies now claimed was scared of the former peasant warlord. Liu's presence in town was an opportunity for Mesny to recycle his tales about the Black Flags for the *Herald*, nettled that his earlier claims of cannibalism amongst them had been doubted: "I see that the humdrum *Daily Press* has been questioning the accuracy of some of my statements". Later in the year, Mesny noted with quiet satisfaction that his long-promised promotion to brevet Lieutenant-General in the Chinese military had been confirmed, which, he hoped, would "put a stop to the captious notes on the General's rank which have been appearing in the *China Mail*."

Events in Yunnan next drew Mesny's attention, and he began to fanatically berate Cen Yuying, the man he believed had been behind the near-fatal assault on him at Qianxi. As Viceroy of Yungui (Yunnan and Guizhou), Cen was Zhang Zhidong's complimentary colleague and was trying to raise capital from Guangdong's wealthy merchants, apparently in order to develop copper mining in his region. Mesny doubted this was his true motive: "All that Cen wants is money, and war materials, avowedly with a view to opposing foreigners, but in reality to serve his own private ends". These ends, according to Mesny, were decidedly sinister, as Cen had "commenced a little war of his own against the hated English in Burma... Hundreds of taels will be offered as a reward for every English devil's head that can be got hold of, even though it be dug out of a grave. The missionaries and traders in Upper Burma are likely to find themselves tracked and hunted like beasts of prey... All this requires money, and Cen believes he can raise it here". While warning off prospective investors, Mesny welcomed the prospect of Cen coming to blows with the British in Burma: his rule in Yunnan had been bitterly resented, and locals would gladly join in an uprising should Britain send in troops to overthrow him. "I believe that the Chinese Government could not possibly do anything better calculated to invoke the invasion and annexation of Yunnan [by Britain], than the retention of [Cen Yuying] as Viceroy".

As 1886 wore on, the tone of Mesny's articles became increasingly caustic towards Zhang Zhidong as well, as he began to lose faith in the viceroy's policies. Much of this was due to Zhang's decision to employ German advisors: the Chinese were looking for allies against France, and had discovered that Germany had won the Franco-Prussian War of 1870. While Mesny plainly resented any foreign competition for the viceroy's attention, he also seems to have had some deep-seated dislike of Germany itself; a few years earlier he had derided the Chinese government's purchase of the *Dingyuan* warship from the Vulcan Company of Stettin, even though China had also ordered two Armstrong cruisers from Britain. He moaned that the deal had only been struck "through some kind of jobbery business" and that unless the Foreign Office picked up its game, British trade and influence in China would lose out to Germany, despite the inferiority of their products.

At first it seemed that Mesny might not have much to worry about: the Germans made a poor first impression with Zhang thanks to the ineptitude of their Malay-born interpreter, who instead of translating their greetings delivered a bewildering lecture on why all foreigners had blue eyes and brown beards. But he was soon reporting glumly that the newcomers had gained influence at Guangzhou by selling obsolete but inexpensive weapons, thereby undercutting legitimate dealers (such as Mesny himself): "If respectable traders in arms had been treated with more consideration by the high provincial authorities, the unscrupulous ones would not have succeeded so easily in deceiving the Viceroys and Governors who have be so easily victimised of late".

Things came to a head in late September 1886, when Zhang Zhidong ordered the summary dismissal of his British advisors for being "troublesome and petulant... Germans are no doubt more pliable fellows than Englishmen. The latter are too fond of telling officials the naked truth, whenever consulted on important matters, and this jars against the nerves of all the Chinese officials who are so fond of vain flattery and hearing pleasant things". Yet just a few days later Zhang offered to reinstate Mesny as Chief Superintendent of Guangzhou's two arsenals, though Mesny haughtily turned down the post of "for reasons which it is not necessary to mention here". Within a month the offer was repeated, the *North China Herald* claiming that the arsenals were in a disgraceful state, with the production of armaments almost at a standstill: "I hear that the Chinese, who alone are in charge, directors and artificers and all, cannot put a decent gun together among them". But several of Mesny's close friends had lost their jobs with Zhang and he was in an unforgiving mood, ranting that no other Chinese official had treated his foreign advisors with as much contempt. "Everything tends to prove that Viceroy [Zhang Zhidong] is totally unsuited for provincial service. His proper place, I should think, would be in the Imperial Library at Peking".

And so, at the start of April 1887, Mesny decided to quit his role of freelance advisor on modernisation and settle down at Shanghai, where he was to spend the best part of the following thirty years.

The city had changed considerably from the war-torn fortress it had been when he had last lived there in the early 1860s, full of refugee peasants, foreign soldiers of fortune and seedy entrepreneurs. Though technically still Chinese territory and never ceded as a foreign concession or treaty port, Shanghai had grown in the interim to become what some described, only half-sarcastically, as a model republic. In the wake of the Taiping Rebellion, the British, American and French residents had established a "Foreign Settlement" alongside the Chinese city, elbowed out the local authorities and elected a municipal council to run the place. Within its boundaries, the foreigner-run council administered its own taxation and laws to a 250,000-strong population – almost exclusively Chinese – and had its own police force, treasury, courts and public works department, and was only loosely answerable to any government back home. With everything geared to making commerce straightforward, Shanghai was well on its way to becoming one of the major trading hubs for Asia, and a visitor arriving up the Huangpu would have found the river teeming with huge European ocean steamers and Chinese vessels of all sizes and description. The mid-river moorings were occupied by a handful of foreign iron-clad warships, alongside four ugly, blunt-ended hulks where Indian opium was stored after being imported; it was clearly too valuable a cargo to risk warehousing it onshore.

The British quarter covered about a square mile, spreading west from the Huangpu to Tibet Road, bounded north and south by Suzhou Creek and the Yangjing canal respectively. Pride of the settlement was the river-front Bund, a functional flood-proof embankment developed into a broad, paved road lined with grand neoclassical buildings. Working south down the Bund from where Suzhou Creek was spanned by the delicately arched, wooden Garden Bridge – replaced in 1908 by China's first steel-girder construction, still in use – were the gardens themselves, with greenhouses, a bandstand, a monument to Margary and a compact area of lawns and flowerbeds. The new British consulate opposite, built in 1882, was a two-storey affair wrapped in shady colonnades as a concession to the subtropical climate. Below here loomed an imposing wall of company offices and warehouses; Jardine Matheson's were at the corner of Peking Road. A few streets inland, sandwiched between Kiukiang and Hankow roads, lurked the enormous Holy Trinity Church, a splendid Victorian red-brick Gothic edifice with wood and granite interior, looking as if it had been transplanted from county England and absurdly out of place given the compact scale of the quarter. In all, "the English part of the settlement is a collection of small palaces [with no] alternation of houses and hovels, of neatness and filth, of luxury and squalor... The private residences, the public banks, the wholesale warehouses, and even the retail shops, are large substantial stone buildings, constructed on a scale of absolute grandeur".

In fact, this grand design was restricted to the eastern half of the British quarter. West of Nanking Road things were more down-to-earth, a world of wood-fronted Cantonese teashops, bustling restaurants, narrow streets, tiny temples, opium salerooms, Chinese men airing their songbirds in ornate wooden cages and less salubrious businesses which one visitor wrote off as "nastier, dirtier, more trumpery, and, in fact, more loathsome shops I have never seen". Major roads, however, were full of energy: rickshaws running in every direction and porters bouncing along, their carefully-balanced bamboo shoulder poles weighted down with their wares; company messengers pushing their way through the crowds; here and there a rare white face given a courteously wide berth amongst all the jostling chaos. Foreign visitors ventured into this melange to visit Chinese theatres and inevitably emerged with baffled but condescending accounts of class-cracking vocals, discordant orchestras, magnificent costumes, raucous audiences and "grossly indecent" plots.

Characteristically, the British looked down on other areas of the foreign settlement. North over Suzhou Creek, the American quarter was patronised as being decent enough but only half-developed, with pretentious mansions, embryonic factories and warehouses, an excellent hotel, and a few middling shops, most of which sold only ordinary Chinese goods. More scorn was reserved for the French district, dismissed as sombre, unprosperous and squalid, weighed down under a heavy-handed administration whose sole achievement had been to drive all commerce elsewhere. As far as the British were concerned, the French quarter's most useful function was as a buffer zone between themselves and the original "native city" to the south. The only place considered more downbeat was Zhoupu, the largely undeveloped south bank of the Huangpu, which Mesny portrayed as "the abode of a large number of smugglers and rowdies, who congregate there to hatch their plans and dispose of their spoils" (and unrecognisable today as an overbuilt financial district actually sinking into the soft bedrock under the weight of its futuristic architecture).

Social life for the city's foreign contingent focused around the Shanghai Club at the southern end of the Bund; here were European newspapers and journals, several dining rooms, billiard tables, a café, and a comfortable lounge, though younger members of the club were rather given to gambling on cards and the ponies. The horse track itself was large and carefully turfed, located just west of town at the end of the city's major promenade, Nanking Road, where crowds gathered on race days to watch jockeys struggle with their tough and unruly Mongolian mounts. Beyond these distractions, Shanghai's entertainment options were limited; there were few unmarried European women in town and conversation amongst the majority, business-minded males revolved around trade – though if you enjoyed shooting, the waterlogged countryside surrounding the city offered plenty of wildfowl and other game.

Shanghai's Chinese spent their leisure time in the semi-rural western outskirts of town beyond the racecourse, which was just beginning to be developed as a fashionable residential district. Here was Jing'an Temple, one of the grandest in the city, which claimed to date back sixteen hundred years and was headquarters for the Chinese Buddhist Association. The nearby Weichun Gardens, "where the native youth and beauty of Shanghai congregate in large numbers every fine afternoon and summer evening", were a classical Chinese affair with rockeries, willows, bamboo groves, lotus ponds, zigzag bridges, pavilions and promenading crowds. The gardens were established not long after Mesny moved to Shanghai by a wealthy businessman named Zhang Shuhe, partly as a retort to the way that Chinese were barred from parks within the European quarters. The similar but much older Yu Yuan Gardens sat just south of the foreign settlement inside the original city, surrounded by a wall designed to look like a massive, coiled dragon and famed for its strangely-shaped ornamental rocks, which were meant to evoke famous landscapes. Foreign tourists were told that the attractive teahouse outside, built on piles in the middle of a pond, had been the setting for the story depicted on "willow pattern" crockery.

Considering the length of time that Mesny lived at Shanghai, he wrote very little about the place and almost nothing – beyond the fact that he became a Mason and attended regular meetings of the Royal Asiatic Society – on how he filled his days there. It's also unclear whether he lived as a Westerner, as a Chinese, or had feet in both camps; his first address was close to the racecourse on Shantou Road and only just within the foreign settlement. Without the stimulus of travel, of life in China's outports and the irritations of working for Chinese officials, his writing dried up; from now on there were no more lengthy newspaper articles, and first-hand accounts of his experiences were only resumed – largely retrospectively – with the publication of the *Miscellany* eight years later.

Occasional glimpses of Mesny in contemporary journals and official documents show himself becoming immersed in several projects. The first of these was continuing to champion the development of railways, a notion which was at last finding favour with some influential officials.

Since the short-lived Shanghai-Wusong line had been dismantled in 1877, the British had managed to "secretly" build a small line from their mines at Tangshan, about a hundred kilometres northeast of Tianjin, to transport coal to barges on the nearby canal. Now, a decade later – just as Mesny arrived at Shanghai – the railway's potential had been grasped by Li Hongzhang and contracts were being offered for anyone wanting to develop it: the first phase would take the line right to Tianjin's sea port at Dagu; and the second would extend the completed Tangshan-Tianjin section west to Beijing and east to military defences at Shanhaiguan, the point where the Great Wall ran into the sea. An immediate scrabble broke out amongst Western powers for a piece of the pie. Though the construction company was Chinese-run, most of the funding was being raised through foreign loans: the rails were produced in Britain and Germany, while Britain and France supplied the engines, surveyors and engineers. The complexities of developing railways and issues over their ownership were to tie up China's internal politics for decades.

Mesny, meanwhile, had gone in a completely different direction and become China representative for the Lartigue Railway Construction Company. "For passenger traffic there is nothing in the world equal to the *Monorail* Electrical Railways, erected by the Lartigue Railway Construction Company, Limited. On these railways it is possible to travel with greater speed, comfort and safety than on any other yet invented." French engineer Charles Lartigue had originally developed his monorail system to cross the Algerian desert, and had exhibited commercial prototypes at exhibitions in Paris and London. The first (and, as it turned out, only) passenger line was currently under construction in Ireland, and Mesny began a campaign to "cover the land and fill the air" with Lartigue's invention. Construction was certainly simple, fast and inexpensive, costing – in ideal circumstances – as little as a third of a conventional narrow-gauge railway. True, the ten-mile-long Irish line had come in at a steep £30,000, but Mesny emphasised the terrible terrain involved, requiring the construction of numerous bridges, embankments and complicated level crossings. In his enthusiasm, he erroneously claimed in the *North China Herald* that a Lartigue track was being built in Britain to carry two thousand passengers and 460 tons of freight daily, and that Russia had already had "lines in practical operation for some time", and were busy testing the system for military purposes.

Mesny now saw potential in a Beijing-Tianjin line, a Shanghai-Wusong line, and a Shanghai-Suzhou-Hangzhou circuit; the company would fund half the cost, if the rest could be raised locally. But it seemed that few shared Mesny's faith in Lartigue; conventional railways had been around for sixty years and everyone else was satisfied with the existing technology. The Irish line was expected to make three thousand pounds a year but in fact never turned a profit; it ended up carrying mostly schoolchildren and sightseers and closed in 1924. Mesny never did raise the necessary capital.

Throughout the late 1880s, provinces along the lower Yangzi were devastated by severe waves of flooding and famine. Exacerbated by earlier warfare, this was part of an ongoing cycle of natural disasters which had begun decades earlier and ran well into the twentieth century, killing more than five million people. Zeng Guochuan, a former Taiping veteran and now the regional viceroy at Nanjing, submitted a harrowing appeal for help to the throne: "During the present year, in the Provinces of Jiangsu and Anhui, while the high lands have been parched with drought, the low lands bordering on the Yellow River have been deluged, causing death and desolation of which the description is painful to hear, and the sight painful to look on". The Emperor took pity and allowed Zeng to divert his annual tribute rice, then being ferried to Beijing along the Grand Canal from central and southern China, and have it redistributed in the famine regions. But when even this Imperial largesse fell short of requirements, Zeng lobbied the governor of Shanghai for aid, who in turn approached the city's business community. After some hesitation – a few cynical Westerners doubted that the famine really was as serious as being reported – a committee of Shanghai's foremost "Foreign and Chinese Gentlemen" launched the North China Famine Relief Fund, which by early 1889 had raised some $80,000 in aid. A grateful Zeng noted this "proof that the foreign merchants take pleasure in benevolent actions, and it is very deeply recorded in my heart".

One of the worst-hit provinces was Anhui, whose ravaged landscape would later inspire the China-raised American novelist Pearl Buck to write her vivid saga of Chinese peasant life, *The Good Earth*. The committee looked around for somebody to report first-hand on the extent of the disaster and found Mesny, who was unable to contribute financially and so offered his services: "This gentleman has an excellent reputation, and his high official rank, Chinese dress, and knowledge of the language will render him thoroughly acceptable to the Chinese officials and people with whom he will be brought into contact".

Buoyed by this praise and a pocketful of introductory letters, Mesny left Shanghai in late January 1889 for a hurried, eighteen-day circuit through central Anhui's bitter winter chill, recording his progress in a bundle of little carbon-copied pages which he duly sent to London's

Royal Geographical Society. The focus of his fact-finding mission was Hefei county, seat of the provincial capital and Li Hongzhang's home town. Mesny reached here aboard a succession of ever-smaller boats – and one large wooden tub – which eventually saw him grounded in a muddy creek outside the city's eastern gate. The canal through the city was dry and the surrounding plain utterly treeless; Mesny's first advice on preventing further droughts was to plant trees, build reservoirs and dredge the river to make it navigable and guarantee a water supply.

The rest of Hefei county appeared fertile enough yet impoverished, the people dressed in rags and frost-bitten, and living with their animals in bare mud huts. At the small market town of Dianpu, Mesny found a third of the population starving after their rice crop had failed, though relief aid was beginning to trickle in; elsewhere villagers were getting by on a winter crop of barley. The continuing absence of trees bothered Mesny; he doesn't seem to have considered the possibility that they had all been cut down for firewood or even eaten by starving farmers. He summed up Hefei as "a poor county despite its very fine plain and the fact that tens of thousands of its sons served during the late civil war at a good pay, many of them rising to rank and opulence and many of them are still holding lucrative posts in various parts of the Empire. The lack of trees, good roads, and canals must always be a great drawback to the place as it has no fuel but straw, and its population being entirely devoted to agriculture are reduced to starvation whenever crops fail".

Aid had so far been effective, thanks to the honesty and efficiency of local officials, but the authorities were at a loss how to raise sufficient funds to keep their efforts going. Mesny estimated that over seven million people had been affected by the famine in Anhui alone, but that a suspension of land-tax and the distribution of two million taels in aid had prevented widespread starvation; this was probably why earlier reports had downplayed the seriousness of the situation. Some towns did indeed have ample stores of grain available from government warehouses, but most peasants were so impoverished by years of failed harvests that they couldn't afford to buy any.

Whatever else Mesny might have busied himself with at Shanghai, he still found time to dish out critical opinions of Chinese officialdom. In June 1889 Cen Yuying died, aged sixty-one, at his headquarters in Yunnan, where he had first sprung to prominence a quarter of a century earlier during the Muslim Uprising. The *Chinese Times* reported that Cen had been worn down by chronic malaria, though Mesny wrapped up his vitriol towards the man with the unlikely assertion that Cen had "died a raving maniac" in Kunming, haunted by guilt for Margary's murder and doomed to be transformed into a mule in the afterlife, to be ridden, whipped and beaten by his victim for all eternity. His Imperial Highness, the emperor Guangxu, begged to differ, proclaiming that "Cen Yuying was a man endowed with a loyal and patriotic nature, combined with solid attainments and tried experience": he was posthumously given the title of Grand Tutor, the imperial treasury donated 1,000 taels towards his funeral expenses and his five sons were all promoted within the civil service. Cen was buried in family tombs on a hillside near his hometown of Guilin; Mesny might have been gratified to know that in 2012 the derelict grave of the man who had perhaps once tried to have him murdered was robbed of its stone guardian figures by antiques thieves.

Zhang Zhidong was next to receive a beating. Having stirred everyone up at Guangzhou with his reforms and modernisations, Zhang now caught "railway fever" and memorialised the throne about building a line from Beijing to Hankou – an ambitious undertaking for what would be China's first long-distance route, not the least because it would have to cross the Yellow River. His proposal cited a raft of advantages that the railway would bring, laden with the hype that always accompanies such projects: trade would increase, there would be military benefits, mining would become more profitable, travel would be easier, and construction would employ millions of people. Zhang estimated the cost at sixteen million taels, to be financed by the treasuries of the provinces it passed through. Although materials would initially need to be imported, iron for the rails could later be mined from rich sources in his old stamping ground, Shanxi province. Whether the usually conservative court actually believed that Zhang's calculations were sound, or whether they were simply happy enough to let him take full responsibility for this risky project, the Beijing–Hankou Railway was approved. In 1889, Zhang was transferred to the governorship of Lianghu, the twin provinces of Hunan and Hubei, with his headquarters at Wuhan, the planned southern terminus of the line.

Almost immediately, however, he was in difficulties. One very traditional Chinese concern with railways was that in *feng shui* terms they were held to draw luck away from a place, especially cemeteries – a serious issue in such a densely populated country where everyone practiced ancestral worship. More pragmatically, railways were also seen as spearheading further foreign interference, and allowing them to run through the countryside was likely to increase growing public resentment against the government. The powerful Empress Dowager also objected, forcing Li Hongzhang – one of the few high-ranking officials in favour of the project – to withdraw his support. The provinces along the route were unanimous in rejecting any idea that they should fund the line, meaning that yet more foreign loans would have to be sought, at ruinous interest. It also turned out that Shanxi's iron mines were too remote to be financially viable; it would still be cheaper to import the rails from Europe. The English-language press began to ridicule Zhang, claiming that he had never seriously wanted to build the railway, only to support the general notion of "progress", and had been aghast when his plans were approved. Zhang seemed to confirm this view, amending his proposal to the effect that China would build no railways until she could do so with her own iron – an unlikely prospect in a country lacking any modern heavy industry.

Yet the viceroy now confounded his critics by announcing that he would open China's first full-scale industrial plant at Wuhan, the Hanyang Iron and Steelworks, with the express purpose of manufacturing rail lines. Though the foundry eventually became plagued by logistical problems and was sold to private interests, it drew in other industries and earned Wuhan the nickname of "Chicago of the East", ultimately producing 74,000 tons of iron annually (though much of this was exported to a rapidly industrialising Japan, who had invested heavily in the project). The economic spinoffs allowed Zhang to reform his provincial finances, doubling revenue. Doubtless much to Mesny's disgust he again employed

Germans, this time as instructors to train Wuchang's garrison in modern warfare.

It's impossible to admire Mesny at this point: instead of congratulating Zhang for having the courage to take on the enormous responsibility of large-scale modernisations – and forgetting his exhortations on just this subject while at Taiyuan thirteen years earlier – he wrote a spiteful article predicting doom for the viceroy's efforts. The works were "a giant folly", badly sited at the foot of a hill and prone to flooding from the Yangzi. Hanyang had no coke nor iron ore – this was true enough – and after factoring in transportation costs for the raw materials, the product would be more expensive than imported steel. Zhang should have listened to his advice back in 1882 and set up the works at Taiyuan, close to iron and coal mines. "And the result of all your operations as an Iron-master will be loss! Great loss!! Irreparable loss!!!"

Perhaps Mesny remained bitter over the lost shipping contract and Zhang's poor treatment of British employees at Guangzhou, but underneath everything was sheer resentment that Zhang had the audacity to introduce modern technology on this scale without consulting a foreign expert – namely, Mesny himself.

In retrospect, 1891 turned out to be a very bad year, the beginning of Mesny's career stall and eventual decline. Things started out moderately well, with an attempt to whip up interest in one of his pet projects – the opening up of Southwest China – by reading a paper on *Yunnan: its Treasures and Trade Routes* to the Royal Asiatic Society in Shanghai. But the audience seemed to miss the point; instead of being inspired or intrigued by Mesny's proposals, they picked over minor details with surprisingly petty, shallow questions which perhaps showed just how little most Shanghailanders knew or cared about life outside the city.

The real rot set in that September. The previous year, Mesny had invested in a successful but short-lived switchback railway, an embryonic roller-coaster, but it had been shut down by the council after irate neighbours complained about the noise. Now a typhoon spun over from the Philippines, bringing gales and torrential rain which dismasted ships, tore down telephone lines and destroyed Mesny's new, grandly-furnished Olympia roller-skating rink on Lloyd Road. Protective matting had been laid over the roof to hold down the tiles, but the straw's waterlogged weight brought the building crashing down, "ruining me financially so that I have never been able to recover".

Yet far worse was Mesny's involvement in the strange affair of Charles Welsh Mason. This young British customs official had been caught running guns to the Gelao Hui, an anti-dynastic society whom some held responsible for a string of murderous attacks on missionaries along the Yangzi valley. The attacks were causing a diplomatic crisis; the Chinese believed them to be the work of random anti-foreign agitators, but the British felt there was a widespread, co-ordinated conspiracy afoot and wanted the ringleaders brought to justice. Mesny, who had first written about the Gelao Hui in his *Shanghai Courier* articles twenty years earlier, disparaged the society as a vague, disorganised association which had been talking about overthrowing the Manchus for decades, if not centuries, but had never actually achieved anything. For his part, Mason saw involvement with the Gelao Hui as an adventure, an escape from the dull drudgery of life in a remote posting with just a handful of fellow foreigners for company. He somehow managed to join the organization and promised them arms and men to further their cause.

As the disturbances escalated in early 1891, Mesny offered to provide a machine gun and 30,000 rounds of ammunition to help protect the foreign concession at Hankou. Hearing of this, Mason wrote to Mesny anonymously, asking if he would source firearms for him too and at the same time recruit a force of foreign freebooters to capture forts near Shanghai. Mason's letter is rich in melodrama, as he tried to conceal his identity as a European by writing in pidgin English: "Kindly to reply by bearer because if you do not we find another. The bearer has ten friends, and if you betray they will shoot you. If you afterwards inform the authority, we must know and punish. If you come in, certain succeed and you great general with Tls. 500 per month. The bearer can to trust if you tell him. Better to write clear, pretend hand, no sign. Write answer immediate. Foreign word in Chinese envelope address &c. X c/o Custom

House Post Office, Chinkiang. Also next Saturday can trust young Chinese on Garden Bridge; he will say "Liang" you say "Chiang."

According to his account in the *Miscellany*, Mesny ignored the letter and so Mason, posing as a staff member from the American consulate (the two men had never met), turned up at his home. Mesny showed him the machine gun, demonstrated how to use it and Mason offered to buy it at some future date, but never returned. Court reports, however, state that Mesny actually went to the bridge as directed, but nobody showed up. At the very least, either version shows Mesny as being – whether naively or cynically – disturbingly willing to pursue the deal, and though he later handed Mason's letter to the British consul, he admitted this was more for his own protection in case Mason's "ten friends" tried to kill him. Mesny therefore had nobody but himself to blame when he was drawn into an embarrassing farce after Mason was arrested attempting to import a large cache of rifles and explosives from Hong Kong; the matter went to trial at Shanghai that October and Mesny was called as a witness.

While it remains unclear how deeply the Gelao Hui were really involved in Mason's plans, the case allowed both the British and Chinese authorities to find a focus for the anti-foreign disturbances. Any Chinese who had known Mason – his house staff, prostitutes and even a former general – were arrested as rebels, tortured and executed. Mason himself was convicted, jailed for nine months and then deported. In his 1924 autobiography, *The Chinese Confessions of Charles Welsh Mason*, he revealed that ingratiating himself with the Gelao Hui was part of a naive dream to overthrow the Manchus and set himself up as emperor. Mesny's view was that Mason was a dim-witted stooge for some manipulative troublemakers and that "nine-tenths of his revelations were unquestionably pure fabrications". Despite Mesny asserting that the trial convincingly cleared him of any wrongdoing, his name was now linked to that of a convicted revolutionary, and many of his Chinese associates began to avoid him.

Mesny still had a few friends, however. In January 1892 he met up with General Liu Heling, his mendacious mentor from the Miao campaign, who was working with Zhang Zhidong at Hankou and offered Mesny a post "organizing some sort of naval brigade". But Mesny scorned the proposal, pompously demanding that Zhang should write to him personally if he was serious, and yet again cutting himself out of a potentially lucrative, influential position. And Liu's well-meant offer was to be the last of its kind that Mesny would ever receive. On May 23, during a trip to Tianjin and Beijing to meet with Manchu officials, Mesny had a disastrous interview with Li Hongzhang. A few weeks earlier, he had written a signed letter to the *North China Herald* describing Li as a diligent, worthy official, whose long experience made him almost irreplaceable – but that Wu Dacheng, a former Guangdong governor, would be a good choice if the need arose. Most other Chinese politicians, Mesny continued, were too set in their ridiculously archaic ways, "better qualified to be clothed in strait jackets than in an official's costume". While Mesny probably intended the article in praise of Li, and to soften him up before their meeting, it was easy enough to interpret it as a suggestion that the viceroy was merely the best of a bad bunch, and that he should really step down in favour of Wu, a man who had once served as his secretary.

Now Mesny walked in on a furious Li Hongzhang, who – in the light of this article and the Mason affair – told him to shut up, settle down and take up a serious post. Mesny suggested that Li offer him one and Li refused, saying that he wasn't even fit for his former lowly position as a customs inspector. He wondered how Mesny, who appeared to have had no obvious source of income since rejecting his offer of employment ten years previously, managed to get by. Mesny could speak fluent Chinese and yet had learned nothing for all his time in China; despite having won high military rank, he had conspired with Mason and secret societies to foment rebellion. He ought to be executed for treason! The meeting ended with the two men on their feet, shouting at one another, and Mesny stormed out between protective ranks of astounded government staff.

Blind to his own shortcomings in the matter and weighed down by anti-German prejudices, Mesny believed that Li had been fed these hostile opinions by Customs Commissioner and long-time China resident Gustav Detring, one of Li's many foreign advisors (and also founder of Tianjin's racetrack). Whatever the truth of the matter, Li Hongzhang was the most powerful statesman in China and not somebody to fall out of favour with. Mesny now found himself shunned by the Chinese officials he had counted on for employment, and after this was never offered another official position.

Li's barb about Mesny's mysterious income highlights the fact that Mesny was rarely explicit about how he made money. He certainly seemed to have lived comfortably enough until this point, despite expenses incurred by a decade of almost non-stop wanderings, when he sometimes had an entourage of thirty or more dependents and had to hire boats, porters and pack animals. He had received generous presents from officials, conducted a little trade at Guizhou and Chongqing, and had presumably been paid for his newspaper articles and perhaps even profited from dealing in antiques and precious stones – not to mention the relatively brief periods at Taiyuan and Guangzhou when he was actually on official payrolls. The Mason affair suggests that Mesny had also continued in the arms trade after settling at Shanghai, and, as it soon turned out, he had made some investments too. But none of this suggests financial security and, having isolated himself politically, Mesny's fortunes now slumped when Hall & Holtz, an upmarket department store in which he held shares, went into liquidation. The company survived restructuring, but Mesny lost his money and in 1893 the *North China Herald* reported him in court, facing eviction by his landlord for unpaid rent. At the same time he was also successfully sued by a Chinese woman named Chow, in a confused case involving a loan, some rental property owned by Mesny, and a counter-claim by his concubine Han Fenglan (or "my housekeeper", as he pointedly described her in court). Mesny had to take out a stiff mortgage on the properties in order to pay off his debts.

1894 turned out to be another momentous year, and not just for Mesny: on July 31, his daughter Marie Wan-er was born, and on the very next day China went to war with Japan.

Japan, which like China had been forcibly opened up by Western powers during the nineteenth century, had proved rather more enthusiastic about embracing the benefits: if Europeans could use their weapons to forge empires and impose their will on others, then perhaps Japan could too. Accelerating out of a feudal cocoon, they reorganized their politics, economy and – especially – their military along Western lines and set out to settle some very old scores.

Just two hundred kilometres west across the sea – and right on China's doorstep – lay Korea, politically split between conservatives surrounding the court and reformist factions in open revolt against them. When Korea appealed to China for military aid to help suppress the uprising, the Japanese decided to step in too, in support of the rebels. Few outside observers had any doubt of the outcome. Europeans saw Japan as "merely a country of beautiful flowers, charming mademoiselles, fantastic parasols, fans and screens", whilst the Japanese themselves were insultingly dismissed in China as "dwarf pirates", a nation of noisy, bragging upstarts who had stolen what little culture they possessed. Furthermore, following the naval debacle at Fuzhou a decade earlier, Li Hongzhang had spent vast sums on modernising China's Northern Navy, sending his officers overseas for training and importing a fleet of armour-plated, foreign-built destroyers, gunboats and cruisers. But the navy had never fought an action, and China's luxury-loving Empress Dowager had secretly skimmed off thirty million taels earmarked for naval funding to resurrect the ruined Summer Palace outside Beijing (renovations which, with inspired cynicism considering where the money had come from, included a giant ornamental stone boat).

On September 15 1894, China's Huai Army met Japanese forces at Pyongyang in Korea and were convincingly beaten. Two days later, the Northern Navy lost five of its ten warships – including the British-built *Zhiyuan* – at the Battle of Yalu River, through a combination of poor tactics, inexperienced leadership and obsolete ammunition. Defeated by land and sea, only the onset of a fiercely cold winter prevented the Japanese military from storming unchecked into China.

Li Hongzhang was blamed and temporarily stripped of his powers; a sadder casualty was Philo McGiffin, an American officer commanding the heavy-hitting Chinese warship *Zhenyuan*. McGiffin was another foreigner whose career paralleled Mesny's: under Li Hongzhang's patronage, he oversaw the construction of Chinese ironclad warships in Britain and was appointed head of the naval college at Weihai. The *Zhenyuan* actually survived the battle but McGiffin was badly wounded and later committed suicide after returning to the United States.

At the outbreak of war, Mesny volunteered for service in Korea and travelled to the Manchurian border at Shanhaiguan, the place where, at the start of the Qing dynasty, Wu Sangui had let the Manchu armies into China. Shanhaiguan was under the control of Imperial military commissioner Liu Kunyi; the two men had last met fifteen years earlier at Guangzhou, where Mesny had disparaged Liu's idea of using a lottery to raise capital for coastal defences. Now the veteran official once more dismissed Mesny and told him to go home. Way back in the Taiping era, Liu had served briefly under Li Hongzhang and Mesny predictably suspected some collusion between them in his rebuttal, vindictively characterising Liu in the *Miscellany* as "a lazy and incapable official who ought to have been forced to retire decades ago in order to make room for a superior man". This is grossly unfair: Liu had, in fact, come out of early retirement in 1890, and on hearing that the Qing government had begun negotiating a peace deal with Japan, urged them to keep fighting instead.

Despite his rejection, a rumour began to circulate that Mesny had in fact been appointed to take over Liu's post in Korea and Manchuria, a story ridiculed by the *Hong Kong Telegraph*, who pointed out that Mesny had "practically retired from active service". In the *Miscellany*, Mesny asserted that he was actually asked to reform the Emperor's personal guards at Beijing, but that – of course – Li Hongzhang had a German drill instructor appointed instead.

Short of funds, with a dwindling reputation and with his career as a troubleshooter and advisor to Chinese officials over, what was Mesny to do next? Obviously, parade his own version of events and gain fame! It was over a decade since Mesny had first mentioned, in the introduction to *Tungking*, that he was compiling an authoritative work on China, and he now decided to publish his opus as a weekly magazine. Priced at thirty cents a copy, or ten dollars for a year's subscription, *Mesny's Chinese Miscellany: A Text Book of Notes on China and the Chinese* launched on

Thursday, September 26 1895, from company offices at No.2, the Bund (a site occupied today by Shanghai's *Waldorf* hotel). Issues appeared in uneven bursts over the following decade, later gathered together into four bound volumes of around five hundred pages each.

Once you got past the daunting first few pages – a dictionary-like list of Chinese characters – the *Miscellany* turned out to be written in a refreshingly direct style, free from colonial condescension. At its core were "Notes on China and Chinese Subjects", where Mesny unburdened his extensive knowledge in thousands of brief entries on language, acupuncture, the theatre, political institutions, mining, folk heroes, pawnshops, alchemy, the military, trade routes, cuisine, marriage customs, botany... the list went on. The lack of direction echoed his earlier *North China Herald* articles from Taiyuan, though Mesny sometimes focused on one particular theme, profiling a province in depth or gathering together "Commercial Notes" for would-be foreign entrepreneurs. There was also some overlap with "Progress in China", a regular section which enlarged on the Nineteen-Point Plan Mesny had presented to Zhang Zhidong back in 1882, developing it into a soapbox for airing his opinions on all aspects of reform and modernisation.

Each issue also featured an exciting instalment of Mesny's autobiography, grandly titled "The Life and Adventures of a British Pioneer in China", beginning with his arrival at Shanghai in 1860. He barely managed to complete twelve years of his story, despite cramming in as much detail as possible by using a smaller font than in the rest of the magazine: the *Miscellany*'s first two volumes cover Mesny's career as a blockade-runner on the Yangzi and his capture by the Taipings, the third features reminiscences of Hankou during the 1860s and the start of his military career in Guizhou, while volume four concludes with his arrival at Guiyang in 1872 after the Chong'an campaign.

In brief then, the *Miscellany* was everything Mesny wanted to say about China, a ramble through thirty years of personal notes, opinions and memories. It wasn't all original (he quotes fifty or more sources), and others had produced similar works – notably the long-running *Chinese Review* magazine, and Dyer Ball's classic *Things Chinese* – but none of these matched Mesny's idiosyncratic approach to such a vast range of subjects, the result of his own restless character and intelligent interest in almost everything. And only the *Miscellany* had a sense of humour which allowed itself to swing between the pedantic and the seemingly ridiculous, such as by reporting a novel approach to gold mining from north China: "The inhabitants of the neighbourhood [of Yongbei] keep large flocks of geese to work the gold fields for them and when the geese are found to be very heavy they are killed and their mauls emptied of the gold therein". As a source of insightful information into practically every facet of domestic and official life in late nineteenth century China (as much about what people of the time believed, rather than what was necessarily true), the *Miscellany* had no peer in English. Even more importantly, without it there would be little record – aside from his largely anonymous newspaper articles – of either Mesny or his extraordinary life.

Mesny's stated purpose in publishing the *Miscellany* was to shed "a little more light" on Chinese culture for his fellow expatriates, though the text was not always reliable. While there is no reason to doubt his bare facts, Mesny's dates are hopelessly inaccurate and he frequently shifted the emphasis of events to serve his own ends. His travels around China between 1879 and 1884, for example, seemed largely self-motivated in his original newspaper articles but by the time of the *Miscellany* had become dignified by a sense of purpose, often dressed up as "special commissions" for the Chinese government. The much-trumpeted Nineteen-Point Plan keeps mutating too, not just compared with the original loose proposals from 1882 but even throughout the *Miscellany* – it finally ends up as "Nineteen Great Propositions", despite actually numbering twenty of them – to increasingly emphasise the credit Mesny felt he deserved for pioneering the cause of modernisation. There are far more subtle shifts as well: for instance, in his detailed account of the Chong'an campaign, Mesny drops any mention of General Liu Heling's meanness towards his troops, though this was a central theme of the original *Shanghai Courier* articles. Perhaps the two men were still in touch.

As already seen, the *Miscellany* could also be fiercely vindictive towards those whom Mesny held a grudge against, such as Li Hongzhang, Cen Yuying and Liu Kunyi. But then Mesny was by now well into middle age and writing at a frustrating, insecure time, when his fortunes were fading and a genuine anti-foreigner sentiment was on the rise in China. For all this his anger was always personal, never stooping to crass racism; it's notable that he never even demonised the Miao or Hui, despite fighting against them for four years and being exposed to the Han Chinese view of these "savages".

With his future riding on the project Mesny clearly needed the *Miscellany* to succeed, and he must have been cheered when reviews proved largely positive. The authoritative *North China Herald* enthused over "a full, even minute, record of a thousand-and-one novel incidents [and] an astonishing collection which illustrates... the inner workings of the Chinese mind and heart". Others were impressed by Mesny's military rank, his long years in China and his experience of remote corners of the country, and saw a time when this distillation of knowledge would be "of the greatest assistance to every consul, merchant, missionary or student" of China. True, there were also quibbles over minor factual errors and poor proofreading, but the most widespread criticisms focused on what were also the *Miscellany*'s strongest points: the extraordinary range of subject matter, and its haphazard presentation. A much-needed index was included with each bound volume, but one baffled reviewer commented, "We have tried in vain to discover the order on which the arrangement of the work is based, but have failed utterly to detect it. Such being the case we haven't the remotest idea of how far the work is to proceed, or when, if ever, the "Miscellany" is to be exhausted". The *Shanghai Mercury* agreed, enlarging on what it saw as the *Miscellany*'s shortcomings: "The information given is useful and interesting, but it is difficult to discover its connection. It is given, in fact, in too discursive a manner... it is rather too egotistic... If General Mesny corrects these slight mistakes we augur a great success for his *Miscellany*".

War with Japan continued through into 1895. Having penned the remnants of China's Northern Navy into Weihai harbour in Shandong province, Japan destroyed them in a combined land and sea assault; the German-built *Dingyuan* warship, pride of the Chinese fleet, was scuttled by its crew and sank after being torpedoed. North across the Gulf of Zhili,

Japanese forces simultaneously broke out of Korea to invade Manchuria, clearly with a view to launch a pincer attack on Beijing. As plans were made to evacuate the Imperial household westwards, Li Hongzhang and his German advisor Gustav Detring were packed off to Japan in April to sue for peace at the Treaty of Shimonoseki. China agreed to recognise Korea's "autonomy" (in fact, Korea became a Japanese protectorate and was later annexed wholesale), four Chinese treaty ports were opened to Japanese merchants and the country was fined a huge war indemnity, eventually set at 230 million taels. But most humiliatingly of all, China was forced to cede territory for the first time since Britain had taken Hong Kong back in 1842: Japan now claimed Manchuria's Liaodong Peninsula, with its strategic, ice-free port at Lushun; and Taiwan, the large island off the Fujianese coast which the Chinese themselves had captured from the Dutch at the start of the Qing dynasty.

For brokering such appalling terms, calls went out across Taiwan to assassinate Li Hongzhang should he dare set foot on the island. Ironically, Li narrowly missed being murdered by a Japanese fanatic whilst arranging the treaty, which worked in China's favour – his hosts were so embarrassed that they actually dropped some of their demands. Mesny joined in the furore, questioning what had become of the seven million rifles apparently purchased by Li, when Chinese soldiers in Manchuria had been armed only with spears and antique matchlocks. He also repeated a scurrilous report that two statues of famous traitors flanking the tomb of the patriot general Yue Fei at Hangzhou had been torn out by the mob and replaced with effigies of Li and Detring, to be urinated on by visitors wanting to show their contempt. Mesny relished the German's imagined humiliation by proxy in an uncharacteristically racist stereotyping: "It is astonishing how well the founders [of the statue] have imitated Detring's bullet head, close cropped hair, and well trimmed moustaches". There's no evidence of these statues today, if indeed they ever existed.

Taiwan might have been abandoned by the mainland, but it wasn't giving in to Japan without a fight. The island now declared its independence as a republic under the Qing governor-general, Tang Jingsong, but when Japanese forces actually landed, Tang fled to the mainland in June 1895, leaving the former Black Flag commander, Liu Yongfu, to head up resistance. Liu engaged in a series of indecisive guerrilla raids against the invaders, though totally fanciful propaganda prints were circulated in China showing his victorious forces capturing and beheading the Japanese general Kabayama Sukenori (who in fact survived the campaign, his head firmly attached, to become Taiwan's first Japanese governor). In October the Taiwanese capital, Taipei, fell, completing Japan's occupation of the island, which lasted until after World War Two. According to popular rumour, Liu Yongfu eluded capture and escaped back to the Chinese mainland by dressing as a woman; the redoubtable warlord later published his memoirs and, outlasting the Qing Empire itself, died in January 1917 at the age of seventy-nine. Mesny once praised Liu's skills as a guerrilla fighter in the *North China Herald*: "Few if any Chinese Generals can show such a splendid record of military service in such a short time... no man in China could come up to him in the way of record of battles fought and won".

Japan didn't get everything it wanted from Shimonoseki. Russia, Germany and France, alarmed at her territorial gains – and in an unusual display of solidarity – coerced Japan into handing back the Liaodong Peninsula to China, an apparent act of goodwill which was in fact used as leverage by the other foreign powers to demand further territorial concessions for themselves. In the meantime Li Hongzhang, to keep him out of the public eye until tempers had cooled, was dispatched as a Special Commissioner to St. Petersburg in Russia, where he attended the coronation of Czar Nicholas II. He also quietly signed a treaty allowing Russia to build a railway through northeastern China, linking the Manchurian capital, Harbin, with the ice-free port of Lushun – effectively giving Russia control of the very territory it had just forced Japan to return to China. Li then extended his mission into a world tour, returning home via Europe, the United States and Britain, where he was, incredibly, knighted by Queen Victoria herself. This accolade could only have confirmed Li's image back home as a stooge to Western powers, and Mesny commented sourly that "Earl Li is the most unpopular though most capable of Chinese officials amongst the conservative anti-foreign party in China".

September 1896 saw the end of the *Miscellany's* original print run; with the first two volumes under his belt, Mesny estimated that he had lost two thousand Shanghai dollars on the business and appealed for advertisers to fund a third volume which he was hoping to launch that October. As he was also being investigated by the Shanghai Customs over an advert in the *Miscellany* offering up a large number of redundant French rifles for sale, it's also likely that Mesny was still topping up his bank balance with a little arms dealing.

Japanese conquest had done nothing to ease anti-foreigner violence in China. Now two German missionaries were killed in Shandong province. In retaliation, Germany seized the port of Qingdao (incidentally, setting up China's first commercial brewery here under the "Tsingtao" label) and demanded sole rights for rail construction and mining operations throughout the province. Other foreign powers jumped on board, forcing fresh concessions that saw China carved up into regional "spheres of influence": the British took the Yangzi valley basin (an enormous land-grab in which they claimed the provinces of Sichuan, Hubei and Hunan, Jiangxi, Anhui and Jiangsu, plus parts of Henan, Yunnan and Guizhou and mining rights for Shanxi); the Russians occupied Manchuria and Mongolia; Japan took control of Taiwan and adjacent Fujian province; and France pushed in to what was left of southwestern China. Not even this was enough. When the contract for constructing Zhang Zhidong's Beijing–Hankou railway was finally won by a Belgian syndicate, the disgruntled British government put pressure on China to grant them the rights to build future rail lines too. Mesny sarcastically reported this new meddling to be "progress of a marvellous nature", glumly listing the number of mines, rail lines and regions that the Chinese had recently ceded to foreign control.

With the political situation deteriorating rapidly, and fearing a popular uprising against the Qing dynasty unless some radical changes were introduced, Zhang Zhidong – ever ready to stick his neck out for the good of the country – published *An Appeal for Reform* in 1898 (abridged and translated into English as *China's Only Hope*). This was something of a belated manifesto for the long-established Self-Strengthening Movement, of which the highest-profile project had been Zhang's iron foundry but which broadly included all ideas that adopted Western technologies for China's benefit. While the *Appeal* was strongly respectful of tradition, there's no doubt that some of Zhang's themes echoed Mesny's original Nineteen-Point Plan, especially in its call to turn temples into classrooms teaching modern subjects; education should reflect the abilities of each student, whether they showed an aptitude in mathematics, art, science, languages or sport (a very modern approach, utterly at odds with the traditional Chinese method of learning-the-classics-by-rote for all). Like Mesny, Zhang also picked out the importance of railways: "Is there any one power that will open the door of learning for the scholar, the farmer, the workman, the merchant, and the soldier? To this question we reply emphatically that there is, and it is the Railway... The Railway is the source of wealth and power of Western countries... how can the Chinese people progress or even exist without railways?" Militarily, Zhang not so much proposed Mesny's idea of modernising China's army, emphasising instead the importance of not relying on International Law or disarmament to bring peace to the nation, but rather in maintaining a viable fighting force that would help keep foreign powers at bay.

The *Appeal* was also bluntly critical of China's failure to face up to foreign aggression. Her initial fault was in attempting a direct confrontation with Britain in 1840, when she had no notion of modern warfare. However, sixty years on she still hadn't modernised her forces, and Zhang berated his fellow-countrymen for the ingrained stupidity, indolence and corruption which had held China back. "We admit that the employment of foreign methods in China has not been a success, but we cannot admit that this is due to our faults. The promoters of these foreign schemes showed no enterprise except to further their own personal and private ends [and were not, therefore, acting in the interests of the country]". Recently China had been beaten by Russia, France and now Japan, and still the government hadn't learned its lesson. The country should send students abroad to be educated in modern ways, and bring that knowledge back to China. But the *Appeal* was certainly not a blueprint for thoughtless Westernisation: Zhang was emphatic that reform, especially the adoption of foreign methods or technologies, should be entirely for China's good and developed along Chinese lines.

Over a million copies of Zhang's *Appeal* were printed, endorsed by no lesser patron than the emperor Guangxu, who proclaimed that it "embodies a fair and candid statement of facts. A diligent perusal of its contents will broaden the mental scope and open up methods of far-reaching usefulness." Fired up by the whole notion of reform, Guangxu turned to an unlikely ally: a political radical named Kang Youwei. Kang, who knew Mesny slightly, was an articulate if rather arrogant scholar whose eclectic philosophy drew inspiration from Chinese, Western and even Japanese sources. Like Zhang Zhidong he sought an expansion of the Self-Strengthening Movement, but had very specific ideas on how this should be achieved: where former attempts at modernisation had been carried out piecemeal, Kang wanted legislated, uniform change introduced across China and proposed a constitutional monarchy, the end of the Imperial examination system in favour of Western-style schools and universities, and a rapid development of industry. Despite the implications for his own position, the emperor quietly approved Kang's suggestions, and on 11 June 1898 launched a barrage of decrees for China's modernisation in what became known as the Hundred Days' Reform.

From the outset, Guangxu realised that he would need more than words to defend his plans against the largely conservative court, who depended on the old order for their positions and were anyway mostly in thrall to his baroque and decidedly sinister aunt, the Empress Dowager Cixi. Vain and deeply ignorant of the world beyond her palace walls, Cixi had been the real power behind the Manchu throne for almost forty years; she hated foreigners and their ideas, rejected anything that loosened Qing control over China and was certainly not going to relinquish her own authority without a struggle. There was no place for her in Kang's modernisations and, if plans for her removal were discovered, Guangxu faced the real possibility that his aunt might depose him and have him quietly murdered. So Guangxu turned for protection to a rising military officer named Yuan Shikai, one of Li Hongzhang's students, whom he hoped would bring the Northern Army to the reformist side. But Yuan turned out to be more loyal to another cause – himself – and betrayed Guangxu to the court: the emperor found himself summarily imprisoned by the Empress Dowager, the Hundred Days' Reform movement was brutally crushed (Kang was sentenced to death by dismemberment, but escaped overseas), and a conservative, anti-foreign backlash swept China.

As the sad drama of these coups and counter-coups played out amongst the Imperial court, Mesny and Han Fenglan were finally married at Shanghai's red-brick Holy Trinity Cathedral on 30 August 1898. Their timing was strategic rather than romantic: a recent attempt to secure a military post at Nanjing had ended with Mesny being denounced to the authorities as "a dangerous character, a friend of Mason, the plotter", and the deteriorating political landscape made Han Fenglan and their children vulnerable; the marriage gave them protection as British subjects. The marriage certificate also describes Mesny as a widower, so perhaps his first wife, Nien, had recently died – they had never legally divorced in Western law – allowing him to remarry without committing bigamy. But he was soon regretting his decision, not least because of the hypocritical snobbery shown by the city's International community towards mixed-race marriages, despite the fact that many foreign men quite openly kept Chinese mistresses.

1898 also proved to be a landmark year for one of Mesny's pet projects – the penetration of southwestern China by river steamer – carried out by another of his adventurous contemporaries, Archibald Little. The two men had led surprisingly similar lives: arriving in China in 1859 as a tea taster, Little had fought against the Taipings, run a mining venture, been taken for a British spy and nearly killed, travelled widely around the country and become convinced that rivers were the surest way of ferrying Western goods into China's remote interior. In 1889 he daringly attempted to captain a steamer up through the Three Gorges to Chongqing, a feat which would, under the terms of the Chefoo Convention, have automatically opened up the city to foreign trade. On this occasion Little was foiled by bureaucracy and got no further than Yichang, where Chinese officials claimed, absurdly, that monkeys throwing stones would be mistaken for hostile peasants, sparking an international incident. But Mesny had been impressed, remembering his own entrepreneurial efforts at Chongqing and awarding Little a notional crown as the city's "resident pioneer of commerce".

Two years later the British overrode the convention and had Chongqing unilaterally declared an open treaty port, though the idea of steaming up through the gorges was still considered suicidal by most experts. Little disagreed and safely steered his purpose-built vessel, the *Leechuan*, through from Yichang in just eleven days (suffering nothing worse than a bent propeller and minor damage to the hull), mooring below Chongqing's Imperial Customs Station on 8 March 1898. Within a year British gunboats had repeated Little's feat, and soon afterwards a regular passenger service began aboard a vessel named, ironically enough, the *Pioneer*. By this time Mesny had taken issue with Little's book, *Through the Yang-Tse Gorges*, large chunks of which he believed had been plagiarised from his own unpublished notes. It's also possible that he had been offended by one of Little's observations: "I do not wonder at those Europeans who have cast their lot in the interior of China appearing eccentric, to say the least, to their fellow-countrymen, when they again emerge into real civilization." But most likely Mesny was simply frustrated that, once again, his long-held ambitions were being realised by others. He later forgave Little and wished him success "with long life and much happiness".

March 1899 saw the *Miscellany* re-appear, two years later than intended, launching under the triumphant banner "The Resurrection!!!". The biggest change from earlier issues – presumably due to the worsening situation in China, which had seen a growing tally of foreigners being murdered – was that Mesny had become stridently right-wing: following local resistance to the British occupation of Hong Kong's New Territories, he ranted that Britain should annex all of southern China, which he believed would be greeted by popular delight. If "progress" – social, political and industrial – meant foreign occupation of China, then it should be occupied, and change forced on the Chinese for their own good. "It is folly and weakness to consult the Chinese and ask them permission to do anything, as the Chinese Government is bound to refuse, but accepts everything imposed upon China by any power".

Another bombastic editorial exhorted Shanghailanders to break away from China and declare the International Settlement as a neutral republican state. "We hold Shanghai by right of conquest, and Chinese officials ought not to have anything to say in the matter... The only satisfactory manner of dealing with the Chinese officials is, generally, to take what we want and just notify them not to interfere". It's difficult to see the younger Mesny here, the man who had shown so much sympathy towards his fellow soldiers; age and frustration were again taking their toll.

There were other changes too. The *Miscellany*'s scope had broadened to include more in the way of news and current affairs, such as a recent counterfeiting case involving the new art of photolithography to forge banknotes (though the fakes were given away by poor paper quality – still a common check for counterfeit currency in China today). There were further personal reminiscences: "From Canton to Turkestan" promised to cover the whole of his 1879–82 travels between Guangzhou and Hami, but only took the reader as far as Guiyang; while "How I made my Fortune" – which told you everything but – was a return to his murky dealings at Shanghai and Hankou during the 1860s. Another not-so-subtle shift saw the *Miscellany* plugging Mesny's new calling as an insurance agent for the China Mutual, whose offices – a heavy neoclassical block still standing in downtown Shanghai – were just around the corner from his home on Sichuan Road. Typically confident despite his inexperience, he offered stern advice for the way European insurance firms conducted business: "The Chinese do not understand it... [believing insurance to be] instituted by foreigners of doubtful reputation, anxious to bleed the Chinese for all they are worth... all respectable Chinese are thoroughly disgusted with the manner in which they have been approached by foreign canvassing agents". He later claimed that rival insurance companies were boycotting the *Miscellany* because of his forthright criticisms.

Across the country it was clear that, despite the failure of the Hundred Days' Reform, the Qing dynasty was crumbling. But what would replace it? The biggest fear amongst Chinese was that, without an effective ruler, the country was doomed to descend into chaos and be carved up, pie-like, by foreign powers. Observing through Western blinkers, Mesny split the alternatives into two camps: reformers who were anti-foreign (or anti-Christian), and those that were friendly. But the situation was far more complex than this. Some "progressives" envisioned a Republican government, some wanted a new Imperial house, others favoured Kang Youwei's idea of a constitutional monarchy. All were patriotic in their own way and only willing to deal with foreigners in as far as they were allowed to set their own terms.

Not that the Empress Dowager Cixi or her conservative faction were admitting defeat just yet. Out in China's famine-struck northeast, discontent at the country's plight was coalescing into the Boxer movement, a society whose members, trained in a martial arts routine that supposedly made them bullet-proof, now launched a violent, xenophobic crusade under the banner "Protect the Qing, Exterminate the Foreigners". Given how domineering the foreign powers had become since the First Opium War in 1840, it's worth noting just how few of their nationals were actually living in China at the time, and how vulnerable they were: a *National Geographic* article of 1900 tallied only 17,193 in the thirty-odd treaty ports, of which around a third were British and the rest a mix of Japanese, American, French, Russian and assorted "European". Given that there were well over seven million Chinese in the treaty ports alone, and some four hundred million in the country as a whole, the Boxers' aims didn't seem too unrealistic.

As the movement erupted out of its base in Shandong province, the Boxers targeted Christians as hated symbols of Western imperialism, launching a bloody pogrom against missionaries and their converts. Impressed, the Empress Dowager issued a string of decrees ordering provincial governors to support the Boxers' cause. In June 1900 the Boxer army marched on Beijing unopposed, killed the German and Japanese ministers and, with the assistance of sympathetic Qing officials, cornered the city's entire foreign population inside their legation quarter, where they sat out the next two months in a state of siege. A triumphant Cixi declared war on all foreign nations, but her victory proved short-lived; in mid-August an 18,000-strong Allied Expeditionary Force reached Beijing, slaughtered the Boxers, relieved the foreign legations and proceeded to methodically sack the city. Utterly humiliated, the emperor and Cixi disguised themselves as peasants and fled west to Xi'an in a cart, from where they called on an increasingly frail and elderly Li Hongzhang to negotiate with the foreign powers on their behalf. Li was still trusted by the foreign community; he had fallen from grace in the aftermath of the Hundred Days' Reform and had been packed off to a post in southern China, and so avoided any involvement with events at Beijing. He duly signed the "Boxer Protocol" on 7 September 1901, which included yet another colossal indemnity, the permanent posting of foreign forces at the capital, a two-year prohibition on arms imports (probably undermining Mesny's remaining interest in the trade), the execution of officials who had supported the Boxers and the opening of another batch of treaty ports.

Though the consequences of the Boxer Uprising cost China dearly in money and prestige, in terms of nineteenth-century rebellions this was a relatively isolated, small-scale affair, limited to Beijing and the surrounding districts. By no means did all officials obey the Empress Dowager's call to arms: Zhang Zhidong and Liu Kunyi made a joint commitment to keeping the Yangzi valley stable during the rebellion and Liu issued specific instructions that foreigners and their property at Shanghai were to be protected, executing two rebels who appeared at Nanjing. Even so, the Boxers did nothing for Mesny's sense of security; perhaps his Chinese friends were feeding him horror stories. During the build-up to the crisis, he wrote: "My own wife has told me hundreds of times that she is in dread of the awful fate that awaits me [on account of the Boxers] and has begged me to grant her a letter of divorce and let her take the children away, she has worried the life out of me the past few months with this clamour for divorce and I believe she is being incited thereto by designing people... and when they have got my wife away from me by divorce she ceases to be British, then they will *do to her* what they dare not do now, and probably kill my children, so that I may die childless".

Even without the Boxer scare, the new century had begun badly for Mesny. Back in 1893 – when he was being evicted and sued – he had taken out a bank loan of 3,000 taels against property he owned at Shanghai, a block of land built up with Chinese-style houses and a large company premises. Interest was set at eight percent and the bank had the right to sell the block without consulting Mesny if he fell behind with repayments. The previous November, the bank, finding three years' worth of interest in arrears, had auctioned the property to one of the residents, but Mesny refused to admit that the sale had been legal and had been harassing workmen sent to renovate the buildings by the new owner. Once more the court found against him; Mesny not only lost his property but had to pay costs too, and was soon hauled back before a judge owing a further $99.99 against what little property he still possessed. Told to pay up or face bankruptcy, he seems to have finally settled the affair out of court.

At last came some satisfaction. On 7 November 1900, Mesny's bugbear Li Hongzhang died, aged 78, shortly after signing the Boxer Protocol. Having risen to power during the Taiping Rebellion on the strength of his undoubted military skills, the general opinion amongst Han Chinese was that Li had let his country down badly by siding with the Manchu court and fawning to foreign interests: he had signed away China's rights to France over Tungking, to Japan over Korea, to Russia in Manchuria and to a whole bag of nations over the Boxers. Mesny, who of course held a personal grudge, stopped just short of calling Li a traitor, though he repeated a rumour that the Japanese, having annexed Korea, planned to invade China and install Li as emperor. From a more distant perspective, Li Hongzhang could be seen as a deeply patriotic man badly let down by the times. Caught between the poles of conservatism and reform, he had a pragmatic sense of China's capabilities, understood the futility of attempting to confront the West on its own terms and wanted to win China time to build up its strength. His reputation was ultimately ruined by being regularly wheeled out as the face of national defeat, the signatory to ever-more ignominious surrenders to foreign interests, so deflecting blame from the Imperial house.

Not that Li was a selfless ascetic who didn't profit from his time in office: he had an eye for investments and owned shares in steamships, railways and telegraph lines. Shanghai's Huashan Road, today a relatively quiet residential avenue west of the centre, was virtually owned by his family during the early twentieth century and even features a memorial hall to Li inside the grounds of Fudan College. Part-way along is Dingxian Gardens, a villa complex built by Li; the gardens are classically Chinese but the house is an unexpected compromise between the tropics and suburban England, with balconies overlooking a neatly mowed lawn, long brick chimneys and shuttered windows. Clearly, all the contact with foreigners over the years had rubbed off on the great statesman.

Li left behind journals and his portrait on the Tientsin Bank's $100 bill, but his real legacy and political successor – inheriting both his former position as viceroy of Zhili, and command of the Huai Army which Li had founded – was Yuan Shikai, the man who had betrayed the emperor during the Hundred Days' Reform.

January 1902 saw the Imperial court return from exile in Xi'an to Beijing where, almost insultingly, the British decided not to try the now-powerless Empress Dowager Cixi for war crimes. Indeed, she became almost moderate, inviting foreigners to private audiences and appointing two Western-educated women as her personal interpreters. As "reform" became a permitted topic at the capital, Liu Kunyi and Zhang Zhidong submitted a fresh proposal to the throne, reiterating their wish to see China's education, military and industry modernised along Western lines. Liu himself died that October; Mesny's final comment was that Liu was "neither bright nor progressive", though Liu scored his grudging approval for objecting to restructuring the Chinese military along German lines. Mesny remained committed to reform too, even if he seems to have abandoned any idea of gaining credit for his views. The following year he met the republican philosopher Xiong Shili and, according to a Chinese website, became involved in trying to get Xiong's reformist friends (and anti-dynastic agitators) Zhang Binglin, Huang Xing and Zhang Shizhao released from prison. All these men went on to play significant political roles in early twentieth-century China.

Meanwhile, foreign powers had begun squabbling over their territorial interests in China. In 1903 Britain briefly invaded Tibet, using machine guns against the poorly-armed peasant armies sent against them and pushing right through to Lhasa in a futile quest for trade agreements and evidence of Russian military infiltration. The Russian-Japanese War of 1904, for control of Manchuria's Liaodong Peninsula, was on a far larger scale and again saw victory for Japan: the first time that a rising Asian power had defeated a developed nation, heralding a fundamental change in International relations. Losing Liaodong was also a personal setback for Russia, who – having been one of the powers that had forced Japan into returning it to China after the Sino-Japanese war – had spent the intervening decade developing the region at her own expense. The Japanese now occupied both Korea and Manchuria, right on China's northeastern doorstep, and soon cemented their authority over the region by building the South Manchurian Railway – and, ostensibly to protect their investment, installing a 10,000-strong military force here. Mesny despaired of the situation: "The Chinese have for years been provoking foreign nations to dismember their fine Empire, and have nearly succeeded in so doing".

But the country wasn't finished yet. In 1905, some twenty years after Zhang Zhidong's original memorial on the subject, the Beijing–Hankou railway finally opened as China's first long-distance passenger line. It had taken less than eight years to actually lay the track, but the project had become bogged down in its early stages over financing. Ultimately, a consortium of Chinese officials and merchants formed a construction company to raise the forty million taels required; for a half-share of the profits, the government chipped in by donating land along the route and allowing the company to acquire more through compulsory purchases. From these beginnings, China's rail network has since expanded into every province, progress that Mesny would definitely have approved of – and probably claimed as his own idea.

As railways began to shrink distances in China, so regional currency variations and exchange rates became increasingly ridiculous. Mesny again pondered the necessity of creating a unified coinage, reminding readers that he had "proposed to mint gold coins worth ten taels or ounces of silver, five taels and one tael each, some years ago". The government now opened a central mint at Tianjin, though it still concentrated on producing copper "cash". Tael weights were finally abolished as late as 1933 with the issuing of a standardised silver dollar; the coins didn't catch on, however, and were soon replaced by paper notes.

Events and age were grinding Mesny down. A photograph taken for his sixtieth birthday in 1902 shows him moustached, bald and bolt upright, dressed in an austere, slightly shabby dark suit – a far cry from the proud image of him as a young military official from thirty years earlier. Not long afterwards he moved north across Suzhou Creek, well outside of the confines of the original International Settlement, to what was presumably cheaper accommodation at 22 Ward Road, not far from the enormous new jail whose Art Deco recessed gateway still opens out on to the busy street. As with most of Mesny's addresses, his home has long-since vanished under demolitions and road-widening schemes, though a contemporary residential block survives nearby, patterned in grey and red brick.

Despite continuing financial woes, Mesny managed to publish the final volume of his *Miscellany* in 1905, after a break of over five years. The preface apologised for the long delay, describing how he had "lost all my savings at one stroke, and seeing that I am already 62 years old, though sound in mind and limb, such a misfortune for a person of my age is no joke". Though he never clearly states the nature of this disaster, scattered through the volume are indications that he and Han Fenglan had at last gone their separate ways; she later successfully applied for a legal separation, taking half of Mesny's remaining property with her.

Volume four of the *Miscellany* featured crisper paper, a professionally thorough index and – for the first time – photographs, though these were used mostly to illustrate potted biographies of famous officials and people of note. The first issue launched with two of these eulogies, one to Zuo Zongtang ("The most Progressive and Patriotic Chinese Statesman of the Nineteenth Century") and one to Mesny himself. Overall, there was far less original material this time around – what had become his "Anglo-Chinese Notes" looked decidedly threadbare next to those in the first volume – the space filled instead with "Telegrams of the Week" and reviews of journals and books, much of it harvested from other periodicals.

Aside from his heartfelt reminiscences of the Miao war, clearly based on notes made on the spot, the *Miscellany*'s whole tone had become far blander and less spirited: every editorial echoed Mesny's foresight, his knowledge, his abilities, and his skill at handling insurance claims; he had finally run out of things to say and was becoming a bore. He must have realised it too. Significantly, the last issue ended not with an appeal for subscribers towards a fresh volume, but only with an unfulfilled promise to publish *Mesny's Commercial Guide*, recycling material that had already appeared in the *Miscellany*.

It's a shame that Mesny's voice fades out at this point, as he would certainly have had plenty to comment about over the following few years. China was on the brink of some startling changes, many of which would vindicate his beliefs. The first of these came in September 1905, just months after the *Miscellany* ceased publication, when the court unexpectedly announced the abolition of Imperial examinations, by which candidates for the civil service had been chosen since A.D. 605, to be replaced with a Western-style education system. As thousands of classically-trained students suddenly found their hard-won knowledge of Confucian texts redundant, the call went out once more to convert temples into modern classrooms – much as Mesny had first suggested to Zhang Zhidong back in 1883, and Kang Youwei had proposed to the emperor during the Hundred Days' Reform.

In December, anti-foreign riots broke out at Shanghai, but this time the causes were very different from the old-style, quasi-religious violence espoused by secret societies such as the Boxers and Gelao Hui. There had been growing public resentment at the way foreign courts inside the International Settlement were increasingly meddling in Chinese law cases, which they weren't entitled to do; now porters had gone on strike in protest, tempers had frayed and fighting swept through a market district. Foreign militias quickly suppressed the unrest, leaving a police station in ruins and a score of protesters sprawled dead on the street ("only Chinese coolies were killed", wrote one paper, as if their deaths hardly counted), but this was the first of a new kind of social uprising, one which saw ordinary Chinese asserting their legal rights in the face of colonial arrogance. Two years later, a Shanghai court awarded Mesny $8, plus costs, for a "good strong hat" which had been ruined during the disturbance, and which in some unexplained way had once saved his life. It all sounded very trivial next to other people's claims – for 18,000 taels in one case – and perhaps Mesny was growing petty with bad fortune.

Another sign of dramatic change came when Britain finally agreed to end its opium trade, the shameful lever by which it had first got its claws into China some seventy years earlier. Moves in this direction had begun back in 1893, when a British Royal Commission was set up to investigate the trade in light of growing social pressure against it at home. Mesny, who – as he had innocently revealed to Gill on their first meeting – had ample first-hand experience with addiction, wrote the Commission a detailed letter, in which he estimated about seventy percent of southwestern China's population were users, including women and children. At its worst, he felt that the drug sapped energy and had doubtless reduced many households to poverty, but in fact only a fraction of smokers became dependent on the drug; the majority simply indulged in a pipe or two to relax at the end of a hard day and otherwise coped perfectly well. While personally against its use, Mesny believed that there was no official will in China to ban the opium trade as such – too much money was involved – only outrage that, with imported Indian opium far superior to home-grown varieties, so much of the profits ended up in foreigners' pockets.

The Commission had been impressed by Mesny's testimony. "How many of the Merchant class of witnesses [making submissions] can either speak or read the Chinese language, or have even the most superficial acquaintance with the manners, customs, and opinions of the Chinese people, it is impossible to say. General W. Mesny is, I think, the only one for whom any claim to special knowledge of this kind is made. He has undeniably had a very extensive experience of Chinese life". However, they continued, his evidence was undermined by the fact that "General Mesny also admits that he himself has been an opium-smoker and got cured" – though it didn't say how this personal insight made his opinions unreliable. The Commission's report, released the following year, outrageously suggested that the Chinese were immune to opium's worst effects, and that its use was no more dangerous or socially unacceptable than alcohol.

Now, fourteen years later, it looked as if the trade – and perhaps even opium use in China – might be on its way out. Under the Opium Agreement of 1907, an imperial edict banned cultivation and Britain agreed to reduce imports by ten percent a year, promising to make China opium-free within a decade. But Mesny had been right: the truth was that officials only wanted imports stopped because they were undermining sales of the domestic poppy crop, which in good years produced a profitable 22,000 tons of the drug. Inevitably, the terms of the Opium Agreement were renegotiated, applied erratically for a while and then ignored. Imports from British India continued, even though selling them became far more complicated; in 1912, six million pounds worth of foreign opium sat in storage for months at Shanghai while merchants haggled with provincial officials over distribution rights. Widespread opium use would persist in China until after the Communists seized power in 1949.

A wave of mortality now swept China, removing some of the nation's most influential personalities and altering the balance of power. First to die was the emperor Guangxu on 14 November 1908, followed a day later by his aunt, the Empress Dowager Cixi. The emperor had remained

under house arrest ever since Yuan Shikai's treachery during the Hundred
Days' Reform movement back in 1898, and he had been sickly for a long
while. Yuan, however, had flourished under the patronage of a grateful
Cixi; despite refusing to support the Boxers he had been promoted to
Viceroy of Zhili and then Generalissimo of all China, a position that even
Li Hongzhang had never achieved. *Who's Who in the Far East* described
him as "the man of power in China at present" and he was allowed to
wear an Imperial sable robe, an extraordinary honour. But now Cixi was
dead and a new emperor, Aisin Gioro Puyi, was on the throne; Puyi
was only two years old and his father and acting regent, Prince Chun –
Guangxu's younger brother – revenged himself against the duplicitous
Yuan by ordering him to resign all his powers and retire on account of a
"lame leg".

A year later on 5 October 1909, while serving as a Grand Councillor
to the court and having survived an assassination attempt by a Wuchang
bookseller, Zhang Zhidong also died, aged 73. Zhang had risen to
power following his forthright criticisms of Russia and France, and tried
to live the life of an ideal official: honest, hard-working and steeped in
Confucian values. He had proved to be audacious too, initiating China's
first full-scale industrial reforms with his railway, mint, and iron foundry,
unperturbed at the frequent scorn aimed at him by both the European
press and conservative Chinese factions. He had also displayed great
courage in keeping the Boxers out of southern China, at the risk of serious
imperial displeasure. For his part, Mesny felt that Zhang was vacillating
and susceptible to flattery, though also intelligent and well-meaning –
on one occasion he even half-seriously proposed him as a replacement
emperor should the Qing dynasty fall. Yet Mesny never forgave Zhang
for not acknowledging the influence that his ideas had played in Zhang's
subsequent career, and could never be wholly complimentary about his
former employer; nor did he ever give him credit for his grand vision.
His final, rather mean-spirited judgement was that Zhang "treated his
subordinates so badly that few people of ability cared to serve under
him".

As the new decade got underway, the Imperial court began to yield to pressure for genuine political reform and offered to establish a constitutional monarchy and parliament by 1913. This willingness to appease reformers was interpreted as a sign of weakness and an open revolt against the throne broke out at Guangzhou.

The regent, Prince Chun, tried to calm the situation by appointing an interim advisory cabinet, but as the majority of its members were Manchu – not Han Chinese – this did nothing to ease popular discontent. Then the government decided to nationalise the country's growing rail system, taking individual lines (and their profits) out of the hands of the regional authorities, who had sunk a huge amount of their own capital into the network's construction. A riot against the proposal in Sichuan escalated into a major anti-Qing uprising at Wuhan in October 1911, in which the German-trained Manchu garrison was slaughtered and half the city burned to the ground during days of furious fighting.

As the whole country tottered once again on the brink of civil war, a desperate Prince Chun recalled Yuan Shikai from rustication as the head of the Northern Army. Yuan restored order but, emphasising that he held the fate of the entire nation in his hands, pointedly refrained from crushing the rebels. Instead, he brokered an extraordinary peace deal: the emperor would abdicate – though still retaining his titles, property and a substantial income – and a republican government would take up the reins of power at Nanjing. The Chinese empire, which had begun over two thousand years earlier with the despotic warlord Qin Shihuang, ended quietly in the aftermath of a revolt over railways on 12 February 1912, under a child emperor too young to understand what was happening.

Across the land, stunned civil servants, whose entire existence had revolved around serving the throne, burst into tears at the fate of their patron. It's unlikely that Mesny joined in their lamentations. Cixi, had she still been alive, would have had the bitter satisfaction of being vindicated in her xenophobia: in the end, it was indeed foreigners and their devious modern technology which had steered the Qing dynasty towards ruin.

A struggle immediately began for control of the country. The Cantonese physician and long-time revolutionary Sun Yatsen, who had been abroad raising funds to overthrow the Manchus when the dynasty actually fell, now returned to China as President-elect of the new republic at Nanjing. This didn't sit well with Yuan Shikai, who pressured Sun to stand down in his favour and then demanded that the government move back to Beijing, where he could use his loyal Northern Army to consolidate power. But when Sun Yatsen's newly-formed Kuomintang – the Nationalist Party – did well during the first governmental elections in February 1913, Yuan began a campaign of violence against them, assassinating key members and forcing Sun into renewed exile. For appearances sake Yuan then handed the presidency to Xiong Xiling, an ethnic Miao from the small town of Fenghuang on the Hunan-Guizhou border. But within a few months the two had fallen out; Xiong resigned and Yuan Shikai dissolved the parliament, assumed the role of dictator and by 1915 had begun to plan a revival of the monarchy, with himself as emperor.

Amid all this excitement of railways, revolution and dynastic collapse, Mesny found himself, mundanely, back in Debtor's Court. He had been keeping busy in recent years as the China representative for the Old Age Pension Trust (one of many such organisations springing up in the wake of Britain's recent Old Age Pensions Act), and had become involved with the International Institute, a Christian association which promoted understanding between followers of the various faiths in China and counted members of Shanghai's business community, and even retired Chinese officials, amongst its members. He had also continued to stand up for Chinese associates in trouble with the law, agitating for the release of two young men whom he felt had been falsely imprisoned for counterfeiting copper coins.

But none of these things, however worthy, had made Mesny any money, and now judgement in a new case had gone against him for $1350 plus costs. As he had done ten years earlier, Mesny claimed to be unable to pay. "My son pays my expenses. Sometimes I make a little money on life insurance, share broking, and the sale of horses and land. I only earned $27½ in two years and a half, and I don't think I shall be able to pay quickly what is due". Challenged that his name appeared on the current Shanghai registry as owning two lots of land, he replied "That must be a mistake, for Mrs Mesny", and denied any knowledge of her affairs: "When we were separated I was obliged to give her half of my property. She has been successful and I have been unsuccessful. The furniture in my house belongs to my son and Mrs Mesny. I am living in the same house as a lodger". Having cheekily asked the judge to find him work, Mesny did admit to owning shares, mostly in Malay rubber plantations, though he considered them almost worthless. He was given a month to discuss how best to sell these investments and so repay some of his debt.

The First World War broke out in Europe in July 1914, and though German interests were affected after China sided with the Allies, the conflict never actually spread to China itself. Mesny – by now in his early seventies – had himself declared fighting fit by a doctor and offered his services to the British Government. The Foreign Secretary, Lord Balfour, good-humouredly commended his zeal and promised to send for his help should Germany invade. This slightly comical episode hides the fact that Mesny was almost certainly feeling lonely and desperate to be useful: his young nephew John had died recently and much of Shanghai's foreign population had returned overseas to take up arms. This might partly explain why, that November, he abandoned Shanghai, his home for the past thirty years, and moved back up the Yangzi to Hankou, Wuhan's north-bank suburb. A pressing need for employment probably played a part too, as he seems to have swiftly found an office job with the trading firm of Reiss & Co, whose waterfront offices were on the corner of what is now Huangpu Street. Hopefully, after spending decades bumping in and out of debt, financial security brought a comfortable stability to Mesny's final years.

Hankou was still picking itself up after being almost levelled during the 1911 revolution, when Imperial forces had torched the city in frustration after a month of hard fighting had failed to dislodge the rebels. The foreign concession, which had grown to monopolise the river frontage in a long band of buildings just a few blocks deep, was being rebuilt in grand style; as at Shanghai, there was a Bund, a stone-face embankment topped by a tree-lined park running along its length, offering the city's neoclassical banks, merchants' homes and warehouses some protection against the Yangzi's regular flooding. The concession – split into various self-governing national districts – was entirely walled off from Hankou's bustling Chinese quarters and, outside the peak tea-trading season in early summer, was surprisingly quiet. Just at the edge of the French quarter rose the French-Gothic facade of Hankou train station, terminus for Zhang Zhidong's line from Beijing, which was already bringing wealth into the city; the extension south to Guangzhou (not completed until the 1930s) would turn Wuhan into central China's main rail hub. Today, using the latest high-speed trains, the city is just six hours away from either Guangzhou or Beijing.

Discontent returned to Hankou in 1916 when another riot, apparently instigated by nationalist agitators, saw parts of the Chinese city once again going up in flames; there was shooting and looting, and around a hundred people were killed. Meanwhile at Beijing, Yuan Shikai's attempts to set himself up as emperor were unravelling: having caved in to yet more bellicose concessions demanded by Japan, he had lost all credibility and been abandoned by his warlord allies, who threatened to throw the provinces into revolt should he ascend the throne. Forced to renounce all claims to the monarchy, Yuan died in June.

As his former bodyguards escorted the marquee-sized bier to Beijing's train station, where a carriage decked in flowers carried it away, Yuan's death plunged China into chaos. The old, stultified order that the foreigners had milked so successfully was gone, and with it the dissembling Imperial-era officials, with their Confucian credentials and love of compromise and inaction. Replacing them was an entirely new breed of warlords, brisk, decisive and cruel, backed by well-trained private militias – the descendants of Zeng Guofan's Hunan Army – all engaged in a struggle for supremacy. With power increasingly localised and with no weak central authority to bully, foreigners found it harder to get their own way and were forced to negotiate for their needs at every turn. The Chinese public was also becoming more assertive, more organised; political and social pressures saw several of the treaty ports returned to Chinese control over the following decades, the country's territory passing back into the hands of its population. Forced out of the interior, foreign businesses retreated to the coast at Hong Kong and Shanghai, which boomed as international markets and investment became focused there. And in the background,

Japan was growing ever-more menacing. After setting up the unfortunate last emperor, Puyi, as head of a puppet state in Manchuria, she was to launch a bloody invasion of eastern China in 1937 which – though rarely recognised as such in Europe, with its focus on Germany and Hitler – marked the beginning of the Second World War.

As the China he knew began to disintegrate around him, Mesny himself died on 11 December 1919 at 7 Rue De Paris – now Huangxing Road – just a short walk from Hankou train station. He was seventy-seven years old, and had kept up cheerful, robust good health to the end, described in his final months as a brisk, white-haired old man, slightly unsteady on his legs but with clear eyes, a strong voice and a "complexion fair and tinted like a winter apple."

His obituary in the *North China Herald* mourned the declining fortunes of his later years, but as his will left money, shares and a small collection of antique scrolls and porcelain worth around £1,500 to be split between his children, it's nice to know that Mesny was by no means destitute at the time of his death. He did, however, specify that his estranged wife Han Fenglan should receive nothing, repeating that he had already given her half of everything he owned at the time of their separation and that she was "well provided for having Real Estate registered in her own name at the British Consulate General, Shanghai, besides other valuable property".

Mesny was probably buried in Hankou's International Cemetery, which was cleared during the 1950s to build government offices. He left behind an impressive record of a long and active life in China: as an entrepreneur along the Yangzi, as a decorated war veteran, as a minor government official, a traveller, plant collector, prospector, correspondent, arms dealer, advisor, observer, and, ultimately, as an author. He also became a unique witness to the terrible struggles that pulled the country apart during the closing years of the Qing dynasty – the Taiping, Miao and Muslim rebellions, the war over Tungking and the Japanese invasion of Manchuria – and knew some of the period's most notable statesmen. Yet he earned very little reward after abandoning his military post in Guizhou to follow Gill across China in 1877. While it's true that this allowed him to become a great traveller, travel was both his strength and his weakness: without it he would have never have acquired his specialist knowledge of Chinese landscape, language and life, and so have had nothing to write about; but with it, he was too restless to forge the lasting official contacts that allowed many of his foreign contemporaries in China to carve out successful careers for themselves.

His plans for the country's modernisation were continually undermined by an unerring ability to shoot himself in the foot, his life a long list of worthwhile official posts turned down, missed financial opportunities and – most of all – a lack of tact towards the patrons who might have helped him realize his schemes. By the time he finally settled at Shanghai he had spent too long out of European society to ever fully fit back in, what with a Chinese mistress and two mixed-race children; and so the loss of reputation amongst his Chinese connections following the Mason debacle must have been a bitter blow. Isolated and with a declining income, at a time when widespread hostility against foreigners was boiling over into outright violence, it's hardly surprising that parts of the *Miscellany* ring with outspoken paranoia, resentment and a reinterpretation of past events to place himself at the centre of things.

Yet, as his surviving journals and newspaper articles show, not all of Mesny's reminiscences in the *Miscellany* are skewed. His Nineteen-Point Plan might not have been the origin of China's reform movement, but Mesny surely deserves a large amount of credit for nurturing Zhang Zhidong's leading role in it, even if it was Zhang's own drive and initiative that got things done. Perhaps if events had worked out differently – if the Hundred Days' Reform of 1898 had succeeded – then today's captains of heavy industry in China might look back to Zhang Zhidong as their founding father, and Mesny, as the man who inspired him, could have claimed a significant place in Chinese history.

With his writings out of print for over a century, Mesny's name remains familiar only to China specialists and botanists, though in 1992 the island of Jersey published an attractive set of six stamps to commemorate a century and a half since his birth. The sole physical monument to his life and travels is the small chain-link suspension bridge that he designed for

Zhou Dawu, which still spans the river just west of Chong'an in Guizhou. Somewhere out there, perhaps Zuo Zongtang's two complimentary scrolls and remnants of the "Mesny Collection" of ethnic jewellery survive as well. But for a man with almost no formal education, and who ran off to sea at the age of twelve, Mesny's finest memorial is his four-volume *Miscellany*, with its first-hand accounts of events, places, personalities and all things Chinese: a rich sample of the cultural fragments that made up China's late nineteenth-century.

EPILOGUE

Han Fenglan died at Shanghai in September 1943, still registered as a British subject; she would have been in her mid-seventies. Shanghai was under Japanese occupation at the time, and her death was reported to the British authorities by the city's neutral Swiss Charge d'Affaires.

Mesny's daughter Marie Wan-er married Frank Watson in 1917. The couple had two children, Ivy and Reggie: after World War II, Reggie settled in Australia while Ivy and her mother both immigrated to the United States. Marie died in California in 1977.

Husheng Pin Mesny spent his entire life in China. He worked for the British American Tobacco Company, became a life-member of the North China branch of the Royal Asiatic Society and was possibly married. According to documents posted on a Chinese website, in 1940 he and his mother still owned a considerable amount of property along what is now Hailun Road in Shanghai's northeastern suburbs, including an apartment called Tongle Li. This would most likely have been confiscated by the Japanese during their wartime occupation of the city, and certainly by the Communists after they came to power in 1950. Husheng died at Shanghai in 1963 aged 78, just as the country teetered on the cusp of anarchy under the Red Guards, leaving £1,200 in a Hong Kong bank account to his adopted god-daughter, Yu Fengying. Between them, father and son clocked up over a century in China, spanning the closing days of the Opium Wars to the first stirrings of Mao's Cultural Revolution.

THE CAST

Bao Dadu (包大肚), died 1872. "Big Belly Bao". Miao military leader who Mesny saw getting seriously wounded during an attack on Jiuzhou, though his men later ambushed the Hunan Army at Huangpiao. He was executed by the Chinese.

Cen Yuying (岑毓英) 1829–1889. Guangxi general who fought against the Muslim Uprising in Yunnan from the 1850s right through until the fall of Dali in 1873, and was responsible for the subsequent slaughter after the city had surrendered. Later appointed viceroy of Yunnan and Guizhou; Mesny met him at Guiyang in 1879. The British held him responsible for Margary's murder in 1875, and Mesny depicted him as a scheming, anti-foreign agitator responsible for the attack on his own life at Qianxi in 1880. According to Mesny, Cen died insane at Kunming. His tomb is outside Guilin.

Chen Shuiqing Sichuan Army general during the Miao war, who covered up his own cowardice by accusing Tang Jiong of abandoning Chong'an in 1870, getting him cashiered.

Cixi 1835–1908. Empress Dowager from 1861, controlling a succession of weak emperors which included her nephew, Guangxu. Her conservative and anti-foreign stance held China back at a time that it needed to reform, contributing to the collapse of the Qing dynasty in 1911.

Cooper, Thomas Thornville 1839–1878. British explorer who turned down Mesny as a guide for his journey from Sichuan to Weixi in Yunnan in 1868. Mesny met him again at Bhamo in 1877, where Cooper was the British Resident, at the end of his travels with Gill. Cooper was shot by his bodyguards a few months later. Author of *Travels of a Pioneer of Commerce, in Pigtails and Petticoats*.

Ding Baozhen (丁寶楨) 1820–1886. Upstanding viceroy of Shandong and Sichuan, where he reformed the provincial salt trade; Mesny met him on several occasions. The popular Chinese dish "Kongpao Chicken" is named after him.

Dupuis, Jean 1829–1912. Merchant, gun-runner and associate of Mesny's at Hankou during the 1860s. In 1868, Dupuis introduced Mesny to the recruiters who employed him into the Sichuan Army in Guizhou. Inspired by the Lagrée expedition, Dupuis subsequently forced his way up along the Red River through Vietnam and into Yunnan, proving that the river was a viable trade route and indirectly precipitating the French annexation of Tungking, northern Vietnam.

Du Wenxiu (杜文秀) 1823–1872. Islamic scholar turned warlord who took Dali in Yunnan as his capital in 1856 during the Muslim Uprising. After surrendering to Chinese forces, he committed suicide on his way to execution by taking an opium overdose.

Gao He (高禾) d.1872. One of the major leaders of the Miao Rebellion, captured after the final battle at Leigong Shan and executed gruesomely by the Chinese.

Garnier, Francis 1839–1873. Eventual leader of the 1866–68 French Lagrée Expedition to explore the Mekong from Vietnam through Laos and into China. In 1873 he was sent to mediate between Vietnamese and French merchants but ended up capturing Hanoi. Garnier was later killed here during a skirmish and the French were drawn into a war with China over control of Tungking which ended with France's annexation of all of Vietnam in 1886.

Gill, William 1843–1882. Officer in the British Royal Engineers who, having inherited a fortune, decided to travel. In 1877 Mesny accompanied him from the Sichuanese capital, Chengdu, to Bhamo in Burma. Gill authored *The River of Golden Sand*, was awarded the Royal Geographical Society's gold medal, worked in intelligence in Turkey and Bulgaria and was killed in Egypt.

Giquel, Prosper 1835–1886. Frenchman who in 1863 led the Ever Triumphant Army, the French version of Ward's Ever Victorious Army, against the Taipings. He was later employed by Zuo Zongtang establishing the Fuzhou naval dockyards which were, ironically, destroyed by French gunboats in 1884.

Gordon, Charles 1833–1885. Officer in the British Royal Engineers who took command of the Ever Victorious Army after Ward's death, and fell out with Li Hongzhang following the slaughter at Suzhou. Mesny was offered a job by Gordon but turned him down as he had become sympathetic to the Taipings. Gordon was famously killed at Khartoum in the Sudan.

Guan Baoniu (aka Wanguan Baoniu, 萬官保牛) 1826–1868. Miao leader killed by Xi Baotian's Hunan Army during the battle at Dingpatang, the first comprehensive victory for Chinese forces since the start of the rebellion.

Han Fenglan (韓鳳蘭) c1866–1943. Mesny's second wife. Anecdotal evidence in the *Miscellany* suggests that he bought her as a concubine around 1882; they had a son Husheng Pin (1885–1963) and daughter Marie Wan'er (1894–1977) before marrying in a church wedding at Shanghai in 1898. They later legally separated, Mesny losing half his property. He wrote her out of his will.

Hill, David (1840–1896). Methodist missionary who spent several years at Wuxue on the Yangzi, where he met Mesny in 1874 and described him in a letter to his father. Hill became a friend of the family, and was executor of John Mesny's will.

Hong Xiuquan (洪秀全) 1814–1864. Failed civil service candidate who formulated his own version of Christianity and from 1850–64 led the Taiping Rebellion, the world's largest civil war. He committed suicide shortly before his capital, Nanjing, fell to Imperial troops.

Hosie, Alexander 1853–1925. British consul, traveller and author of *Three Years in Western China*. Mesny met him at Chengdu and again in Kunming.

Hou Guansheng (侯管勝) 1829–1865. Taiping general, titled the Forest King, who along with his brother chaperoned Mesny during his captivity. After the fall of Nanjing, he changed his name to Hou Yutian and fled to Hong Kong, but the British had him arrested and handed over to the Chinese authorities at Guangzhou for execution.

Jin Dawu (金大五) aka Li Kaiyuan, d.1872. Miao leader in Southeast Guizhou during the rebellion. Mesny saw him when Miao forces attacked Jiuzhou.

Kang Youwei (康有为) 1858–1927. Reformer who proposed a constitutional monarchy, the end of the Imperial Examination system and rapid modernisation of industry and education. He was proscribed after the failure of the Hundred Days' Reform movement but escaped execution by fleeing overseas. Mesny knew him slightly.

Li Hongzhang (李鴻章) 1823–1901. A scholar who rose to fame as a general and founder of the Huai Army during the Taiping Rebellion; later, he became a powerful statesman and politician, though his numerous capitulations to foreign nations lost him credit with the general public. Following the Mason case in 1892 Li accused Mesny of being a traitor, and seems to have ensured that he never found work with Chinese officials again. Unsurprisingly, Mesny paints a mean picture of him in the *Miscellany*.

Li Xietai (aka Li Zhenguo, 李珍國) d.1888. One-time bandit and Chinese-sponsored guerilla along the Yunnan-Burmese border during the Muslim Uprising who, many believed, was directly involved in the murder of Margary at Mangyun in 1875. Mesny and Gill met him two years later on their way to Burma.

Little, Archibald 1838–1908. Lived in China from 1859 and, like Mesny, travelled widely. After Little successfully navigated a purpose-built steamer through the Three Gorges to Chongqing, Mesny claimed that Little's earlier book *Through the Yang-tse Gorges* had plagiarised his own unpublished notes. Little's wife Alicia (1845–1926) was a driving force behind the anti-footbinding movement for Chinese women which eventually saw the practice banned; she also wrote a biography of Li Hongzhang.

Liu Chin-hsiang d.1885? Miao prisoner that Mesny saved from execution at Jiaba Niuchang in 1870 and took as an understudy. Liu later investigated the situation in Tungking on Mesny's behalf and became a blood brother of Liu Yongfu, the Black Flag commander. Anecdotal evidence in the *Miscellany* suggests he was killed defending Sontay against the French.

Liu Heling (刘鹤龄), died after 1891. Sichuan Army general stationed in Guizhou 1868–71; Mesny served directly under him. He appeared to tire of Mesny's frequent advice and after an embarrassing defeat headed home for unapproved leave, though this might have been an attempt to destabilise a likely peace and so prolong both the war and his military career. His withdrawal forced Tang Jiong to retreat from the Chong'an area. Liu returned, only to quit the campaign in a fury on hearing his rival, Zhou Dawu, had been appointed Commander-in-Chief for all Guizhou. Mesny's newspaper articles from the 1870s describe Liu as an unprincipled profiteer, though he toned down this aspect in the *Miscellany*.

Liu Jintang (劉錦堂) 1844–1894. A protégé of Zuo Zongtang who fought with him in the northwest, took over after Zuo was recalled to Beijing and in 1884 was appointed first governor of Xinjiang. Mesny met him at Hami in 1881, when Liu seemed keen to fund his operations with the French loan. But Russia's withdrawal from Ili ended the northwest conflict, and the need for a Chinese military presence in the area.

Liu Kunyi (劉坤一) 1830–1902. Fought under Li Hongzhang against the Taipings and was then given various provincial governorships. Liu offered Mesny employment at Guangzhou, but funding was to come through a lottery and Mesny turned the job down. Liu later sent Mesny back home when he tried to enrol for service during the first Sino-Japanese War. Though Mesny disliked him, Liu and Zhang Zhidong also kept southern China stable during the xenophobic Boxer rebellion by refusing to support the militants, despite an Imperial command to do so.

Liu Yongfu (劉永福) 1837–1917. Leader of the Black Flags in Tungking; initially a bandit, then employed by the Chinese to tackle the French on their behalf. After Tungking was annexed and the Black Flags disbanded, Liu became a government official in Guangdong and, briefly, Taiwan.

Lovatt, William Nelson 1838–1904. British Royal Artilleryman who taught Mesny gunnery at Shanghai in 1862. Like Mesny, Lovatt later joined the Imperial Maritime Customs Service and, having spent most of his life orbiting between Korea, China and America, died at Hankou.

Ma Hualong (馬化龍) d. 1871. Muslim warlord at the head of the Tungan Revolt in northwest China.

Margary, Augustus Raymond 1846–1875. British diplomat at Shanghai, from where he surveyed route to Bhamo in Burma via Guizhou, Sichuan and Yunnan. Returning to Tengchong in Yunnan, he was killed at the village of Mangyun. British outrage led to the Chefoo Convention of 1876, in which the Chinese government apologised for the murder, promised to provide protection for British subjects in China and were required to make the Treaty Ports duty-free enclaves. Details were posted around the country as the Margary Proclamation.

Mason, Charles Welsh 1866–after 1924. British customs official, whose attempt to smuggle guns to rebel groups in 1891 indirectly implicated Mesny and turned Li Hongzhang against him. His autobiographical *Chinese Confessions of Charles Welsh Mason*, published thirty years after the events, are full of self-loathing despite the passage of time. On his release from prison in China, Mason ended up in New York and enjoyed success as a newspaper columnist and novelist. But he somehow drifted into a life of vagrancy, leaving his job to try his luck as a gold miner and labourer in Canada. During the First World War he enlisted in the British army and was wounded at Gallipoli, but in 1920 a journalist found him back in America, working on a road gang. He vanished for good after *Confessions* was published.

Mesny, William (麥士尼, *maishini*; originally written 梅尼, *meini*, after the Jersey pronounciation) 1842–1919.

Nien Suey Tsen 1852–? Mesny's first wife, the daughter of a minor official at Guiyang. Mesny says little about her, and implies that he divorced her around 1882 after the birth of his son, Husheng Pin, to his concubine. She possibly died in the mid-1890s.

Riviere, Henri 1827–1883. French naval officer who captured Hanoi in 1882, before being killed during a sortie the following year.

Su Yuanchun (蘇元春) 1844–1908. Chinese general who fought against the Miao in Guizhou and the French in Tungking. He was one of the survivors of the Huangpiao ambush and later had the bodies of the fallen Chinese soldiers buried in a mass grave outside Shidong village, not far from the battle site. The ruins of his mansion and wife's grave also survive at Shidong.

Tang Jiong (唐炯) 1829–1909. Mesny's Commander-in-Chief during the Chong'an campaign. Mesny describes him as virtuous, generous, and brave, and was disgusted when he was sent back to Sichuan in disgrace. Tang was later given further official appointments in Sichuan, Shanxi and Yunnan. In 1885 he was blamed for the loss of Sontay in northern Vietnam to France and sentenced to death; Mesny and many high-ranking officials petitioned the throne for clemency and Tang was pardoned.

Ward, Fredrick Townsend. 1831–1862. An American mercenary engaged by Li Hongzhang to drill Chinese troops in modern military tactics; his force was known as the Ever Victorious Army. Ward became a Chinese military official but was killed in September 1862, after which the EVA was taken over by Gordon.

Wu Sangui (吳三桂) 1612–1678. Ming dynasty general who, following the suicide of the last Ming emperor in 1644, let the Manchu armies through the Great Wall and into China. The Manchus rewarded Wu with governorship of Guizhou and Yunnan provinces, but then became worried over his growing popularity and recalled him, provoking Wu to rebel in 1673. There are temples dedicated to him at Tianlong, outside Anshun in Guizhou, and on the northern outskirts of Kunming.

Wu Tang (吳棠) 1813–1876. Viceroy of Sichuan during the later stages of the Miao war; Mesny paints him as an idler who withholds much-needed pay and supplies from the Sichuan Army in Guizhou.

Xi Baotian (席寶田) 1829–1889. Hunan Army commander based at Zhenyuan during Mesny's campaign in Guizhou. His forces were defeated by Bao Dadu's

Miao at Huangpiao. He was later reprimanded for apparent corruption and retired due to illness.

Yakub Beg 1820–1877. Muslim warlord, born in what is now Uzbekistan, who declared himself Emir of Kashgar in 1867, with his territory (Kashgaria or Chinese Turkestan) spread across western Xinjiang. He was defeated a decade later by Zuo Zongtang and Liu Jintang and died the same year.

Yang Yuke (杨玉科) 1838–1885. An ethnic Bai from Yingpan village, northwest of Dali, who fought for the Chinese against Du Wenxiu during the Muslim Uprising in Yunnan; it was his forces that actually captured Dali at the end of the war. Killed in Tungking at the Battle of Dong Dang.

"Yellow Tiger" Zhang Xianzhong (张献忠) 1606–1647. Soldier turned bandit who took advantage of nationwide chaos at the end of the Ming dynasty to rampage through central China, finally taking Sichuan as his own kingdom. He was relentlessly cruel and ransacked both Chongqing and Chengdu before being defeated in northeastern Sichuan by the rising Qing dynasty.

Yuan Shikai (袁世凯) 1859–1916. Duplicitous Generalissimo who engineered the abdication of the last Manchu emperor, broke up the subsequent Republic and attempted to found his own dynasty. Having destabilised the country, his death precipitated a warlord era which lasted until Mao Zedong's communists came to power in 1950.

Zeng Guofan (曾國藩) 1811–1872. Founded the Hunan Army during the Taiping Rebellion, the first time the Manchu government had allowed a Chinese to raise a formal provincial force.

Zhang Xiumei (張秀眉) 1822–1872. Miao leader during their rebellion 1855–72; sources differ as to his exact role in the conflict. Despite fighting Miao forces for eighteen months, Mesny never mentions him.

Zhang Zhidong (張之洞) 1837–1909. Technocrat who instigated China's first large-scale industrial plant and long-distance railway, and became Mesny's patron after the two men met outside Beijing in 1882. It's likely that Zhang was inspired to become a reformer by Mesny's own Nineteen-Point Plan, though Zhang never acknowledged the fact and the two men eventually fell out, partly over Zhang's employment of German staff.

Zhou Dawu (周達武) 1813–1895. General appointed in late 1870 as commander-in-chief for operations in Guizhou. He employed Mesny for the remaining Guizhou campaigns, taking him to Chengdu in 1873. The suspension bridge in Chong'an was built by Zhou to Mesny's design.

Zuo Zongtang (左宗棠) 1812–1885. Military statesman who rose to prominence during the Taiping Rebellion, founded the naval arsenal and shipyards at Fuzhou, suppressed the Nian rebels and campaigned for twenty years against Muslim insurgents in northwest China. Mesny met him in Hankou in 1866 but missed him later at Lanzhou, Hami, Beijing and Fuzhou. Zuo recommended Mesny for military rank during the Miao Rebellion in 1869 and, shortly before his death, presented Mesny with two scrolls of his calligraphy.

Bibliography

Online newspaper archives: britishnewspaperarchive.co.uk; Hong Kong Public Library (http://mmis.hkpl.gov.hk/web/guest); National Library of Australia (trove.nla.gov.au); National Library of New Zealand (http://paperspast.natlib.govt.nz); National Library, Singapore (newspapers.nl.sg); newspaperarchive.org.

The Miscellany online *Mesny's Chinese Miscellany* is available to view at Deutsche Digitale Bibliothek (www.deutsche-digitale-bibliothek.de).

Many out-of-print titles below were downloaded as pdfs from the Internet Archive (http://archive.org).

Alcock, Sir Rutherford *The Journey of Augstus Raymond Margary* (Macmillan 1876)

All About Shanghai (University Press, Shanghai 1934)

Allan, James *Under the Dragon Flag* (William Heinemann 1898)

Bailey, Frederick M. *China–Tibet–Assam* (Jonathan Cape 1945)

Balleine, George *Biographical Dictionary of Jersey* (Staples Press 1948)

Bird, Isabella *The Yangtze Valley and Beyond* (John Murray 1899)

Blakiston, Thomas *Five Months on the Yang-tsze* (John Murray 1862)

Boerschmann, Ernst *Old China in Historic Photographs* (Dover 1982)

Boulger, Demetrius Charles *The Life of Yakoob Beg* (William Allen 1878)

Bretschneider, Emil *History of European Botanical Discoveries in China* Vol 2 (Sampson Low 1898)

Broomhall, Marshall

 – *The Chinese Empire: A General and Missionary Survey* (China Inland Mission 1907)

 – *Islam in China: A Neglected Problem* (China Inland Mission 1910)

Bruce, Clarence Dalrymple *In the Footsteps of Marco Polo* (William Blackwood 1907)

Chen Quanming and others *A Chinese-English Guide to Qiandongnan Tourism* (Guizhou, 2003)

Chen Tong *A Glimpse of Old China* (Zhongguo Huabao 2005)

China Directory *Chronicle & Directory for China, Japan & the Philippines* 1862–1906 (Hong Kong)

China Mail
  – newspapers, 1870–1920
  – *Who's Who in the Far East* (Hong Kong 1906)

Chinese Times (5 volumes; Tientsin Printing Co. 1886–1891)

Ch'u Tung-tsu *Local Government in China under the Ch'ing* (Stanford University Press 1969)

Clark, G. W. *Kweichow and Yün-nan Provinces* (Shanghai 1894)

Clarke, Samuel R. *Among the Tribes of South-West China* (Morgan & Scott 1911)

Colborne, Baber Edward *A Journey of Exploration in Western Szechuan 1881*, including three Lolo (Yi) manuscripts collected by Mesny (Royal Geographical Society archives JMS/10/83)

Colquhoun, Archibald *Across Chrysê* (Sampson Low 1883)

Cooper, Thomas Thornville *Travels of a Pioneer of Commerce, in Pigtails and Petticoats* (John Murray 1871)

Crow, Carl *Travelers' Handbook for China* (Shanghai, 1922)

Daqing Diguo Fensheng Jingtu (大清帝國分省精圖, Provincial Atlas of the Qing Empire, Toyama Publishing House, Tokyo c1908)

Darwent, Charles Edward *Shanghai Handbook* (Kelly & Walsh c1903)

Deal and Hostetler *Art of Ethnography: A Chinese "Miao Album"* (University of Washington 2006)

de Carné, Louis *Travels in Indo-China and the Chinese Empire* (Chapman & Hall 1872)

Desk Hong List for Shanghai (Shanghai, 1904)

Dillion, Michael *China's Muslims* (Oxford University Press 1996)

Dyer Ball, James *Things Chinese* (Samson Low Marston 1892)

Dzengseo *Diary of a Manchu Soldier in Seventeenth Century China* (translated by Nicola Di Cosmo; Routledge 2006)

Edkins, Joseph *Chinese Currency* (Kelly and Walsh 1901)

Farrer, Reginald *The Rainbow Bridge* (Edward Arnold & Co 1926)

Fitzgerald, C. P. *The Tower of Five Glories* (Cresset Press 1941)

Foreign Languages Press *The Taiping Revolution* (Foreign Language Press, Beijing 1976)

Forsyth *Mission to Yarkund* (Calcutta, 1875)

Fortune, Robert *Three Years' Wanderings in China* (John Murray 1847)

Foster, Arnold *Report of the Royal Commission on Opium Compared with the Evidence from China that was Submitted to the Commission* (Eyre and Spottiswoode, Hankou 1899)

Geil, William Edgar *Eighteen Capitals of China* (Constable, London 1911)

Giles, Herbert *A Chinese Biographical Dictionary* (Kelly & Walsh 1898)

Gill, William
 – *The River of Golden Sand* (Cambridge University Press 2010)
 – Diaries, volumes 5 & 6 (Royal Geographical Society archives RGS 213357)

Hadland, Tony *Glimpses of a Victorian Hero* (Hadland Books 2002)

Hake, Egmont *The Story of Chinese Gordon* (John W Lovell 1883)

Hart, Virgil *Western China: A Journey to the Great Buddhist Centre of Mount Omei* (John Wilson & Son 1888)

Hickey, William *The Memoirs of William Hickey*, volume 1 (Hurst & Blackett c1925)

Hill, David
 – letter to his father, late 1874, describing meeting Mesny at Wuxue (School of African and Oriental Studies, Wesleyan Missionary Society Archive, China Papers of David Hill, H-2723 Box 632 (3), microfiche #1099)

Holt, Henry
 – Unpublished manuscript describing Mesny's journey from Guangzhou to Guiyang, Chongqing, Hami and Beijing 1879–82, based on Mesny's notes (Royal Geographical Society archives JMS/10/79)
 – *Mr. Mesny's Route from Chungching Fu to Lan Chou Fu & part of his route from Lan Chou Fu to Peking*, eight maps (Royal Geographical Society archives MR CHINA S.172)

Hosie, Alexander *Three Years in Western China* (George Phillip 1899)

Hummel, Arthur *Eminent Chinese of the Ch'ing Period* (US Government 1943)

Hsü, Immanuel C.Y. *The Rise of Modern China* (Oxford University Press 2000)

Israeli, Raphael *Muslims in China* (Curzon Press 1980)

Jackson and **Hugus** *Ladder to the Clouds: Intrigue and Tradition in Chinese Rank* (Ten Speed Press 1999)

Jenks, Robert D. *Insurgency and Social Disorder in Guizhou: The "Miao" Rebellion, 1854–1873* (University of Hawaii Press 1994)

Jernigan, Thomas *Shooting in China* (Methodist Publishing House, Shanghai 1908)

Johnston, Reginald *Twilight in the Forbidden City* (Victor Gollancz 1934)

Knollys, Major Henry *English Life in China* (Smith, Elder & Co, London 1885)

Kuropatkin, A. N. *Kashgaria* (translated by Walter Gowan; Thacker, Spink & Co 1882)

Launay Adrien, *Histoire des Missions de Chine, Mission du Kouy-Tcheou* (Société des Missions-Etrangères 1908)

Leavenworth, Charles *The Arrow War with China* (Sampson Low Marston 1901)

Lindley, Augustus Frederick *Ti-ping Tien-kwoh* (Day & Son 1866)

Lin Yutang *Lady Wu* (Foreign Language Teaching and Research Press, Beijing 2009)

Li Xiucheng *The Autobiography of the Chung-Wang* (translated by W.T. Lay; Presbyterian Press 1865)

Little, Alicia *A Marriage in China* (F.V. White & Co 1896)

Little, Archibald
 – *Mount Omei and Beyond* (Heinemann 1901)
 – *Through the Yang-tse Gorges* (Sampson Low Marston 1898)

Lorge, Peter *Chinese Martial Arts from Antiquity to the Twenty-First Century* (Cambridge University Press 2012)

Madrolle Guidebooks *Northern China* (Hachette 1912)

Maclellan *Story of Shanghai* (North China Herald 1889)

MacMurray, John *Treaties and Agreements with and Concerning China 1894–1919* (Oxford University Press 1921)

Margary, Augustus *Notes of a Journey from Hankow to Tali-fu* (Walsh, Shanghai 1875)

Mason, Charles Welsh *The Chinese Confessions of Charles Welsh Mason* (Grant, Richards 1924)

Mayers, William Frederick
 – *The Chinese Government, A Manual of Chinese Titles* (Kelly & Walsh, Shanghai 1897)
 – *A Chinese Reader's Manual* (Probsthain & Co 1910)
 – *Treaty Ports of China and Japan* (with N. B. Dennys and Charles King, Trübner and Co 1867)

McAleavy, Henry *Black Flags in Vietnam* (Allen & Unwin 1968)

Mesny, William

– correspondence between General William Mesny and Jardine Matheson (Jardine Matheson archives, Cambridge MSS JM/B7/12, JM/B7/37, JM/C42/2)

– correspondence between Mesny and the Royal Geographical Society, 1875 (RGS/CB6/1572)

– *Mesny's Chinese Miscellany* vols I–IV (Shanghai, 1895–1905)

– *Notes of a journey from Shanghai to Su chow fu* (Royal Geographical Society archives JMS/10/92)

– *Notes on a journey from Canton to Hami via Kuei Yang fu and Chung ching fu*, including several loose letters by Gill and others, Mesny's climate observations for the Chongqing–Beijing leg of his travels, his daily log for the Chongqing–Hami trip, and loose notes for the Guiyang–Chongqing journey (Royal Geographical Society archives JMS/10/79)

– *Notes on a Journey from Canton to Kwei-Yang-Fu up the Canton River* (Report of the British Association for Advancement of Science, 1880)

– partial transcript of a letter to Henri Cordier dated Kuei-hsien 16 July 1883 (Bibliothèque nationale de France, Extr. de R. E. O. 1883. II. 582–584, FRBNF39423728)

– *Tungking* (Noronha, Hong Kong 1884)

National Geographic *The Complete National Geographic* (National Geographic DVD 2010)

Nguyễn Thuật 往津日記 ("Journey to Tianjin", Chinese University Press, 1980)

North China Herald (Shanghai, 1850–1920)

Osbourne, Milton *River Road to China* (George Allen & Unwin 1975)

Parker, E.H. *Chinese Account of the Opium War* (Kelly & Walsh 1888)

Piasetskii, Dr. Pavel Iakovlevich *Russian Travellers in Mongolia and China* (translated by J. Gordon-Cumming; Chapman & Hall 1884)

Rowe, William T. *China's Last Empire: The Great Qing* (Belknap Harvard 2012)

Scott, James George *France and Tongking* (Fisher Unwin 1885)

Shanghai Courier

– *The Tientsin Massacre* (articles published 16 June–10 September 1870 and collected into a book)

– microfilm of the complete *Shanghai Evening Courier* 1874–75 at the British Library (SN 013913680 / MFM.MF1473)

– numerous *Shanghai Courier* articles by Mesny, 1869–77, reconstructed through attributed accounts in other newspapers

Sladen & Browne *Mandalay to Momien* (Macmillan 1876)

Smith, Richard J. *The Employment of Foreign Military Talent: Chinese Tradition and Late Ch'ing Practice* (Journal of the Royal Asiatic Society Hong Kong Branch, Vol 15, 1975)

Stanford, Edward
  – *Atlas of the Chinese Empire* (Stanford & China Inland Mission 1908)
  – *Complete Atlas of China* (China Inland Mission 1917)

Stevens, Keith
  – *A Jersey Adventurer in China* (Journal of the Royal Asiatic Society Hong Kong Branch, Vol 32, 1992)
  – *The American Soldier of Fortune Frederick Townsend Ward Honoured and Revered by the Chinese with a Memorial Temple* (Journal of the Royal Asiatic Society Hong Kong Branch, Vol 38, 1998)
  – *A Tale of Sour Grapes: Messrs. Little and Mesny and the First Steamship through the Yangzi Gorges* (Journal of the Royal Asiatic Society Hong Kong Branch, Vol 41, 2001)
  – *William Mesny: A Jerseyman who rose to the rank of general in the Chinese army* (recording of 1993 lecture; Hong Kong Central Library)

Stringer, Harold *The Chinese Railway System* (Kelly & Walsh 1922)

Thomson, John *China and its People in Early Photographs* (Dover 1982)

Waley, Arthur *The Opium Wars through Chinese Eyes* (Stanford University Press 1968)

Wei, Alice *The Moslem Rebellion 1855–73* (University of Chicago thesis T24908, 1974)

White, Trumbull, *The War in the East* (McDermid & Logan 1895)

Williams, Clement *Through Burmah to Western China* (Blackwood and Sons 1868)

Wilson, Andrew *The "Ever Victorious Army"* (Blackwood and Sons 1868)

Wood, Frances *No Dogs and Not Many Chinese: Treaty Port Life in China 1843–1943* (John Murray 1998)

Woodhill, William *Land of the Lamas* (Century 1891)

Worcester, George Raleigh Gray *Sail & Sweep in China* (HMSO 1966)

Zelin, Madeleine *The Merchants of Zigong* (Columbia University Press 2005)

Zhang Zhidong *China's Only Hope* (abridgement of 勸學篇, translated by S. I. Woodbridge; Fleming H. Revell Company 1900)

EXPLORE ASIA WITH BLACKSMITH BOOKS

From retailers around the world or from *www.blacksmithbooks.com*